SUITE 303
DENVER, CO 80202
303.292.0801
FAX 292.0959

GRAPHIS ANNUAL REPORTS 3

GRAPHIS ANNUAL REPORTS 3

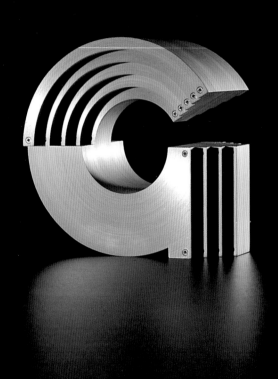

GRAPHIS ANNUAL REPORTS 3

THE INTERNATIONAL YEARBOOK OF ANNUAL REPORTS

DAS INTERNATIONALE JAHRBUCH ÜBER JAHRESBERICHTE

LE RÉPERTOIRE INTERNATIONAL DES RAPPORTS ANNUELS

EDITED BY · HERAUSGEGEBEN VON · RÉALISÉ PAR:

B. MARTIN PEDERSEN

PUBLISHER AND CREATIVE DIRECTOR: B. MARTIN PEDERSEN

EDITOR: JOY AQUILINO

ASSOCIATE EDITORS: HEINKE JENSSEN, ANNETTE CRANDELL, DAVID BOURGEOIS

ART DIRECTOR: ADRIAN PULFER

DESIGNERS: ERIC GILLETT, MARY JANE CALLISTER, ADRIAN PULFER

"G" FROM THE ALUMINUM ALPHABET DESIGNED BY TAKENOBU IGARASHI

GRAPHIS PRESS CORP., ZÜRICH (SWITZERLAND)

GRAPHIS PUBLICATIONS

GRAPHIS, THE INTERNATIONAL BI-MONTHLY JOURNAL OF VISUAL COMMUNICATION
GRAPHIS DESIGN, THE INTERNATIONAL ANNUAL OF DESIGN AND ILLUSTRATION
GRAPHIS PUBLICATION 1, THE INTERNATIONAL SURVEY OF EDITORIAL DESIGN
THE GRAPHIC DESIGNER'S GREEN BOOK, ENVIRONMENTAL CONCERNS OF THE DESIGN AND PRINT INDUSTRIES
ART FOR SURVIVAL: THE ILLUSTRATOR AND THE ENVIRONMENT, THE CATALOG FOR AN EXHIBITION
SPONSORED BY THE UNITED NATIONS ENVIRONMENTAL PROGRAMME IN COOPERATION WITH
EARTH ISLAND INSTITUTE AND THE SOCIETY OF ILLUSTRATORS, INC.
GRAPHIS PHOTO, THE INTERNATIONAL ANNUAL OF PHOTOGRAPHY
GRAPHIS POSTER, THE INTERNATIONAL ANNUAL OF POSTER ART
GRAPHIS PACKAGING, AN INTERNATIONAL SURVEY OF PACKAGING DESIGN
GRAPHIS LETTERHEAD, AN INTERNATIONAL SURVEY OF LETTERHEAD DESIGN
GRAPHIS DIAGRAM, THE GRAPHIC VISUALIZATION OF ABSTRACT, TECHNICAL AND
STATISTICAL FACTS AND FUNCTIONS
GRAPHIS LOGO, AN INTERNATIONAL SURVEY OF LOGOS
GRAPHIS PUBLICATION DESIGN, AN INTERNATIONAL SURVEY OF THE BEST
IN MAGAZINE DESIGN
GRAPHIS ANNUAL REPORTS, AN INTERNATIONAL COMPILATION OF THE BEST DESIGNED
ANNUAL REPORTS
GRAPHIS CORPORATE IDENTITY, AN INTERNATIONAL COMPILATION OF THE BEST IN
CORPORATE IDENTITY DESIGN

GRAPHIS PUBLIKATIONEN

GRAPHIS, DIE INTERNATIONALE ZWEIMONATSZEITSCHRIFT DER VISUELLEN KOMMUNIKATION
GRAPHIS DESIGN, DAS INTERNATIONALE JAHRBUCH ÜBER DESIGN UND ILLUSTRATION
GRAPHIS PUBLICATION DESIGN, EINE INTERNATIONALE ZUSAMMENSTELLUNG DES BESTEN
ZEITSCHRIFTEN-DESIGNS
THE GRAPHIC DESIGNER'S GREEN BOOK, UMWELTANLIEGEN DER DESIGN- UND DRUCKINDUSTRIE, VON ANN CHICK
ART FOR SURVIVAL: THE ILLUSTRATOR AND THE ENVIRONMENT, DER KATALOG FÜR EINE AUSSTELLUNG IM
RAHMEN DES UMWELT-PROGRAMMS DER UNO, IN ZUSAMMENARBEIT MIT DEM EARTH ISLAND INSTITUTE UND
DER SOCIETY OF ILLUSTRATORS, INC.
GRAPHIS LETTERHEAD, EIN INTERNATIONALER ÜBERBLICK ÜBER BRIEFPAPIERGESTALTUNG
GRAPHIS LOGO, EINE INTERNATIONALE AUSWAHL VON FIRMEN-LOGOS
GRAPHIS PHOTO, DAS INTERNATIONALE JAHRBUCH DER PHOTOGRAPHIE
GRAPHIS POSTER, DAS INTERNATIONALE JAHRBUCH DER PLAKATKUNST
GRAPHIS PACKAGING, EIN INTERNATIONALER ÜBERBLICK ÜBER DIE PACKUNGSGESTALTUNG
GRAPHIS DIAGRAM, DIE GRAPHISCHE DARSTELLUNG ABSTRAKTER TECHNISCHER UND
STATISTISCHER DATEN UND FAKTEN
GRAPHIS ANNUAL REPORTS, EIN INTERNATIONALER ÜBERBLICK ÜBER DIE GESTALTUNG
VON JAHRESBERICHTEN
GRAPHIS CORPORATE IDENTITY, EINE INTERNATIONALE AUSWAHL DES BESTEN
CORPORATE IDENTITY DESIGNS

PUBLICATIONS GRAPHIS

GRAPHIS, LA REVUE BIMESTRIELLE INTERNATIONALE DE LA COMMUNICATION VISUELLE
GRAPHIS DESIGN, LE RÉPERTOIRE INTERNATIONAL DE LA COMMUNICATION VISUELLE
GRAPHIS PUBLICATION DESIGN, LE RÉPERTOIRE INTERNATIONAL DU DESIGN DE PÉRIODIQUES
THE GRAPHIC DESIGNER'S GREEN BOOK, L'INDUSTRIE GRAPHIQUE FACE AUX PROBLÈMES D'ENVIRONNEMENT, PAR ANN CHICK
ART FOR SURVIVAL: THE ILLUSTRATOR AND THE ENVIRONMENT, CATALOGUE D'UNE EXPOSITION SPONSORSÉE PAR LE
PROGRAMME DES NATIONS-UNIES POUR L'ENVIRONNEMENT, EN COLLABORATION AVEC LE EARTH ISLAND INSTITUTE
ET LA SOCIETY OF ILLUSTRATORS, INC.
GRAPHIS LETTERHEAD, LE RÉPERTOIRE INTERNATIONAL DU DESIGN DE PAPIER À LETTRES
GRAPHIS LOGO, LE RÉPERTOIRE INTERNATIONAL DU LOGO
GRAPHIS PHOTO, LE RÉPERTOIRE INTERNATIONAL DE LA PHOTOGRAPHIE
GRAPHIS POSTER, LE RÉPERTOIRE INTERNATIONAL DE L'AFFICHE
GRAPHIS PACKAGING, LE RÉPERTOIRE INTERNATIONAL DE LA CRÉATION D'EMBALLAGES
GRAPHIS DIAGRAM, LE RÉPERTOIRE GRAPHIQUE DE FAITS ET DONNÉES ABSTRAITS,
TECHNIQUES ET STATISTIQUES
GRAPHIS ANNUAL REPORTS, PANORAMA INTERNATIONAL DU MEILLEUR DESIGN DE RAPPORTS
ANNUELS D'ENTREPRISES
GRAPHIS CORPORATE IDENTITY, PANORAMA INTERNATIONAL DU MEILLEUR DESIGN D'IDENTITÉ CORPORATE

PUBLICATION NO. 210 (ISBN 3-85709-431-1)
© COPYRIGHT UNDER UNIVERSAL COPYRIGHT CONVENTION
COPYRIGHT © 1992 BY GRAPHIS PRESS CORP., DUFOURSTRASSE 107, 8008 ZURICH, SWITZERLAND
JACKET AND BOOK DESIGN COPYRIGHT © 1992 BY PEDERSEN DESIGN
141 LEXINGTON AVENUE, NEW YORK, N.Y. 10016 USA

PRINTED IN JAPAN BY TOPPAN PRINTING CO., LTD

CONTENTS · INHALT · SOMMAIRE

REMARKS

OUR SINCERE THANKS ARE EXTENDED TO ALL CONTRIBUTORS THROUGHOUT THE WORLD WHO HAVE MADE IT POSSIBLE FOR US TO PUBLISH AN INTERNATIONAL SPECTRUM OF OUTSTANDING WORK.

ENTRIES: GRAPHIS PRESS CORP., DUFOURSTRASSE 107, CH-8008 ZÜRICH, SWITZERLAND

ANMERKUNGEN

UNSER HERZLICHER DANK GILT EINSENDERN AUS ALLER WELT, DIE ES UNS MÖLICH GEMACHT HABEN, EIN BREITES, INTERNATIONALES SPEKTRUM DER BESTEN ARBEITEN ZU VERÖFFENTLICHEN.

TEILNAHMEBEDINGUNGEN: GRAPHIS VERLAG AG, DUFOURSTRASSE 107, 8008 ZÜRICH, SCHWEIZ

AVERTISSEMENT

NOS SINCERES REMERCIEMENTS VONT À TOUS LES COLLABORATEURS DU MONDE ENTIER, QUI NOUS ONT PERMIS DE PUBLIER UN VASTE PANORAMA INTERNATIONAL DES MEILLEURS TRAVAUX.

DEMANDE DE PARTICIPATION: EDITIONS GRAPHIS SA, DUFOURSTRASSE 107, 8008 ZÜRICH, SUISSE

INTRODUCTION

VORWORT

PRÉFACE

A Z I Z C A M I PEOPLE ARE SAID TO LOOK AT AN ANNUAL REPORT FOR JUST FOUR MINUTES. I HAVE HEARD THIS DUBIOUS STATISTIC MANY TIMES, THOUGH NO ONE HAS YET BEEN ABLE TO CITE THE SOURCE. PERHAPS IT'S TRUE. SO OFTEN THE TEXT IS TURGID, AND FOUR MINUTES IS ALL YOU NEED TO LOOK AT THE PICTURES AND READ THE BIG WORDS AT THE FRONT. ☐ AT EVERY ANNUAL REPORT PRESENTATION WE MAKE, WHATEVER WE SAY ABOUT DESIGN, WE ALWAYS STRESS THE IMPORTANCE OF GOOD WRITING. GETTING THE WORDS TOGETHER IS A DIFFICULT TASK FOR COMPANIES WITH DIVERSE INTERESTS. SOMETIMES YOU CAN ALMOST SEE THE SCISSORS AND PASTE. ACTIVITIES WILL BE

reviewed division by division, with each subdivision getting its own paragraph. Yet shareholders or people researching the company do not want to read about each individual component and then try to understand the whole. That's a bit like taking a car apart and asking someone to look at all the bits and say what shape it's in. Showing what shape the company is in is the job of the annual report. ☐ The designer's concern is not the minutiae of the company but its main thrust. Most businesses are complicated, and chief executives usually want to cover too many issues. What the designer has to battle for is an overall message: the distillation of a whole series of important and generally interrelated points. ☐ I see designers as more than people who just go off and do things. They also discuss things. They need to be able to sustain a cogent argument with the intelligent people who run companies. Some people think that if designers concentrate too much on business issues, they lose creativity. I think the reverse is true. Creativity becomes easier. Learning about the company's ambitions steers you toward ideas and solutions. You understand the strategic idea, and then you visualize it. The core idea is what the whole job is going to be about. ☐ There has to be one big thrust, because an annual report is a small document. But most companies are too complex to be expressed in a single idea. The primary message must be clear, but there can be subtexts. An annual report is not a one-dimensional form of communication. The designer can weave in many signals, but keeping it all in balance will be a challenge. An annual report often fails to communicate not because the information is missing, but because different parts cancel each other out. If the report is not to be frantic, the designer must put all the messages in their proper places

☐ For example, in the 1989 annual report we designed for Bowater, one theme was the holding company's respect for the individual characters of all its businesses. That democratic approach was signaled in the photography: Every picture, whether of the chairman or of a logger, was the same size. ☐ Each decision the designer makes—on shape, size, paper, imagery, layout or cover—can be aligned with the messages to be conveyed. For example, if a company wants to be seen as international, the designer can use a format outside standard European or American sizes. Every design element plays a precise part. It sounds unemotional, almost surgical, but that's not the result. You could say it's the difference between an orchestra dissecting each phrase of a work in rehearsal and performing it on opening night. ☐ The process that the designer goes through with an annual report is a version of what happens with corporate identity, albeit in a simplified form. There's the same need to understand. For that reason I'm a great believer in long-term relationships, which I think explain the notable success of some reports in the States. It's not only that designers and writers can build on previous knowledge and experience. In a world barraged with information, it helps to be consistent. Most companies are not in such a dynamic market that they should look different every year. They're like tankers that slowly chew up the sea miles: They don't suddenly heel over and go in another direction. They need to reinforce the message, not start again each year. Consistency allows readers to find their way around, and gives people confidence that the company is steady. ☐ Long-term relationships can also be good news on fees. The principle that fees rise every year is unsound. For several of our annual report clients they have consistently gone down. Morgan Grenfell is one example. Because it is a fast-moving merchant bank, people work in a way that requires constant change to the text, which pushes up design costs. We suggested that they install their own Apple Macintosh, and it paid for itself within a year. □ Public companies in the United Kingdom have made great strides since the days when they regarded annual reports as an obligation rather than an opportunity. The overall standard in Europe is not nearly as high, and the economic importance of major countries is simply not reflected in the quality of literature.

Nonetheless, there are some very bright beacons. The Dutch in particular are giving a strong creative lead. □ Reports in the United States still lead on production quality, but Britain is closing the gap. British companies will really surge ahead, perhaps, when they set more ambitious objectives for their annual reports. I don't mean increasing the share price, but clarifying the company. A well-designed report can articulate a point of view and put over a solid concept to the right people in the right way. When designers succeed, the print run usually leaps the following year. ■

AZIZ CAMI WAS TRAINED AT CAMBERWELL AND THE LONDON COLLEGE OF PRINTING. HE WAS A FOUNDING MEMBER OF THE PARTNERS, A GRAPHIC-DESIGN FIRM SPECIALIZING IN CORPORATE LITERATURE, CORPORATE IDENTITY AND PACKAGING. HIS WORK HAS RECEIVED SEVERAL NOMINATIONS AND AWARDS IN *DESIGN AND ART DIRECTION*, AND HAS BEEN RECOGNIZED BY OTHER NOTED DESIGN ORGANIZATIONS. CAMI IS A MEMBER OF THE DBA COUNCIL OF MANAGEMENT COMMITTEE, AND SERVED AS CHAIRMAN OF THE 1991 DONSIDE GRAPHIC DESIGN AND PRINT AWARDS. ■

AZIZ CAMI ES WIRD BEHAUPTET, DASS EIN JAHRESBERICHT IM SCHNITT NUR VIER MINUTEN LANG ANGESEHEN WIRD. ICH HABE OFT VON DIESER FRAGWÜRDIGEN STATISTIK GEHÖRT, ABER BISHER WAR NIEMAND IN DER LAGE, DIE QUELLE ZU NENNEN. VIELLEICHT STIMMT SIE. OFT IST DER TEXT ZIEMLICH GESCHWOLLEN, UND MAN BRAUCHT NUR VIER MINUTEN, UM DIE GROSSEN WORTE IN DER EINFÜHRUNG ZU LESEN. □ BEI DER PRÄSENTATION VON JAHRESBERICHTEN REDEN WIR NICHT NUR ÜBER DESIGN, SONDERN HEBEN IMMER WIEDER DIE BEDEUTUNG EINES GUTEN TEXTES HERVOR. FÜR FIRMEN MIT VIELEN INTERESSENSBEREICHEN WIRD DER TEXT ZUM PROBLEM. MANCHMAL SIEHT

man förmlich Schere und Klebstoff vor sich. Jede Abteilung wird den sie betreffenden Text prüfen, wobei jeder Unterabteilung ein Absatz zusteht. Aber die Aktionäre und die an dem Unternehmen interessierten Leute wollen nicht über jeden einzelnen Bestandteil der Firma informiert werden, um sich dann ein Bild zu machen. Das ist, als nähme man ein Auto auseinander und verlange dann von jemandem, alle Teile anzuschauen und zu sagen, wie das Auto aussieht. □ Der Designer muss sich nicht um alle Einzelbelange des Unternehmens kümmern, sondern um das Wesentliche. Die meisten Unternehmen sind recht kompliziert, und häufig will die Geschäftsführung im Jahresbericht zu viele Aspekte berücksichtigen. Also muss der Designer um eine umfassende Botschaft kämpfen – eine Destillation einer ganzen Reihe von nicht unwichtigen und miteinander verbundenen Punkten. □ Ich sehe Designer nicht nur als Leute, die losziehen und Dinge erledigen. Es sind Leute, die Dinge auch besprechen. Sie müssen in der Lage sein, in den Diskussionen mit sehr intelligenten Leuten, der Geschäftsführung von Unternehmen, überzeugende Argumente zu vertreten. Manche sind der Meinung, dass Designer, die sich zu sehr mit Geschäftsinteressen befassen, etwas von ihrer Kreativität verlieren. Ich glaube, das Gegenteil ist der Fall. Kreativität wird einfacher. Je besser man die Ziele einer Firma versteht, desto leichter findet man Lösungen. Man versteht die Strategie und kann sie visualieren. Der ganze Job dreht sich im Prinzip um die Grundidee. □ Es muss ein grosses Thema geben, denn ein Jahresbericht ist ein kleines Dokument. Aber die meisten Firmen sind zu komplex, als dass sie sich durch eine einzige Idee darstellen liessen. Während die Hauptbotschaft als solche erkannt werden muss, sind untergeordnete Texte

durchaus möglich. Ein Jahresbericht ist keine eindimensionale Form der Kommunikation. Der Designer kann viele Signale setzen. □ Er oder sie muss sich um Ausgewogenheit bemühen. Häufig kommt die Botschaft eines Jahresberichts nicht zum Tragen, und das nicht, weil es keine Information gäbe, sondern weil die verschiedenen Teile sich gegenseitig aufheben. Um zu vermeiden, dass der Bericht überladen wirkt, muss der Designer alle Ebenen der Botschaft an den richtigen Platz setzen. □ Beim Jahresbericht 1989 für Bowater ging es zum Beispiel u.a. darum, dass die Holding-Gesellschaft die Eigenständigkeit aller ihrer Unternehmen respektiert. Diese demokratische Haltung wurde dadurch signalisiert, dass alle Aufnahmen die gleiche Grösse hatten, ob es sich um ein Porträt eines Mitglieds der Geschäftsleitung oder um das eines Arbeiters handelte. □ Jede Entscheidung, die ein Designer fällt – sei es hinsichtlich des Formats, des Umfangs, des Papiers, der Illustrationen, des Layouts, des Umschlags – kann auf die zu vermittelnden Botschaften abgestimmt werden. Bei einer Firma, die sich als internationales Unternehmen präsentieren möchte, kann der Designer z.B. ein Format verwenden, das weder dem europäischen noch den US-Standardformaten entspricht. Jedes Gestaltungselement erfüllt eine bestimmte Aufgabe. Das klingt sehr nüchtern, das Ergebnis ist es keineswegs. Es ist wie der Unterschied zwischen Orchesterproben und dem anschliessenden Konzert. □ Bei einem Jahresbericht ist der Arbeitsprozess für den Gestalter ähnlich wie bei der Entwicklung eines Firmenerscheinungsbildes, wenn auch in vereinfachter Form. In beiden Fällen ist Verstehen eine Voraussetzung. Aus diesem Grund bin ich von den Vorteilen langjähriger Geschäftsverbindungen überzeugt, die auch den Erfolg einiger Jahresberichte aus den USA erklären. □ Designer und Texter können auf vorhandenem Wissen und ihrer Erfahrung aufbauen und somit bessere Arbeit leisten. Die meisten Firmen sind nicht in einer so dynamischen Branche tätig, dass sie sich jedes Jahr anders präsentieren müssten. Sie sind wie Tanker, die sich langsam ihren Weg durch die Fluten bahnen, sie machen keine plötzlichen Manöver, um eine andere Richtung einzuschlagen. Die Firmen müssen die Botschaft untermauern und nicht jedes Jahr neu beginnen. Beständigkeit ermöglicht den Lesern, sich zurechtzufinden und vermittelt einen Eindruck der Stabilität der Firma. □ Langjährige Verbindungen können auch in finanzieller Hinsicht Vorteile bedeuten. Das Prinzip, dass die Honorare jedes Jahr steigen müssen, ist ungesund. Für viele unserer Auftraggeber haben sich die Kosten für den Jahresbericht konstant verringert. Morgan Grenfell ist ein Beispiel. Es handelt sich um eine sehr aktive Handelsbank, und das bedeutet, dass es im Text ständig Änderungen gibt, was wiederum die Designkosten erhöht. Wir schlugen ihnen deshalb vor, einen Apple Macintosh anzuschaffen, der sich tatsächlich bereits innerhalb eines Jahres amortisierte. □ Aktiengesellschaften in Grossbritannien haben grosse Fortschritte gemacht, nachdem sie in der Vergangenheit Jahresberichte eher als eine Verpflichtung als eine Chance gesehen haben. Im Vergleich ist das Niveau auf dem europäischen Festland nicht annähernd so gut; die wirtschaftliche Bedeutung der grossen Länder zeigt sich kaum in der Qualität der Unternehmensliteratur. Es gibt aber auch einige Ausnahmen. Besonders die Holländer zeichnen sich durch Einfallsreichtum aus. □ Die Jahresberichte aus den USA sind hinsichtlich der Produktionsqualität führend, aber die Briten holen auf. Die britischen Firmen könnten vielleicht noch mehr Ehrgeiz hinsichtlich der Zielsetzung in ihren Jahresberichten entwickeln. Damit meine ich nicht die Erhöhung der Aktienkurse, sondern eine klare Definition des Unternehmens. Was ein gut gestalteter Bericht vermag, ist die Artikulierung eines Standpunktes und die Vermittlung eines soliden Konzepts an die richtigen Leute, auf die richtige Art. Wenn die Gestalter dies erfolgreich bewältigen, erhöht sich gewöhnlich die Auflage des Berichtes im nächsten Jahr. ∎

AZIZ CAMI WURDE IN CAMBERWELL UND DEM LONDONER COLLEGE OF PRINTING AUSGEBILDET. ER IST GRÜNDUNGSMITGLIED DER GRAPHIK-DESIGNFIRMA THE PARTNERS, DIE SICH AUF FIRMENPUBLIKATIONEN, C.I.-DESIGN UND VERPACKUNGEN SPEZIALISIERT HAT. ER HAT VERSCHIEDENEN AUSZEICHNUNGEN ERHALTEN, U.A. DREI SILBERMEDAILLEN VON DESIGN AND ART DIRECTION (D&AD). AZIZ CAMI IST MITGLIED DES KOMITEES DES DBA COUNCIL OF MANAGEMENT UND WAR 1991 VORSITZENDER BEI DER PREISVERGABE DER DONSIDE GRAPHIC DESIGN AND PRINT AWARDS. ∎

AZIZ CAMI ON DIT QUE LES GENS NE CONSULTENT EN MOYENNE UN RAPPORT ANNUEL QUE PENDANT QUATRE MINUTES. J'AI ENTENDU CETTE STATISTIQUE DOUTEUSE UNE QUANTITÉ DE FOIS, BIEN QUE PERSONNE N'AIT JAMAIS ÉTÉ CAPABLE DE M'EN CITER LA SOURCE. PEUT-ÊTRE EST-CE VRAI. LE STYLE DU TEXTE EST SOUVENT SI EMPHATIQUE! IL NE FAUT PAS PLUS DE QUATRE MINUTES POUR REGARDER LES IMAGES ET LIRE LES GROS TITRES. □ À CHAQUE PRÉSENTATION DE RAPPORT ANNUEL QUE NOUS FAISONS, QUOIQUE NOUS DISIONS SUR LE DESIGN, NOUS INSISTONS TOUJOURS SUR L'IMPORTANCE D'UNE BONNE RÉDACTION. PARVENIR À COMBINER LES MOTS EST UN PROBLÈME DIFFICILE POUR

des entreprises qui ont des intérêts multiples. Quelquefois, on voit presque les ciseaux et la colle. Les activités sont passées en revue, département après département, chaque subdivision faisant l'objet d'un paragraphe. Pourtant, les actionnaires ou les gens qui font des recherches sur l'entreprise n'ont pas besoin d'être informés de tous les détails pour comprendre le tout. C'est un peu comme si vous preniez une voiture, que vous demandiez à quelqu'un de regarder toutes les pièces et de dire quelle forme elle a. □ Le rôle du rapport annuel, c'est de montrer quelle forme elle a. □ Le rôle du designer n'est pas de se préoccuper des menus détails d'une société, mais du principal. La plupart des affaires sont assez compliquées et les directeurs veulent généralement embrasser trop de questions. Le designer doit lutter pour un message global – un condensé de tous les points qui ne sont pas négligeables et qui sont généralement en corrélation. □ Je ne vois pas les designers uniquement comme des gens qui se lancent et font des choses. Ils savent aussi discuter. Ils doivent être capables de soutenir un argument convaincant devant les gens très intelligents qui font marcher l'entreprise. Certains pensent que les designers qui se concentrent trop sur les questions commerciales perdent de leur créativité. Je pense que c'est le contraire qui arrive: la créativité devient alors plus facile. Essayer d'adhérer aux ambitions de l'entreprise vous amène à certaines idées et solutions. Vous comprenez l'idée stratégique, puis vous la visualisez. L'idée-force constitue le sujet même de la recherche. □ Un rapport annuel est un petit document, aussi faut-il un grand sujet. Mais la plupart des entreprises sont trop complexes pour être résumées en une seule idée. Alors que le message principal doit être respecté à sa juste mesure, il peut y avoir des subdivi-

sions. Un rapport annuel n'est pas une forme de communication en une seule et unique dimension. Le designer peut associer divers messages. □ Il n'est pas si difficile de garder l'équilibre. Bien souvent, un rapport annuel ne réussit pas à communiquer l'information; non pas qu'elle fasse défaut, mais certaines de ses composantes annulent toutes les autres. Si le rapport ne veut pas être débridé, le designer doit mettre tous les niveaux du message à leur place. □ Par exemple, dans le rapport annuel 1989 que nous avions conçu pour Bowater, le thème, c'était le respect de l'entreprise pour le caractère individuel de toutes ses activités. Cette approche démocratique était signalée dans la photographie: chaque photo avait un format identique, que ce soit celle du président ou d'un ouvrier. Toute décision que prend le designer – concernant la forme, la taille, le papier, l'image, la mise en pages, la couverture – peut s'aligner sur le message qui doit être transmis. Par exemple, pour une entreprise qui veut être considérée comme internationale, le designer peut utiliser un format qui soit en dehors des normes européennes ou américaines. Chaque élément du design joue un rôle précis. On peut dire que c'est ce qui fait la différence entre la répétition d'un orchestre, où chaque phrase musicale est disséquée, et la représentation finale le soir même. □ Pour le designer, réaliser un rapport annuel n'est pas tellement différent au niveau du processus que de concevoir une identité visuelle, bien que cela soit sous une forme simplifiée. Ils obéissent à la même condition de compréhension. Pour cette raison, je crois fermement aux relations à long terme, qui expliquent, à mon avis, le succès notable de quelques rapports annuels américains. □ Les designers et les rédacteurs peuvent se baser sur une connaissance et une expérience préalables, et donc faire un meilleur travail. Cela aide à être conséquent dans un monde où nous subissons un vrai déluge d'informations. Le marché n'est pas si dynamique pour que les entreprises aient un nouveau look chaque année. Elles sont comme ces tankers qui avalent lentement les distances sur les océans: ils ne peuvent rebrousser chemin subitement. Les entreprises ont besoin de renforcer le message, et non de repartir de zéro chaque année. La cohérence permet au lecteur de trouver son chemin et donne une impression de stabilité. □ Les relations à long terme peuvent être aussi bénéfiques pour les honoraires. Le principe qui veut que ceux-ci augmentent chaque année est aléatoire. Pour plusieurs de nos clients, ils ont considérablement baissé. Morgan Grenfell est un exemple typique. Parce que c'est une banque d'affaires qui bouge vite, les gens travaillent de telle manière qu'il y a constamment des changements dans le texte, ce qui fait grimper les coûts du design. Nous leur avons donc suggéré d'installer leur propre Apple Macintosh: les frais ont été amortis en une année. □ Les sociétés par actions de Grande-Bretagne ont fait de grands progrès le jour où elles ont considéré les rapports annuels comme une obligation plutôt que comme une opportunité. En comparaison, le niveau général est loin d'être aussi élevé dans le reste de l'Europe et l'importance économique de la plupart des pays ne se reflète pas simplement dans la qualité de la littérature. Malgré tout, on trouve des exceptions remarquables. La Hollande en particulier est en train de suivre une nouvelle voie créative très intéressante. □ Les rapports annuels aux Etats-Unis viennent en tête de la production au niveau de la qualité, mais la Grande-Bretagne est en train de réduire l'écart. Les entreprises anglaises vont peut-être vraiment faire und bond en avant si elles posent des objectifs plus ambitieux à leurs rapports annuels. Je ne veux pas dire en faisant monter en flèche le prix des actions. Mais en clarifiant les buts de l'entreprise. Ce qu'un rapport annuel bien conçu peut faire, c'est d'articuler un point de vue et faire comprendre un concept sérieux d'une certaine manière à un certain public. Quand les designers y réussissent, d'ordinaire, les tirages grimpent l'année suivante. ∎

AZIZ CAMI A FAIT SES ÉTUDES À CAMBERWELL ET IL A FRÉQUENTÉ LE LONDON COLLEGE OF PRINTING (ÉCOLE DES MÉTIERS DE L'IMPRIMERIE). IL EST MEMBRE FONDATEUR DE THE PARTNERS, UN STUDIO DE DESIGN GRAPHIQUE SPÉCIALISÉ DANS LES PUBLICATIONS D'ENTREPRISES, LES PROGRAMMES D'IDENTITÉ CORPORATE ET LA CRÉATION D'EMBALLAGES. IL A REÇU DE NOMBREUSES DISTINCTIONS, NOTAMMENT TROIS MÉDAILLES D'ARGENT DÉCERNÉES PAR DESIGN AND ART DIRECTION (D&AD). AZIZ CAMI EST MEMBRE DU COMITÉ DU DBA COUNCIL OF MANAGEMENT ET EN 1991, IL A ÉTÉ ÉLU PRÉSIDENT DU JURY DU CONCOURS DONSIDE GRAPHIC DESIGN AND PRINT AWARDS AUX ÉTATS-UNIX. ∎

MARK MANSON ONCE UPON A TIME AND MANY YEARS AGO, IN HIS INTRODUCTORY LECTURE, AN ACCOUNTING PROFESSOR HELD UP COPIES OF A SINGLE COMPANY'S ANNUAL REPORTS FOR THREE CONSECUTIVE YEARS. THE FIRST COVER PORTRAYED SMILING, HELPFUL PEOPLE AND PRODUCTS, SIMPLY LAID OUT. THE SECOND WAS ADORNED WITH A STEEPLY RISING ESCALATOR, EACH STEP OF WHICH WAS A DIFFERENT COLOR, DEPICTING THE GROWTH IN THE COMPANY'S SALES AND EARNINGS. THAT ILLUSTRATION WAS CAPTIONED "THE BEST IS YET TO COME!" THE THIRD ANNUAL REPORT CARRIED ONLY THE COMPANY'S NAME AND DATE IN BLACK PRINT ON A WHITE BACKGROUND, AND APPEARED

to be less bulky than the others. The accounting professor shouted at the class: "You people are dolts! You don't know anything! You certainly don't know how to read or understand what is in these books. But even dolts like you can read the story set out by the patterns of these three annual-report covers. Part one: Company runs its business. Part two: Hubris usurps work ethic. Part three: Failure. Study these documents and report back tomorrow." He smacked the annual reports down on his desk and stormed out of the classroom. □ In the feature film industry, where accounting procedures are Byzantine at best, quantitative results only occasionally reflect the financial condition of any given company accurately; when they do, that accuracy is often the result of happy accident rather than intent. The way a company qualitatively chooses to portray itself, or what it unconsciously reveals by its self-presentation, can be more telling than the numbers. □ Consider the 1989 annual reports of the three major American entertainment companies, Time Warner, Paramount Communications and The Walt Disney Company. In 1989, Time Inc. and Warner Communications attempted a friendly merger. Paramount bid for Time Inc.— an action that both Time and Warner viewed as hostile. As a defense, Time acquired Warner and an enormous load of debt in the process. Paramount erased much of its reported operating profit for the year with a write-down of about $100 million for costs associated with its aborted takeover effort. Disney ignored the turbulence, did not become engaged in the acquisition orgy of the period, and reported record profits by a wide margin. □ Time Warner's annual report (which I loved for its bravery and intent as much as for its conceptualization and execution) boasted a shocking lime green with

the word "WHY" in heavy bold type at its center. The body of the report was subdivided into sections titled "HOW," "WHAT" and "WHO." The presentation style extended more than emulated the work of Marshall McLuhan, with fragmented text presented in circles, in the borders and superimposed on pictures. Photographs and drawings carried the message. The "straight" text, in which management explained the "why" of the business combination of Time and Warner, was punctuated by such quotes as "Wait 'til they get a load of me!" by Jack Nicholson as The Joker in the Time Warner film *Batman*. The annual report effectively communicated the point that media were merging, that print, television, film and electronic data were simply various distribution systems for transmitting information—and that Time Warner could win in the communications industry because the company was a global leader boasting all of those capabilities. Not necessarily hidden, but not leaping out at the reader, were the financial results for the year. Time Warner lost $987 million in 1989. □ Paramount stuck to the facts. In the year just completed, the company had changed its name from Gulf and Western; sold its most profitable operating business, financial services, in an effort to streamline and concentrate on its communications business; taken substantial write-downs in publishing, one of its two remaining businesses; and lost the Time Warner takeover battle. Paramount's uncluttered and handsome visual presentation style befitted a company with a newly found focus on communications. The text acknowledged the aborted Time takeover, but moved quickly to stress the company's renewed vision. Paramount earned $1.47 billion in 1989, almost entirely a gain sale of its divested division. One could find in the text, if one looked, that the company had lost about $100 million in the Time escapade, that it had taken a write-down of $140 million in publishing (effectively deleting all earnings in that division) and that entertainment had put on a flat performance. The company's crisp presentation and the emphasis on its new direction and opportunities, however, left the reader with an optimistic look. □ The Walt Disney Company whistled while it worked in 1989, went about business without apparently paying much attention to the struggles all around it, and published an annual report following the tradition that Disney has established. Against a plain, all white cover, with a banner reading "Disneyland Celebrates 35 Years of Magic," the company presented a modest collage of company mementos, including a photograph of Uncle Walt himself, a Mickey Mouse doll and a Disneyland admission ticket. The letter to shareholders from the chairman, Michael Eisner, rambled to include the performance of his 11-year-old son on a spelling test ("His performance gives me the opportunity to pay tribute to our employees, who likewise accomplish the impossible") and a letter he had received from an elderly couple who had brought their retirement home on profits from Disney stock. Only then—and without bragging or ranking—did Eisner list the company's achievements for the year, which were substantial. □ Near the end of the letter, Eisner commented on the merger of yet another son's school with a neighboring girls' school, and the emotional trauma that had ensued. The point, apparently, was that it was better to do no deals than bad deals. In 1989 The Walt Disney Company earned $703 million versus $522 million the year before. □ As a financial analyst whose job is to discern inefficient pricing in the valuation of publicly traded securities, I need hard data as much as a masochist needs a beating. Without solid information, analysis can lead to painful conclusions and losses. Too many bits and bytes, however, clog the system and prevent any profitable action from ever being taken. The qualitative message—the statement of WHY, HOW, WHAT and WHO—underlies the numbers. The guiding concept behind an annual report often tells more about a company's place in that world than is intended. From Time Warner, the ultimate message was that the company saw its role as giving order to the chaos in which it, too, was swimming. For Paramount the task was to batten down the hatches, dig a deeper foxhole and regroup before initiating another assault. And Disney, thank you very much, seemed to be perfectly content with the status quo. The company, in its own mind, had a better mousetrap, and saw no point in fixing something that clearly was not broken. All three annual reports accurately reflected their companies' radically different places in the same industry. Each was telling, and each was helpful. As for the accounting professor, perhaps his pontificating also revealed more than he had intended. ■

MARK MANSON IS A VICE PRESIDENT WITH THE SECURITIES FIRM OF DONALDSON LUFKIN & JENRETTE INC, SPECIALIZING IN THE ENTERTAINMENT INDUSTRY. HE IS A MEMBER OF THE *INSTITUTIONAL INVESTOR* ALL-AMERICA RESEARCH TEAM. ■

MARK MANSON

VOR VIELEN JAHREN ZEIGTE EIN PROFESSOR FÜR BETRIEBSWIRTSCHAFT BEI SEINER EINFÜHRUNGSVORLESUNG DREI AUFEINANDERFOLGENDE JAHRESBERICHTE EINER EINZIGEN FIRMA. AUF DEM ERSTEN UMSCHLAG SAH MAN LÄCHELNDE, HILFREICHE LEUTE UND PRODUKTE, EINFACH DARGESTELLT. DEN ZWEITEN, IN LEUCHTENDEN FARBEN GEDRUCKT, SCHMÜCKTE EINE STEIL ANSTEIGENDE TREPPE, VON DER JEDE STUFE ANDERS AUSSAH, ZWECKS DARSTELLUNG DER STEIGENDEN VERKÄUFE UND EINNAHMEN. UNTER DIESER ILLUSTRATION STAND DER MUTIGE SATZ: «DAS BESTE KOMMT ERST NOCH!» AUF DEM DRITTEN JAHRESBERICHT STAND NUR DAS JAHR UND

der Firmenname, Schwarz auf Weiss, und er schien dünner als die anderen zu sein. Der Professor rief ins Auditorium: «Sie sind Ignoranten. Sie wissen gar nichts. Ganz sicher wissen Sie nicht, wie man diese Berichte liest, und sie verstehen nicht, was gesagt wird. Aber selbst Ignoranten verstehen die Botschaft, die sich von den Umschlägen dieser Berichte ablesen lässt.» Dann fügte er hinzu: «Nr. 1: Die Firma geht ihren Geschäften nach. Nr. 2: Überheblichkeit statt Arbeitsethik. Nr. 3: Misserfolg. Schauen Sie sich diese Berichte bis morgen an.» Dann schmetterte er die Jahresberichte auf sein Pult und stürmte aus dem Auditorium. □ In der Spielfilmindustrie, in der Buchhaltungsmethoden bestenfalls als undurchschaubar zu bezeichnen sind, geben die quantitativen Ergebnisse nur selten genauen Aufschluss über die finanzielle Situation einer Firma; wenn es tatsächlich der Fall ist, war meistens eher ein glücklicher Zufall als Absicht im Spiel. Die Art, wie eine Firma sich qualitativ darstellt oder was sie unbewusst durch ihre Selbstdarstellung verrät, sagt mehr als die Zahlen aus. Sehen Sie sich die Jahresberichte von den drei grössten Unternehmen der amerikanischen Unterhaltungsindustrie an: Time Warner, Paramount Communications und die Walt Disney Company. Im Jahre 1989 hatten Time Inc. und Warner Communications eine Fusion angestrebt. Paramount machte ein Angebot für Time Inc., eine Aktion, die sowohl Time als auch Warner als unfreundlich betrachteten. Im Gegenzug übernahm Time deshalb Warner und lud sich dabei enorme Schulden auf. Paramount benötigte einen grossen Teil der ausgewiesenen Betriebsergebnisses des Jahres für die Abschreibung von ungefähr $ 100 Millionen an Kosten für den missglückten Übernahmeversuch. Disney ignorierte den Wirbel, hielt sich aus der Akquisitionsorgie der Zeit heraus und konnte Rekordgewinne verzeichnen. □ Der Jahresbericht von Time Warner (den Mut und Intention nach Meinung des Autors ebenso auszeichnen wie Konzept und Ausführung) präsentierte sich mit einem knallgrünen Umschlag, und mitten darauf stand in schwerer, fetter Schrift das Wort «Why» (warum). Der Inhalt des Berichtes war in Abschnitte unterteilt – mit den Titeln «How» (wie), «What» (was) und «Who» (wer). Die Art der Plazierung von Textteilen in Kreisen, am Rand und über Bildern war eine Weiterführung der Arbeit von Marshall McLuhan. Photos und Zeichnungen waren die Hauptträger der Botschaft. Der klare Text, in dem sich das Management zu dem «Warum» der Zusammenlegung von Time und Warner äusserte, war mit bekannten Zitaten aus Filmen gespickt («The Joker and Prince» mit Jack Nicholson und Time Warners «Batman»). Was der Jahresbericht wirkungsvoll ausdrückte, war die Tatsache, dass Medien sich zusammenschliessen, dass Print, TV, Film und elektronische Datensysteme einfach verschiedene Systeme sind, die alle Informationen vermitteln, und dass Time Warners Chancen in der Kommunikationsindustrie ausgezeichnet seien, weil das Unternehmen einmalig und in allen diesen Bereichen weltweit führend sei. Nicht gerade versteckt, aber auch nicht so offensichtlich, dass der Leser direkt darauf stossen musste, wurden die vorläufigen finanziellen Ergebnisse des Jahres präsentiert. Time Warner hatte 1989 einen Verlust von $ 987 Millionen. □ Paramount berief sich auf Fakten. In dem gerade abgeschlossenen Jahr war aus dem Namen Gulf + Western Paramount Communications geworden; die Firma hatte ihre finanziell erfolgreichsten Unternehmungen im Betriebs- und Finanzberatungsbereich verkauft, um sich auf die Kommunikationsbranche zu konzentrieren; und sie verlor die Time-Warner-Schlacht. Der schlichte und ansprechende Stil des Paramount-Berichtes eignete sich ausgezeichnet für eine Firma, die sich neuerdings auf Kommunikation spezialisiert. Im Text wurde der fehlgeschlagene Übernahmeversuch erwähnt, man ging aber schnell zur neuen Ausrichtung der Firma über. Paramount verdiente 1989 $ 1,47 Milliarden, die fast ausschliesslich aus dem erwähnten Verkauf stammten. Wenn man genau hinsah, konnte man dem Text entnehmen, dass die Firma durch die Time-Eskapade ungefähr $ 100 Millionen Verlust hinnehmen musste, dass sie im Verlagsgeschäft Abschreibungen von $ 140 Millionen hatte (wodurch alle Gewinne dieses Bereiches aufgezehrt wurden), und dass die Ergebnisse im Unterhaltungsbereich schwach waren. Die frische Darstellung der Firma und die Betonung der neuen Richtung und Möglichkeiten vermittelten dem Leser jedoch optimistische Aussichten. ☐ Die Walt Disney Company liess sich 1989 nicht aus der Ruhe bringen, den Kämpfen um sie herum schenkte sie offenbar keine Beachtung und veröffentlichte einen Jahresbericht ganz in der Disney-Tradition. Ein schlichter weisser Umschlag, auf dessen Kopf in sanfter Kursivschrift stand: «Disneyland feiert 35 zauberhafte Jahre», mit einer bescheidenen Collage mit einer Aufnahme von Walt Disney, einer Mickey-Mouse-Puppe und einer Eintrittskarte für Disneyland. Im Brief an die Aktionäre erwähnt Chairman Michael Eisner den Erfolg seines elfjährigen Sohnes bei einer Rechtschreibeprüfung und geht dann auf die Leistungen der Mitarbeiter ein, «die ebenfalls das Unmögliche möglich machten». Ausserdem berichtet er von dem Brief eines älteren Ehepaares, das sich mit den Dividenden aus seinen Disney-Aktien ein Haus finanzieren konnte. Erst danach – und ohne Prahlerei oder Gewichtung – führt er die beachtlichen Leistungen der Firma im abgeschlossenen Jahr

auf. Gegen Ende des Briefes spricht Mr. Eisner über den Zusammenschluss der Schule eines weiteren Sohnes mit einer benachbarten Mädchenschule und dem daraus entstandenen seelischen Schock. Damit will er offenbar sagen, dass es besser sei, sich auf keine Geschäfte einzulassen als auf schlechte. «Gemischte Schulen sind eine Sache für sich. Etwas zu teuer zu bezahlen, das man nicht in den Griff bekommen kann, ist eine andere Sache», so die Schlussfolgerung von Michael Eisner. 1989 verdiente die Walt Disney Company $ 703 Millionen gegenüber $ 522 Millionen im vorhergehenden Jahr. ☐ Als Finanzanalytiker, dessen Aufgabe es ist, uneffiziente Preisfestsetzung in der Bewertung von an der Börse gehandelten Wertpapieren zu erkennen, brauche ich hieb- und stichfeste Daten. Ohne solide Information kann die Analyse zu ziemlich schmerzhaften Folgerungen und Verlusten führen. Zu viele Bits und Bytes blockieren jedoch das System und verhindern jegliche profitable Aktion. Die qualitative Botschaft in der Feststellung WARUM, WIE, WAS und WER eine Firma in einem dynamischen Umfeld ist und sein möchte, steht hinter den Zahlen und besagt, ob man sich überhaupt mit den Zahlen herumschlagen soll. Das Grundkonzept eines Jahresberichtes sagt oft mehr als beabsichtigt über den Platz der Firma in jenem Umfeld aus. Bei Time Warner war die Botschaft, dass das Unternehmen seine Rolle darin sieht, Ordnung in das Chaos zu bringen, in dem auch es sich befindet. Für Paramount bestand die Aufgabe darin, sich neu zu formieren, bevor sie einen neuen Angriff wagt. Disney wiederum schien mit dem Status quo vollkommen zufrieden zu sein. Diese Firma sah nicht ein, warum sie etwas reparieren sollte, was offenbar nicht zerbrochen war. Alle drei Jahresberichte reflektierten die vollkommen verschiedenen Positionen, die diese Unternehmen in der gleichen Industrie einnehmen. Jeder Bericht sagte etwas aus und war dadurch im Endeffekt nützlich. ∎

MARK MANSON, EINER DER VIZEPRÄSIDENTEN DER ANLAGEFIRMA DONALDSON, LUFKIN & JERETTE INC. IN NEW YORK, IST ANALYTIKER FÜR DIVIDENDENPAPIERE, AUF DIE UNTERHALTUNGSINDUSTRIE SPEZIALISIERT. ER IST MITGLIED DES INSTITUTIONAL INVESTOR ALL-AMERICA RESEARCH TEAM (AMERIKANISCHER AUSSCHUSS FÜR INSTITUTIONELLE ANLEGER).∎

MARK MANSON VOICI DES ANNÉES DE CELA, DANS SON COURS D'INTRODUCTION, UN PROFESSEUR DE GESTION D'ENTREPRISES PROPOSA EN EXEMPLE LES TROIS DERNIERS RAPPORTS ANNUELS D'UNE SOCIÉTÉ. LE PREMIER MONTRAIT EN COUVERTURE DES GENS SOURIANTS, SERVIABLES, ET DES PRODUITS, DANS UNE MISE EN PAGES TRÈS SIMPLE. LE SECOND ÉTAIT ORNÉ DE LA PHOTO D'UN ESCALATOR DONT CHAQUE MARCHE, D'UNE COULEUR DIFFÉRENTE, REPRÉSENTAIT LA CROISSANCE DES VENTES ET DES GAINS DE LA COMPAGNIE. CETTE ILLUS-TRATION ÉTAIT ACCOMPAGNÉE D'UNE LÉGENDE AUDACIEUSE: «LE MEILLEUR EST À VENIR!» LE TROISIÈME DE CES RAPPORTS ANNUELS PORTAIT

seulement le nom de l'entreprise et la date, imprimés en noir sur fond blanc, et il avait l'air plus mince que les précédents. Le professeur interpella alors ses élèves d'une voix retentis-sante: «Vous êtes tous des ânes. Vous n'arriveriez certaine-ment pas à lire ou comprendre le contenu de ces publica-tions. Mais même les ânes peuvent saisir le message qui s'ex-prime sur ces trois couvertures.» Puis il ajouta: «Première-ment, l'entreprise fait des affaires. Deuxièmement, l'arro-gance prend le pas sur l'éthique de travail. Troisièmement, c'est l'échec. Etudiez ces documents jusqu'à demain.» Et jetant les rapports sur son bureau, il sortit précipitamment de la classe. □ Dans l'industrie cinématographique la comp-tabilité est d'une extrême complication, les bilans reflètent l'état des finances d'une société. Quand c'est le cas, cette exactitude est souvent le résultat d'un heureux hasard. La manière dont une société choisit de se présenter, ou bien ce qu'elle révèle insconsciemment, peuvent en dire plus long que les chiffres. Regardons par exemple les rapports annuels 1989 des trois plus grandes sociétés de cinéma, la Time War-ner, Paramount Communications et la Walt Disney Compa-ny. En 1989, Time Inc. et Warner Communications avaient poursuivi une politique de fusion amicale. La Paramount fit une offre d'achat à Time Inc., ce que Time et Warner virent d'un mauvais œil. Time riposta en achetant Warner, s'endet-tant formidablement à cette occasion. Paramount dut em-ployer la plupart de ses bénéfices de l'année pour amortir les quelques 100 millions de dollars de dettes qu'avait occasion-nés cette tentative de rachat avortée. La Walt Disney Com-pany resta en dehors de toute cette agitation, indifférente à la vogue de rachats d'entreprises qui marquait cette période, et la firme enregistra des bénéfices record. □ Le rapport annuel de la Time Warner (que j'ai aimé en raison de son audace et de ses intentions, du concept et de l'exécution) présentait une couverture vert vif avec, au milieu, en caractères gras, monumentaux, le mot Why («Pourquoi»). Le contenu de ce rapport était divisé en chapitres qui portaient les titres sui-vants: How («Comment»), What («Quoi») et Who («Qui»). Le style de la présentation, des blocs de texte circulaires dis-posés dans les marges et superposés aux images, complétait en quelque sorte les illustrations de Marshall McLuhan. Les photographies et les dessins venaient renforcer le message. Rédigé dans un style direct, le texte, dans lequel la direction expliquait le pourquoi de cette alliance entre Time et War-ner, était ponctué de citations tirées de films («The Joker and Prince» avec Jack Nicholson et «Batman», de la Time & Warner). Ce rapport réussissait particulièrement bien à ex-primer le fait que les médias sont en train de fusionner, que l'édition, la TV, le cinéma et les systèmes informatiques ne sont que différents organes de distribution servant à la transmission de l'information; dans le secteur de l'industrie de la communication, la société Time Warner a donc toutes les chances, parce qu'elle est unique et qu'elle est le n° 1 de la branche dans le monde. Bien qu'ils n'aient pas été vraiment dissimulés, les résultats financiers provisoires de l'année n'étaient pas mis en relief de manière à ce que le lecteur tombe tout de suite dessus. Les pertes de la Time Warner en 1989 se chiffraient à 987 millions de $. □ La Paramount s'ap-puyait sur les faits. Au cours de l'année qui venait de se ter-miner, cette société avait abandonné son ancien nom, Gulf + Westen, adoptant celui de Paramount Communications; la firme avait revendu ses entreprises les plus profitables et ses services financiers afin de se concentrer sur le secteur de la communication; et elle avait perdu la bataille de la Time Warner. La présentation claire et attrayante du rapport annuel de la Paramount était parfaitement adaptée à une firme qui vient de se spécialiser dans le domaine de la communication. Le texte mentionnait la tentative infructueuse de rachat, mais abordait aussitôt la nouvelle stratégie de l'entreprise. Paramount avait gagné 1,47 milliard de dollars en 1989, qui provenaient presque entièrement des ventes dont nous avons parlé. En lisant le texte encore plus attentivement, on découvrait que l'entreprise avait perdu environ 100 millions de dollars dans l'aventure du rachat de Time, qu'elle enregistrait 140 millions de dollars de déficit dans le domaine de l'édition (tous les autres bénéfices de ce secteur ayant servi à les renflouer), et que les résultats du secteur des loisirs étaient plutôt faibles. Le ton direct de la présentation de la firme et l'accent mis sur la nouvelle direction et ses projets donnaient cependant au lecteur l'impression de perspectives optimistes. □ La Walt Disney Company ne se laissa pas troubler par les luttes qui faisaient rage autour d'elle en 1989 et elle publia un rapport annuel dans la tradition des précédents. Une couverture toute simple, avec un titre écrit en italiques sur fond blanc: «Disneyland célèbre 35 années magiques», ornée d'un collage discret de photos-souvenirs, y compris celle de Walt Disney, une poupée aux traits de Mickey et un ticket d'entrée à Disneyland. Dans la Lettre aux actionnaires, Michael Eisner, le président, fait même allusion à la réussite de son fils de onze ans à un examen de calcul, passant ensuite aux performances accomplies par ses collaborateurs «qui, eux aussi, rendent l'impossible possible». Il parle en outre de la lettre d'un vieux couple de retraités qui a pu se financer une maison grâce aux dividendes provenant de leurs actions Disney. Ensuite seulement, sans plastronner ni insister lourdement, M. Eisner présente les succès appré-

ciables de la firme au cours de l'année. Vers la fin, il parle de la fusion de l'école que fréquente un autre de ses fils avec une école de filles voisine et du choc psychique que cela a engendré. Avec cette allusion, il veut apparemment faire remarquer qu'il vaut mieux ne pas se lancer à l'aventure que de faire de mauvaises affaires. «La mixité est une chose. Payer trop cher quelque chose que vous ne pouvez pas contrôler en est une autre», conclut M. Eisner. En 1989, la Walt Disney Company a gagné 703 millions de dollars, contre 522 l'année précédente. □ Analyste financier, j'ai besoin de données irréfutables. Sans une information solide, une analyse peut avoir des conséquences désastreuses et conduire à des pertes. Quoi qu'il en soit, un excès de jargon informatique est rédhibitoire et empêche de se lancer dans des entreprises fructueuses. Le message qualitatif contenu dans l'affirmation de ce qu'est, ou de ce que désire être une entreprise dans un monde dynamique, le POURQUOI, le COMMENT, QUI et QUOI se trouve derrière les bilans: eux seuls indiquent si cela vaut la peine de se batailler avec les chiffres. Le concept directeur d'un rapport annuel en dit souvent plus qu'on ne le croit sur la position de la firme dans le monde des affaires. Chez Time Warner, en définitive, le message était que la firme considère qu'il lui faut remédier au chaos dans lequel elle est plongée. Quant à la Paramount, il lui faut boucher les trous, assurer ses arrières et se restructurer avant de se lancer dans de nouveaux assauts. A l'évidence, Disney s'est contenté du statu quo. Cette firme ne voit pas pourquoi elle devrait réparer ce qui manifestement n'a pas été détruit. Ces trois rapports annuels reflétaient les positions absolument différentes d'entreprises d'une même branche. Chacun exprimait quelque chose et était finalement utile. C'est comme pour notre professeur de gestion d'entreprises, sa leçon pontifiante révélait elle aussi beaucoup plus qu'il ne l'avait cru. ■

MARK MANSON EST VICE-PRÉSIDENT DE LA FIRME D'INVESTISSEMENTS DONALDSON, LUFKIN & JENRETTE INC. À NEW YORK, OÙ IL EST ANALYSTE SPÉCIALISÉ DANS LES DIVIDENDES PROVENANT DE L'INDUSTRIE DES LOISIRS. MEMBRE DE L'INSTITUTIONAL INVESTOR ALL-AMERICA RESEARCH TEAM (COMMISSION D'INVESTITEURS INSTITUTIONNELS AUX USA). ■

JURY COMMENTS

KOMMENTARE DER JURY

COMMENTAIRES DU JURY

THE JUDGING OF ANNUAL REPORTS 3, COVERING FISCAL YEARS 1989 AND 1990, TOOK PLACE AT THE SCHOOL OF VISUAL

ARTS IN NEW YORK CITY DURING THE SUMMERS OF 1990 AND 1991. EACH COLLECTION OF 25 REPORTS WAS CHOSEN

FROM OVER 1,000 INTERNATIONAL ENTRIES, WITH "BEST OF SHOW" AWARDS THEN SELECTED FROM EACH YEAR'S GROUP. ■

1 9 8 9 THE 25 REPORTS CHOSEN FOR THIS YEAR'S SELECTION EXCELLED IN ALL CATEGORIES: CONCEPT, TYPOGRAPHY, ILLUSTRATION AND PHOTOGRAPHY. THIS MADE THE SELECTION OF A SINGLE BEST REPORT EXTREMELY DIFFICULT. AS A RESULT, AWARDS WERE GIVEN TO TWO REPORTS LAUDED AS "CUTTING EDGE" AND "OUTSTANDING" BY THE JUDGES. ■

ARMANDO MILANI

ADRIAN PULFER

GREGORY SAMATA

ARMANDO MILANI, principal of Milani Design in New York City, studied at Scuola Umanitaria of Design in Milan. He has collaborated with many important designers, including Massimo Vignelli, and in 1978 he founded his own design studio in New York, specializing in corporate identity programs and logo, book and poster design. Milani's work has been published in several annuals and included in major graphic exhibitions in Milan, Paris, London, New York and Los Angeles. ■ A native of Melbourne, Australia, **ADRIAN PULFER** is current-ly the principal of Adrian Parry Design in Salt Lake City, Utah. He moved to the United States in 1970, and opened his first design studio in Salt Lake City in 1975. He then moved to New York in 1982, where he was a partner in the design firm Jonson, Pedersen, Hinrichs & Shakery, and where he also worked with Parry Merkley to complete their textile collection. Pulfer has directed design projects in a variety of areas, and has received many awards. He currently teaches at the design school of Brigham Young University. ■ Since founding his own design firm in the early 1970s, **GREGORY SAMATA**, currently principal and designer of Samata Associates in Dundee, Illinois, has created annual reports, corporate trademarks and identity programs for numerous *Fortune*-500 companies. His work has been recognized in every major design publication, and he has received hundreds of awards in various shows and annuals. Samata received his B.F.A. from the Chicago Academy of Art, is a national board member of the AIGA, and is also a member of the American Center for Design. ■

1 9 9 0 THIS YEAR'S 25 ANNUAL REPORTS REFLECT A VARIETY OF STYLES, AND WERE CHOSEN ON THE BASIS OF THEIR INNOVATIVE AND INTELLIGENT CONCEPTS AND THEIR EXPRESSIVE USE OF PHOTOGRAPHY AND ILLUSTRATION. THE JUDGES DESCRIBED THE BEST OF SHOW AS "SUBTLE" AND "ELEGANT," A HARMONY OF PRESENTATION AND ELEMENTS. ■

RICHARD DANNE

BENNETT ROBINSON

DON SHANOSKY

TYLER SMITH

RICHARD DANNE is currently president and creative director of Richard Danne & Associates in New York City. He studied at the UCLA Graduate School of Design after graduating from Oklahoma State University. He and his firm are engaged in three fundamental areas of design–annual reports, corporate identity programs, and environmental graphics–for which they have won many awards. Danne's work has been exhibited in several one-man shows and invitational exhibitions. He was the founding president of AIGA/NY, the New York chapter of the institute, and now serves as president of the United States delegation of Alliance Graphique Internationale. ■ **BENNETT ROBINSON** is the group chairman and creative director of Corporate Graphics Inc. in New York City, a group of which he is a cofounder. Corporate Graphics has offices in New York, London, and Los Angeles, and specializes in the production of annual and quarterly reports, capabilities brochures and corporate identity programs. Robinson and his team of designers have garnered numerous major awards and honors, and have been the subject of feature articles in several leading design publications. ■ **DON SHANOSKY**, principal of Cook and Shanosky Associates in Princeton, New Jersey, which he cofounded in 1967 with Roger Cook. The firm specializes in corporate and institutional communications and serves a diverse list of clients. Cook and Shanosky has been profiled in major design publications, and is a recipient of The Presidential Award for Design. ■ **TYLER SMITH**, principal of Tyler Smith, Art Direction in Providence, Rhode Island, has won numerous national and international graphic-design awards, including gold and silver medals from the New York Art Directors Club. He has lectured at the Smithsonian Institution and has judged various design, advertising and photography competitions throughout the United States. His work is represented in the permanent collection of the Cooper-Hewitt Museum in New York, and has also appeared in numerous leading design publications. ■

AUBREY BALKIND, PRESIDENT AND CEO

KENT HUNTER, CREATIVE DIRECTOR, FRANKFURT GIPS BALKIND

TIME WARNER ANNUAL REPORT 1989

A CPA, a Columbia MBA and an Arthur Young management consultant before becoming a designer, Aubrey Balkind has a background that is particularly suited to strategic communications. He is the architect of Frankfurt Gips Balkind as a communications agency, and is its chief strategist for MCI Communications and Time Warner, among many other *Fortune*-500 clients. □ Aubrey takes an active role in the design community. He is founding director of the Association of Professional Design firms and the International Design by Electronics Association. He has lectured for these groups and others, such as Broadcast Promotion & Marketing Executives, the American Institute of Graphic Arts, the Design Management Institute, *Financial World*'s annual report seminars, the New York Macintosh Users Group, the Women's National Book Association, and various colleges around the country. ■ As creative director of Frankfurt Gips Balkind, an integrated communications agency, based in New York and Los Angeles, Kent Hunter directs a team of designers on assignments that include annual reports, corporate magazines and newsletters, book projects, posters and multimedia presentations. His work has been recognized by the Mead Show, AR 100, *Communication Arts*, the American Center for Design, *Graphis* and the New York Art Directors Club. He has recently won awards for his annual reports for Time Warner, the Associated Press and The Limited. □ Hunter serves on the board of the New York chapter of the American Institute of Graphic Arts, has judged numerous design shows and has given many lectures around the country. ■

MICHAEL VANDERBYL, PRINCIPAL, VANDERBYL DESIGN

THE L.J. SKAGGS AND MARY C. SKAGGS FOUNDATION ANNUAL REPORT 1989

Michael Vanderbyl received a Bachelor of Fine Arts degree in graphic design from the California College of Arts and Crafts in 1968. Today he is dean of the School of Design at his alma mater. □ Since being established in San Francisco in 1973, Vanderbyl Design has evolved into a multidiscipline firm with expertise in graphics, packaging, signage, interiors, showrooms, furniture, textiles and fashion apparel. A partial client list includes Amaco, the American Institute of Architects, Bernhardt Furniture Company, Esprit, IBM, Polaroid, Simpson Paper Company, and the San Francisco Museum of Modern Art. □ Vanderbyl has gained international prominence in the design field as a practitioner, educator, critic and advocate. He has served on the National Board of Directors of the AIGA and the group's Education Committee, and is a founding member of the San Francisco chapter of the AIGA. The United States Information Agency invited Vanderbyl to act as a consultant on "Design USA: A Cultural Exchange Exhibition with the USSR." In 1987 Vanderbyl was elected to become a member of the Alliance Graphique Internationale, an international design organization in Zürich. □ Vanderbyl's printed work has gained recognition in every major design competition in the United States and Europe. His work is part of the permanent collections of the Cooper Hewitt Museum (Smithsonian Institution) and the Library of Congress. *Time* magazine selected Vanderbyl's line of Esprit home textiles for its "Best of '87" design issue. Vanderbyl and his sheet collection for Esprit were also featured in an interview on the Today Show. ∎

DANA ARNETT, PRINCIPAL, VSA PARTNERS INC.

CHICAGO BOARD OF TRADE ANNUAL REPORT 1990

Dana Arnett is a principal with the design firm VSA Partners, located in the historic Printers Row district of Chicago. Arnett, who joined the firm in 1985, shares the responsibility for running the office with the partners, Robert Vogele, Ted Stoik and Jamie Koval. □ The work of Arnett and VSA Partners has received recognition in a variety of publications and competitions, including *Graphis, Communication Arts, Print Magazine,* the AIGA, the American Center for Design, the New York Art Directors Club, the IABC and the Chicago Financial Advertisers. Recently, VSA Partners was recognized by *ID Magazine* as "...representing some of the best corporate identity in America." □ Arnett currently serves as a board member of DIFFA/Chicago (the Design Industries Foundation for AIDS) and other groups. ■

89

ANNUAL REPORT DESIGN

GESTALTUNG VON JAHRESBERICHTEN

DESIGN DES RAPPORTS ANNUELS

WHY?

TIME WARNER INC.

. . . .

▲ The annual report is the one, major, hard-copy piece that we, as an entire company, put out during the year; otherwise, all of our divisions publish autonomously. Our annual report serves as the company's one big, current identity piece. There's a diverse audience for any annual, but I think this is especially true in our case. The primary readership is split equally between the existing shareholders and the investment community and our employees, most of whom are shareholders (and, in general, I feel any company's annual report should be for the employees). Then there is the secondary, larger audience, consisting of all the people we do business with: artists, journalists, other companies, and the United States and foreign governments. Finally there's the function of the annual report as a general public relations document. This report, the first from the company created by the merger of Time, Inc. and Warner Communications, is meant to answer the question stated on the front cover: Why? Why did we merge? The answer is: To position the company as the global leader in media and entertainment, both in creation and in distribution of creative product. The report is designed in layers, each relating back to the question and answers, so that even a surface reader can grasp the main points. From a design standpoint, we didn't want something that looked like either a Time or a Warner annual report; we wanted it to look unlike anything that's been done in the past, and we wanted to communicate a lot of information in a succinct but intriguing way. We feel that designers should not be hired to create artwork; they should be hired to aid effective communication through their talents.

. . . .

■ Der Jahresbericht ist das eine grosse Schriftstück, das wir als Gesamtunternehmen während des Jahres herausgeben; ansonsten sind alle unsere Abteilungen autonom. Jahresberichte haben grundsätzlich ein sehr gemischtes Publikum, und das trifft wohl ganz besonders in unserem Fall zu. Die Hauptzielgruppe besteht gleichermassen aus den gegenwärtigen Aktionären und Investoren und unseren Angestellten, die zum grossen Teil auch Aktionäre sind (ich glaube übrigens, dass sich alle Jahresberichte auch an die Angestellten richten sollten). Die zweite, grössere Gruppe setzt sich aus all den Leuten zusammen, mit denen wir geschäftlich verbunden sind: Künstler, Journalisten, andere Unternehmen und die Regierungen der USA und anderer Länder. Zu guter Letzt dient der Jahresbericht als allgemeines Public-Relations-Dokument. Der aktuelle Bericht ist gleichzeitig der erste Bericht des Unternehmens, das durch die Fusion von Time Inc. und Warner Communications zustande kam, und er soll die auf der Titelseite gestellte Frage beantworten: Warum haben wir fusioniert? Der Bericht ist in verschiedenen Schichten entworfen, die sich allesamt auf die eingangs gestellte Frage und die Antworten darauf beziehen, so dass selbst bei oberflächlichem Lesen die wichtigsten Punkte klar werden. Die Aktionäre sollten etwas bekommen, das aus der Masse anderer Jahresberichte herausragt. Das Design sollte weder an einen Time- noch an einen Warner-Jahresbericht erinnern: Wir wollten etwas absolut Neuartiges, einen Bericht, der sich von allem bereits Dagewesenen unterschied, und wir wollten gleichzeitig eine Menge Information in knapper aber ansprechender Form vermitteln.

. . . .

● Le rapport annuel de gestion est l'imprimé le plus important que nous ayons à publier durant l'année. Tout l'entreprise partcipe à cet effort alors que, habituellement, chaque section est autonome. Le public des rapports annuels est toujours très varié, mais je pense que c'est particulièrement vrai dans notre cas. Ce rapport est principalement conçu pour les actionnaires, les investisseurs, et nos employés, qui sont pour la plupart actionnaires (et j'ai d'ailleurs le sentiment que tout rapport annuel d'entreprise devrait être conçu en priorité pour les employés). Nous tenons compte ensuite d'une audience plus large, constituée par tous ceux avec qui nous traitons: les artistes, les journalistes, les autres entreprises, ainsi que les gouvernements américain et étrangers. Ce rapport, le premier de la société créée à la suite de la fusion de Time, Inc. et Warner Communications, est destiné à répondre à la question posée sur la page de couverture: «Pourquoi avons-nous fusionné?» Le rapport est conçu «en strates», renvoyant chaque fois à la question principale et à ces réponses, pour que même un lecteur superficiel puisse appréhender l'essentiel. Pour les actionnaires et les investisseurs, nous voulions quelque chose qui sorte de l'ordinaire, qui soit vraiment différent des rapports qu'ils reçoivent habituellement. Du point de vue conception, il était hors de question qu'il y ait la moindre ressemblance avec ceux de Time ou de Warner. Nous voulions qu'il ne rappelle en rien ce qui avait été fait auparavant, et notre but était de communiquer un maximum d'informations, de façon concise, mais de manière à piquer la curiosité du lecteur.

[JOAN NICHOLAS]

TIME WARNER INC.: 1271 AVENUE OF THE AMERICAS, NEW YORK, NY 10020

75 ROCKEFELLER PLAZA, NEW YORK, NY 10019 USA 212.484.8000

FRANKFURT GIPS BALKIND

▲ Frankfurt Gips Balkind had been the design firm for the Time, Inc. annual report and was chosen to continue in this role for the newly merged Time Warner company. Because the job was controlled internally by former Warner personnel, it was like working for a new client, even more so with their concern that the report stress that this was a new company, not a merger where either absorbed the other. Warner, in past reports, had taken visual imagery to the limit, but had been less interested in copy. This year, they wanted to create a new language—one that incorporated words and pictures. Despite its distinctive design, we had no difficulty in selling the final concepts to the client; after all, their main objective was to garner attention. The result sparked conversation in the press and along company corridors. All of our books contain "markers" that help the reader remember what the report's about—they serve as milestones, highlighting the main themes. In this case, we wanted to create an interactive report, one that integrated words and pictures, while reflecting the global hunger for information and entertainment. In many ways, this was one of the most difficult reports we've ever done. Despite the enormous attention received by this book, budget guidelines were very strict; they wanted it done for what it had cost the previous year. The innovative look was actually created to keep the book in line with budget demands.

■ Frankfurt Gips Balkind war zuvor schon die Design-Firma für den Jahresbericht von Time Inc., und wir wurden ausgewählt, in dieser Rolle auch für den neu fusionierten Time-Warner-Konzern zu arbeiten. Da die interne Verantwortung für den Auftrag bei ehemaligen Warner-Angestellten lag, mussten wir uns gewissermassen auf einen völlig neuen Kunden einstellen. Hinzu kam, dass Time Warner in dem Bericht betonen wollte, dass es sich hier um ein neues Unternehmen handelte, nicht um eine Fusion, bei der einer den anderen geschluckt hatte. Warner hatte in seinen früheren Berichten den visuellen Elementen absoluten Vorrang vor dem Text gegeben. Dieses Jahr sollte eine neue Sprache kreiert werden – eine Sprache, in der Wort und Bild eine Einheit ergaben. Trotz seines ungewöhnlichen Designs hatten wir keine Schwierigkeiten, dem Kunden das endgültige Konzept zu verkaufen – das wichtigste Ziel des Jahresberichts ist es schliesslich, Aufmerksamkeit zu erregen. Das Endergebnis sorgte in der Presse und auch bei den Angestellten des Unternehmens für einiges Aufsehen. In diesem Fall wollten wir einen interaktiven Bericht entwerfen, einen Bericht, der Worte und Bilder integriert und dabei den globalen Hunger nach Information und Unterhaltung zum Ausdruck bringt. Trotz dem hohen Stellenwert, der diesem Buch eingeräumt wurde, erlaubte das Budget wenig Spielraum; der Kunde wollte nicht mehr Geld ausgeben, als der Bericht des Vorjahres gekostet hatte. Der innovative Look ergab sich letzlich aus dem Zwang, mit einem engen Budget auszukommen.

● Frankfurt Gips Balkind, qui avait conçu les rapports annuels de Time, Inc., a été choisie pour accomplir cette même tâche au sein de la nouvelle société Time Warner. Etant donné que le travail était sous la responsabilité interne de l'ancien personnel de la Warner, c'était un peu comme de travailler pour un nouveau client; de plus, il était bien précisé dans le rapport qu'il s'agissait d'une entreprise totalement nouvelle, et non pas d'une simple fusion où l'une ou l'autre des sociétés aurait absorbé l'autre. Dans ses précédents rapports, la Warner avait exploité toutes les possibilités de l'imagerie visuelle au détriment de la rédaction. Time Warner a voulu créer un nouveau langage, un langage qui puisse inclure à la fois mots et images. En dépit de son design particulier, nous n'avons eu aucune difficulté à vendre le concept final au client. Après tout, l'objectif principal était d'attirer l'attention. Le résultat déclencha des polémiques dans la presse aussi bien que dans les couloirs de l'entreprise. Toutes nos publications contiennent des «jalons» qui aident le lecteur à ne pas perdre de vue le sujet du rapport. Ils servent de points de repère, mettant l'accent sur les thèmes essentiels. Dans ce cas précis, nous voulions un rapport interactif qui intégrerait le mot et l'image, tout en reflétant cette soif d'information et de divertissement. Ce fut à maints égards le rapport le plus difficile que nous ayons jamais produit. Malgré l'attention particulière dont le livre a été l'objet, la marge budgétaire était très étroite, le coût global devant rester le même que celui de l'année précédente. Finalement, nous avons dû créer ce «look» innovateur selon le budget imparti.

[AUBREY BALKIND]

FRANKFURT GIPS BALKIND: 244 EAST 58TH STREET, NEW YORK, NEW YORK 10022 USA 212.421.5888

Global ization

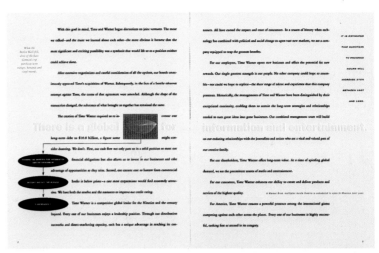

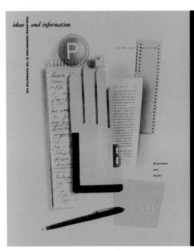

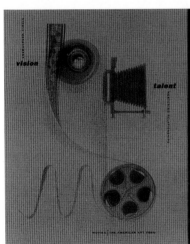

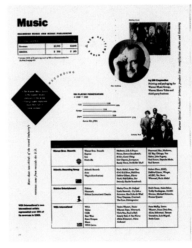

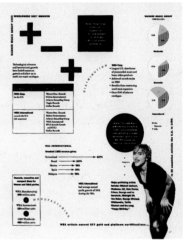

CLIENT: TIME-WARNER INC. ■ DESIGN FIRM: FRANKFURT GIPS BALKIND ■ CREATIVE DIRECTORS: AUBREY BALKIND, KENT HUNTER ■ DESIGNERS: KENT HUNTER, RIKI SETHIADI ■ PHOTOGRAPHERS: SCOTT MORGAN, GEOF KERN, CHRIS SANDERS ■ WRITER: TIME-WARNER INC. ■ PRODUCTION MANAGER: BONNIE GOLDBERG ■ TYPOGRAPHER: FRANKFURT GIPS BALKIND ■ PAPER SELECTION: CENTURA GLOSS COVER, REFLECTIONS GLOSS WEB AND SUNDANCE VELLUM SPECIAL BRIGHTNESS ■ TRIM SIZE: 9⅞ x 11 INCHES ■ TYPE SELECTION: FRANKLIN GOTHIC, GARAMOND NUMBER 3 ■

THE L.J. SKAGGS AND MARY C. SKAGGS FOUNDATION

▲ The purpose of this annual report is to satisfy the legal requirements of reporting on the activities of the Foundation as well as to relay information on programming within the various granting areas. The primary audience is divided between those who have received support from the Foundation during the year of reporting and those who would like to approach the Foundation for funding. The secondary audience would include other foundations that are interested in our activities. Each year our annual report has focused on one particular area of grants, with an essay and illustrations to support the written material. The current issue attempts to-communicate a philosophy on "the effect of mass media on human behavior and decision making." This is the seventh and last report we are preparing with Michael Vanderbyl's assistance. The visuals, along with the typography, which is very difficult to read, lead us to revise our thinking in producing a design-oriented report. In this particular case, the design became a larger part of the message than we had wanted. The relationship with the designer became strained, as the client felt that its wishes were being overlooked in favor of "cutting edge" design. Ironically, the program has subsequently been cancelled by the trustees of the Foundation. In short, while we respect Mr. Vanderbyl's design integrity, we felt in the final analysis that this book was "his" more than it was ours.

■ Der Zweck dieses Jahresberichts ist einerseits, die gesetzlichen Vorschriften zu erfüllen, die uns verpflichten, die Aktivitäten unserer Stiftung offenzulegen. Gleichzeitig soll er darüber informieren, welche Programme innerhalb der verschiedenen Subventionsbereiche stattgefunden haben. Der Bericht wendet sich in erster Linie an die Leute, die während des Berichtsjahres Stipendien erhalten haben, und an all diejenigen, die mit der Bitte um Unterstützung an die Stiftung herantreten wollen. Eine weitere Zielgruppe sind verwandte Stiftungen, die an unseren Aktivitäten interessiert sind. Unser Bericht konzentriert sich jedes Jahr auf ein ganz bestimmtes Schwerpunktgebiet, das in einem Essay abgehandelt und anhand von Illustrationen verdeutlicht wird. Die gegenwärtige Ausgabe versucht, eine Philosophie über «die Wirkung der Massenmedien auf unser Verhalten und unsere Entscheidungen» zu vermitteln. Es ist der siebte und letzte Bericht, den wir gemeinsam mit Michael Vanderbyl erarbeitet haben. Die visuelle Aufbereitung und das ausserordentlich schwer lesbare Schriftbild haben uns veranlasst, unsere ursprüngliche Absicht, einen designorientierten Bericht zu produzieren, zu revidieren – das Design wurde hier zu einem weitaus wichtigeren Teil der Aussage, als uns eigentlich lieb gewesen wäre. Die Beziehung zwischen dem Designer und uns wurde immer angespannter, da wir den Eindruck hatten, dass unsere Wünsche zugunsten eines avantgardistischen Designs vernachlässigt wurden. Ironischerweise wurde das Programm später von den Treuhändern der Stiftung abgesetzt. Kurz gesagt: Wir respektieren Mr. Vanderbyls Integrität als Designer, fanden aber letztendlich, dass dieser Bericht eher «sein» Werk war als unseres.

● Le but de ce rapport annuel est de répondre aux exigences légales concernant les activités de la Fondation, aussi bien que de relayer l'information sur la programmation des différents domaines de subvention. Le public visé est composé de ceux qui ont reçu des subventions pendant l'année en cours, et ceux qui aimeraient en savoir davantage sur ces même subventions. Notre deuxième cible représente les fondations intéressées par nos activités. Notre rapport annuel s'est toujours concentré sur un type particulier de subvention, comprenant un texte, et des illustrations mettant en valeur le rapport. La présente publication tente de communiquer une certaine conception de «l'effet des mass médias sur le comportement humain et la prise de décision». Ceci est le septième et dernier rapport que nous préparons avec Michael Vanderbyl. Les visuels, de même que la typographie, qui est très difficile à lire, nous ont amené à revoir notre objectif qui était de produire un rapport plutôt tourné vers le design. Dans ce cas particulier, le design a pris une part beaucoup plus grande dans le message que nous le désirions. Les relations avec le designer sont devenues tendues parce que le client sentait que ses désirs étaient outrepassés en faveur d'une création plus «tranchée». Ironiquement, le programme fut annulé par les administrateurs de la Fondation. Bref, bien que nous respections l'intégrité des créations de M. Vanderbyl, nous avons eu le sentiment que ce livre était beaucoup plus «le sien» que le nôtre.

[DAVID KNIGHT]

L.J. SKAGGS AND MARY C. SKAGGS FOUNDATION: 1221 BROADWAY, 21ST FLOOR
OAKLAND, CALIFORNIA 94612-1837 USA 415.451.3300

VANDERBYL DESIGN

▲ The annual report is the only print piece published by the Foundation each year, so it serves as an image piece, while fulfilling the legal obligation of explaining where grant money has gone in the past year and describing how the money has been used. Each annual report highlights a particular area of grant-giving by the foundation and that area determines the theme of the report. It is important to remember that this is a small endowment, but the Foundation is one of the few that concentrates its attention on the arts. The theme of each year's report is based on a collaboration between the foundation and myself, but the visual direction is mine alone. This has been a long-standing client, and they're wonderful to work with—we've had a good relationship. The report has been well-received. It has won a number of awards and been the subject of much recognition—from the design community and other such forums. The budgets constraints on this project are tight, of course, given the nonprofit nature of the Foundation. Each year's budget is based on the previous one, with a slight increase allowed for inflation. We were able to put more money into the printing of this report because of the way it was designed, which was a nice change.

■ Der Jahresbericht ist die einzige Publikation, die jedes Jahr von der Stiftung herausgegeben wird, und dient daher ebenso als Selbstdarstellung wie als offizielle Erklärung, wohin die Unterstützungsgelder gegangen sind und wie sie verwendet wurden. Der Bericht hebt jedes Jahr einen besonderen Subventionsbereich heraus, der dann als Schwerpunktthema präsentiert wird. Man sollte nicht vergessen, dass dies eine kleine Stiftung ist, die allerdings zu den wenigen zählt, deren Unterstützungsgelder ausschliesslich für künstlerische Belange verwendet werden. Die Stiftung erarbeitet das Thema in Zusammenarbeit mit mir, aber die visuelle Leitung liegt ganz in meinen Händen. Ich arbeite schon seit langer Zeit mit diesem Kunden zusammen, und es war immer eine gute, erfolgreiche Beziehung. Der diesjährige Bericht hat viel Anerkennung gefunden und mehrere Design- und andere Preise gewonnen. Da die Stiftung gemeinnützig ist, müssen wir freilich innerhalb eines ziemlich engen Budgets arbeiten, das jeweils dem Budget des Vorjahres entspricht, und mehr oder weniger proportional zur Inflationsrate erhöht wird. Bei diesem Bericht liess uns die besondere Art des Designs etwas mehr Geld für den Druck übrig, was zur Abwechslung einmal ganz nett war.

● Le rapport annuel est la seule publication produite chaque année par la Fondation. En tant que pièce maîtresse, il a donc pour fonction de justifier les subventions de l'année précédente, en décrivant la façon dont l'argent a été utilisé. Chaque année, la Fondation met en valeur un secteur particulier de subvention, qui détermine le thème du rapport. Il est important de rappeler que ces donations sont limitées, mais la Fondation est l'une des rares institutions de la sorte qui s'intéresse aux arts. Le thème de chaque rapport annuel est basé sur une collaboration entre la Fondation et moi-même, sauf en ce qui concerne la direction visuelle qui m'est réservée. Nous travaillons ensemble depuis longtemps et nos relations étaient satisfaisantes. Ce dernier rapport a été favorablement accueilli par le public, gagnant plusieurs prix aussi bien dans le monde du design que parmi les compétiteurs, lui valant ainsi une reconnaissance méritée. Les contraintes budgétaires pour ce projet ont été très fortes, bien sûr, compte tenu du fait que la fondation est une organisation à but non lucratif. Chaque année, le budget est basé sur celui de l'année précédente, incluant une légère augmentation qui suit l'inflation. Cette année nous avons pu consacrer plus d'argent à l'impression de ce rapport, grâce à la manière dont il a été créé, ce qui était plutôt positif.

[MICHAEL VANDERBYL]

VANDERBYL DESIGN: 539 BRYANT STREET, SAN FRANCISCO, CALIFORNIA, USA 415.543.8447

36

SENSE OF SMELL
SENSE OF TOUCH
SENSE OF SIGHT
SENSE OF HEARING
SENSE OF TASTE

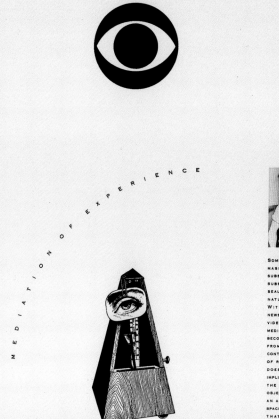

MEDIATION OF EXPERIENCE

SOME EXPERTS THEORIZE THAT MASS MEDIA HAS CREATED A SUBSTITUTE REALITY WHICH IS SUBSUMING THE MYSTERIOUS BEAUTY AND PRIMACY OF OUR NATURAL TACTILE SENSES. WITH RADIO, TELEVISION, NEWSPAPERS, MAGAZINES, FILM, VIDEO AND OTHER FORMS OF MEDIA PROLIFERATING, WE ARE BECOMING WALLED IN—CUT OFF FROM DIRECT KNOWLEDGE OF, CONTACT WITH AND EXPERIENCE OF REALITY. IN FACT, MEDIA DOES JUST WHAT THE WORD IMPLIES: IT MEDIATES BETWEEN THE PERSON AND THE REAL OBJECT. DISCONNECTED, LIKE AN ASTRONAUT FLOATING IN SPACE, WE MAY NOT RECOGNIZE THAT OUR NEW MEDIATED ENVIRONMENT IS A FALSE ONE.

PRESIDENT'S LETTER

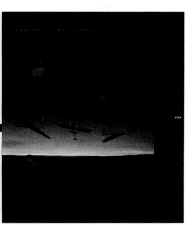

SOLIDARNOŚĆ

| BALANCE SHEET | STATEMENT OF REVENUE, EXPENSES AND | STATEMENT OF CASH FLOWS | NOTES TO FINANCIAL STATEMENTS |

CLIENT: THE L. J. SKAGGS AND MARY C. SKAGGS FOUNDATION ■ DESIGN FIRM: VANDERBYL DESIGN ■ ART DIRECTOR/DESIGNER: MICHAEL VANDERBYL ■ PHOTOGRAPHERS: VARIOUS ■ WRITER: LAURA J. LEDERER ■ TYPOGRAPHER: ANDRESEN TYPOGRAPHERS ■ PAPER SELECTION: CENTURA DULL, SPECKLETONE ■ PRINTER: GEORGE RICE & SONS ■ NUMBER OF PAGES: 78 ■ TRIM SIZE: 8½ x 9½ INCHES ■ PRINT RUN: 3,000 ■

National

Rural

Utilities

1 9 8 9 ANNUAL REPORT

Cooperative

Finance

Corporation

NATIONAL RURAL UTILITIES COOPERATIVE FINANCE

▲ Our annual report primarily serves as a marketing and image piece, directed for the most part to our member-ship, which is the one thousand rural cooperatives across the country to which we lend money. We also direct the report toward the financial community, from which we get money. We don't solicit funding through printed materi-als, but this report does have to serve both audiences. Most of our reports are future oriented, and deal with issues facing our industry. This year was different; it reflected our twentieth anniversary. The report took an historical look at CFC and the entire rural electric program. Anyone could pick up the report and get a good understanding of what we're about. We felt the design of this report was particularly successful because it incorporated historical photographs and captures typical rural scenary. This was our first report with Graffito. It's important for us to be able to sit down and familiarize a firm with our company and what we want in a report, and they grasped it very well. We start to plan early, largely because we have a very limited budget. When we look at a design firm, we're very interested in their project management. We want our annual report controlled and on budget—we can't afford surprises. This firm not only got us the most for our money, we think they hit a home run the first time at bat.

■ Unser Jahresbericht dient hauptsächlich als Marketing- und Image-Dokument und richtet sich vor allem an unsere Mitglieder: die rund tausend landwirtschaftlichen Genossenschaften im ganzen Land, denen wir Darlehen geben. Die zweite grosse Zielgruppe ist die Finanzwelt, die in uns investiert. Unsere Druckdokumente sind keine Werbemittel zu Subventionszwecken, aber dieser Bericht muss beide Gruppen ansprechen. Die meisten unserer Berichte sind zukunftsorientiert und beschäftigen sich mit Fragen und Problemen, die auf unsere Industrie zukommen. Dieses Jahr war eine Ausnahme, und der Bericht konzentrierte sich auf unser zwanzigjähriges Bestehen. Er gibt einen historischen Überblick über die CFC sowie das gesamte ländliche Elektrifizie-rungsprogramm und erklärt in allgemein verständlicher Form, worin unsere Arbeit besteht. Wir halten das Design dieses Berichts für ganz besonders gelungen, weil es mit seinen historischen Photos eine spezifisch ländliche Atmosphäre widergibt. Es war unser erster Bericht mit Graffito. Es ist wichtig für uns, uns mit der Design-Firma zusammenzusetzen und sie mit unserem Unternehmen und unseren Wünschen vertraut zu machen, und das klappte mit Graffito ganz ausgezeichnet. Wir beginnen schon früh mit der Planung, weil wir nur ein äusserst knappes Budget zur Verfügung haben. Wenn wir uns nach einer Design-Firma umschauen, sind wir zunächst einmal an ihrer Projektleitung interessiert. Die Produktion unseres Jahresberichts soll möglichst geregelt verlaufen und innerhalb des Budgets bleiben. Wir können uns keine Überraschungen leisten.

● Notre rapport annuel est essentiellement utilisé pour le marketing et comme image de marque; il s'adresse plus par-ticulièrement à nos adhérents qui représentent 1.000 coopératives rurales, essaimées dans tout le pays, auxquelles nous prêtons de l'argent. Nous destinons également ce rapport à la communauté financière grâce à laquelle nous obtenons de l'argent. Nous ne sollicitons pas de subventions par écrit, mais ce rapport doit pouvoir aussi remplir cet objectif. La plupart de nos rapports sont tournés vers l'avenir et concernent les divers problèmes auxquels notre industrie doit faire face. Cette année c'était différent: le rapport se devait d'évoquer le vingtième anniversaire de notre société, en donnant un aperçu vision historique sur la CFC et sur l'ensemble du programme électrique rural. N'importe qui pouvait jeter un coup d'œil au rapport et comprendre rapidement de quoi il était question. Nous avons le sentiment que son succès était surtout dû aux photographies anciennes de scènes typiques de la vie rurale. C'était la première fois que nous travaillions avec Graffito. Il est important pour nous de pouvoir prendre le temps de connaître le studio de design avec lequel nous allons collaborer, et de faire savoir ce que nous voulons, ce qu'ils ont très bien saisi. Nous avons commencé à nous organiser assez tôt, surtout parce que notre budget était très limité. Nous désirons garder un contrôle sur le rapport et respecter le budget, car nous ne pouvons pas nous permettre d'avoir de mauvai-ses surprises. Chez Graffito, ils ont su en tirer le maximum, et nous pensons qu'ils ont touché la cible du premier coup.

[VICKI ALBIZO]

NATIONAL RURAL UTILITIES COOPERATIVE FINANCE CORPORATION: 1115 30TH STREET, N.W.

WASHINGTON, D. C. 20007 USA 202.337.6700

GRAFFITO

. . . .

▲ The concept for this report was definitely built around the budget. The client wanted to touch on their anniversary, but not dwell on it—their original idea was to use a timeline, but we suggested the old and new theme and they bought into the concept very quickly. Once that was settled, they were an enthusiastic client—even going so far as to help us with the picture research. Working with black-and-white and color was part of the original concept, and as the idea grew, we began to think of the photographs taken by the government-sponsored Farm Security Administration program back in the 1930s. That led us to the Library of Congress, which provides prints of all photographs in their files for free. This worked perfectly with the budget. The designer, Joe Parisi, Vicki Albizo, and I spent the day in Washington, D.C., going through the files and looking at photographs—our only criteria was that they be rural in subject matter, and it would be nice if they dealt with electricity. We augmented the file photographs with four-color stock photos, and ran the black-and-white as four-color, which really improved the quality on a lot of the old prints. This was our first report with the client, but the flow between us went really well.

. . . .

■ Das Konzept für diesen Bericht wurde eindeutig um das knappe Budget herum entwickelt. Der Kunde wollte auf sein Firmenjubiläum hinweisen, aber nicht bis zur Erschöpfung darauf herumreiten – er dachte ursprünglich daran, das Motiv einer historischen Entwicklungslinie zu verwenden, aber wir schlugen das Thema Alt/Neu vor, und dieses Konzept fand dann auch ziemlich schnell Anklang. Nachdem das entschieden· war, erwies sich National Rural als ausgesprochen enthusiastischer Kunde – seine Leute halfen uns sogar bei der Photosuche. Das ursprüngliche Konzept sah Schwarzweiss- und Farbphotos vor, aber als die Idee Gestalt annahm, kamen wir auf den Gedanken, die Photos zu verwenden, die in den 30er Jahren von der Farm Security Administration während ihres Bauernhilfsprogramms aufgenommen wurden. Das führte uns in die Library of Congress, die kostenlos Abzüge ihrer Archivphotos zur Verfügung stellt, was natürlich perfekt zu unserem Budget passte. Die Designer, Joe Parisi, Vicki Albizo und ich verbrachten einen ganzen Tag in Washington DC, gingen durch die Archive und suchten Photos mit ländlichen Motiven heraus, die nach Möglichkeit auch mit Elektrizität zu tun haben sollten. Wir fügten vierfarbiges Archivmaterial hinzu und druckten die Schwarzweissphotos als Vierfarbbilder, was in vielen Fällen die Qualität der alten Abzüge um einiges verbesserte. Es war unser erster Bericht für den Kunden, aber die Zusammenarbeit lief wunderbar.

. . . .

● Le concept de ce projet a été d'emblée déterminé en fonction du budget. Le client voulait parler du vingtième anniversaire de la société, il ne voulait pas s'appesantir sur ce sujet. Au départ, ils avaient eu l'idée de choisir un tableau temporel, mais nous avons suggéré le thème de «l'ancien et le nouveau», auquel ils ont rapidement adhéré. Une fois ceci mis en place, ils étaient très enthousiastes, allant jusqu'à nous aider dans la recherche de photos. Travailler avec du noir et blanc ainsi que de la couleur faisait partie du concept original, mais à mesure que nous avancions, l'idée d'utiliser les photos prises par la Farm Security Administration, dont le programme était sponsorisé par le gouvernement dans les années trente, nous séduisait de plus en plus. Ce qui nous conduisit à la bibliothèque du Congrès, qui nous fournit obligeamment et gratuitement toutes les photos qui avaient été conservées. Cette idée convenait parfaitement à notre sujet. Le designer, Joe Parisi, Vicki Albizo et moi-même, nous passâmes la journée à Washington, sélectionnant des photos dans de vieux dossiers, recherchant plus spécialement des sujets ruraux ayant trait à l'électricité en général. Nous avons ensuite enrichi notre documentation de photos en couleurs, imprimant le noir et blanc en quadrichromie, ce qui a réellement amélioré un grand nombre de vieux clichés. Si l'on considère que ceci était notre premier travail pour ce client, on peut dire que les choses se sont très bien passées.

[TIM THOMPSON]

GRAFFITO: 601 NORTH EUTAW STREET, BALTIMORE, MARYLAND 21201 USA 301.837.0070

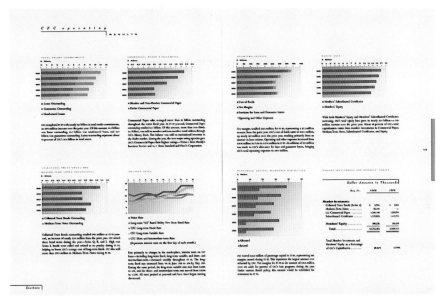

SAN FRANCISCO

INTERNATIONAL

A I R P O R T

◈

G A T E W A Y

TO THE PACIFIC

◈

N I N E T E E N

EIGHTY-NINE

ANNUAL REPORT

▲ The city of San Francisco has historic ties to the Pacific, and continuing trade between the Bay Area and the entire Pacific Rim is very important to the economy of both the airport and the metropolitan area we serve. In our annual report, we have tried to emphasize San Francisco's role as a departure point for Pacific destinations. We are especially pleased with the illustrations in this year's book, as well as the cover. Each has a strong Japanese feel, which is significant when you consider that the average Japanese visitor to the airport spends $400 in our duty-free shops and that duty-free shops are responsible for 10 percent of the airport's total revenue. The audience for this report falls equally into three categories: the bond investment community, the general aviation community (airlines, other airports, and the aviation industry at large), and the general public. We always want our report to reflect the high level of passenger service that we offer as well as the overall quality of our airport. Jennifer always gives us a report with a quality look and we get a very positive response to the design.

■ San Francisco hat historische Bindungen zum pazifischen Raum, und der Handel zwischen unserer Gegend und der gesamten Pazifikküste ist von grosser wirtschaftlicher Bedeutung für den Flughafen und sein Einzugsgebiet. In unserem Jahresbericht haben wir versucht, San Franciscos Rolle als Ausgangspunkt zu pazifischen Zielorten zu unterstreichen. Am diesjährigen Bericht haben uns besonders die Illustrationen und der Umschlag gefallen. Sie haben ein unverkennbares japanisches Flair, was durchaus von Bedeutung ist, wenn man bedenkt, dass jeder japanische Flughafenbesucher durchschnittlich $400 in unseren Duty-Free-Shops ausgibt - und 10 Prozent der Gesamteinkünfte des Flughafens kommen aus den Duty-Free-Shops. Die Zielgruppe für den Bericht lässt sich in drei Kategorien unterteilen: Das Anlagepublikum, Luftfahrtunternehmen (Fluggesellschaften, andere Flughäfen und die Luftfahrtindustrie) und die allgemeine Öffentlichkeit. Es kommt uns darauf an, dass der Bericht unseren ausgezeichneten Passagierservice sowie die hohe Gesamtqualität unseres Flughafens zum Ausdruck bringt. Jennifer gibt uns immer einen erstklassig gestalteten Bericht, und unser Publikum reagiert jedes Jahr ausgesprochen positiv auf das Design.

● L'histoire de la ville de San Francisco est étroitement reliée à l'océan Pacifique; le commerce incessant entre la région de la baie de San Francisco et toute la bordure Pacifique est essentiel, aussi bien pour l'aéroport que pour la zone métropolitaine que nous desservons. Nous avons essayé dans notre rapport annuel de souligner le rôle de San Francisco en tant que point de départ pour les destinations du Pacifique. Nous sommes tout particulièrement contents des illustrations de cette année et de la couverture. Celles-ci traduisent bien l'importance de l'élément japonais, surtout si l'on considère qu'un touriste japonais moyen dépense environ 400 dollars dans nos boutiques hors taxes, lesquelles représentent dix pour cent du revenu total de l'aéroport de San Fransisco. Le public visé par ce rapport se divise en trois catégories: les investisseurs financiers, l'ensemble de la communauté aérienne (les compagnies aériennes, les autres aéroports et l'industrie aéronautique en général) et le grand public. Notre objectif constant est de refléter l'excellence des services offerts aux passagers, de même que la qualité de notre aéroport. Jennifer nous donne toujours un très bon rapport, dont le design suscite la plupart du temps des échos positifs.

[JOHN MARTIN]

SAN FRANCISCO AIRPORTS COMMISSION: P.O. BOX 8097, SAN FRANCISCO, CALIFORNIA 94128 USA 415.876.2100

MORLA DESIGN

. . . .

▲ The client gave us the basic direction of "Pacific-Rim Countries," and from that, we unified the concept with the visuals. In this book, we dealt with destinations, rather than shots of airplanes, which really breaks with the traditional airport annual report. There's a very tight budget on this report, and by choosing illustration over photography, I always feel you get "more bang for your buck." We did have to do very tight presentations to get them to accept illustration, though. I wanted an Asian feel in the artwork, and Guy Billout's two-dimensional style reflects that influence. We used cranes on the cover because the bird is the Japanese symbol for flight. This has been a very successful report, even though I feel it pushed to the limit the clients' expectations of what an annual report could be. I think that's okay in this case, because it's unusual for an airport to produce an annual report in the first place, and they use it for a number of purposes, such as publicity and advertising, as well as financial reporting.

. . . .

■ Die Themenvorgabe lautete dieses Jahr «Länder am Pazifik», und wir entwickelten dieses Konzept zu einer einheitlichen visuellen Aussage. Wir haben uns in diesem Bericht entgegen aller Tradition von dem üblichen Flugzeugmotiv verabschiedet und statt dessen die Zielorte in den Vordergrund gestellt. Das Budget für diesen Bericht ist sehr eng, und indem wir uns für Illustrationen anstelle von Photos entschieden, konnten wir wesentlich mehr aus unserem Etat herausholen. Wir mussten allerdings bis ins letzte ausgefeilte Designvorschläge präsentieren, um den Kunden von den Illustrationen zu überzeugen. Ich wollte eine asiatische Atmosphäre, und Guy Billouts zweidimensionaler Stil weist deutliche fernöstliche Einflüsse auf. Wir verwendeten Kraniche als Umschlagmotiv, das japanische Symbol für Fliegen. Es war ein sehr erfolgreicher Bericht, obwohl er nicht unbedingt so aussieht, wie der Kunde sich seinen Jahresbericht vorstellte. Ich glaube, das ist in diesem Fall in Ordnung: Zum einen ist es ungewöhnlich für einen Flughafen, einen Jahresbericht herauszubringen, und zum anderen soll dieser Bericht nicht nur über finanzielle Aspekte informieren, sondern dient auch als Werbe- und Anzeigenprospekt.

. . . .

● Pour ce rapport, le client nous a donné comme point de départ «les pays de la bordure Pacifique». A partir de cela, nous avons unifié le concept en utilisant des moyens visuels. Dans ce rapport, nous esssayons de proposer des destinations plutot que des photos d'avions, ce qui sort complètement du schéma habituel en ce qui concerne les aéroports. Le budget de cette année était très réduit et, en privilégiant l'illustration au lieu de la photographie, je suis persuadée que l'impact est plus grand, compte tenu de l'argent investi. Cependant, nous avons dû concevoir des présentations très précises afin qu'ils acceptent les illustrations. Je désirais que ce rapport ait un style asiatique: le style bidimensionnel de Guy Billout a fort bien réussi à suggérer cette influence. Nous avons choisi des grues pour la couverture, car au Japon cet oiseau est le symbole du vol. Ce rapport a eu beaucoup de succès, bien que j'aie le sentiment qu'il ait un peu bousculé l'image que cette société se fait de ce type de publication; mais je ne pense pas que ce soit un gros problème dans ce cas précis, parce qu'il est assez inhabituel pour un aéroport de produire un rapport annuel. De plus, ils ont pu l'utiliser aussi bien pour leur publicité et les relations publiques que pour leurs bilans financiers.

[JENNIFER MORLA]

MORLA DESIGN: 463 BRYANT STREET, SAN FRANCISCO, CALIFORNIA 94107 USA 415.543.6548

A notable feature of Fiscal Year 1988/89 at San Francisco International Airport was continuing growth in international traffic. Since the International Terminal opened in 1983, international passenger traffic has increased by 81%. More than 3.6 million international passengers passed through the Airport in Fiscal Year 1988/89, representing a 7.2% increase over the previous fiscal year. ✧ To plan for further growth, staff continued to work on the Airport Master Plan. This guiding document, which outlines planned developments through 2006, was updated in June 1989, and balances a variety of concerns. With this plan, the Airport considers economic, environmental, noise, and growth impacts as it prepares for the future. ✧ In conjunction with the Master Plan, the Airport has proposed the construction of a new International Terminal which would close the loop between the North and South terminals. The new facility would have 26 gates and the ability to handle 5,000 arriving passengers per hour. ✧ Although it is owned and operated by the City and County of San Francisco, the Airport receives no support from the City's General Fund. Instead, the Airport relies on highly diversified sources of revenue to meet its expenditures. Since 1981, concession revenues have increased by over 100%, while airline landing fees have been reduced—in real terms—by over 58%. San Francisco now has the second lowest landing fee among major airports in the U.S. ✧ Despite its passenger growth, the Airport has remained an efficient and often frugal operation. Since 1981, the Airport's operating cost per enplaned passenger has actually decreased from $3.71 to $3.26 (in constant 1980 dollars). This sound fiscal performance is reflected by high bond ratings: San Francisco International Airport bonds are rated "A+" by Standard & Poor's and "A1" by Moody's.

Pilots flying for twenty-one airlines serve more than thirty-five international destinations from San Francisco International.

Service to destinations in the Asia/Pacific region is convenient, frequent, and direct from San Francisco International Airport. Currently, passengers can fly direct to twelve primary Pacific Rim cities including Seoul, Shanghai, Singapore, and Sydney.

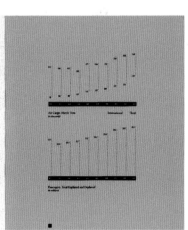

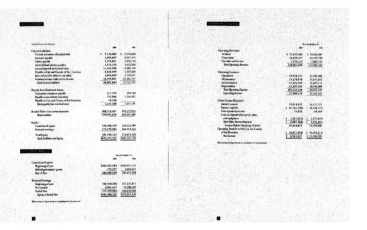

CLIENT: SAN FRANCISCO AIRPORT ■ DESIGN FIRM: MORLA DESIGN ■ ART DIRECTOR: JENNIFER MORLA ■ DESIGNERS: JENNIFER MORLA, MARIANNE MITTEN ■ PHOTOGRAPHER: TOM TRACY ■ ILLUSTRATOR: GUY BILLOUT ■ WRITER: STEVEN FALK ■ PRODUCTION MANAGER: MARIANNE MITTEN ■ TYPOGRAPHER: ANDRESEN ■ PAPER SELECTION: SIGNATURE, FRENCH RAYON ■ PRINTER: THE JAMES H. BARRY CO. ■ TRIM SIZE: 8½ x 9 ½ INCHES ■ NUMBER OF PAGES: 32 PLUS COVER ■ TYPE SELECTION: FUTURA BOLD, COPPERPLATE GOTHIC 33B, JANSON ROMAN/ITALIC ■ PRINT RUN: 3,000 ■

THE MACNEAL-SCHWENDLER CORPORATION

▲ Last year's report broke the bank, so we wanted to stick to a tight budget this year—we wanted a report that could be produced as cheaply as possible. And we are absolutely happy with this report. The words and the graphics are excellent. My only objection was to the black cover. I hadn't seen this until the last moment, when the report was on press, and when I did, I blew my stack. The cover was changed from black to white, and now I'm very happy. This report had to serve a wide audience: the investor community, clients and potential clients, employees, and business partners or potential business partners. It had to show that we're a very good company with which to work. We're not wasteful of our resources, and we work as an arm of the engineering companies that are our clients to make them work better. We spend money where it will do us and those who work with us the most good. The report also had to show that we are not just taking care of existing clients and projects, but future ones as well. I am not an artistic person, I'm a scientist, but I'm very proud of this report.

■ Der Bericht des Vorjahres hat zu viel gekostet, daher haben wir dieses Jahr ein ziemlich knappes Budget veranschlagt - wir wollten einen Bericht, der so billig wie möglich produziert werden konnte. Und wir sind absolut glücklich mit dem Ergebnis. Der Text und die graphische Gestaltung sind ausgezeichnet. Mein einziger Einwand betraf den schwarzen Umschlag. Ich bekam ihn erst in letzter Minute zu Gesicht, als der Bericht in den Druck ging, und mir lief erstmal die Galle über. Die Umschlagfarbe wurde von Schwarz auf Weiss umgeändert, und jetzt bin ich vollauf zufrieden. Der Bericht wendet sich an ein breitgefächertes Publikum: Anleger, Kunden und potentielle Kunden, Angestellte, Geschäftspartner und potentielle Geschäftspartner. Er sollte zeigen, dass es eine gute Idee ist, mit unserem Unternehmen ins Geschäft zu kommen. Wir gehen bedachtsam mit unseren Mitteln um und sehen uns als verlängerten Arm unserer Konstruktionsfirmen. Der Bericht sollte ausserdem zeigen, dass wir uns nicht nur um unsere gegenwärtigen Projekte und Kunden kümmern, sondern uns bereits jetzt auf zukünftige Aufgaben einstellen. Ich bin kein künstlerischer Mensch, ich bin Wissenschaftler, aber ich bin sehr stolz auf diesen Bericht.

● Le rapport de l'année dernière nous a ruiné, c'est pourquoi nous voulions à tout prix respecter un budget limité cette année. En fait, nous désirions un rapport aussi bon marché que possible. Et nous sommes absolument ravis de celui-ci dont le texte et le graphisme sont excellents. Ma seule objection concernait la couverture noire. Je ne l'avais pas vue jusqu'au dernier moment, alors que le rapport était déjà à l'imprimerie. Et lorsque je l'ai vue, j'étais furieux. Ils l'ont finalement changée pour une couverture blanche, ce qui me convenait beaucoup mieux. Le rapport doit toucher une large audience: les investisseurs, les clients actuels et les clients potentiels, les employés, ainsi que nos partenaires actuels ou futurs. Il devait montrer que nous sommes une société idéale avec laquelle on peut faire des affaires. Nous ne gaspillons pas nos ressources et nous travaillons de concert avec nos sections d'ingénierie afin d'améliorer encore la qualité du travail. Nous plaçons notre argent là où ce sera le plus rentable pour nous et pour nos clients. Ce rapport doit également montrer que nous ne nous contentons pas de nous préoccuper de nos clients et de nos projets actuels, mais aussi de nos futurs clients. Bien que n'étant pas artiste mais scientifique, je suis très fier de ce rapport.

[DR. JOSEPH F. GLOUDEMAN]

THE MACNEAL-SCHWENDLER CORPORATION: 815 COLORADO BOULEVARD

LOS ANGELES, CALIFORNIA 90041-1777 USA 213.258.9111

ROBERT MILES RUNYON & ASSOCIATES

. . . .

▲ The client had had a profitable, but not a great year. They wanted a black-and-white book, a book that would look like they were holding back. They also wanted their audience to know they were broad in terms of their client base and not just dependent on Defense Department contracts. We came up with the idea of highlighting five different client groups and the software that has been created to serve each group. The three-dimensional models shown throughout the book are actually the products—that's how an engineer would see them on the computer screen. We began with a tight budget and the initial figure was cut back twice in the process of actually doing the report. We had originally designed the book with the black cover and this had been approved throughout the process. A sheet was pulled when we were at the engraver and sent to the client. At this point, the client said no to the cover and it was changed to white. We show copies of the book with the black cover for our own purposes, but the client is very happy with the report in its final version.

. . . .

■ Der Kunde hatte ein profitables, aber keineswegs grossartiges Jahr hinter sich. Er wollte ein schwarzweisses Buch, das den Eindruck unternehmerischer Zurückhaltung vermitteln sollte. Er wollte seinem Publikum ausserdem erklären, dass das Unternehmen über eine breite Kundenbasis verfügt und nicht allein von Aufträgen des Verteidigungsministeriums abhängt. Wir hatten die Idee, fünf verschiedene Kundengruppen herauszustreichen und die jeweils für sie produzierte Software zu präsentieren. Die dreidimensionalen Modelle, die in dem Buch gezeigt werden, stellen die eigentlichen Produkte dar, wie ein Ingenieur sie auf dem Computer-Bildschirm sehen würde. Wir begannen mit einem engen Budget, das im Verlauf unserer Arbeit noch zweimal gekürzt wurde. Wir hatten das Buch ursprünglich mit einem schwarzen Umschlag entworfen, gegen den bis zum Schluss keinerlei Einwände bestanden. Als wir beim Graveur waren, machten wir einen Abzug, den wir dem Kunden schickten. Das Unternehmen entschied sich in letzter Minute gegen den schwarzen und für einen weissen Umschlag. Bei unseren Präsentationen zeigen wir das Buch mit seinem ursprünglichen schwarzen Umschlag, aber der Kunde ist mit der endgültigen Version des Jahresberichts sehr zufrieden.

. . . .

● Notre client a eu une année profitable, mais pas excellente. La société désirait un livre noir et blanc, un livre qui donne une impression assez discrète de la firme. Elle voulait aussi que le public sache qu'il y avait une clientèle de base diversifiée, et que l'entreprise n'était pas simplement dépendante de ses contrats avec le Ministère de la Défense. Nous nous sommes finalement décidés pour mettre en valeur cinq différents groupes de clients, ainsi que les logiciels créés pour servir chacun de ces groupes. Les modèles tridimensionnels montrés tout au long du rapport sont effectivement les produits eux-mêmes, exactement tels que les ingénieurs les verraient sur l'écran de l'ordinateur. Nous avions démarré avec un budget serré, et par la suite, le montant de départ fut réduit de moitié alors que nous étions en plein milieu du projet. A l'origine, il avait été décidé que la couverture serait noire, ce qui avait été approuvé tout au long du processus. Alors que nous étions chez le graveur, nous en avons envoyé un exemplaire au client. C'est à ce moment là qu'il a refusé la couverture noire et que nous avons opté pour du blanc. En ce qui nous concerne, nous avons gardé quelques copies du rapport avec la couverture noire, mais le client est ravi de la version finale du rapport.

[GARY HINSCHE]

ROBERT MILES RUNYON & ASSOCIATES: 4223 GLENCOE AVENUE, SUITE A223

MARINA DEL REY, CALIFORNIA 90292 USA 213.823.0975

CLIENT: THE MACNEAL SCHWENDLER CORPORATION ■ DESIGN FIRM: RUNYAN.HINSCHE.ASSOCIATES ■ ART DIRECTORS: ROBERT MILES RUNYAN, MICHAEL MESCALL ■ DESIGNER: MICHAEL MESCALL ■ PHOTOGRAPHER: BURTON PRITZKER ■ ILLUSTRATORS: PAUL BICE, JR., PATTY KARASAWA ■ PRODUCTION MANAGER: PATTY KARASAWA ■ TYPOGRAPHER: COMPOSITION TYPE ■ PAPER SELECTION: CURTIS FLANNEL, CENTURA DULL (TEXT) ■ PRINTER: LITHOGRAPHIX ■ NUMBER OF PAGES: 32 PLUS COVER ■ TRIM SIZE: 8 x 11⅝ INCHES ■ TYPE SELECTION: BEMBO ■ PRINT RUN: 15,000 ■

CENTRE REINSURANCE

CENTRE REINSURANCE

. . . .

▲ We're a new company in an old business. Two and a half years ago we started with two employees and now we have assets of over one billion dollars. Centre Reinsurance is a private company, so this report was specifically designed for the dual purpose of marketing and financial reporting. We're considered unique in the business because we started from scratch and we market insurance in nontraditional ways—we wanted the report to show that we react creatively to problems. The response to this report has been exceptional. It provided the basis for an advertising campaign and our marketing program for the year. The success of the report was largely due to our relationship with the design firm. We had a lot of trust in them because we knew their work, but there was also a lot of back-and-forth between us. We gave them latitude, but we were involved in every page. The designer really listened to what we were saying and came back with changes that reflected what we wanted. This was very important, because the concept had to reflect the company and this particular concept could have been a very dangerous one for us if it wasn't well-balanced. The idea of board games and insurance don't necessarily go together. They brought us different concepts when we started out, and this was not the first choice, but once we made the committment we stayed with it and it has garnered a lot of positive attention.

. . . .

■ Wir sind ein neues Unternehmen in einem alten Geschäftszweig. Vor zweieinhalb Jahren haben wir mit zwei Angestellten angefangen, und jetzt besitzen wir Aktiva von mehr als einer Milliarde Dollar. Centre Reinsurance ist eine Personengesellschaft, und daher wurde dieser Bericht sowohl zu Marketing-Zwecken als auch zur Darlegung unserer finanziellen Aktivitäten entworfen. Wir nehmen eine Sonderstellung in diesem Geschäftszweig ein, weil wir das Unternehmen aus dem Nichts aufgebaut haben und Versicherungen auf nicht traditionelle Weise vermarkten – der Bericht sollte zeigen, dass wir kreativ auf Probleme reagieren. Dieser Jahresbericht fand ein ausserordentliches Echo und bildete die Grundlage für eine Werbekampagne und unser gegenwärtiges Marketing-Programm. Der Erfolg des Berichts ist zum grossen Teil unserer Beziehung mit der Design-Firma zu verdanken. Wir gaben der Firma Spielraum, waren aber am Entwurf jeder einzelnen Seite beteiligt. Der Designer machte sich wirklich Gedanken über unsere Vorschläge und kam dann mit Änderungen zurück, die unsere Wünsche und Vorstellungen reflektierten. Das war ausserordentlich wichtig, da das Konzept das Wesen des Unternehmens widerspiegeln sollte, und dieses Konzept ein grosses Risiko für uns dargestellt hätte, wenn es nicht perfekt ausgewogen gewesen wäre. Die Idee eines Brettspiels ist nicht so ohne weiteres mit einem Versicherungsunternehmen unter einen Hut zu bringen. WYD brachte uns anfangs mehrere verschiedene Konzepte, und dies war zunächst nicht unsere erste Wahl, aber nachdem wir uns einmal dafür entschieden hatten, blieben wir dabei, und der Anklang, den der Bericht fand, war ausgesprochen positiv.

. . . .

● Nous sommes une nouvelle compagnie sur un vieux marché. Il y a deux ans et demi, nous avons démarré avec deux employés et maintenant nous avons plus d'un milliard de dollars de capital. Centre Reinsurance est une entreprise privée, c'est pourquoi ce rapport a été créé spécifiquement pour le marketing et les bilans financiers. Nous sommes considérés comme uniques sur le marché parce que nous sommes partis de zéro, et que nous vendons maintenant des assurances de manière totalement nouvelle. Nous voulions donc que le rapport montre que nous réagissons aux problèmes de manière créatrice. Le résultat a été exceptionnel. Il a servi de base à une campagne de publicité et à notre programme de marketing de cette année. Le succès de notre rapport a été dû largement au relations que nous avions avec le studio de design. Nous leur avons donné pas mal de latitude, tout en étant toujours très attentif à chaque étape. Le designer était vraiment à l'écoute de nos suggestions et revenait avec des modifications qui reflétaient nos désirs. Ceci était extrêmement important, car le concept devait symboliser et représenter la compagnie, et cela aurait pu être très dangereux pour nous si ce dernier n'avait pas été correctement pensé. Les jeux de société et les assurances ne vont pas forcément très bien ensemble. Au départ, le studio de design avait proposé differents concepts; celui qui fut retenu n'était pas le premier, mais, et une fois engagés dans ce projet, nous nous y sommes tenus, ce qui nous a valu des réactions très positives.

[STEVEN M. GLUCKSTEIN]

CENTRE REINSURANCE: CUMBERLAND HOUSE, ONE VICTORIA STREET, HAMILTON, BERMUDA 809.295.8501

▲ This was Centre Reinsurance's first annual report. They're not a public company, and therefore don't have to produce an report, but they were really open about wanting something different in a document. They wanted to stress that they are "the innovators in reinsurance." But innovative does not mean frivolous—they will take on projects that most others wouldn't, but stress that this is because of innovation, not because they're risk-takers. They're solid—but different. Credit for this report has to be shared equally with the client; the concept would never have flown without their acceptance and support. We presented two concepts in one meeting—all of the principals were together and ideas were discussed for two-and-a-half hours. The theme "re-writing the rules of the game" went in and out of the window three or four times. Once they were finally comfortable with the concept, we did full-blown comps on the computer and they approved. And this is what made them a great client: they never lost their vision of what they wanted in the beginning—in fact, they became more enthusiastic as time went on. And because we gave them such distinct comps on the computer, they knew exactly what they were going to get. As with all our clients, we establish the budgets up-front, and we stick with it. Here we were no more than 5 percent over. A lot of clients just don't know what things cost. In this case, the spiral binding, double cover, and paper stock added to the costs, but the client was able to understand what they were getting for their money, so they approved it.

■ Dies war der erste Jahresbericht von Centre Reinsurance. Es ist ein privates Unternehmen und muss daher keinen Geschäftsbericht herausbringen, aber gleichzeitig herrschte eine grosse Bereitschaft, etwas wirklich Neues zu versuchen. Die Leute von Centre Reinsurance wollten betonen, dass sie «die Innovatoren im Rückversicherungsgeschäft» sind. Innovativ heisst freilich nicht leichtsinnig – sie übernehmen Projekte, die die meisten anderen ablehnen würden, aber das liegt ausdrücklich daran, dass sie Innovatoren sind, und nicht daran, dass sie übertrieben risikofreudig wären. Sie sind solide – aber anders als die anderen Versicherungsunternehmen. Der Erfolg des Berichts ist zu 50 Prozent das Verdienst des Kunden. Ohne seinen Zuspruch und seine Unterstützung wäre das Konzept nie zustande gekommen. Wir präsentierten zwei Konzepte bei einer Besprechung – die gesamte Geschäftsleitung war anwesend, und wir diskutierten zweieinhalb Stunden lang alle möglichen Ideen. Das Thema «Die Spielregeln umschreiben» wurde drei- oder viermal verworfen und wieder aufgenommen. Nachdem der Kunde schliesslich mit dem Konzept zufrieden war, haben wir ein vollständiges Muster auf dem Computer entworfen, und das wurde dann angenommen. Die Zusammenarbeit mit dem Kunden lief einfach grossartig: Er verlor seine ursprünglichen Vorstellungen nie aus den Augen – sein Enthusiasmus wuchs sogar, während das Projekt Gestalt annahm. Und weil wir ihm detaillierte Computer-Entwürfe gegeben hatten, wusste er genau, was er am Ende bekommen würde.

● C'était le premier rapport annuel de Centre Reinsurance. C'est une entreprise privée, ils n'ont donc pas besoin de produire de rapport; mais ils étaient réellement ouverts à toute nouvelle approche pour un document de ce type. Ils désiraient souligner le fait qu'ils sont «les innovateurs de l'assurance». Mais innovation ne signifie pas pour autant frivolité. Ils ont opté par exemple pour des projets que la plupart des gens auraient refusés, non par amour du risque, mais bien plutôt par esprit d'innovation. Centre Reinsurance est une entreprise solide, mais différente des autres. Tout le mérite de ce rapport est à partager entre nous et le client. La réalisation du projet n'aurait jamais si bien marché sans le soutien de la compagnie. Présentant deux projets durant une seule réunion, nous avons discuté pendant deux heures et demie de tous les principes et les idées que nous avions. Le thème: «réécrire les règles du jeu» fut contesté à trois ou quatre reprises. Les essais que nous fîmes ensuite sur l'ordinateur furent approuvés. Et c'est exactement ce qui fait d'eux des clients fantastiques: ils n'ont jamais perdu de vue ce qu'ils voulaient depuis le début. En fait, ils sont même devenus de plus en plus enthousiastes au fur et à mesure que le projet avançait. Et puisque nous leur avions montré des exemples concrets de la mise en pages sur l'ordinateur, ils savaient exactement ce qu'ils allaient obtenir. Comme avec tous nos clients, nous avions établi un budget à l'avance et nous nous y sommes tenus, sans le dépasser de plus de cinq pour cent.

[RANDY SMITH]

WEISZ YANG DUNKELBERGER (WYD): 61 WILTON ROAD, WESTPORT, CONNECTICUT 06880 USA 203.227.2627

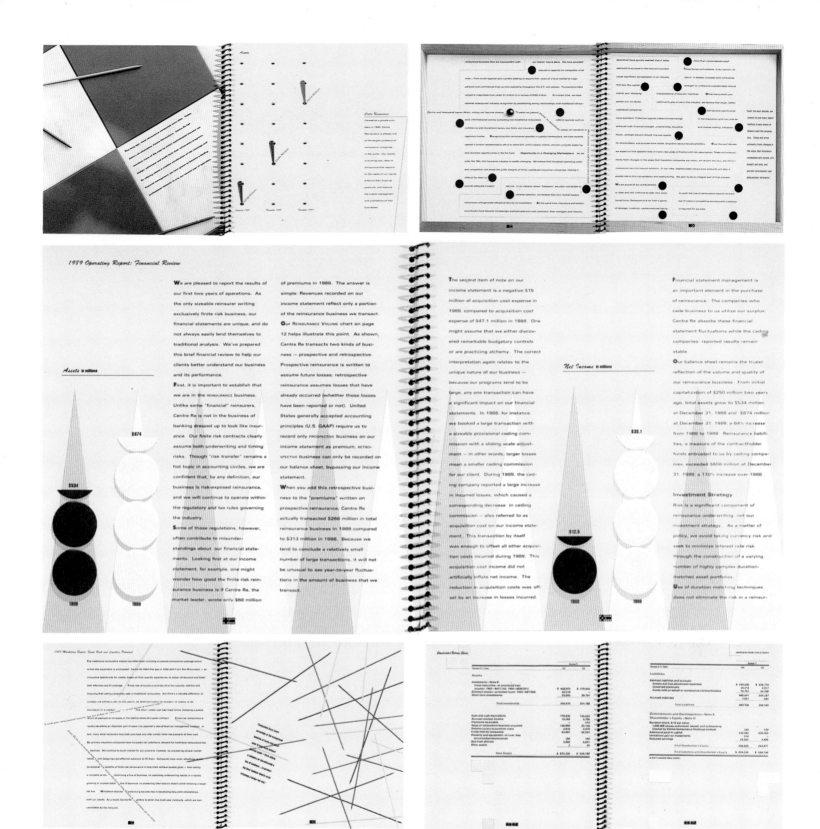

CLIENT: CENTRE REINSURANCE ■ DESIGN FIRM: WEISZ YANG DUNKELBERGER (WYD) ■ ART DIRECTORS: RANDY SMITH, FRANK OSWALD ■ DESIGNER: RANDY SMITH ■ PHOTOGRAPHER: JOHN STILL ■ ILLUSTRATOR: RANDY SMITH ■ WRITER: FRANK OSWALD ■ PRODUCTION MANAGER: SUZIE YANNES ■ TYPO-GRAPHERS: TYPEHOUSE, PROTYPE ■ PAPER SELECTION: ROYAL BRILLIANCE, ROYAL SILK, STARWHITE VICKSBURG HI-TECH ■ PAPER MANUFACTURERS: DONSIDE, SIMPSON PAPER CO. ■ PRINTER: SANDERS PRINTING ■ NUMBER OF PAGES: 24 PLUS COVER ■ TRIM SIZE: 9½ x 9½ INCHES ■ TYPE SELECTION: BRUSH SCRIPT, UNIVERS 53, 63, AND 73; HELVETICA COMPRESSED, FUTURA EXTRA BOLD ■ PRINT RUN: 5,000 ■

GOLD GREENLEES TROTT PLC

GOLD GREENLEES TROTT PLC

. . . .

▲ We wanted this report to show a serious, businesslike company producing a range of advertising and marketing services noted for their creativity. The challenge was to combine the excitement of the product with the seriousness of the business approach. We think the design communicates this very well to our audience, which includes of course investors and potential investors, as well as employees, clients, banks, and acquisition targets.

. . . .

■ Dieser Bericht sollte ein seriöses, erfahrenes Unternehmen präsentieren, das eine Vielzahl von Werbe- und Marketing-Diensten anbietet und für seine Kreativität bekannt ist. Die Herausforderung für den Designer bestand darin, den phantasievollen Charakter unserer Produkte mit der Seriosität unserer Geschäftsphilosophie zu verbinden. Das Design vermittelt diese doppelte Aussage ausgezeichnet an unser Publikum, zu dem nicht nur Investoren und potentielle Investoren, sondern auch Angestellte, Kunden, Banken und potentielle Kunden zählen.

. . . .

● Le but de ce rapport était de montrer que notre société est une société sérieuse, produisant une va-riété de services marketing et publicité connus pour leur créativité. Le défi était de pouvoir allier l'enthousiasme du produit et le sérieux requis pour une approche commerciale. Nous pensons que la conception de ce rapport a parfaitement communiqué ce message à notre public, constitué surtout par les investisseurs actuels et potentiels, aussi bien que nos employés, clients, banques et acquéreurs.

[MATTHEW ALLEN]

GOLD GREENLEES TROTT PLC: 82 DEAN STREET, LONDON, W1V 5AB GBR 01.437.0434

PAVILION COMMUNICATIONS SERVICES

▲ This report is the fruit of a collaboration between design firm and client, and everyone on both sides is very pleased with the results. Along the way the design was referred to the company's executives for their reactions, and all-in-all the client was most cooperative and helpful, even supplying at times useful creative suggestions. The budget was determined beforehand, but it was very comprehensive and generous. This is not typical for us these days. Companies are demanding an exact budget up-front and presenting alternative quotations that are very low. One of the adjustments we've made is that our typesetting is computer generated in total.

■ Dieser Bericht entstand in direkter Zusammenarbeit zwischen uns und dem Kunden, und beide Seiten sind mit dem Ergebnis ausgesprochen zufrieden. Während der Entwicklungsphase wurde das Design mehrmals von der Unternehmensleitung begutachtet, und alles in allem war der Kunde äusserst kooperativ und hilfsbereit, und lieferte manchmal sogar nützliche kreative Ideen. Das Budget wurde im voraus festgesetzt, aber es war ausgesprochen umfassend und grosszügig. Das ist heutzutage keineswegs die Regel. Die meisten Unternehmen verlangen exakte Kostenvoranschläge und präsentieren billige Alternativofferten von anderen Designfirmen. Um uns dieser Entwicklung anzupassen, lassen wir die Schrift jetzt vollständig auf dem Computer setzen.

● Ce rapport, fruit de la collaboration entre le studio de design et le client, a été très satisfaisant pour chacune des parties. Durant tout le processus, nous avons continuellement soumis le projet aux responsables de l'entreprise; je dois dire que le client était particulièrement coopératif, suggérant même parfois des idées très utiles. Le budget établi à l'avance était généreux et bien calculé, ce qui est plutot surprenant de nos jours. Les entreprises demandent généralement à connaître le budget exact à l'avance, avec diverses solutions bon marché. L'entière informatisation de la composition a été l'unique compromis que nous ayons fait.

[MATTHEW ALLEN]

PAVILION COMMUNICATION SERVICES LIMITED: 15 SHIELD DRIVE, WARDLEY

WORSLEY, MANCHESTER M28 5PR GBR 061.794.4267

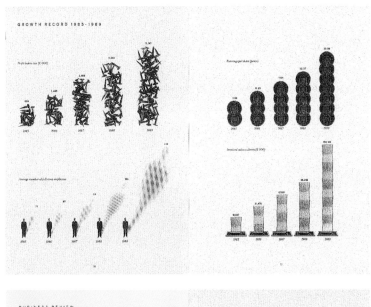

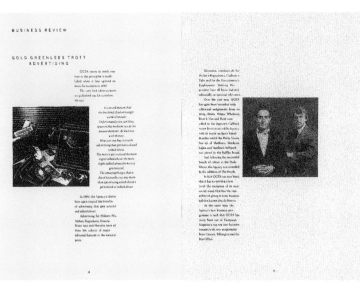

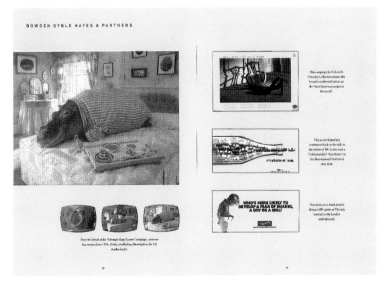

CLIENT: GOLD GREENLEES TROTT PLC ■ DESIGN FIRM: PAVILION COMMUNICATION SERVICES LTD ■ DESIGNERS: JOHN BRACKEN, SARA ROCHMOND, KATHY SMITH ■ ILLUSTRATOR: STEVE LIVESEY ■ WRITER: GRAEME ARKELL ■ PRODUCTION MANAGERS: REG REDMOND, SARA LATTEY ■ TYPOGRAPHER: PHILIP MACALEAVY ■ PAPER SELECTION: GB BRIGHTWATER FLANNEL, ICONOREX SPECIAL MATTE ■ PAPER MANUFACTURERS: GB PAPERS, ZANDERS ■ PRINTER: DOYLE QUAYS ■ NUMBER OF PAGES: 68 ■ TRIM SIZE: 210 MM x 297 MM (A4) ■ TYPE SELECTION: BERLING ■

1989

Expeditors

International

Report

EXPEDITORS INTERNATIONAL

. . . .

▲ The audience for our report consists of shareholders, the financial community, and the staff, and customers for our offices around the world. In the beginning, our annual report served as our only sales/marketing/image piece. The success of Expeditors has been the strength of its international network, along with a high level of service. The approach Van Dyke Company has taken with our reports has helped position us as a leader in our industry. Our reports have been well received by the financial community, and by our business affiliates in the principal countries in which we do business.

. . . .

■ Unser Jahresbericht richtet sich sowohl an die Aktionäre und die Finanzwelt als auch an unsere Kunden und Angestellten in unseren Niederlassungen in aller Welt. Ursprünglich war der Jahresbericht unser einziges Kommunikationsmittel für Verkauf, Marketing und Image-Werbung. Expeditors' Erfolg ist auf die Stärke seiner internationalen Präsenz und auf seine ausgezeichneten Dienstleistungen zurückzuführen. Die von der Van Dyke Company gestalteten Jahresberichte haben unser Image als führende Firma in unserem Bereich unterstützt. Unsere Berichte sind von der Finanzwelt und auch von unseren Filialen in den wichtigen Ländern, in denen wir tätig sind, gut beurteilt worden.

. . . .

● Notre rapport annuel s'adresse à un public d'actionnaires, à la communauté financière, au personnel de nos entreprises, ainsi qu'à nos clients du monde entier. Au début, il constituait le seul document disponible pour la vente, le marketing ou notre image de marque. Le succès d'Expeditors est dû à un solide réseau international, auquel vient s'ajouter la haute qualité de ses prestations. La présentation adoptée par l'agence Van Dyke a contribué à renforcer notre position de leader dans la branche. Nos rapports annuels ont été bien accueillis par la communauté financière et par nos filiales dans les principaux pays où nous faisons des affaires.

[PETER ROSE]

EXPEDITORS INTERNATIONAL: 19119 16TH SOUTH, SEATAC, WA 98188 206.246.3711

VAN DYKE COMPANY

▲ I've been with this client since they went public, so there's a long history behind this report. When we started, we established a certain look that would reinforce their positioning as an international company. The tradition of world trade and commerce is well-established in Europe and Asia, but, as with everything else, is fairly new in the United States. An important audience for this company's report has always been offshore, and they wanted to keep this in mind. Right from the beginning I've gone for a classic, traditional look. Expeditors is a service company, which means there's no product to show—unless we wanted to be very clichéd and show people sitting at their computers. Instead, I concentrate on studio set-ups that create a strong impression of the company and its services. This year's book was a continuation of this approach, with added visual elements that relate to the company's customers and what they ship. The fact is, the company works with some important companies, and they wanted to drop some names. Expeditors has always been a good client. They're high-road and very sophisticated. Nonetheless, this is a modest book: one form, sixteen pages, six-color; they get a strong image within a limited budget.

■ Ich arbeite für dieses Unternehmen, seit es in eine AG umgewandelt wurde; hinter diesem Jahresbericht steht also eine lange Geschichte. Am Anfang entwarfen wir einen bestimmten Look, der Expeditors' Position als internationales Unternehmen unterstreichen sollte. Firmen, die sich ausschliesslich mit dem Handels- und Warenverkehr beschäftigen, haben eine lange Tradition in Europa, stellen aber in den Vereinigten Staaten etwas ziemlich Neuartiges dar. Der Jahresbericht zielt auf ein Auslandspublikum, und Expeditors wünschte sich ein Design, das dort Anklang finden würde. Ich habe mich von Anfang an um einen klassischen, traditionellen Look bemüht. Expeditors ist ein Dienstleistungsunternehmen, das heisst, wir können kein konkretes Produkt vorführen - wenn wir nicht gerade in Klischees verfallen und Leute an ihren Computern zeigen wollen. Ich konzentriere mich statt dessen auf Studioarrangements, die einen aussagekräftigen Eindruck von dem Unternehmen und seinen Dienstleistungen vermitteln. Der diesjährige Bericht setzte dieses Thema fort, fügte aber einige neue visuelle Elemente hinzu, in denen die Kunden des Unternehmens und ihre Waren dargestellt werden. Expeditors arbeitet mit mehreren wichtigen Unternehmen zusammen und wollte ein paar grosse Namen einstreuen. Die Firma war immer ein guter Kunde. Sie hat ein kultiviertes, elitäres Profil. Der Jahresbericht wirkt dennoch schlicht: ein einheitliches Format, sechzehn Seiten, sechs Farben. Ein starkes Image im Rahmen eines begrenzten Budgets.

● Nous travaillons avec cette société depuis qu'elle est côtée en Bourse public; ce rapport a donc une longue histoire. A l'origine, nous avions établi une certaine image qui renforcait sa position en tant que groupe international. Alors qu'en Europe, l'expérience commerciale est très ancienne, c'est encore une conception assez nouvelle aux Etats-Unis. La clientèle de ce rapport a toujours été une clientèle étrangère, et la société tenait à le souligner. Dès le début, j'ai donc opté pour une image traditionnelle. Expeditors International est une entreprise de prestation de services, ce qui signifie qu'il n'y a pas de produits à vendre, sauf si l'on veut sombrer dans le cliché et montrer des gens assis devant leur ordinateur. Au lieu de cela, je me suis concentré sur les créations d'atelier qui donnent une image forte de la société et de ses services. Le rapport de cette année est la continuation de ce thème; auquel on y a ajouté certains éléments visuels concernant les clients et ce qu'ils envoient. Elle travaille avec d'importantes entreprises et tenait à citer quelques noms. C'est une société véritablement sophistiquée et de haut niveau. Néanmoins ce modeste rapport, à la formule simple, comprenant seize pages, dont six en coleurs, donne une image forte de l'entreprise et ce, pour un budget limité.

[JOHN VAN DYKE]

VAN DYKE COMPANY: 611 POST AVENUE #15, SEATTLE, WASHINGTON 98104 USA 206.621.1235

Financial Highlights

(In thousands, except per share data)	1989	1988	1987	1986	1985
Revenues	$193,602	147,460	146,823	108,774	66,029
Net earnings	9,311	7,206	5,843	4,062	2,865
Net earnings per share	1.60	1.25	1.02	.73	.56
Working capital	34,501	26,553	20,201	13,498	8,601
Total assets	64,968	52,389	44,826	36,366	21,552
Long-term debt	1,722	1,906	2,506	2,699	1,752
Shareholders' equity	44,504	34,695	27,171	19,643	11,076
Weighted average shares outstanding	5,821	5,774	5,747	5,553	5,073

All share and per share information has been adjusted to reflect a 3-for-2 stock split effected in September 1986.

In a highly competitive business environment, nothing is more important to a corporation than earning the trust and support of its customers. Our 1989 annual report is dedicated to our customers, who during the past decade have helped make Expeditors a leader in the industry. At Expeditors, we believe our customers are second to none when it comes to talent, loyalty and integrity. We are proud to serve them.

Consistent with past performance, Expeditors International experienced another profitable year in 1989 as the Company continued to benefit from strong exports, made significant gains in ocean and air forwarding, and improved and expanded operations worldwide. ■ By aggressively adhering to our strategy for growth, the Company in 1989 continued to outpace much of our competition. Earnings per share increased 28 percent, from $1.25 in 1988 to $1.60 in 1989. Total revenues were $193.6 million, compared to $147.5 million the preceding year. Net earnings increased 29 percent to $9.3 million. ■ Airfreight exports, which accounted for approximately 34 percent of the Company's net airfreight revenues, continued as one of the Company's top net revenue producers. However, our ocean, import airfreight, and custom house brokerage segments grew significantly as well, reflecting the Company's heightened reputation among customers as a leading full service provider in the industry. New leadership at the helm of Pac Bridge Shipping Ltd., our NVOCC (Non-Vessel Operating Common Carrier) operation, helped turn ocean freight forwarding into one of the fastest growing lines of service in the Company. ■ To meet growing demand for our services, we opened new offices in strategic locations throughout the world and expanded existing facilities. We opened new offices in Cincinnati, Ohio and Birmingham, England, and added sales representatives in Dhaka, Bangladesh, and Kuala Lumpur, Malaysia to meet the needs of customers entering those areas to take advantage of low labor costs. We also formed an agency agreement in Brazil with an eye toward expansion should the Brazilian market prove profitable. ■ Major expansions of the Company's Chicago and London facilities, coupled with substantial leases for larger buildings in San Francisco and Los Angeles, further enhanced our ability to satisfy customer requirements. Expansion of our Seattle headquarters building to double its original size made room for increased operating efficiency as well as training facilities for Company personnel and our customers and vendors. ■ Our state-of-the-art computer capabilities were strengthened with the completion of a new export air program. Next on the agenda is development of a Company-wide Electronic Data Interface (EDI) system. Our staff of skilled computer professionals will continue to perfect new programs to meet the expanding needs of our customers for innovative and efficient service through automation. ■ Last year marked our tenth anniversary in business. In just one decade we have grown from a small ocean forwarding company to a mature industry front-runner. During the past five years alone, our net earnings have increased over three-fold. Our inclusion in the Forbes listing of the "200 Best Small Companies in America" reflects our success. ■ We recognize, however, that only through continued hard work and attention to a sound strategy for growth can we maintain our position of leadership. Even as we grow, our strategy will continue to emphasize quality service and personal attention to our customers. We believe that consistent efforts to maintain a small company atmosphere with a highly trained and motivated work force will provide the competitive edge. ■ Expeditors enters the new decade with confidence. Thanks to attention to our customers and investment in the tools necessary to deliver superior service, we believe the Company will maintain its leadership position. We look forward to continued strong performance as we sustain our efforts to earn the trust and commitment of our customers and shareholders.

■ Peter J. Rose, President

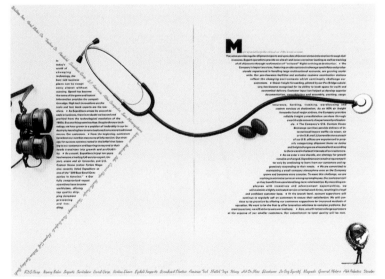

CLIENT: EXPEDITORS INTERNATIONAL ■ DESIGN FIRM: VAN DYKE COMPANY ■ ART DIRECTOR/DESIGNER: JOHN VAN DYKE ■ PHOTOGRAPHER: CLIFF FIESS ■ WRITER: RICK MOSS ■ TYPOGRAPHER: TYPEHOUSE ■ PAPER SELECTION: ICONOLUX ■ PAPER MANUFACTURER: ZANDERS FEINPAPIERE ■ PRINTER: GRAPHIC ARTS CENTER ■ NUMBER OF PAGES: 16 ■ TRIM SIZE: 8 1/4 x 11 3/4 INCHES ■ TYPE SELECTION: UNIVERS 75 ■ PRINT RUN: 8,500 ■

WPP Group plc

Annual Report and Accounts 1989

"The purpose of all WPP Group companies
is to add value and worth to clients' businesses through
the management of the imagination"

WPP GROUP PLC

· ·

▲Our annual report is aimed at a diverse audience that includes financial analysts, journalists, financial institutions, clients, employees, potential employees, and vendors. What is more, we are an organization with a complex corporate structure—many well-known subsidiaries with distinct identities—and we provide a wide variety of services in the areas of advertising, marketing, and public relations. The common element that unites these companies is given in the statement on the front covers of the two books: "The purpose of all WPP Group companies is too add value and worth to clients' businesses through the management of the imagination." It was important that the look and style of the annual report should reflect this sentiment, that the company should be seen to practice what it preaches. We also wanted to put across that this is the group in the marketing and communications sector that knows more about the field than any other, that is aware of trends and changes. And we wanted to present the finacial information clearly and simply, but with imagination. This report succeeded in all respects. From many conversations and letters, we know that it was admired and appreciated by all elements its diverse audience.

· ·

■ Unser Jahresbericht wendet sich an ein vielschichtiges Publikum, das sich aus Finanzexperten, Journalisten, finanziellen Institutionen, Kunden, Angestellten, potentiellen Angestellten und Händlern zusammensetzt. Zudem sind wir eine Organisation mit einer komplexen Unternehmensstruktur - wir haben viele bekannte Tochtergesellschaften, die sich in ihrem Charakter deutlich voneinander unterscheiden - und wir bieten eine brei-te Palette von Dienstleistungen im Werbe-, PR-, und Marketing-Bereich. Diese Unternehmen haben ein gemeinsames Merkmal, das auf der Titelseite der beiden Bücher in einem Satz zusammengefasst wird: «Es ist das Ziel aller Gesellschaften der WPP-Group, durch angewandtes kreatives Denken den Wert von Unternehmen zu steigern.» Es war uns wichtig, dass der Stil und das Design des Jahresberichts diesen Vorsatz gewissermassen in die Praxis umsetzten, um unsere Aussage konkret zu untermauern. Wir wollten ausserdem herausstreichen, dass unsere Gruppe sich besser im Marketing- und Public-Relations-Bereich auskennt als alle anderen Firmen in dieser Branche, und dass sie ihren Finger am Puls der Zeit hat. Und wir wollten die Bilanzen klar und deutlich, aber in einfallsreicher Form präsentieren. Dieser Bericht war in jeder Hinsicht ein durchschlagender Erfolg. Wir wissen aus vielen Briefen und Gesprächen, dass er bei unserem Publikum auf breitester Front Anerkennung und Bewunderung fand.

· ·

● Notre rapport annuel vise un public très divers comprenant analystes financiers, journalistes, institutions financières, clients, employés actuels et employés potentiels ou vendeurs. De plus, notre organisation a une structure commerciale très complexe (plusieurs filiales assez connues avec des identités bien distinctes) et nous proposons un large éventail de services dans les domaines de la publicité, du marketing et des relations publiques. L'élément commun à ces compagnies est révélé sur la page de couverture des deux livres: «Le but de toutes les compagnies WPP Group est d'augmenter la valeur des entreprises de chaque client à travers la gestion de l'imagination.» Il était important que l'image et le style du rapport annuel reflètent cette évidence: notre société fait exactement ce qu'elle prône. Nous voulions aussi mettre en lumière le fait que ce groupe est bien plus informé qu'aucun autre en matière de marketing et de changements. Nous voulions également présenter le côté financier de façon claire et simple, mais avec imagination. Ce rapport a été un succès dans tous les domaines. A partir de conversations ou de lettres, nous avons pu constater qu'il a été admiré et apprécié par notre public, et la relation que nous avons avec le designer a été crucile dans la réalisation de ce succès. Nos designers l'ont parfaitement compris et, de fait, ils ont totalement contribué. Des solutions imaginatives ont été apportées au fur et à mesure que les problèmes se soulevaient. Les designers ont parfaitement réussi à garder son intégrité au design tout en respectant la personnalité du rapport.

[FEONA McEWAN]

WPP GROUP PLC: 27 FARM STREET, LONDON W1X 6RD GREAT BRITAIN 071.408.2204

SAMPSON TYRELL LTD

▲ We felt very strongly that the concept of "management of the imagination," as depicted by the pencil sharpener and pencil and in the form of two books, met the client's communications objectives, and, indeed, they loved the idea. we presented varying levels of the concept, the most powerful of which demonstrated the versatility with which we could we interpret it to make specific points throughout the report. This is what "sold" the execution to our client. The abstraction of the two images on the front covers was debated at length but ultimately met with unanimous approval. We worked with the client on three previous reports and knew the budget parameters. The execution was based on a fixed figure that was set once the concept was approved. Although we see budget concerns in some areas, most of our clients still recognize the value of a good annual report, and they regard the cost as an important investment. We feel that, as designers, it is up to us to demonstrate cost-effectiveness through proper budget management and intelligent use of resources.

■ Wir waren davon überzeugt, dass das Konzept des «angewandten kreativen Denkens», das in dem Bild des Bleistifts und des Bleistiftspitzers und im Design der zwei Bücher zum Ausdruck kommt, der Aussageabsicht des Kunden entsprach, und der Vorschlag fand dann auch sofort Anklang. Wir präsentierten das Konzept aus mehreren Perspektiven, und unser stärkstes Argument war seine vielseitige Interpretierbarkeit im Hinblick auf die verschiedensten Punkte innerhalb des Berichts. Dieses Argument gab dann den Ausschlag. Der Abstraktionsgrad der zwei Bilder auf dem Umschlag wurde lange debattiert, fand aber letztlich uneingeschränkte Zustimmung. Wir hatten schon zuvor drei Berichte für den Kunden entworfen und kannten die Grenzen des Budgets. Die Ausführung beruht auf einer bestimmten Summe, die festgesetzt wurde, nachdem das Konzept angenommen war. Hin und wieder müssen wir uns zwar nach der Decke strecken, aber die meisten unserer Kunden erkennen den Wert eines guten Jahresberichts und betrachten die Kosten als gute Investition. Es liegt dann an uns, durch gute Ausnutzung des Budgets und intelligenten Einsatz unserer Ressourcen so kostengünstig wie möglich zu arbeiten.

● Nous avons eu le sentiment que le concept de «gestion de l'imagination» ainsi illustré par le taille-crayon, le crayon, et sous la forme de deux livres, correspondait exactement aux objectifs de communication de client et, bien sûr, ils ont adoré cette ideé. Nous avons présenté différents niveaux du concept, dont le plus marquant démontrait les différentes façons dont nous pouvions l'interpréter afin de souligner certains points spécifiques tout au long du rapport. C'est cela qui a «vendu» le concept au client. L'abstraction des deux images sur la couverture a été longuement débattue, mais à la fin, elle a fait l'unanimité. Nous avions déjà travaillé sur trois rapports précédents avec le client, et nous connaissions bien les paramètres budgétaires. L'exécution du projet fut basée sur un chiffre fixe, établi une fois le concept approuvé. Bien que nous ayons d'habitude de problèmes budgétaires dans certains domaines, la plupart de nos clients reconnaissent tout de même la valeur d'un bon rapport annuel, et ils en considèrent le coût comme un investissement important. C'est à nous de démontrer l'efficacité des coûts, en gérant intelligemment et adroitement les ressources attribuées.

[DAVID FREEMAN]

SAMPSON TYRELL LIMITED: 6 MERCER STREET, LONDON WC2H 9QA GBR 071.379.7124

CONTENTS

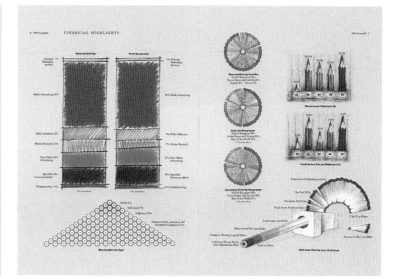

FINANCIAL HIGHLIGHTS

The Grass Roots Group PLC

Grass Roots has a special position within the WPP Group in that its role is that of a catalyst. Its function is to ensure that, when customers show interest in any product or service, the human faces of the business are capable and keen.

Any company that advertises faces a major point of weakness in their strategy if the human point of customer contact is not aware of the strategy, is not able to translate it into action and is not doing so on a regular basis. In short, motivation is an ongoing issue.

Grass Roots provides advertisers with the communications, training, incentive strategies and systems to help them make their media expenditure that much more effective.

The areas of activity are wide ranging. From sales team effectiveness to dealer network standards. From customer service research to launching a new product. In every case the one common purpose is to get the corporate strategy in place at the point of customer contact.

P & L International Vacationers Ltd

International Vacationers has grown in size and in the services it provides since coming into the WPP Group infrastructure.

The creation, planning and operations of incentives, conferences, product launches, special interest programmes and corporate entertaining remain the core business. In the past two years, however, many of our blue chip clients have asked our accounts directors to help them make a greater impact in the market place. As a result we now have a rapidly expanding team who devote their time to producing events, sponsorship and fund raising.

We have recently welcomed David Mills to our incentive and motivation division, which trades under the name of PLIV. David has an excellent reputation for putting together the most innovative and successful overseas programmes. During the coming year we shall further develop our client list, creative services and our wide selection of imaginative and exciting destinations.

Anspach Grossman Portugal

With twenty-one years of experience in corporate, brand and retail identity, we have worked with over 300 organizations worldwide. We help create a competitive advantage for our clients through thorough analysis, systematic planning and innovative design. Our experience has proven over time that a carefully planned and executed identity program is an indispensable business tool.

We view identity in its broadest sense. It is the distinctive capabilities and values of the client which are clarified during analysis, developed into a comprehensive communications plan and expressed through design at all levels of business activity.

We create identity programs for companies large and small, regional, national and international, bringing to each the highest level of innovation and personal care.

Our clients' success is the best measure of our success.

Brouillard Communications

Niccolò Machiavelli understood how one's reputation influences all other aspects of life.

So he would have appreciated Brouillard Communications.

We're an agency committed to reflecting and enhancing corporate reputations.

Through coordinated campaigns of advertising and public relations, Brouillard has served scores of leading companies and financial institutions.

And while we embody the personal service and esprit de corps of a small agency, at $70 million we're a giant in our speciality.

Our staff is made up of people who've chosen this kind of communications as their career. People who, as a group, have created scores of award-winning advertising and public relations campaigns.

Machiavelli would have understood our commitment to producing the best corporate and financial services advertising in America.

CLIENT: WPP GROUP PLC ■ DESIGN FIRM: SAMPSONTYRRELL LTD ■ CREATIVE DIRECTOR: DAVID FREEMAN ■ ACCOUNT DIRECTOR: SARAH RITCHIE CALDER ■ DESIGNERS: PAUL BARLOW, DAVID FREEMAN, LINDA WESTON ■ PRINCIPAL ILLUSTRATORS: KARIN LITTLEWOOD, JENNY POWELL, JULIE SMITH ■ WRITER: MARTIN SORRELL ■ PRODUCTION MANAGER: MARTIN BARLEY ■ PAPER SELECTION: CANALETTO CONSORT, ROYAL SILK PAPER ■ PRINTERS: ROYLE CITY, BALDING & MANSELL ■ NUMBER OF PAGES: 64 EACH VOLUME ■ TYPE SELECTION: GARAMOND, STEMPEL, HELVETICA ■

Komag Annual Report 1989

KOMAG

. . . .

▲ We wanted this report to make three key points to our investors. First, that we are a technology leader in a technology based market. Second, we are the largest independent manufacturer of our product (high-capacity data storage disks), and third, we are well-positioned for future growth. This last point was extremely important because of our recent financial history. The first half of 1989 was lousy, but the second half was good. This report had to stress recovery and positioning for 1990, as well as highlight our strong customer base and alliances, particularly its affiliations with Japanese companies, which are unusual in this industry. In a tough year, you have to live with the annual report. This one was elegant and tasteful, and that's a tribute to our designer. We're a company of engineers, and we know we need creative talent, but anyone who works with us has got to be able to moderate their style to suit ours. Steve is great at adding enough squares and cubes to the book to suit us as engineers, but with enough creative flair to produce a good-looking annual report.

. . . .

■ Wir wollten mit diesem Bericht unseren Anlegern drei Schlüsselpunkte vermitteln: Wir sind in unserem speziellen Marktbereich technologisch führend, wir sind der grösste unabhängige Hersteller von Platten-speichereinheiten, und wir sind in einer guten Ausgangsposition für zukünftiges Wachstum. Dieser letzte Punkt war angesichts unserer Finanzlage während des letzten Jahres besonders wichtig: Die erste Hälfte von 1989 war lausig, aber die zweite Hälfte war gut. Der Bericht musste unterstreichen, dass wir uns erholt hatten und uns in einer guten Startposition für 1990 befanden. Gleichzeitig sollte er unsere solide Kundenbasis her-vorheben und auf unsere Allianzen mit anderen, insbesondere japanischen Unternehmen hinweisen, was ziemlich ungewöhnlich ist. In einem schwierigen Jahr muss man das Beste aus seinem Jahresbericht machen. Dieser Bericht war elegant und geschmackvoll, und das ist das Verdienst des Designers. Wir sind ein Unternehmen von Ingenieuren, und wir wissen, dass wir auf kreative Leute angewiesen sind, aber der Designer, der mit uns zusammenarbeitet, muss sich auf unseren Geschmack einstellen. Steve weiss das, und er gibt uns all die Quadrate und Kuben, die wir als Ingenieure erwarten, und schafft es dabei doch, soviel kreatives Flair einzubringen, dass am Ende ein visuell ansprechender Jahresbericht zustande kommt.

. . . .

● Avec ce rapport, nous cherchions à démontrer trois choses à nos investisseurs. Tout d'abord, que nous sommes un des leaders sur le marché de la technologie. Nous sommes également les plus gros fabricants indépen-dants de notre produit (des disques de stockage de données haute capacité), et nous sommes bien placés pour une future croissance. Ce dernier point était particulièrement important, compte tenu de notre très récent passé financier. Le premier semestre 1989 a été désastreux, mais heureusement le deuxième était meilleur. Ce rapport se devait de souligner cette amélioration ainsi que la nouvelle politique de l'année 1990; il devait parler de notre clientèle de base aussi bien que des alliances que nous avons, particulièrement avec le Japon, ce qui est très inhabituel dans ce domaine. Pendant une année difficile, il faut vivre avec le rapport financier. Celui-ci était particulièrement élégant et tout le mérite en revient à notre designer. Nous sommes une entreprise d'ingénieurs et nous savons que nous avons besoin de talents créatifs, mais quiconque travaille pour nous doit savoir oublier son propre style au profit du nôtre. Steve a su nous donner suffisamment de formes géométriques pour plaire à nos esprits scientifiques, tout en privilégiant la créativité qui a permis de produire un bon rapport annuel.

[HUNT PAYNE]

KOMAG: 275 SOUTH HILLVIEW DRIVE, MILPITAS, CALIFORNIA 95035 USA 408.946.2300

. . . .

▲ This report was the third we had done with Komag, and we're starting on the fourth. As with any client, there's been a process of education and a building of trust. Now there's a strong sense of collaboration between us, the CEO, and the company writer. This year's report built on themes established in the previous book. In 1988 we had divided the book into four segments, covering manufacturing technology, materials technology, strategic alliances, and a stong customer base. The four sections were tied together by a strong company statement. This year, we kept the same basic structure, but wanted to take it further. We used the idea of allowing a hypothetical third party observer, say an industry analyst, to comment on the industry. These independent statements are used as the openings to each section. Then the company responds to that statement, following it with detailed information on the four segments we're highlighting. This report contains a lot of the elements that I like to have in all the reports I do. I believe in levels of information in annual reports—people should be able to find exactly the amount of information they need. If they want a surface reading, or a detailed study, they still can find out what they need to know. I also go for a lower grade stock for the financial section, highlighting the information with colors. In this way, I can put more money up in the front of the book, where it should be. Here, this allowed us to use the metallics, which are not just a pretty design element, but a reflection of the company's product.

. . . .

■ Dieser Bericht war unser dritter für Komag, und wir beginnen gerade mit dem vierten. Wie bei jedem Kunden fand zunächst ein Prozess des Lernens und der Vertrauensbildung statt. Inzwischen herrscht ein starkes Gefühl kollegialer Zusammenarbeit zwischen uns, dem Vorstand und dem Werbetexter der Firma. Der diesjährige Bericht setzt Themen fort, die in dem vorausgegangenen Buch eingeführt wurden. 1988 unterteilten wir den Bericht in vier Abschnitte unter den Oberbegriffen «Fertigungstechnik», «Materialtechnik», «Strategische Allianzen» und «Eine solide Kundenbasis». Die vier Abschnitte verbanden sich zu einer starken Firmenaussage. In diesem Jahr verwendeten wir die gleiche Grundstruktur, bauten sie aber weiter aus. Der Bericht enthält viele der Elemente, die ich gerne in allen Jahresberichten unterbringe, an denen ich arbeite. Nach meiner Überzeugung sollten Jahresberichte ihre Informationen gestaffelt darbieten - die Leser sollten in der Lage sein, genau die Menge an Informationen zu finden, die sie brauchen, egal ob sie den Text nur kurz überfliegen oder sorgfältig studieren wollen. Ich bin ausserdem dafür, billigeres Papier für den finanziellen Teil zu verwenden und die einzelnen Informationen farblich hervorzuheben. Auf diese Weise kann ich mehr Geld in den vorderen Teil stecken, wo es hingehört. In diesem Fall konnten wir so Metallfarben verwenden, die nicht nur ein hübsches Designelement ergeben, sondern auch das Produkt des Unternehmens widerspiegeln.

. . . .

● Ce rapport était le troisième depuis que nous travaillons avec Komag, et nous démarrons déjà le quatrième. Comme avec tout client, nous sommes passés par une phase de connaissance qui a finalement abouti à une confiance mutuelle. A présent, il y a un fort esprit de collaboration entre nous, le directeur général et le rédacteur de la société. Le rapport de cette année a été construit sur les thèmes établis dans les précédents rapports. En 1988, nous avions divisé la publication en quatre sections, couvrant la technologie de fabrication, celle des matériaux, les alliances stratégiques et une solide clientèle de base. Ces quatre sections étaient reliées ensemble sous la forme d'un solide bilan d'entreprise. Cette année, nous avons gardé la même structure fondamentale en la poussant un peu plus loin. Ce rapport contient un grand nombre d'éléments que j'aimerais retrouver dans tous les rapports financiers auxquels je collabore. Je pense que plusieurs niveaux d'information sont nécessaires dans un rapport annuel. Les lecteurs devraient pouvoir y trouver l'exacte quantité d'information dont ils ont besoin. Qu'ils désirent simplement parcourir le livre ou l'étudier de manière plus approfondie, ils doivent pouvoir trouver ce qu'ils ont besoin de savoir. Je préconise aussi l'usage de papiers bon marché pour la partie financière, les couleurs venant simplement souligner l'information. De cette façon, je peux consacrer plus d'argent aux premières pages, là où c'est le plus important. Dans ce cas précis, nous avons pu utiliser des papiers métalliques, qui sont non seulement un élément esthétique de la création, mais qui reflètent surtout les produits de l'entreprise.

[STEVEN TOLLESON]

TOLLESON DESIGN: 444 SPEAR STREET #204, SAN FRANCISCO, CALIFORNIA 94105 USA 415.626.7796

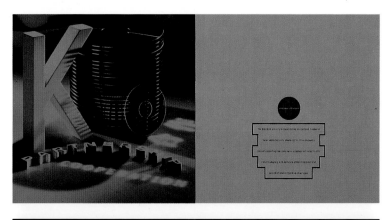

Komag, Incorporated designs, manufactures, and markets the data storage industry's most advanced metallic disks for use in small-diameter, high-capacity Winchester disk drives. Founded in 1983, Komag has grown to become the world's largest independent supplier of sputtered, thin-film disks with manufacturing facilities in California and, through a joint venture, in Japan.

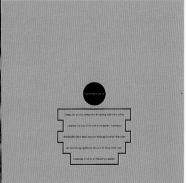

CLIENT: KOMAG ■ DESIGN FIRM: TOLLESON DESIGN ■ ART DIRECTOR: STEVEN TOLLESON ■ DESIGNERS: STEVEN TOLLESON, BOB AUFULDISH ■ PHOTOGRAPHER: HENRIK KAM ■ WRITER: LINDSAY BEAMAN ■ TYPOGRAPHERS: TOLLESON DESIGN, SPARTAN TYPOGRAPHY ■ PAPER SELECTION: CELESTEA, CHAMPION OFFSET ■ PRINTER: LITHOGRAPHIX ■ NUMBER OF PAGES: 48 ■ TYPE SELECTION: MATRIX, GILL SANS ■ PRINT RUN: 10,000 ■

TRENWICK

1989 ANNUAL REPORT

TRENWICK GROUP, INC.

. . . .

▲ The primary audience for our annual report is our stockholders (who are mainly institutional investors), with a secondary audience of potential investors. We believe our annual report should simply and concisely tell shareholders how their company is doing, not be a self-congratulatory or flashy advertising document. We want our report to impart three basic messages about the company, which are here stressed both visually and in the text: one, we follow a simple and consistent business strategy; two, our report presents financial information in a straightforward manner; and three, we take a logical, well-reasoned, and controlled approach to running our business. Reinsurance is a highly competitive business and we don't make anything—our report has to reflect the strict business plan we follow. Reinsurance is also perceived as a highly technical and archaic business—we want a report that is crisp and functional, but at the same time interesting. The theme of consistency is underscored by using the same basic format for three years in a row. Its functional design makes the company easy to understand. The design, which is workbook-like, encourages use, not just perusal. We like that and have no plans to change the format. It not only works for us, but design-wise runs counter to both the boring gray reports usually put out by financial institutions and the razzle-dazzle reports of other corporations. The function of this report is information, not entertainment. Frank listened to us in our initial meetings and this design was his response to us. Unlike other designers we interviewed, he didn't try to impose a design on us, but created a design that suited our needs.

. . . .

■ Unser Jahresbericht wendet sich hauptsächlich an unsere Aktionäre (die grösstenteils institutionelle Anleger sind) und zielt in zweiter Linie auf potentielle Investoren. Unser Jahresbericht soll den Aktionären schlicht und einfach erklären, wo ihr Unternehmen wirtschaftlich steht; wir sind weder an lautem Eigenlob noch an einem protzigen Werbedokument interessiert. Das Rückversicherungsgeschäft ist stark wettbewerborientiert und insofern eine abstrakte Sache, als wir nichts Konkretes herstellen - unser Bericht muss also den strengen Geschäftsplan reflektieren, dem wir folgen. Rückversicherungen gelten ausserdem als ziemlich technische und trockene Angelegenheit - wir wollen also einen Bericht, der einerseits knapp und funktionell, aber andererseits auch interessant ist. Das Thema «Beständigkeit» wird dadurch unterstrichen, dass wir zum nunmehr dritten Mal das gleiche Format verwendet haben. Der funktionelle Aufbau macht unsere Aussage leicht verständlich, und das schulbuchartige Design ermuntert dazu, den Bericht zu benutzen und nicht nur zu überfliegen. Das gefällt uns, und wir haben keinerlei Pläne, dieses Format zu ändern. Es erfüllt nicht nur seine Aufgabe, sondern bildet auch einen Kontrast zu der grauen Ödnis der üblichen bilanzorientierten Geschäftsberichte und zu dem buntgescheckten Design der Jahresberichte anderer Unternehmen. Die Hauptfunktion dieses Berichts ist Information, nicht Unterhaltung. Im Gegensatz zu anderen Designern, mit denen wir uns unterhielten, versuchte Frank nicht, uns ein bestimmtes Design aufzudrängen, sondern entwickelte etwas, das unseren Bedürfnissen entspricht.

. . . .

● Nos actionnaires (dont la plupart sont des investisseurs institutionnels) sont les premiers intéressés par notre rapport annuel, tandis que les investisseurs potentiels constituent un auditoire secondaire. Nous pensons qu'un rapport annuel devrait informer de manière simple et concise les actionnaires du fonctionnement de l'entreprise, et non pas être une expression de sa propre autosatisfaction, une publication trop tape-à-l'œil. Les assurances sont un domaine ultra-compétitif, et nous ne faisons aucun produit. Notre rapport doit refléter les règles commerciales rigoureuses que nous suivons. Les assurances sont également un marché perçu comme quelque chose de très technique et archaïque: c'est pourquoi nous désirons un rapport concis et fonctionnel, mais en même temps intéressant. Le thème de la cohérence est souligné par l'utilisation, pour la troisième fois consécutive, du même format de base. Son design fonctionnel rend la compagnie facile à appréhender. Il se présente sous la forme d'un cahier, ce qui encourage l'utilisation. C'est ce que nous aimons et c'est la raison pour laquelle nous n'avons aucunement l'intention de changer de format. Non seulement cela marche très bien pour nous, mais une conception avisée est beaucoup plus payante à long terme que les habituels rapports incolores habituellement produits par les institutions financières, ou les éblouissants rapports d'autres entreprises. La fonction primaire de ce rapport est d'informer, pas de divertir. Frank nous a écouté et, contrairement aux autres designers que nous avons entendus, il n'a pas essayé de nous imposer un design, mais en a crée un qui correspondait à nos besoins.

[PAUL FELDFHER]

TRENWICK GROUP, INC.: METRO CENTER, ONE STATION PLACE, STAMFORD, CONNECTICUT 06902 USA 203.353.5500

FRANK C. LIONETTI DESIGN

▲ This is our third year with Trenwick; the concept has been the same since its inception, and we're now in the process of working on the fourth, again with no change to the basic concept. Trenwick is the first annual report we ever did. We approached it with the desire to do something different in this area, and once we met with the people there, we knew it had to be simple. All of the type for this report has been produced right off a 300 dpi laser printer. Still, this is not an inexpensive report to produce, but it looks practical. Each year we make a subtle change in the design, but not in the format. For example, this year the heads, the tabs, and the cover were set in Univers. This has become the most difficult task—to come up with the something different, not just to be different, but to improve the information. For a report that appears to be basic, there are a lot of subtleties involved here.

■ Dies ist unser drittes Jahr mit Trenwick; das ursprüngliche Konzept ist das gleiche geblieben und wird auch für den vierten Jahresbericht übernommen werden, an dem wir im Moment arbeiten. Der Trenwick-Bericht war unser erster Jahresbericht überhaupt, und wir wollten zunächst einmal etwas völlig Neuartiges versuchen. Als wir uns dann mit den Leuten von Trenwick trafen, wussten wir, dass wir das Design so schlicht wie möglich halten mussten. Das gesamte Schriftbild für den Bericht wurde auf einem 300 dpi Laser-Drucker produziert. Das heisst nicht, dass der Bericht in der Herstellung billig ist, aber er sieht ausgesprochen zweckmässig aus. Wir nehmen jedes Jahr subtile Veränderungen am Design vor, während das Format gleich bleibt. Dieses Jahr wurden zum Beispiel die Überschriften, die Tabellen und der Umschlag in Univers gesetzt. Und hier liegt auch die eigentliche Schwierigkeit - wir müssen uns Jahr für Jahr etwas Neues einfallen lassen, und zwar nicht einfach, um Abwechslung in das Design zu bringen, sondern um die Information besser zu präsentieren. Man glaubt kaum, wie viele Feinheiten in einen scheinbar so schlichten Bericht eingehen.

● Ceci est notre troisième année de travail en collaboration avec Trenwick. Le concept est resté le même depuis le début, et nous sommes actuellement en train de préparer le quatrième rapport, sans grands changements majeurs. Le rapport annuel pour Trenwick fut le premier que nous ayions fait. Notre approche pour ce projet était motivée par le désir de réaliser quelque chose de différent dans ce domaine, et notre recontre avec les gens de Trenwick nous a prouvé que ce quelque chose devait être simple. Toute la partie texte de ce rapport a été effectuée sur une imprimante laser de type dpi 300. Bien que ce procédé ne soit pas bon marché, il est fort pratique. Chaque année nous modifions imperceptiblement le design, sans changer le format. Cette année, par exemple, les titres, les tableaux, ainsi que la couverture ont été composés sur Univers. Il est trés difficile de proposer quelque chose de vraiment différent, non pas pour être différents, mais dans le but d'améliorer réellement l'information. Derrière son apparence modeste, ce rapport a demandé beaucoup de travail.

[FRANK C. LIONETTI]

FRANK C. LIONETTI DESIGN, INC.: 3 LEDGE ROAD, OLD GREENWICH, CONNECTICUT 06870 USA 203.637.4152

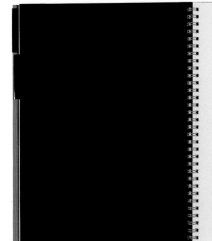

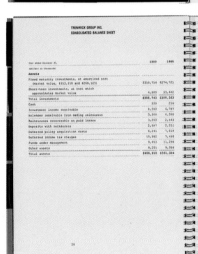

Client: TRENWICK GROUP, INC. ■ Design Firm: FRANK C. LIONETTI DESIGN, INC. ■ Art Director: FRANK C. LIONETTI ■ Designer: MEG SHERMAN ■ Photographer: FRANK WHITE PHOTOGRAPHY ■ Typographer: LOW KEY TYPOGRAPHERS, INC. ■ Paper Selection: CHROMOLUX 700 , POSEIDEN ■ Paper Manufacturers: ZANDERS, MOHAWK ■ Printer: BEAUVAIS PRINTING ■ Number of Pages: 52 PLUS COVER ■ Print Run: 4,000 ■

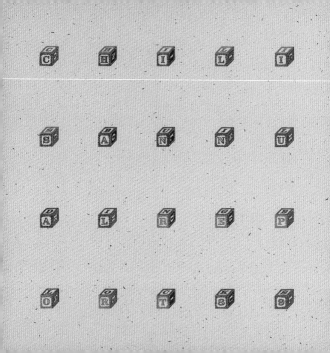

▲ Chili's Inc. uses its annual report primarily for the traditional purpose of reaching shareholders, financial analysts, and real estate developers, and secondarily as an aid to employee recruitment. The company has experienced a tremendous growth, but we wanted to emphasize that we are building the company on a solid base; we are a stable and solid company. We always receive a good response to our annual report and this year was no exception. Much of this is due to our relationship with our design firm. They are very interested in who we are and what our business is—in fact, working with them is like having a partner in our company. We like unusual twists in our annual report and they manage to give us a new one every year.

■ Der Jahresbericht von Chili's Inc. erfüllt die traditionelle Aufgabe, unsere Aktionäre, Finanzanalytiker und Immobilienunternehmer zu informieren und dient in zweiter Linie dazu, Angestellte zu rekrutieren. Das Unternehmen hat sich während der letzten Jahre gewaltig vergrössert, und wir wollten unterstreichen, dass dieses Wachstum auf einer soliden Grundlage stattfindet, dass wir ein stabiles, solides Unternehmen sind. Unsere Jahresberichte finden immer viel Anklang, und dieses Jahr bildete keine Ausnahme. Das liegt zu einem grossen Teil an unserer guten Beziehung zu unserer Design-Firma. Die Designer sind sehr daran interessiert, wer wir sind und worin unser Geschäft besteht – wir arbeiten mit ihnen zusammen, als wären sie Teilhaber an unserem Unternehmen. Wir haben gerne ein paar ungewöhnliche, überraschende Elemente in unserem Jahresbericht, und unsere Designer lassen sich jedes Jahr etwas Neues einfallen.

● Chili's Inc. utilise son rapport annuel à la fois dans le but de toucher ses actionnaires, les analystes financiers et les promoteurs immobiliers, aussi bien qu'à des fins de recrutement du personnel. L'entreprise a connu une croissance considérable, aussi avons nous voulu souligner que ce développement se faisait sur des bases solides, et que nous sommes une entreprise saine et sérieuse. Nous avons toujours eu de bons échos de nos rapports annuels, il en a été de même cette année. Une grande part de ce succès est due à la bonne entente qui règne entre le bureau de design et nous-mêmes. Ce que nous faisons les intéresse énormément, et en fait, c'est presque comme si nous avions de nouveaux associés. Nous aimons la surprise et la nouveauté, et ils n'en manquent jamais.

[KEN DENNIS]

CHILI'S, INC.: 6820 LBJ FREEWAY, SUITE 200, DALLAS, TEXAS 75240 USA 214.980.9917

RICHARDS BROCK MILLER MITCHELL & ASSOC.

. . . .

▲ People look at this report and think it's very elaborate, but in fact, it gives the impression of being expensive when it really isn't. We have a good budget, but the sky's not the limit. The thermography used in the printing process was actually cheaper than running a varnish over a four-color photograph. This report is always based on close collaboration with the client, this year more so than ever. Last year we emphasized the company's growth, and this year their suggestion was that we stress *controlled* growth—good management and a solid financial base. Hence the idea of the building blocks. This concept actually came from Chili's marketing department, but we initially discarded it as being too often used; a bit of a cliché. However, once we discovered that the block has six sides and there are six letters in Chili's, we started to run with it. This was the fourth report we've done for them. They trust us, and each year we try to reflect their corporate culture while creating a strong financial document.

. . . .

■ Die Leute schauen sich diesen Bericht an und denken: «Das war bestimmt furchtbar aufwendig», aber Tatsache ist, dass er viel kostspieliger aussieht, als er in Wirklichkeit war. Wir haben ein gutes Budget zur Verfügung, aber es ist keineswegs unbegrenzt. Das Thermo-Verfahren, das wir beim Druck einsetzten, war tatsächlich die preisgünstigere Alternative zu einem Lackieren der Vierfarbphotos. Der Chili-Jahresbericht kommt immer in enger Zusammenarbeit mit dem Kunden zustande, und das traf ganz besonders in diesem Jahr zu. Letztes Jahr haben wir das Wachstum des Unternehmens betont, und dieses Jahr sollten wir unterstreichen, dass es ein kontrolliertes Wachstum auf einer durchdachten und finanziell gesunden Grundlage ist. Daher auch die Idee mit den Bauklötzen. Das Konzept stammte ursprünglich aus Chilis Marketing-Abteilung, und wir lehnten es anfangs als zu abgegriffen ab. Als wir aber entdeckten, dass ein Bauklotz sechs Seiten und das Wort «Chili's» sechs Buchstaben hat, fanden wir Gefallen daran. Es war unser vierter Jahresbericht für Chili's. Der Kunde hat Vertrauen zu uns, und wir versuchen jedes Jahr, Chili's Unternehmenskultur zum Ausdruck zu bringen und gleichzeitig ein aussagestarkes finanzielles Dokument zu entwerfen.

. . . .

● Les gens examinent ce rapport et s'imaginent qu'il est très élaboré, alors qu'en fait, il a seulement l'air d'avoir coûté très cher. Certes, notre budget est large, mais pas illimité. Le procédé thermographique utilisé pour l'impression était en fait moins cher que l'utilisation d'un vernis sur une photo quatre couleurs. Ce rapport est toujours basé sur une collaboration étroite avec le client, ce qui était particulièrement vrai cette année. Alors que l'année dernière, nous avions mis l'accent sur la croissance de l'entreprise, cette année, ils ont décidé de montrer que cette croissance est contrôlée: une direction avisée, combinée à une solide base financière. D'où le concept de fondations constituées par des cubes. Cette idée est en fait venue du département «marketing» de Chili's, mais au départ nous l'avions écartée comme étant trop commune. Cependant, lorsque nous nous sommes rendus compte que les cubes ont six faces, et qu'il y a justement six lettres dans Chili's, nous avons foncé. C'était le quatrième rapport que nous faisions pour eux. Ils nous font confiance, et chaque année, nous nous efforçons de refléter fidèlement la personnalité de l'entreprise, tout en réalisant un sérieux dossier financier.

[BRIAN BOYD]

RICHARDS BROCK MILLER MITCHELL & ASSOC.: 7007 TWIN HILLS #200, DALLAS, TEXAS 75231 USA 214.987.3662

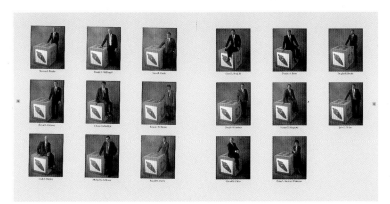

CLIENT: CHILI'S INC. ■ DESIGN FIRM: RICHARDS BROCK MILLER MITCHELL & ASSOC. ■ ART DIRECTOR: BRIAN BOYD ■ DESIGNER: BRIAN BOYD ■
PHOTOGRAPHER: ROBERT LATORRE ■ ILLUSTRATOR: JOHN CRAIG ■ WRITER: KEVIN ORLIN JOHNSON ■ TYPOGRAPHER: CHILES & CHILES ■ PAPER
SELECTION: VINTAGE ■ PRINTER: HERITAGE PRESS ■ NUMBER OF PAGES: 40 PLUS COVER ■ TYPE SELECTION: CLARENDON BOLD, GOUDY OLD STYLE ■

THE CABOT CORPORATION

. . . .

▲ One of the greatest challenges in the creation of our annual report stems from the fact that we are a Fortune 300 company, but still small in terms of our size. We're a diverse company with many far-flung divisions around the world; an old company in the midst of organizational change. We wanted this report to address the questions: What does the new Cabot mean? What is our strategy for dealing with these changes? How are we upholding the tradition while adapting to change? Ultimately, this report could only lay the groundwork for the explanation, because this was a real transition year, in terms of both management and the public's perception of the company. In a period such as this, it's important to realize that no document can accomplish everything we might like. But this report planted the seed, which was good. The feature section explained the technology of what we do, which is manufacture and supply specialty chemicals, materials, and energy. This approach was different and got a very good response. Weymouth Design has been doing our reports for some time now, and this history has been extremely helpful; their knowledge of our company made a last-minute concept decision go smoothly. The report was produced during a very busy period for us and the firm was able to manage a lot of work without heavy direction. They devised a flexible format that allowed us to drop in changes at the last minute. We could concentrate on the quality of the copy without having to worry about how it would fit. In recent years, Cabot has been willing to look at new ways of communicating. Weymouth Design has been great in their response.

. . . .

■ Eine der grössten Herausforderungen bei der Entwicklung unseres Jahresberichts liegt darin, dass wir einerseits ein Fortune 300-Unternehmen, aber andererseits dem Umfang nach klein sind. Wir sind ein breitgefächertes Unternehmen mit vielen, rund um die Welt verstreuten Zweigstellen. Cabot ist ein altes Unternehmen, das viele organisatorische Veränderungen durchlaufen hat. Wir wollten mit unserem Bericht drei verschiedene Fragen ansprechen: Was bedeutet die Neuorganisation von Cabot? Welche Strategie verwenden wir bei der Auseinandersetzung mit diesen Veränderungen? Und wie bleiben wir unserer Tradition treu und passen uns gleichzeitig der veränderten Situation an? Letzten Endes konnte dieser Bericht nur ansatzweise Erklärungen liefern, da es sich im Hinblick auf die Unternehmensleitung und im Auge der Öffentlichkeit um ein Übergangsjahr für Cabot handelte. In einer solchen Übergangsperiode ist es wichtig zu erkennen, dass kein Dokument all das leisten kann, was einem vorschwebt. Doch dieser Bericht legte ein solides Fundament. Der Reportageteil erklärt die technologischen Grundlagen unserer Arbeit – der Herstellung und Lieferung von Spezialchemikalien und -materialien und Energie. Das war etwas Neuartiges und fand viel Anklang. Weymouth Design entwirft bereits seit einiger Zeit unsere Jahresberichte, und das stellte sich als ausserordentlich hilfreich heraus. Weymouth war mit unserem Unternehmen vertraut, so dass eine Änderung in letzter Minute absolut glatt über die Bühne ging. Weymouth entwarf ein flexibles Format, das es uns ermöglichte, in letzter Minute Veränderungen einzufügen.

. . . .

● L'un des plus grands défis dans la création de notre rapport annuel est basé sur la dichotomie existant entre le fait que nous soyons une entreprise «Fortune 300», et dans le même temps, petits par la taille. Notre société est très diversifiée et comprend de nombreuses filiales, réparties dans le monde entier. Cabot est une vieille maison qui est passée par plusieurs changements au niveau de l'organisation. Nous voulions que ce rapport réponde aux questions suivantes: qu'est-ce que la nouvelle société Cabot représente exactement? quelle est notre stratégie vis-à-vis de ces changements? comment maintenons-nous notre tradition tout en nous adaptant aux transformations? En définitive, ce rapport ne peut que proposer une ébauche réponse, puisque cette année était une époque transitoire, aussi bien pour la direction, que pour la manière dont l'entreprise est perçue par le public. Dans une telle situation, il est important de prendre conscience qu'aucun imprimé ne peut satisfaire à toutes nos exigences. Cependant, ce rapport a posé les premiers jalons, ce qui est positif. Depuis assez longtemps déjà, l'agence Weymouth Design est chargée de la création de notre rapport et cette collaboration aura été extrêmement utile. Une bonne connaissance de notre société leur a permis de prendre des décisions importantes à la dernière minute, sans que cela pose de problème majeur. Ce rapport a été produit pendant une période où nous étions très occupés, et l'agence a pu accomplir énormément de travail sans trop avoir besoin de nous. Ils ont imaginé un système assez souple pour nous permettre d'opérer des changements au dernier moment.

[SCOTT ESLER]

CABOT CORPORATION: 950 WINTER STREET, P.O. BOX 9073, WALTHAM, MASSACHUSETTS 02254-9073 USA 617 890 0200

▲ This was not our first report for Cabot Corporation, but we worked very closely with them again this year. The initial concept was theirs—they told us they wanted to focus the report on the specialty chemicals area of their business. Based on this premise, we provided three different approaches for the report. The final selection was made by a committee made up of representatives of both our firm and Cabot. We felt all three approaches were valid and weren't trying to sell one over another, so we were happy with their decision. In the end, its flexibility worked quite well, as there were a number of last-minute changes because of reorganization within the corporation. That can sometimes make a report very difficult, but I think our familiarity with the client went a long way in smoothing the process. Both we and the client were very happy with the report.

■ Dies war nicht unser erster Bericht für die Cabot Corporation, und wir haben auch in diesem Jahr wieder eng mit ihren Leuten zusammengearbeitet. Das ursprüngliche Konzept kam vom Kunden – er wollte, dass der Bericht sich auf den Geschäftsbereich der Spezialchemikalien konzentrierte. Auf dieser Grundlage erarbeiteten wir drei verschiedene Vorschläge. Die Endauswahl wurde dann von einem Komitee vorgenommen, das sich aus Vertretern von Cabot und unserer Firma zusammensetzte. Wir hielten alle drei Vorschläge für gleichwertig und gaben keinem den Vorzug, so dass bei der endgültigen Entscheidung keinerlei Unstimmigkeiten aufkamen. Die Flexibilität des Designs stellte sich als grosser Vorzug heraus, da wir wegen der Reorganisation des Unternehmens in letzter Minute einige Änderungen vornehmen mussten. Das kann manchmal recht problematisch sein, aber da wir mit dem Kunden vertraut waren, verlief alles ziemlich glatt. Sowohl Cabot als auch wir sind mit dem Bericht sehr zufrieden.

● Ce n'était pas notre premier rapport pour la Cabot Corporation, mais une fois de plus, nous avons collaboré très étroitement avec eux cette année. Le concept initial était le leur, puisqu'ils voulaient que le rapport se concentre sur le caractère particulier de leurs produits chimiques. Nous basant sur ces prémisses, nous avons proposé trois approches différentes pour le rapport. La sélection finale fut faite par un comité composé de représentants de notre agence et de la Cabot société. Nous avons été heureux de leur décision, car il nous est apparu que les trois approches étaient également valables. Finalement, cette flexibilité a bien fonctionné, étant donné le nombre de changements de dernière minute causés par la réorganisation interne de l'entreprise. Cela peut parfois poser des problèmes pour la réalisation d'un rapport, mais je pense que notre connaissance du client fut pour beaucoup dans la bonne marche du travail. Le client et nous-mêmes sommes très satisfaits de ce rapport annuel.

[TOM LAIDLAW]

WEYMOUTH DESIGN, INC.: 332 CONGRESS STREET, BOSTON, MASSACHUSETTS 02210 USA 617.542.2647

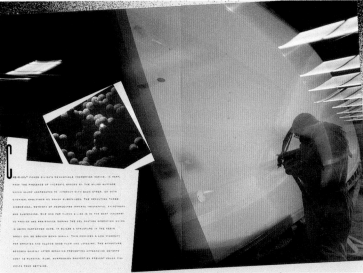

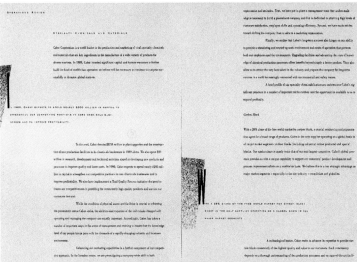

CLIENT: CABOT CORPORATION ■ DESIGN FIRM: WEYMOUTH DESIGN ■ ART DIRECTORS: TOM LAIDLAW, MICHAEL WEYMOUTH ■ DESIGNER: CORY FANELLI ■ PHOTOGRAPHERS: LARRY LONG, MICHAEL WEYMOUTH, CHIP FANELLI ■ WRITERS: SCOTT ESLER, MARIO CORNACCHIO ■ TYPOGRAPHER: ACME PRINTING CO. ■ PAPER SELECTION: INSPIRATION, CARDIGAN ■ PAPER MANUFACTURERS: WESTVACO, HOPPER ■ PRINTER: ACME PRINTING CO. ■ NUMBER OF PAGES: 68 ■ TRIM SIZE: 8¼ x 11¾ INCHES ■ TYPE SELECTION: BODONI BOOK, EUROSTILE ■ PRINT RUN: 35,000 ■ BUDGET: $185,000 ■

Annual Report

s

n

a

u

SNUG HARBOR CULTURAL CENTER

1989

Letter from the Chairman

SNUG HARBOR CULTURAL CENTER, INC.,
MADE DRAMATIC STRIDES IN 1989. WE SIGNED OUR LICENSE AGREEMENT
WITH THE CITY OF NEW YORK, MARKING AN ERA OF TREMENDOUS
COOPERATION. THE AGREEMENT REINFORCES A SERIES OF THE VITAL
PARTNERSHIP RELATIONSHIPS BETWEEN
THE CITY OF NEW YORK, REPRESENTED BY THE DEPARTMENT OF
CULTURAL AFFAIRS AND THE DEPARTMENT OF PARKS AND RECREATION.
WE ARE DEEPLY GRATEFUL TO THE ENLIGHTENED CIVIC LEADERS
WHO HAVE RECOGNIZED THE CATALYTIC POTENTIAL
OF SNUG HARBOR AS ESSENTIAL TO ECONOMIC DEVELOPMENT
ON STATEN ISLAND: MAYOR EDWARD I. KOCH, DURING WHOSE
ADMINISTRATION, THE HARBOR HAS PROGRESSED FROM STAGES OF
STRUGGLE AND SURVIVAL TO ONE OF GROWING SUCCESS;
BOROUGH PRESIDENT RALPH J. LAMBERTI WHOSE MANY INITIATIVES
HAVE PROVIDED UNSWERVING SUPPORT AND
RESOURCEFUL LEADERSHIP.

1989 IS A YEAR ALSO THAT HAS SEEN
THE FINALIZING OF THE COMPREHENSIVE SITE PLAN AND THE

SNUG HARBOR CULTURAL CENTER

▲ The Snug Harbor Cultural Center is an eighty-acre historic landmark district situated on Staten Island, within the City of New York. First built in 1831 as a private estate and then converted to a retired sailors home, buildings on the site represent over one hundred fifty years of U.S. architectural history, including such styles as Greek Revival, Beaux Arts, and Italianate. The buildings were literally saved from the wrecking ball ten years ago when the site was purchased by the city to house a cultural foundation and was granted landmark status. The Cultural Center itself is an enormous work in progress—we are less than half-way through our twenty-five-year plan of restoration. This annual report was a mosaic; it had to reflect the wide variety of cultural programs already in progress and at the same time present the monumental task ahead of us in completing our restoration. We compete with such large cultural institutions as Lincoln Center and the Brooklyn Academy of Music for the Manhattan-based corporate contributions. We're not as familiar to these patrons as the more established groups, but I know if we can actually get them here to the site they won't turn us down. With this report, we wanted to bring a piece of Snug Harbor to them. And, of course, the report is also sent to other foundation, to private donors who need a little nudge, and to the community as a P.R. piece. The report was very well received by our primary audience, the corporate community; the rest of our audience was fairly divided, other foundations loved it, but many of our board members did not. The board of directors has never had approval over the annual report before, but they've requested having a say in the future.

■ Snug Harbor Cultural Center ist ein 30 Hektar grosser historischer Bezirk. Er liegt in Staten Island und gehört somit zu New York City. Snug Harbor wurde 1831 als Landgut angelegt und diente später als Altenheim für Seefahrer. Heute befinden sich auf seinem Gelände Beispiele aus 150 Jahren amerikanischer Architektur, von neogriechischen bis hin zu Beaux-Arts-Bauten. Das Zentrum ist im Augenblick noch eine riesige Baustelle, und wir sind mit unserem auf 25 Jahre angesetzten Restaurierungsplan noch nicht einmal auf halber Strecke angelangt. Der Jahresbericht sollte die Idee eines Mosaiks zum Ausdruck bringen und gle- ich-zeitig erklären, was für eine gewaltige Aufgabe die vollständige Restauration ist. Wir sind unter den Spendern aus der Grossindustrie noch nicht sehr bekannt, aber sobald sie einmal auf uns aufmerksam gewor- den sind, werden sie uns sicherlich unterstützen. Mit diesem Bericht wollten wir Snug Harbor bei ihnen ins Gerede bringen. Der Bericht fand viel Anklang bei unserer wichtigsten Zielgruppe, den grossen Unternehmen - sie meinten, sie hätten das Buch als echten Anreiz empfunden, nach Staten Island zu kommen und uns zu besuchen. Diese Gruppe ist visuell sehr anspruchsvoll, und das Design des Berichts ist auf ihren Geschmack zugeschnitten. Die Reaktionen des restlichen Publikums waren eher gemischt: die meisten anderen Stiftungen waren begeistert, aber viele Ausschussmitglieder waren weniger angetan. Die Entscheidung über den Jahres- bericht liegt bislang nicht bei unserem Ausschuss, aber er würde in Zukunft gern ein Wörtchen dabei mitreden.

● Le centre culturel de Snug Harbor est un célèbre quartier historique de d'environ 33 hectares, situé sur l'île de Staten Island, dans la ville de New York. Propriété privée à l'origine en 1831, puis maison de retraite pour marins, le site contenait des vestiges de plus de cent cinquante ans d'histoire architecturale américaine, du «Greek Revival» au style «Beaux-Arts», sans oublier l'architecture italianisante. Le centre lui-même est toujours en travaux, et nous ne sommes qu'à la moitié de notre programme de restauration, qui durera au total vingt-cinq ans. Ce rapport annuel devait donner une idée de mosaïque (idée traditionnelle, mais passionante dans ce cas pré- cis), tout en témoignant du travail monumental que représente un projet tel que la restauration. Nous ne sommes pas très familiers avec les principaux donateurs, mais je sais que si je peux les amener jusqu'ici, ils ne nous lais- seront pas tomber. En fait, avec ce rapport, nous voulions vraiment leur apporter un morceau de Snug Harbor. Le rapport est également envoyé à d'autres fondations et aux donateurs privés qui ont besoin d'un peu de publi- ité. Le rapport a été très bien reçu par notre principal public, les entreprises, qui on déclaré qu'il donnait vrai- ment envie de visiter le site. Il existe également une audience plus sophistiquée, c'est pourquoi nous avons particulièrement travaillé notre approche visuelle dans le rapport. Différentes fondations nous ont dit combien l'avoir énormément apprécié, contrairement à un grand nombre de membres du conseil d'administration. Le conseil n'est pas là pour approuver ou refuser un projet, même si maintenant ses membres aimeraient pouvoir le faire.

[BARBARA KAVANAUGH]

SNUG HARBOR CULTURAL CENTER, INC.: 100 RICHMOND TERRACE

STATEN ISLAND, NEW YORK 10301 USA /18.448.2500

JOHN KLOTNIA DESIGN

. . . .

▲ Barbara gave me a lot of control with this project; the direction was mine, and I'd in fact wanted to go with the poster format even before I knew what the budget constraints were going to be. As it turns out, with the budget being extremely limited, the format worked very well. Snug Harbor can't compete with most of the other, more well-endowed institutions in the city, but this stood out because it was different. The original idea behind the poster was to have all of Snug Harbor unfold before the viewer. The only difficulty in this is that so much of the site is still under restoration, so the poster had to give an idea of the what the center will be. Each of the six panels were created as one page, and the poster conveniently folds to 8 ½ by 11 inches. The report was created completely on a Macintosh. Barbara Kavanaugh was my primary contact. She was enthusiastic and stuck by the concept. I know she is very happy with the report, as are others on the staff. But there are also some that are not so pleased with it. I think that's good too—it gets them thinking about what they really want in their annual report.

. . . .

■ Barbara hat mir bei diesem Projekt ziemlich freie Hand gegeben; das Konzept stammte von mir, und ich entschloss mich für das Posterformat, als die Grenzen des Budgets noch unklar waren. Wie sich herausstellte, war dieses Format für unser extrem knappes Budget genau das Richtige. Snug Harbor kann mit den besser dotierten Institutionen in dieser Stadt nicht konkurrieren, stellt aber eben deswegen etwas Besonderes dar. Das Poster sollte sich ursprünglich als Gesamtansicht von Snug Harbor vor den Augen des Betrachters entfalten. Das ist insofern schwierig, als der Grossteil der Gebäude noch restauriert wird. Das Poster musste also zeigen, wie Snug Harbor einmal aussehen wird. Jedes der sechs Felder stellt eine Seite dar, und das Poster lässt sich auf Schreibbogenformat zusammenfalten. Der Bericht wurde vollständig auf einem Macintosh entworfen. Barbara Kavanaugh war meine wichtigste Kontaktpartnerin. Sie war wirklich enthusiastisch und setzte sich von Anfang bis Ende für das Konzept ein. Ich weiss, dass sie und viele andere Mitglieder von Snug Harbor mit dem Bericht sehr zufrieden sind. Es gibt natürlich auch ein paar, denen er nicht besonders gefällt. Das stört mich allerdings keineswegs - es zwingt sie dazu, sich darüber Gedanken zu machen, wie ihr Jahresbericht aussehen soll.

. . . .

● Pour ce projet, Barbara m'a donné beaucoup de liberté: la direction des opérations me revenait, j'avais déjà choisi le format d'affiche avant même de connaître les contraintes financières auxquelles nous allions devoir faire face. En fait, malgré le budget extrêmement limité, ce format se révéla être parfait. Snug Harbor ne peut lutter avec les autres institutions importantes de la ville, mais ce rapport s'est détaché du lot parce qu'il était différent. L'idée originale derrière cette affiche était de pouvoir offrir une vision d'ensemble de Snug Harbor. La seule difficulté résidait dans le fait que le site est toujours en pleine restauration, et nous avons donné une idée de ce que le centre serait une fois les travaux terminés. Chacun des six panneaux conçus correspondait à une page et l'affiche pliée ne mesurait plus que 21,5 x 28 cm. La réalisation du rapport s'est faite entièrement sur Macintosh. Barbara Kavanaugh, mon premier contact, était enthousiaste et très emballée par le concept. Je sais que le rapport lui a beaucoup plu, ainsi qu'aux autres membres de l'équipe. Mais il y a également ceux qui ne l'ont pas apprécié, et je pense que c'est bien aussi. Cela les pousse à s'interroger sur ce qu'ils veulent vraiment dans un rapport annuel.

[JOHN KLOTNIA]

JOHN KLOTNIA DESIGN: 803 WASHINGTON STREET, NEW YORK, NEW YORK 10014 USA 212.683.2789

CLIENT: SNUG HARBOR CULTURAL CENTER, INC. ■ DESIGN FIRM: JOHN KLOTNIA ■ ART DIRECTOR: JOHN KLOTNIA ■
DESIGNER: JOHN KLOTNIA ■ PHOTOGRAPHERS: U. AMESSE, BILL HIGGINS ■ WRITER: BARBARA KAVANAUGH ■
PRODUCTION MANAGER: JOHN KLOTNIA ■ TYPOGRAPHER: TYPOGRAM ■ PAPER SELECTION: COUGAR WHITE OPAQUE ■
PRINTER: WILLIAMS PRINTING, INC. ■ FORMAT: 33 x 51 INCHES ■ TYPE SELECTION: ENGLISHE, FRUTIGER, BODONI ■

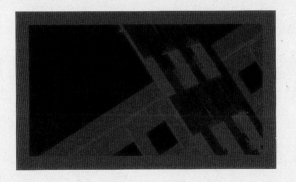

Annual Report 1989

ELECTRO RENT CORPORATION

▲ Our report is developed to report to shareholders and potential shareholders the state of the company at a fixed moment in time. It is also sent to customers, will be reviewed very carefully by our vendors, who are interested in our financial condition and our plans for the coming year. Finally, our report is perused very carefully by our competitors, who will use it to judge their own performance and will try to figure out where we are headed. I wanted this report to communicate that we are in excellent financial condition, that we had weathered a tough business climate very ably. And I wanted to stress our move into new corporate headquarters. To me, the pictures of our new building represent the excitement of change and the sound foundation of our business and our building, which give that change stability. Our designer, Jim Berté, was given a clearly focused but difficult assignment—to work with given photographs. He gave us four excellent alternatives that combined the photography with his strong sense of design. I would have been satisfied with any one of them, but the one we used was the clear winner. We continued sharing ideas and improving until we went to press. It was a very satisfying process.

■ Unser Bericht soll unsere Aktionäre und potentiellen Aktionäre über die Situation unseres Unternehmens zu einem gegebenen Zeitpunkt informieren. Er wird auch an Kunden versandt und ist ein wichtiges Dokument für unsere Händler, die ihn sorgfältig durchlesen, um sich ein Bild von unserer finanziellen Lage und unseren Plänen für das kommende Jahr zu machen. Ausserdem dient er unseren Konkurrenten dazu, ihre Leistung im Vergleich zu uns einzuschätzen und Anhaltspunkte über unseren zukünftigen Kurs zu finden. Ich wollte mit diesem Bericht darlegen, dass wir in ausgezeichneter finanzieller Verfassung sind und uns in einem widrigen geschäftlichen Klima hervorragend behaupten konnten. Ausserdem wollte ich unseren Umzug in ein neues Hauptquartier herausstreichen. Für mich repräsentieren die Bilder von unserem neuen Gebäude die aufregenden Veränderungen in unserem Unternehmen, aber auch das solide Fundament, das unserem Geschäft und unserem Gebäude zugrunde liegt. Unser Designer, Jim Berté, hatte eine klar umrissene, aber schwierige Aufgabe - er musste mit vorgegebenen Photos arbeiten. Er erarbeitete vier exzellente Alternativen, in denen er die Photos in ein aussagekräftiges Design eingliederte. Ich wäre mit jedem einzelnen Vorschlag voll zufrieden gewesen, aber das Design, das wir am Ende nahmen, ragte eindeutig heraus. Zwischen uns herrschte ein ständiger Ideenfluss, und wir fügten bis zum Schluss immer neue Verbesserungen ein. Es war eine äusserst befriedigende Zusammenarbeit.

● Notre rapport est principalement destiné à informer nos actionnaires actuels existants et potentiels de l'état de la société à un moment donné. Il est également envoyé aux clients, et lu très soigneusement par nos vendeurs, qui sont interessés par notre situation financière et nos projets pour l'année future. Enfin, le rapport est examiné très attentivement par nos concurrents qui l'utiliseront pour juger de leur propres performances et tâcheront d'anticiper nos projets. Je voulais que ce rapport montre que notre situation financière est excellente et que nous avons surmonté un climat économique particulièrement difficile. Je désirais également que ce rapport montre notre évolution vers de nouveaux domaines commerciaux. A mon avis, les photos de notre nouvel immeuble représentent l'excitation du changement, ainsi que la solidité de notre entreprise d'où l'idée de stabilité dans le changement. La tâche de notre designer, Jim Berté, était claire mais difficile: il devait travailler avec des photographies déjà existantes. Il nous a offert quatre solutions excellentes, combinant toutes la photographie avec son sens très aigu du design. En fait, toutes ces options me convenaient, mais celle que nous avons finalement retenue était décidément la meilleure. Nous avons ensuite continué à échanger nos idées afin d'améliorer encore la qualité du produit jusqu'au moment de l'impression. Ce fut une opération très satisfaisante.

[DANIEL GREENBERG]

ELECTRO RENT CORPORATION: 6060 SEPULVEDA BOULEVARD, VAN NUYS, CALIFORNIA 91411-2501 USA 818.786.2525

RUNYAN HINSCHE ASSOCIATES

▲ Electro Rent was one of those dream clients—I worked directly with Dan Greenberg, the CEO. Dan did have a requirement that was key in shaping the report: he was personally very involved in the new corporate head-quarters, and he asked us to use exisitng photos of the building, shot at various stages of construction. He wanted the photos to be presented in a graphically strong, straight-forward manner. Presently, most of our clients are cutting back, not in quality, but in quantity—fewer pages, fewer photos, fewer total books printed. But I don't recall any specific numbers or "not to exceeds" being discussed here. Dan essentially asked for a quality project in the same price range as the previous year. Everyone was very pleased with the end result.

■ Electro Rent war einer von den Traumkunden, bei denen man direkt mit dem Vorstandschef zusammenarbeitet. Dan Greenbergs starkes persönliches Engagement für das neue Firmen-Hauptquartier gab die Leitidee für den Bericht ab, und Dan bat uns, bereits existierende Fotos von dem Gebäude zu verwenden, die während verschiedener Bauphasen aufgenommen worden waren. Er wollte, dass die Photos auf graphisch prägnante, direkte Art präsentiert würden. Zur Zeit treten die meisten unserer Kunden kürzer - nicht, was die Qualität anbelangt, aber im Hinblick auf die Quantität - weniger Seiten, weniger Photos, geringere Auflagen. Doch in diesem Fall wurden keinerlei konkrete Zahlen oder Obergrenzen diskutiert. Dan bat mich im Grunde nur, einen Qualitätsbericht zu produzieren und mich dabei am Budget des Vorjahres zu orientieren. Mit dem Endresultat waren alle vollauf zufrieden.

● Electro Rent est un de ces clients de rêve, où l'on peut travailler directement avec le responsable, comme je l'ai fait avec Dan Greenberg, le Président Directeur Général. Dan avait posé une condition essentielle à la con-ception de ce rapport: étant personnellement très impliqué dans les nouveaux bureaux commerciaux, il nous a demandé d'utiliser des photos qu'il possédait de l'immeuble, à différentes étapes de la construction. Il voulait que ces photos créent une forte impression graphique. Habituellement, nos clients tentent d'économiser non pas sur la qualité mais sur la quantité, réduisant les pages, les photos et le nombre d'exemplaires à imprimer. Mais je ne me souviens pas avoir discuté de cela avec Electro Rent. Dan tenait essentiellement à un projet de qualité qui corresponde au même budget que l'année précédente. Finalement, tout le monde était satisfait du résultat.

[JIM BERTÉ]

RUNYAN HINSCHE ASSOCIATES: 4223 GLENCOE AVENUE, SUITE A223

MARIAN DEL REY, CALIFORNIA 90292 USA 213.823.0975

All in all, the past year was a good one for Electro Rent, replete with accomplishment and important progress toward our strategic goals, and these gains were all the more meaningful because the business climate remained less than positive for our industry.

Milestones of the past year included:

▫ A 24 percent improvement in per share earnings
▫ Successful completion of our $44 million stock repurchase program
▫ Occupancy of our new Corporate headquarters
▫ Further enhancement in the quality of our people
▫ Significant expansion of our operating lease equipment management program

All of this was accomplished despite the fact that Electro Rent's dominant business, the rental, sale and lease of electronic test and measurement equipment, has been impacted for the third consecutive year by slowing defense expenditures. This led our customer base to reduce its requirements for the equipment our industry provides. This trend is reflected by our competitors and suppliers, who show a shrinking volume of business and reduced profits in comparable lines of business.

Financial Review
Revenues amounted to $114.5 million, essentially unchanged from $114.9 million a year ago. For the year ended May 31, 1989, income before interest and taxes rose to $20,154,000, up 5.4 percent from $19,130,000 the year before; however, pretax income decreased four percent to $13,226,000 from $13,813,000 in the previous year. Net income declined modestly to $7,936,000 from $8,168,000.

It is a pleasure to report that net earnings per share advanced to $1.74 from $1.40 in the prior year, reflecting the substantially lower number of shares outstanding as a result of the stock repurchase program.

Share Repurchase Program
The year saw the successful completion of our ambitious program to reduce the number of shares outstanding and thereby increase values for our present shareholders. We repurchased 3,634,000 shares over a period of more than two years at an average price of $12.18 a share for a total cost of approximately $44 million. The number of shares outstanding was reduced 46 percent to 4,192,000 from 7,789,000 when the program began.

In addition, the Company was able to purchase at an average price of 85 percent of face value, $843,300 of its outstanding subordinated debentures this year, reducing the total outstanding to $6,948,700. We shall continue our program to buy our debentures at market prices, and replace those funds by the other debt mechanisms that we now have in place.

dollars in millions	85	86	87	88	89
	$89.9	$105.0	$111.3	$114.9	$114.5

Upon completion of coding, we shall take great care to provide our people with the appropriate training and documentation for transition to the new system. The new system is customer and market driven, rather than equipment oriented, and will provide us with a broad, flexible and powerful tool for future expansion.

Extension of TRW Relationship/Addition of Lockheed
Our unique operating lease equipment management program with TRW is the cornerstone of our equipment management activities, an area in which the Company has consistently excelled. During the year we worked closely with TRW to support their efforts and further develop our relationship with them. As a result, the time frame of that relationship again has been lengthened, this time to 1993.

Over the years, Electro Rent has been a pioneer in large scale operating lease programs, developing an impressive set of key concepts that affect equipment management parameters, and helping customers manage their equipment more efficiently and more effectively. Reflecting our long experience and demonstrated expertise, we were successful this summer in adding what we hope will be a significant new customer in this area, Lockheed Missiles & Space Company, Inc., with whom we signed a multi-year leasing agreement that will allow us to work closely with them in the future. While it is not possible to quantify this new activity, we are optimistic about its potential and significance.

New Product Offerings
We have continued to refine our sales and marketing operations, giving special emphasis to expanding our penetration in areas that are rapidly growing such as personal computers, engineering workstations, point-to-point data communications and local area networks.

We have centralized our Data Rentals credit and information retrieval operation in Los Angeles and our data communications division in Florida.

The Company has been very successful this past year renting engineering workstations. The response to our offering of Sun Microsystems' new workstations has been tremendous, and we have been successful in placing these sophisticated units at many of our present aerospace and defense customers, as well as at a number of new customers in the financial services and banking arena.

On the plus side, rental rates and utilization for this highly volatile equipment are substantially better than those for our traditional inventory. On the other side, our ability to dispose of this equipment profitably has yet to be tested.

International Activities
We continue to grow our business in Japan at a very rapid rate and operations have begun to show a slight profit. The market is competitive, but our management group is gaining in stature, experience and capa-

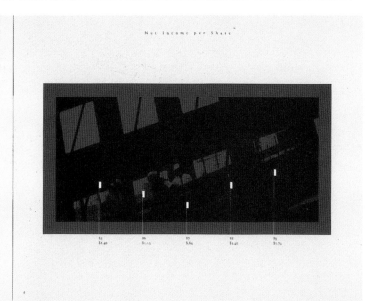

	85	86	87	88	89
	$1.40	$1.15	$.84	$1.40	$1.74

Electro Rent Corporation — Consolidated Statements of Shareholders' Equity — (in thousands)

Three Years ended May 31, 1989

	Number Shares of Common Stock	Common Stock	Additional Paid-in Capital	Retained Earnings
Balance, May 31, 1986	7,772	$ 4,268	$13,722	$52,009
Exercise of stock options	23	50	—	—
Repurchase of common stock	(942)	(520)	(1,659)	(8,797)
Net income for the year ended May 31, 1987	—	—	—	6,029
Balance, May 31, 1987	6,853	3,798	12,063	49,241
Exercise of stock options	24	4	—	—
Repurchase of common stock	(1,736)	(962)	(3,055)	(16,407)
Net income for the year ended May 31, 1988	—	—	—	8,168
Balance, May 31, 1988	5,141	2,840	9,008	41,002
Exercise of stock options	6	23	—	—
Repurchase of common stock	(955)	(528)	(1,674)	(16,650)
Net income for the year ended May 31, 1989	—	—	—	7,936
Balance, May 31, 1989	4,192	$ 2,335	$ 7,334	$38,288

See accompanying notes.

Electro Rent Corporation — Consolidated Statements of Cash Flows — (in thousands)

	Year ended May 31		
	1989	1988	1987
Cash flows from operating activities: Net income	$ 7,936	$ 8,168	$ 6,029
Adjustments to reconcile net income to net cash provided by operating activities:			
Depreciation and amortization	32,718	34,616	33,032
Provision for losses on accounts receivable	678	679	1,005
Gain on sale of equipment	(6,705)	(6,251)	(5,696)
Gain on retirement of subordinated debentures	(126)	—	—
Change in operating assets and liabilities:			
(Increase) decrease in accounts receivable	(116)	3,638	(5,328)
Decrease in inventory	567	565	93
(Increase) decrease in other assets	(1,732)	(1,362)	604
Increase (decrease) in accounts payable	2,268	665	(4,006)
Increase in deferred income taxes	489	3,028	2,386
Increase (decrease) in accrued expenses	(1,865)	1,379	842
Net cash provided by operating activities	32,312	45,125	28,963
Cash flows from investing activities: Proceeds from sale of equipment	26,934	24,401	25,158
Payment for purchase of rental and lease equipment	(35,793)	(65,155)	(39,947)
Payment for purchase of other property	(7,445)	(2,045)	(5,562)
Net cash used in investing activities	(16,304)	(42,799)	(20,351)
Cash flows from financing activities: Increase (decrease) in bank borrowings	(2,785)	18,328	1,984
Payment for retirement of subordinated debentures	(717)	—	—
Proceeds from issuance of common stock	23	4	50
Payment for repurchase of common stock	(12,852)	(20,424)	(10,076)
Net cash used in financing activities	(16,331)	(2,092)	(8,042)
Net increase (decrease) in cash	(323)	234	(330)
Cash at beginning of year	743	509	839
Cash at end of year	$ 420	$ 743	$ 509
Supplemental disclosures of cash flow information:			
Cash paid during the year for:			
Interest (net of amount capitalized)	$ 6,856	$ 5,307	$ 4,666
Income taxes	$ 6,471	$ 4,024	$ 4,130

Supplemental schedule of non-cash investing and financing activities:
The Company acquired equipment and inventory at $5,818, $4,953 and $3,115 at May 31, 1989, 1988 and 1987, respectively, which were paid for during the subsequent year.

See accompanying notes.

CLIENT: ELECTRO RENT CORPORATION ■ DESIGN FIRM: RUNYAN.HINSCHE.ASSOCIATES ■ ART DIRECTOR: JIM BERTÉ ■ DESIGNER: JIM BERTÉ ■ PHOTOGRAPHER: MAXINE GOMBERG ■ PRODUCTION MANAGER: PATTY KARASAWA ■ TYPOGRAPHER: COMPOSITION TYPE ■ PAPER SELECTION: KROMECOAT, KARMA ■ PRINTER: LITHOGRAPHIX ■ NUMBER OF PAGES: 26 PLUS COVER ■ TRIM SIZE: 8½ x 11 INCHES ■ TYPE SELECTION: BEMBO ■

NORCEN ANNUAL REPORT 1990

. . . .

▲ Since we had just been listed on the American Stock Exchange, with this report we were trying to reach American financial analysts and institutional investors. We wanted the report to establish that we are apart from the pack, international in scope, and a cut above the ordinary oil company. For example, in Canada, the company is very well known for its support of living Canadian artsts and has one of the largest corporate art collections in the country. We're always searching for perfection, so we're difficult to please. The design of the graphs was criticized by the financial community because a type style was used that didn't allow the numbers to line up—it was felt that this was an obvious example of design superseding function and readability. We received other complaints that the gray type in the front section was hard to read on the high gloss paper. In addition, the content of the photo essay was criticized because there's a man in every photo and the captions could have been construed as sexist. Our answer to this last comment, which did not come from the financial community, is that this is what life is like on an offshore rig. Personally, I'm happy with the report, and I feel that a strong personal relationship with the designer was key to the success of this report. My senior management and the director felt that too much trust was given, but the oil industry is a conservative lot. It's the team that works together bringing multiple ideas to a project and is willing to take risks that does good, and on that level, the response to this report has been overwhelming.

. . . .

■ Wir waren erst vor kurzem an der amerikanischen Börse notiert worden und versuchten, mit diesem Bericht amerikanische Finanzanalytiker und institutionelle Anleger zu erreichen. Der Bericht sollte den Lesern klarmachen, dass wir uns von der Masse unterscheiden, auf internationaler Basis operieren und eine Klasse besser sind als die gewöhnlichen Ölgesellschaften. Wir sind Perfektionisten und daher schwer zufriedenzustellen. Das Design der Graphiken wurde von der Finanzwelt kritisiert, weil eine Type verwendet worden war, die keine exakte Aufreihung der Zahlen zuliess – es hiess, hier habe das Design ganz offensichtlich den Vorrang gegenüber Funktionalität und Lesbarkeit gehabt. Andere beklagten sich darüber, dass die grauen Lettern im vorderen Teil nur mit Mühe auf dem Hochglanzpapier gelesen werden konnten. Ausserdem wurde der Inhalt des Photoessays kritisiert, weil jedes einzelne Photo einen Mann zeigt, und die Überschriften als sexistisch verstanden werden könnten. Unsere Antwort auf diese letzteren Kommentare, die nicht aus der Finanzwelt kamen, lautet, dass das Leben auf einer Bohrinsel nun einmal so aussieht. Ich persönlich bin vollauf zufrieden mit dem Bericht. In meinen Augen ist er das erfolgreiche Ergebnis einer starken persönlichen Beziehung mit dem Designhaus. Die Geschäftsleitung und der Direktor meinten, ich hätte dem Designer mehr auf die Finger schauen sollen, aber in der Ölindustrie sind die Leute eben sehr konservativ. Ein Team, das die verschiedensten Ideen in ein Projekt einbringt und bereit ist, Risiken in Kauf zu nehmen, ist letztlich der beste Erfolgsgarant, und in dieser Hinsicht war das Echo auf den Bericht überwältigend.

. . . .

● Etant donné que nous venons juste d'être cotés à la Bourse américaine, nous avons tenté d'utiliser ce rapport pour toucher les analystes financiers et les investisseurs institutionnels. Nous voulions démontrer que nous sortons de l'ordinaire, que notre rayon d'action est international et que nous sommes légèrement au-dessus de la moyenne des compagnies pétrolières. Nous recherchons sans cesse la perfection, c'est pourquoi nous sommes très difficiles à satisfaire. Les graphiques ont été vivement critiqués par toute la communauté financière, à cause des caractères utilisés qui ne permettaient pas d'aligner correctement les chiffres. Il nous a semblé que ceci illustrait parfaitement la trop grande importance que prend parfois le design, au détriment de la lisibilité. Nous avons également reçu des critiques à propos des caractères gris sur fond brillant, très difficiles à dechiffrer. De plus, le contenu des photos lui-même a été désapprouvé: en effet, il a été sujet à critiques, puisqu'il y a quasiment un homme dans chaque cliché et les légendes auraient pu être qualifiées de sexistes. Notre réponse à ce dernier reproche, qui ne proprient pas d'ailleurs de la communauté financière, est qu'il y a effectivement très peu de femmes sur une plate-forme off-shore. En ce qui me concerne, je suis très content du rapport et je pense qu'une collaboration très étroite avec le designer a été la clé du succès. L'ensemble de la direction, y compris le PDG, ont le sentiment que nous avons trop fait confiance à l'agence, mais il est vrai que l'industrie pétrolière est plutôt conservatrice. Je pense que ce sont ceux qui travaillent en équipe, apportent des idées multiples et prennent des risques qui ont raison. Et à ce niveau là, les résultats obtenus par ce rapport ont dépassé notre attente.

[KEITH WILSON]

NORCEN: 715 FIFTH AVENUE S.W., CALGARY, ALBERTA T2P 2X7 CANADA 403.231.0111

VAN DYKE COMPANY

· ·

▲ Norcen was an interesting report. It was our first time with them as a client. They had been doing rather "typical" reports in the past, and Keith Wilson wanted to do something different. They had just been listed on the American Stock Exchange, so they were going to a large US audience for the first time. In my opinion, this company has very good managers. Norcen is a smart company that has always managed to do well in a volatile industry. There is a lot of tabular material, and it's very important. We wanted to make that clear and readable. Keith wanted a solid, confident, very businesslike tone in the book. We gave them more white space to create a document look and used color to highlight the maps, showing the geographic scope of the company. The black in the report represents the idea that they're in the oil business. This is a very two sided company: these are good managers who also know how to drill an oil well. The photo essay of life on a rig was used to show what hard work there is on each side of the business. This is a classic, straightforward book, one that is not easily dismissed—I specifically wanted to use the dust jacket to emphasize that. I think this book accomplished what they wanted. But it was also a very different book for management. It's like giving someone a new suit of clothes; at first they're not sure, for some of them it's perhaps too much of a change. But now they're getting good feedback, so the suit fits better.

· ·

■ Der Norcen-Bericht war ein interessantes Projekt. Es war unsere erste Zusammenarbeit mit dem Kunden. Das Unternehmen hatte in der Vergangenheit ziemlich «typische» Berichte produziert, und Keith Wilson wollte etwas Neues probieren. Norcen war gerade an der amerikanischen Börse notiert worden und wendete sich zum ersten Mal an ein grosses Publikum in den USA. Meiner Meinung nach hat das Unternehmen ausgezeichnete Manager. Norcen hat es immer verstanden, sich in einem unbeständigen Industriezweig zu behaupten. Es gibt eine Menge Tabellenmaterial, das ausgesprochen wichtig ist. Wir wollten es klar und übersichtlich präsentieren. Keith wollte einen soliden, selbstsicheren, sehr geschäftsmässigen Grundton für das Buch. Wir haben dem Kunden viel weissen Raum gegeben, um einen dokumentarischen Look zu erreichen. Die Landkarten sind farblich herausgehoben und unterstreichen die geographische Ausdehnung des Unternehmens. Schwarz repräsentiert die Idee, dass der Kunde im Ölgeschäft ist. Norcen hat zwei markante Merkmale – die Manager sind gute Geschäftsleute, die aber auch wissen, wie man nach Öl bohrt. Das Essay über das Leben auf einer Bohrinsel sollte zeigen, dass hinter dem Erfolg des Unternehmens harte Knochenarbeit steckt. Es ist ein klassisches, schnörkelloses Buch, über das man nicht so ohne weiteres hinweggehen kann – der Schutzumschlag verstärkt diesen Eindruck noch. Ich glaube, das Buch ist Norcens Zielvorstellungen gerecht geworden. Das Management musste sich natürlich erst einmal an das neue Design gewöhnen. Es ist das gleiche, wie wenn man jemanden in einen neuen Anzug steckt; zunächst ist er sich nicht ganz sicher oder fühlt sich sogar unwohl. Aber inzwischen bekommen sie ein gutes Echo, und der Anzug passt schon besser.

· ·

● Le rapport Norcen était très intéressant; c'était la première fois que nous travaillions avec eux, en tant que client. Jusqu'à présent, leurs rapports étaient assez traditionnels; or Keith Wilson désirait quelque chose de différent. La société venait juste de faire son apparition en Bourse, c'était donc la première fois qu'elle s'adressait à un large public. Selon moi, cette compagnie a une excellente direction. Norcen est une entreprise intelligente, qui s'est toujours bien comportée dans une industrie instable. Ils ont beaucoup de matériaux tabulaires, c'est très important et nous voulions que cela soit clair et lisible. Keith voulait que le rapport donne une image sérieuse, solide et compétente de la compagnie: cela nous a conduit à laisser davantage d'espace blanc pour donner l'image d'un rapport et à utiliser la couleur pour mettre les cartes en valeur, montrant ainsi la répartition géographique de la compagnie. Le noir représente l'idée qu'ils sont dans l'industrie pétrolière. Norcen est une compagnie à deux visages; les directeurs extrêmement compétents savent également comment forer du pétrole. Les photos illustrant la vie sur une plate-forme pétrolière ont été utilisées pour montrer que le travail est aussi dur des deux côtés de la barrière. Ce rapport est plutôt classique, du genre que l'on ne rejette pas facilement. Je voulais d'ailleurs qu'on utilise une jaquette afin de le souligner. C'était également un ouvrage nouveau pour la direction. C'est un peu comme de donner à quelqu'un un nouveau costume: au début on n'est pas très sûr du résultat, et pour certains, c'est peut-être même un changement trop radical. Mais une fois qu'on obtient des compliments, on se sent tout de suite mieux.

[JOHN VAN DYKE]

VAN DYKE COMPANY: 611 POST AVENUE #15, SEATTLE, WASHINGTON 98104 USA 206.421.5888

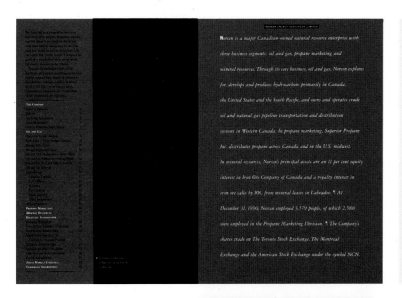
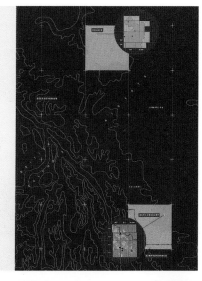

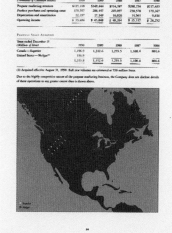

CLIENT: NORCEN ENERGY RESOURCES ■ DESIGN FIRM: VAN DYKE COMPANY ■ ART DIRECTOR: JOHN VAN DYKE ■ DESIGNER: JOHN VAN DYKE ■ PHOTOGRAPHER: JEFF CORWIN ■ WRITER: KEITH WILSON ■ TYPOGRAPHER: TYPEHOUSE ■ PAPER SELECTION: REFLECTIONS ■ PAPER MANUFACTURER: CONSOLIDATED ■ PRINTER: MACDONALD PRINTING ■ NUMBER OF PAGES: 70 ■ TRIM SIZE: 8¼ x 11¾ INCHES ■ TYPE SELECTION: GALLIARD ■ PRINT RUN: 4,500 ■

1
9
8
9

MASSACHUSETTS HIGHER EDUCATION ASSISTANCE

▲ Any annual report has to fulfill certain practical functions for its company, but it also casts the company in a certain light. We're very happy with all the aspects achieved by this year's report. We wanted a report that would describe the process of getting a student loan. Our primary audience is lenders, schools, and students, with the financial community and state and local governments filling only a secondary role. We wanted them to understand what's involved, and we wanted to make the lending process seem as "user friendly" as possible. We particularly wanted the report to explain the technological advances that have improved our operations, using a "before" and "after" format. We're unique in that our President actually writes our report. He sits in on all of the meetings with the designer. We like to have a continuing relationship with a design firm. Because our procedures are so complicated, we like to save ourselves the time of reeducation each year. And Clifford is very familiar with us by now. This saves us time and money because he knows what we like and what we don't like.

■ Jeder Jahresbericht muss gewisse praktische Funktionen erfüllen, aber er präsentiert gleichzeitig ein bestimmtes Bild des Unternehmens. Wir sind mit dem diesjährigen Bericht in jeder Hinsicht mehr als zufrieden. Wir wollten einen Bericht, der beschreibt, wie man ein Studentendarlehen bekommt. Unser Hauptpublikum setzt sich aus Darlehensgebern, Schulen und Studenten zusammen, und der Bericht wendet sich erst in zweiter Linie an die Finanzwelt und die staatlichen und örtlichen Behörden. Wir wollten die notwendigen Schritte für einen Darlehensantrag aufzeigen, um das System so «benutzerfreundlich» wie möglich zu machen. Es kam uns vor allem darauf an, die technischen Fortschritte zu erklären, die wir inzwischen gemacht haben, und wir verwendeten eine «Vorher-Nachher»-Form, um die Verbesserungen zu erläutern, die auf diese Weise zustande gekommen sind. Wir weichen insofern von der Norm ab, als unser Präsident den Bericht persönlich verfasst. Er nimmt an sämtlichen Besprechungen mit dem Designer teil. Wir arbeiten lieber kontinuierlich mit einer Design-Firma zusammen, als unsere komplizierten Verfahren jedes Jahr neu zu erklären. Clifford ist mittlerweile gut mit unserem Unternehmen vertraut. Das erspart uns eine Menge Zeit und Geld, denn Clifford weiss, was uns gefällt und was uns nicht gefällt.

● Quel qu'il soit, un rapport de gestion doit remplir certaines fonctions pour l'entreprise et la mettre en valeur. Nous sommes très heureux de la façon dont ce dernier rapport annuel a été conçu. Nous désirions qu'il décrive le processus d'obtention de prêts pour les étudiants. Nos principaux auditeurs sont les organismes de crédit, les écoles et les étudiants eux-mêmes, tandis que la communauté financière, l'état et les municipalités forment un public secondaire. Nous voulions qu'ils comprennent ce qui est en jeu, et ainsi, rendre toute la procédure aussi simple que possible. Notre objectif principal dans ce rapport était d'inclure et d'expliquer les progrès technologiques actuels, en mettant tout particulièrement l'accent sur la situation générale avant notre arrivée, et les améliorations apportées. Nous sommes uniques en ce sens que notre président rédige lui-même notre rapport, participant à toutes les réunions avec le designer. Nous aimons être en rapport constant avec le studio de design (car nos procédures sont assez compliquées), ce qui nous permet d'économiser le temps passé chaque année à se remettre dans le bain. Et comme Clifford nous connaît bien maintenant, nous évitons une perte de temps, puisqu'il sait exactement ce que nous voulons et ce que nous ne voulons pas.

[JOE CLAYTON]

MASSACHUSETTS HIGHER EDUCATION ASSISTANCE CORPORATION:
330 STUART STREET, BOSTON, MASSACHUSETTS 02116 USA 617.426.9434

CLIFFORD STOLTZE DESIGN

▲ This is the fourth annual report we've done for this client, and it was our first opportunity to do something really different for them. They had come up with the theme for the copy, and it was a subject that would be very hard to do photographically. This enabled us to go with illustration, whereas in the past we'd had to rely on stock or file photography. The budget still did not leave any room for hiring a big-name illustrator, but we liked Tim Carroll's line-art style, which also worked well with the budget. In fact, the design was built largely around the budget and by using the line art, we were actually able to cut some costs. That's important, because there are a lot of student loan organizations in the same building as our client and they all compare annual report costs in the elevators. The client liked the cartoon aspect of it, but by adding the shapes, we were able to get more design-oriented. We were able to control the colors we used and, all in all, it made the budget go a long way. This client trusts us, and they feel this is the one area they can be creative. They're very happy with the report, and we thought it might get into some shows. It's an odd one—you're either going to like it or you're not.

■ Dies ist unser vierter Jahresbericht für diesen Kunden, und es war unsere erste Gelegenheit, das Projekt von einer völlig neuen Seite anzupacken. Der Kunde lieferte das Thema für den Text, der sich nur sehr schwer photographisch darstellen liess. Das gab uns Gelegenheit, mit Illustrationen zu arbeiten, während wir früher auf Archivmaterial zurückgreifen mussten. Das Budget liess zwar nicht genug Spielraum, um einen der bekannteren Illustratoren zu beauftragen, aber wir mochten Tim Carrolls Strichzeichnungen, die auch ansonsten gut in unser Budget passten. Das Design wurde letztlich dem Budget angepasst, und indem wir Strichzeichnungen verwendeten, konnten wir sogar einige Kosten kürzen. Das ist wichtig, denn das Gebäude, in dem unser Kunde sein Büro hat, beherbergt eine Menge anderer Darlehensorganisationen, und sie vergleichen die Kosten für ihre Jahresberichte gerne während der Fahrt im Aufzug. Der Kunde mochte den Cartoonstil, aber indem wir solide Formen hinzufügten, konnten wir eine mehr designorientierte Wirkung erzielen. Wir hatten freie Hand bei der farblichen Gestaltung und kamen alles in allem gut mit dem Budget aus. Der Kunde vertraut uns; für ihn ist dies das eine Gebiet, auf dem er seine Kreativität ausleben kann. Wir hoffen, dass wir den Bericht auf einigen Ausstellungen zeigen können. Er ist ziemlich ungewöhnlich - entweder man mag ihn oder man mag ihn nicht. Der Kunde ist jedenfalls sehr zufrieden.

● C'est le quatrième rapport que nous faisons pour ce client: cela aura été pour nous l'occasion de créer quelque chose de vraiment différent pour eux. Ils avaient trouvé le thème, qui promettait d'être très difficile à illustrer au moyen de la photographie. Ceci nous donna une certaine liberté dans l'illustration, alors qu'auparavant, nous devions nous débrouiller avec ce qu'ils avaient en stock. Le budget restreint ne nous a laissé aucune liberté pour engager un illustrateur connu, néanmoins nous avons aimé le style de Tim Carrol qui, de plus, s'est très bien accomodé du budget. En fait, nous avons conçu le design en fonction du budget et en jouant sur la partie artistique, nous avons pu réduire les coûts. Ceci est important, car il y a de nombreuses organismes de prêts pour les étudiants dans le même immeuble que notre client, et bien entendu, ils comparent tous les rapports annuels lorsqu'ils se rencontrent dans les ascenseurs. Le client a aimé le côté bande dessinée de celui-ci, mais en y ajoutant d'autres formes, nous avons eu la possibilité de nous orienter davantage vers le design. Nous avons également eu toute latitude de choisir les couleurs que nous désirions utiliser et, tout compte fait, cela a permis de rendre le budget plus élastique. Cette société nous fait confiance; ils savent que ce rapport est la seule occasion pour eux d'être créatifs. Ils en sont d'ailleurs tout à fait satisfaits, et nous pensons même que le rapport pourra participer à des expositions. Il est assez singulier: il plaît, ou il ne plaît pas.

[CLIFFORD STOLZE]

CLIFFORD STOLTZE DESIGN: 49 MELCHER STREET, BOSTON, MASSACHUSETTS 02210 USA 617.350.7109

MHEAC provides services to lenders, schools, several levels of government, and to individual students and parents. The future offers many options for enhanced productivity.

- The more rapid exchange of student information to the federal government and to regional and national credit bureaus on the status of students seeking a loan or in default but who may be in repayment.
- The use of electronic transfer of information from sources such as the College Scholarship Service to ease the application burdens on families and financial aid officers.
- Assistance to the state scholarship office of the Board of Regents of Higher Education, which previously used MHEAC to process scholarship applications and to mail out the decisions on a timely basis.
- Collaboration with other states in New England and elsewhere in improving the flow of student loan information.

As the 1990's begin MHEAC staff explores frontiers of technologies including electronic imaging, fibre-optics, and new ways to store, exchange and retrieve data inexpensively and quickly. As Peter Drucker advises, the time to prepare for the twenty-first century has already begun.

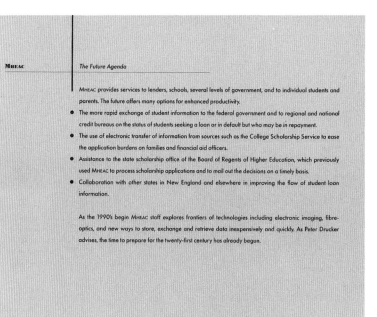

Loan Volume by Institution Type (Stafford)	
Independent Four-Year Institutions	54.8 %
Public Four-Year Institutions	12.0
Proprietary Schools	21.0
Technical and Nursing Schools	3.7
Graduate and Professional Schools	4.5
Two-Year Institutions	3.8
All Other	.2

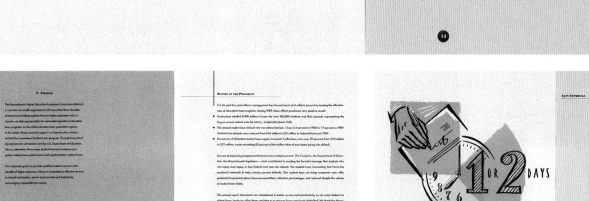

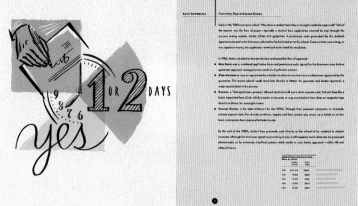

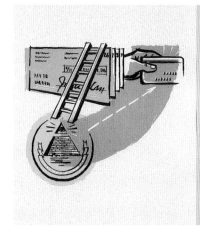

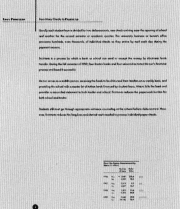

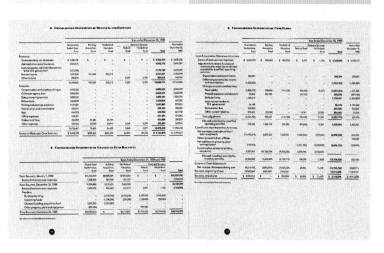

CLIENT: MASSACHUSETTS HIGHER EDUCATION ASSISTANCE CORP. ■ DESIGN FIRM: CLIFFORD STOLTZE DESIGN ■ ART DIRECTOR: CLIFFORD STOLTZE ■ DESIGNERS: CLIFFORD STOLTZE, KYONG CHOE ■ ILLUSTRATOR: TIM CARROLL ■ TYPOGRAPHER: LITHOCOMP ■ PAPER SELECTION: CONFETTI ■ PRINTER: MERCHANTS PRESS ■ NUMBER OF PAGES: 24 PLUS COVER ■ TYPE SELECTION: FUTURA POSTER, BODONI ■ PRINT RUN: 2,500 ■

M c D O N N E L L

D O U G L A S

F I N A N C E

C O R P O R A T I O N

A N N U A L   R E P O R T

1 9 8 9

McDONNELL DOUGLAS FINANCE CORPORATION

....

▲ We're not required to file an annual report. We use the document as a public relations and marketing piece and this year, in particular, our report was directed to our employees as well. The book also has the traditional audience of our customers, along with banks, lenders, and shareholders. Because of very rapid growth, the company has undergone a number of organizational changes over the previous year. We're a small company, but we have over 1,000 employees in far-flung divisions. We needed a document that would give them information on the reorganization and soothe their concerns—and we needed to clearly present the new structure of responsibilities. An annual report is never an easy project; the last-minute changes can be frustrating. Overall, this report went smoothly. The use of sumarized financials made the whole process a lot easier.

....

■ Wir sind gesetzlich nicht dazu verpflichtet, einen Jahresbericht herauszugeben. Wir benutzen unseren Bericht als Public-Relations- und Marketing-Dokument, das sich - besonders in diesem Jahr - auch an unsere Angestellten richtet. Das traditionelle Publikum des Buches sind unsere Kunden sowie Banken, Investoren und Aktionäre. Wegen unseres schnellen Wachstums gab es im letzten Jahr eine Reihe von organisatorischen Veränderungen. Wir sind ein kleines Unternehmen, haben aber über tausend Angestellte in weit verstreut liegenden Fachgruppen. Wir brauchten ein Dokument, das ihre Sorgen über die Reorganisation beschwichtigen und gleichzeitig über die Veränderungen informieren würde. Wir wollten die neue Verantwortlichkeitsstruktur so klar wie möglich aufzeigen. Ein Jahresbericht ist kein einfaches Projekt; die Änderungen in letzter Minute können ziemlich frustrierend sein. Dieser Bericht ging insgesamt glatt über die Bühne. Der Prozess wurde auch dadurch vereinfacht, dass wir einen rein summarischen Finanzbericht verwendeten.

....

● Nous ne sommes pas tenus de produire un rapport annuel de gestion. Nous utilisons ce document en tant qu'élément de relations publiques ou de marketing, et cette année, il était tout particulièrement destiné à nos employés. Cette publication a également la qualité d'intéresser nos clients, ainsi que les banques, les actionnaires et les organismes de crédit. A cause d'une croissance rapide, notre compagnie a connu un grand nombre de changements au niveau de l'organisation au cours de l'année passée. Nous sommes une petite société, mais nous avons plus de 1.000 employés répartis dans différents secteurs. Nous avions donc besoin de quelque chose qui rassure leurs inquiétudes au sujet de la restructuration, tout en donnant des informations sur les divers changements. Nous avions également besoin de présenter la nouvelle répartition des responsabilités d'une manière claire et précise. Un rapport annuel n'est jamais un projet simple; les changements de dernière minute peuvent être très frustrants. En fin de compte, nous pouvons tout de même dire que celui-ci s'est très bien déroulé, surtout grâce à l'utilisation des tableaux financiers récapitulatifs qui ont grandement facilité notre tâche.

[FRANK LABARBA]

MCDONNELL DOUGLAS FINANCE CORPORATION: 340 GOLDEN SHORE

LONG BEACH, CALIFORNIA 90802-4296 USA 213.491.3000

RUNYON HINSCHE ASSOCIATES

. . . .

▲ This was a difficult report to handle; the directive itself was a difficult one to execute. The direction, in terms of concept, came directly from the senior management of the company, but there was internal dissension, not only with regard to the concept but also in relation to the decision to scale down the report from previous years. This decision was not financially based; the finance company is doing very well despite the problems of its parent. We did not create this report on the computer, but Frank LaBarba ran full-size type pages off his Macintosh to show to management. Perhaps there's something about looking at those pages in live type that helps things along, because we had minimal changes in copy. That always makes a report easier.

. . . .

■ Dieser Bericht stellte uns vor einige Probleme; es war allein schon schwierig, den Richtlinien des Unternehmens zu folgen. Das Konzept kam direkt von der Unternehmensspitze, aber es gab einige interne Unstimmigkeiten, die nicht nur das Konzept selbst betrafen, sondern auch damit zu tun hatten, dass der Bericht gegenüber den Vorjahren um einige Nummern kleiner ausfallen sollte. Diese Entscheidung hatte keine finanziellen Gründe — die Finanzierungsgesellschaft war trotz der Probleme ihres Mutterunternehmens ausserordentlich erfolgreich. Wir haben den Bericht nicht auf dem Computer entworfen, aber Frank LaBarba hat Musterseiten auf seinem Mac kreiert, um sie der Geschäftsleitung zu zeigen. Es ist wahrscheinlich hilfreich, diese Seiten fertig gedruckt vor sich zu sehen, denn wir hatten kaum Änderungen im Text. Das macht die Arbeit an einem Jahresbericht natürlich immer einfacher.

. . . .

● Ce rapport financier nous a donné beaucoup de mal; les directives elles-mêmes étaient difficiles à exécuter. Les instructions en termes de concept venaient directement de la direction générale de l'entreprise; il y avait des dissensions internes concernant non seulement le concept lui-même, mais aussi à cause de la décision de réduire le volume du rapport en comparaison de l'année précédente. Ce n'était pas uniquement pour des raisons financières, car cette société est financièrement très saine en dépit des problèmes de la maison mère. Nous n'avons pas conçu ce rapport sur ordinateur, mais Frank LaBarba montra à la direction quelques exemples de pages réalisées sur son Mac. Peut-être que de voir la mise en pages grandeur nature a facilité les choses, car ensuite, nous n'avons pas eu de changements importants à faire. Ce qui rend toujours la création d'un rapport annuel, plus aisée.

[GARY HINSCHE]

RUNYAN HINSCHE ASSOCIATES: 4223 GLENCOE AVENUE, SUITE A223

MARINA DEL REY, CALIFORNIA 90902 USA 213.823.0975

Commercial Equipment Leasing 1989 volume $305 million　McDonnell Douglas Finance Corporation's Commercial Equipment Leasing operation specializes in leasing and financing transportation equipment and productive assets. The General Equipment Leasing Group provided financing of $212 million in 1989. This operation also includes medical equipment and franchisee equipment financing. In 1989, these two businesses generated volumes of $48 million and $43 million, respectively.

At year-end 1989, this group had approximately $1 billion in receivables and continues to be a leader in business aircraft and truck and trailer leasing, and is aggressively pursuing growth in other lines. The people of our Commercial Equipment Leasing operation are known in their markets for rapid turnaround of customer inquiries, for competitive rates on most kinds of equipment, and for special expertise in transportation equipment.

Market Securities Investments 1989 portfolio $120 million　Market Securities Investments, which manages the MDFC portfolio of high-yield corporate bonds, increased the Company's holdings of these securities by $64 million in 1989, to a total of $120 million, or 3.8 percent of the Company's total portfolio. Investment operations weathered some turbulence in high-yield debt markets, but we continue to select and trade securities carefully and have experienced no losses through default. Investment returns through year-end were excellent.

McDonnell Douglas Bank Limited 1989 volume £71.6 million　McDonnell Douglas Bank Limited grew to £129 million in assets in 1989, and to a record volume of £71.6 million. During 1989, the Bank produced a record amount of vendor financing business, including £15 million written through its relationship with McDonnell Douglas Information Systems Limited. During the year, MD Bank also began offering leasing denominated in U.S. dollars and Swiss francs for customers who have revenues in those currencies.

In the year's second half, MD Bank started what is known as "back-to-back" financing, involving the portfolios of smaller finance and leasing companies. With its knowledge of leasing and installment credit, the Bank now arranges fixed-rate loans to these companies, aligning amortization of its financing with repayments of the underwritten companies' own receivables. Volume for the first partial year in this business totaled £6 million, and is expected to be substantially greater in 1990. Also last year, McDonnell Douglas Bank financed three executive jet airplanes and two helicopters, and made further strides in the expansion of real estate financing.

Daniel O. Anderson,
Senior Vice President.
Leads the Company's
largest operating
group, Commercial
Equipment Leasing.
Has served the
McDonnell Douglas
organization since
1967.

CLIENT: MCDONNELL DOUGLAS FINANCE CORPORATION ■ DESIGN FIRM: RUNYAN.HINSCHE.ASSOCIATES ■ ART DIRECTORS: ROBERT MILES RUNYAN, MICHAEL MESCALL ■ DESIGNER: MICHAEL MESCALL ■ PHOTOGRAPHER: CYNTHIA MOORE ■ WRITER: FRANK LABARBA ■ PRODUCTION MANAGER: PATTY KARASAWA ■ TYPOGRAPHER: COMPOSITION TYPE ■ PAPER SELECTION: REFLECTIONS, CENTURA DULL ■ PAPER MANUFACTURER: CONSOLIDATED PAPER ■ PRINTER: LITHOGRAPHIX ■ NUMBER OF PAGES: 20 PLUS COVER ■ TRIM SIZE: 7¾ x 11 INCHES ■ TYPE SELECTION: ALDUS ■

REMEMBER THE LITTLE GUY WITH THE CAP AND HIS MOTORCYCLE LOOKING VEHICLE DELIVERING A LETTER, THE GUY ON THE "SPECIAL DELIVERY" STAMP SEVERAL LIVES AGO? THE SAME guy, a bit larger and in full motion, came by my home every Sunday afternoon. My mom would receive a letter from her sister who lived in Indiana. My mom and her sis' were extremely close and wrote long letters to each other. It was a Sunday ritual, along with roast beef, lemon icebox pie, Drew Pearson, and The Colgate Comedy Hour.

Predictably there was always a newspaper clipping in the letter: an award, a business venture going great, or going bust. A wedding, another birth, and sometimes a clipping that brought sad news, but strengthened the ties between two sisters who dearly loved each other and were separated by fourteen years and hundreds of miles. The letters, clippings and the occasional snapshot were a glue that kept their bond for many years.

The keeping of articles represents a need to hold, keep and carefully maintain our memories in the attic of our soul. Those clippings, snipped, saved, yellowed reminders, are so vital in sustaining our everyday sense of being and seeing. Tomorrow will bring another event that will be cherished, and neatly pressed for posterity. And celebrated forever.

SPECIAL DAY AT THE HAWKINS HOME

MEMBERS OF THREE GENERATIONS OF THE HAWKINS FAMILY were present on Monday to welcome home the newest member, Daniel Allen Hawkins, born December 27th. Proud parents are Mr. and Mrs. Nelson Hawkins. Mrs. Hawkins is the former Miss Betty McCrary of Dothan, Alabama. Pictured above are (left to right) grandfather Charles Hawkins, great grandfather Allen L. Hawkins (holding Daniel Allen) and happy new father Nelson Hawkins.

CRACKER BARREL OLD COUNTRY STORE

....

▲ This report is primarily directed to the company's stockholders, many of whom became investors because they were customers. They've eaten in the restaurants, liked them, watched the stock, seen that it does well, and purchased it. They also come back to the restaurants often. And of course we're trying to reach institutional investors, who have also watched the stock and seen it do well. We were trying to achieve three things with this report. First, we wanted to show that this is a successful company. This is demonstrated by the numbers. We also wanted to show that the restaurants are high-quality. We demonstrate this every year with a well-done annual report. Finally, we want to show that Cracker Barrel Old Country Stores are unique in the restaurant industry. They are trying to maintain a uniquely American experience, and the same feeling that is created in other restaurants runs throughout the annual reports. Every year we present the designer with the challenge of maintaining the quality of tradition while pushing the design to new limits. Tom and his associates always meet this challenge. This is Cracker Barrel's ninth report with his firm. People look forward to receiving this report each year, and the earliest books have, in fact, become collectors items among customers and stockholders.

....

■ Der Bericht wendet sich in erster Linie an die Aktionäre des Unternehmens, die zum grossen Teil Kunden sind, die später zu Anlegern wurden. Sie haben in unseren Restaurants gegessen, waren positiv beeindruckt, haben unsere Aktien beobachtet, erkannten ihr Potential und haben sie gekauft. Sie zählen ausserdem zu den regelmässigen Gästen der Restaurants. Und natürlich versuchen wir, institutionelle Anleger anzusprechen, die ebenfalls den Erfolg unserer Aktien beobachtet haben. Wir haben versucht, mit diesem Bericht drei Dinge zu erreichen: Zunächst einmal wollten wir demonstrieren, dass wir ein erfolgreiches Unternehmen sind. Die Zahlen sprechen hier für sich. Wir wollten ausserdem zeigen, dass die Restaurants qualitativ erstklassig sind. Dies kommt jedes Jahr in der ausgezeichneten Qualität des Berichts zum Ausdruck. Zuletzt wollten wir darlegen, dass Cracker Barrel Old Country Store in der Restaurantindustrie einzigartig ist. Unsere Restaurants versuchen, ein charakteristisches amerikanisches Flair zu bewahren, und eben dieses Flair zieht sich durch die Gestaltung unserer Jahresberichte. Wir stellen den Designer Jahr für Jahr vor die Aufgabe, die traditionelle Grundatmosphäre beizubehalten und gleichzeitig in seinem Design neue Wege einzuschlagen. Tom und seine Partner werden dieser Aufgabe stets gerecht, und wir haben mittlerweile neun Berichte mit seiner Firma produziert. Die Leute freuen sich jedes Jahr auf den Bericht, und die ersten paar Ausgaben sind inzwischen bei unseren Aktionären und Kunden zu Sammlerstücken geworden.

....

● Ce rapport est principalement destiné aux actionnaires de la compagnie, dont un grand nombre sont devenus investisseurs après avoir été clients. Ils ont mangé dans nos restaurants et les ont aimés, ils ont examiné nos actions et voyant que tout marchait bien, ils ont acheté. Souvent d'ailleurs, il arrive qu'ils retournent dans ces restaurants. Bien sûr, nous essayons d'atteindre les investisseurs institutionnels qui ont également remarqué que nos actions allaient bien. Nous avons essayé d'accomplir trois choses dans ce rapport. Tout d'abord, nous désirions montrer que cette entreprise est en plein essor. Les chiffres sont là pour le prouver. Nous voulions également faire savoir que ces restaurants sont des établissements haut de gamme. Nous démontrons cela chaque année au moyen d'un bon rapport annuel. Et troisièmement, nous voulions souligner que Cracker Barrel Old Country Store est quelque chose d'unique dans l'industrie de la restauration. Nous nous efforçons de maintenir une tradition américaine unique en son genre, et ce même sentiment d'unicité, partagé par tous les autres restaurants, se retrouve tout au long des rapports annuels. Chaque année, nous mettons le designer au défi de conserver la qualité de la tradition tout en repoussant sans cesse les limites de la création. Tom et ses associés ont toujours relevé le gant avec succès, et ceci est le neuvième rapport de Cracker Barrel avec eux. Chaque année, les gens sont impatients de recevoir le nouveau rapport; les tout premiers sont en fait déjà devenus des pièces de collection pour les clients et les actionnaires.

[MATT HAMILTON]

CRACKER BARREL OLD COUNTRY STORE: P.O. BOX 787, HARTMANN DRIVE

LEBANON, TENNESSEE 37088-0787 USA 615.444.5533

THOMAS RYAN DESIGN

▲ This was the ninth Cracker Barrel annual report done by the firm (we're now starting on the tenth), and I started on the account three years ago. I come from a small town in Maine, so it's very easy for me to relate to the qualitites that this company and its report represent. We work with a long list of ideas and review it to cull the strongest concepts. When Tom and I feel we have the best concept on the list roughed out, we have lunch with Corporate Communications and get their approval. After that, we show them comps of the cover and a few sample spreads. Once these have been approved, they see final page layouts, and even then they make very few changes. It's a pretty special relationship; they're a great client, and they place a lot of trust in us. But of course, we're not presenting a radical change in concept from year to year, either. The company is based on the consistency of high quality food and the experience people have of eating in the restaurants and, because they're so successful, we're able to stress these qualities in the report. People have the impression that this is an open-ended budget, but it's not—we have some very strict confines to work within. We often have to rely on family and friends for the props and photographs contained in the reports. That makes it more fun, but it also serves the real purpose of saving a lot of money. Still, Cracker Barrel is a rare client, and it really is a privilege to work on their annual report.

■ Dies war der neunte Cracker-Barrel-Jahresbericht, den die Firma entworfen hat (wir beginnen gerade mit dem zehnten). Ich selber bin seit drei Jahren dabei. Ich komme aus einer kleinen Stadt in Maine, und daher fällt es mir leicht, eine Menge persönliche Bezugspunkte zu den Qualitäten zu finden, die dieses Unternehmen und sein Bericht repräsentieren. Wenn ich mit meiner Ideenliste fertig bin, setze ich mich normalerweise mit Tom zusammen, und wir gehen die einzelnen Vorschläge durch und diskutieren, welche Konzepte stärker und welche schwächer sind. Nachdem wir uns auf das beste Konzept geeinigt haben, treffen wir uns mit Cracker Barrels PR-Leuten zum Lunch und präsentieren es ihnen. Danach zeigen wir ihnen Umschlagmuster und Muster-Layouts für ein paar Doppelseiten, und wenn diese ihnen gefallen, entwerfen wir die endgültigen Seiten-Layouts, an denen es meistens nur wenige Änderungen gibt. Wir haben ein ausgesprochen gutes Verhältnis zu diesem Kunden; er hat volles Vertrauen zu uns, und die Zusammenarbeit klappt wunderbar. Wir präsentieren natürlich auch nicht jedes Jahr ein radikal neues Konzept. Cracker Barrel ist so erfolgreich, dass es kaum nötig ist, in dem Jahresbericht extra darauf hinzuweisen; daher können wir uns darauf konzentrieren, die Atmosphäre und die Qualität der Restaurants zu unterstreichen. Wegen unseres Erfolges glauben die Leute, wir hätten ein unbegrenztes Budget, was nicht der Fall ist - wir arbeiten mit ziemlich wenig Spielraum. Wir sind oft darauf angewiesen, die Requisiten und Photos für den Bericht von Freunden zu borgen. Das macht das Ganze im Grunde noch interessanter.

● Ce rapport annuel pour Cracker Barrel est le neuvième que nous ayons produit (nous sommes en train de travailler sur le dixième), et il y a seulement trois ans que j'ai commencé à m'occuper personnellement de ce client. Comme je viens d'une petite ville du Maine, il m'était relativement facile d'appréhender ce que cette entreprise et ce rapport représentent. Ensuite, Tom et moi nous avons discuté de ces idées afin de déterminer quelles étaient les plus faibles ou les plus intéressantes. Cependant, en ce qui concerne le dernier rapport, j'avais senti que je tenais vraiment quelque chose de très bon, et nous nous sommes lancés. Une fois que Tom et moi avons une idée assez précise du concept, nous déjeunons avec les responsables du service Corporate Communications afin d'obtenir leur approbation. Ensuite, nous leur montrons les premièrs projets de la couverture ainsi que quelques exemples des doubles pages. Après cette première étape, ils examinent la mise en pages finale et, en général, ils n'ont que très peu de changements à suggérer. C'est une collaboration assez spéciale. Cracker Barrel est une entreprise formidable et ils nous font complètement confiance. Le succès est tel qu'il n'est même pas nécessaire d'en parler dans le rapport annuel, ce qui nous permet de nous concentrer sur la qualité et l'ambiance de ces restaurants. A cause de notre succès, les gens ont l'impression que notre budget est illimité, ce qui est faux, car les marges qui nous sont allouées sont très étroites. Il arrive très souvent que nous soyons obligés de faire appel à la famille ou aux amis pour obtenir les accessoires et les photos destinés au rapport. Ce qui peut être très agréable et permet également d'économiser beaucoup d'argent.

[CATHY WAYLAND]

THOMAS RYAN DESIGN: 400 EIGHTH AVENUE SOUTH, NASHVILLE, TENNESSEE 37203 USA 615.254.5374

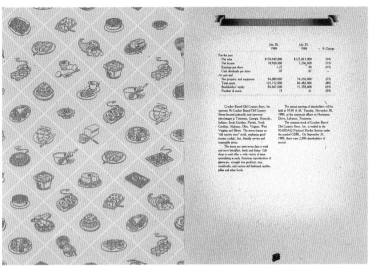

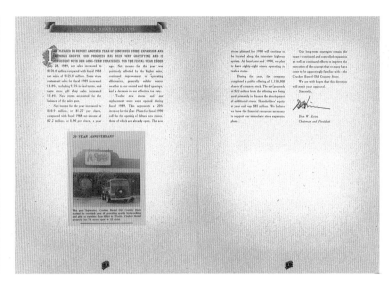

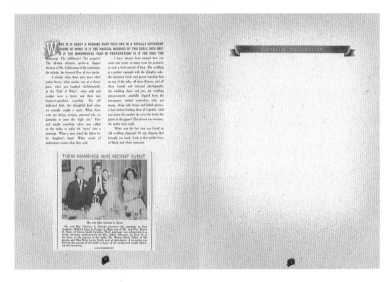

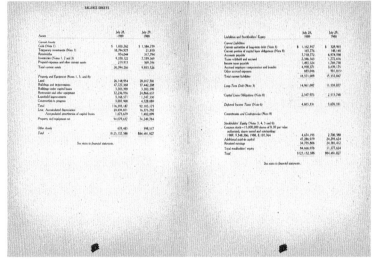

CLIENT: CRACKER BARREL OLD COUNTRY STORE ■ DESIGN FIRM: THOMAS RYAN DESIGN ■ ART DIRECTOR: THOMAS RYAN ■ DESIGNER: CATHY WAYLAND ■ PHOTOGRAPHER: MCGUIRE ■ ILLUSTRATOR: CATHY WAYLAND ■ WRITER: JOHN BAEDER ■ PRODUCTION MANAGER: MATT HAMILTON, CORPORATE COMMUNICATIONS, INC. ■ TYPOGRAPHER: ALAN WALKER AND ASSOCIATES ■ PAPER SELECTION: SPECKLETONE MADERO BEACH, CREAM ■ PRINTER: JONES PRINTING ■ NUMBER OF PAGES: 32 PLUS COVER ■ TYPE SELECTION: CHELTENHAM OLDSTYLE, MEMPHIS CONDENSED ■

MIND BODY SPIRIT YMCA

YMCA CHICAGO

. . . .

▲ In general, the audience for our report is people who can help us accomplish our mission of improving people's lives. This generally means foundations, civic and political leaders, members of the Y, and our employees. We want to reach people who can assist us in doing our work, be it financially or by volunteering their
time and leadership qualities. So this is an image and education piece as much as it is a financial report; it
tells people what we stand for. In the past, we have focused on specific programs, but this year we wanted to
report on the achievements of a five-year plan. The designers pointed out that this could be handled in the the
letters by the president and chairperson. They wanted the visuals to be more reflective of the Y's philosophy,
represented in the idea of a triangle of the body, mind, and spirit. The report is therefore also reflective of
our philosophy of caring for the whole individual, and in this sense is more symbolic than specific. We really
feel this report captured the philosophy and mission of the Y and the spirit behind our organization while giving a lot of information. A lot of this success is due to our relationship with the Samatas. We completely trust
each other, and we appreciate them as problem solvers and advisors. After all, design is what we hire them
for, and we operate on a principle of mutual respect. And from their point of view, there are not a lot of layers
for approval. Given the same organization, they come up with a different report every year—that always surprises me.

. . . .

■ Die Zielgruppe für unseren Bericht besteht grob gesagt aus Leuten, die uns dabei helfen können, das Leben von
Menschen zu verbessern. Der Bericht wendet sich also hauptsächlich an Stiftungen, Politiker, engagierte
Mitmenschen, Mitglieder des YMCA und unsere Angestellten. Wir wollen Leute erreichen, die uns bei unserer Arbeit
finanziell oder durch ihren persönlichen Einsatz unterstützen können. Insofern ist unser Jahresbericht nicht nur
eine Bilanzaufstellung, sondern gleichzeitig eine Werbe- und Imagebroschüre; er erklärt den Leuten, worin unsere
Arbeit und Ziele bestehen. Früher haben wir uns hauptsächlich auf spezielle Programme konzentriert, aber dieses
Jahr wollten wir über die Ergebnisse unseres Fünf-Jahres-Plans berichten. Die Designer meinten, dass wir diese
Mitteilungen am besten im Brief des Präsidenten und des Vorsitzenden unterbringen könnten. Die Illustrationen
sollten dagegen die Philosophie des YMCA widerspiegeln, die in dem symbolischen Dreieck aus Körper, Geist und
Seele zum Ausdruck kommt. Der Bericht legt daher auch unsere Philosophie der Fürsorge für den ganzen Menschen
dar und ist in diesem Sinne eher symbolisch als spezifisch. Wir sind mit diesem Jahresbericht sehr zufrieden: Er
bringt die Philosophie und die Zielsetzung des YMCA erfolgreich auf einen Nenner und vermittelt gleichzeitig eine
Menge Information. Dieser Erfolg beruht zu einem grossen Teil auf unserem Verhältnis zu den Samatas. Es ist ein
Verhältnis völligen gegenseitigen Vertrauens, und wir können uns auf ihre Ratschläge und Problemlösungen stets
verlassen. Design ist nun einmal ihre Domäne, und wir arbeiten auf der Grundlage gegenseitigen Respekts.

. . . .

● La catégorie de population généralement concernée par notre rapport annuel est représentée par tous ceux qui peuvent
nous aider à accomplir notre mission: tenter d'améliorer la vie des gens. Sont donc concernées les foundations, les
responsables municipaux et politiques, les membres du YMCA ainsi que nos employés. Nous désirons sensibiliser ceux qui
peuvent nous aider à faire notre travail, que ce soit par une aide financière, ou en nous donnant un peu de leur temps et de
leur talent. C'est pourquoi ceci est non seulement un rapport financier, mais également le moyen d'éduquer les gens, de
leur transmettre une certaine image de nous-même, et d'informer le public sur notre travail. Alors que quelques années
auparavant nous nous étions concentrés sur des programmes spécifiques, cette année nous désirons montrer les résultats
d'un plan qui a duré cinq ans. Nos concepteurs nous ont fait remarquer que nous pouvions très bien réaliser cela à travers
la rédaction des lettres écrites par le président et le vice-président. Ils désiraient que la partie visuelle soit plus
représentative de la philosophie du YMCA, traduite par un triangle dont les trois côtés correspondent au corps, à l'esprit
et à l'âme. Le rapport reflète ainsi notre philosophie, notre intérêt pour l'individu dans sa totalité, et dans ce sens, il est
donc plus symbolique que vraiment spécifique. Nous avons le sentiment que ce rapport a parfaitement apprehendé la
philosophie et la mission du YMCA, ainsi que l'esprit de notre organisation, tout en laissant une large part à
l'information. Cela est dû en grande partie à la relation que nous entretenons avec les Samatas. Nous avons une totale
confiance en eux, et nous apprécions leur talent de conseillers tout autant que leurs facultés à résoudre les problèmes.

[PATRICE BOYER]

YMCA OF METROPOLITAN CHICAGO: 755 WEST NORTH AVENUE, CHICAGO, ILLINOIS 60610 USA 312.280.3400

▲ This is our eighth year with the YMCA of Chicago, and they're a good client. Of course it's a trade-off; they really can't pay a lot of money for the report, but we're given lots of creative freedom. And it's a good working relationship, too, with a lot of collaboration; we meet each year for a lunch during which we brainstorm, trying out ideas for the theme. This year it was based on the mind, body, and spirit and how the Y contributes to the health of each. There's a good give and take with this client, and we really like doing the report each year.
· ·

■ Wir arbeiten seit nunmehr acht Jahren für den YMCA Chicago, und unser Verhältnis war immer ausgezeichnet. Eine Hand wäscht hier die andere: Der YMCA kann nicht besonders viel für den Bericht bezahlen, aber dafür gibt er uns eine Menge kreative Freiheit. Ausserdem herrscht ein gutes Arbeitsverhältnis zwischen uns; wir treffen uns jedes Jahr zum Lunch und diskutieren alle möglichen Themenvorschläge. Dieses Jahr drehte sich der Bericht um Körper, Geist und Seele und darum, wie der YMCA sich für die Gesundheit des ganzen Menschen einsetzt. Hinter unserer Zusammenarbeit steht eine Philosophie des Gebens und Nehmens, und wir freuen uns jedes Jahr auf dieses Projekt.
· ·

● Ceci est notre huitième année avec le YMCA de Chicago, un très bon client. Etant donné qu'ils ne peuvent pas investir beaucoup d'argent dans le project, nous avons conclu une sorte de marché: en échange, ils nous laissent beaucoup de liberté dans le domaine de la créativité. Nous entretenons également une bonne relation professionnelle dûe à une étroite collaboration. Nous nous rencontrons chaque année au cours d'un déjeuner pendant lequel nous nous torturons les méninges, tâchant de trouver des idées pour le nouveau thème. Cette année le rapport était basé sur le corps, l'esprit et l'âme, et sur la façon dont le YMCA contribue à la santé de chacun. Nous avons d'excellentes relations avec ce client, et c'est un plaisir de travailler chaque année sur ce rapport.

[PAT SAMATA]
SAMATA & ASSOCIATES: 101 SOUTH FIRST STREET, DUNDEE, ILLINOIS USA 60118 708.428.8600

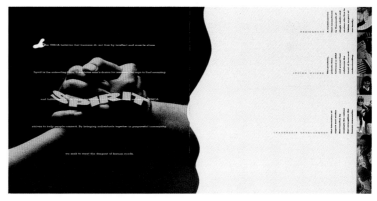

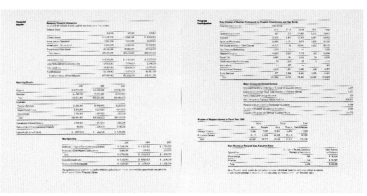

CLIENT: YMCA OF GREATER CHICAGO ■ DESIGN FIRM: SAMATA ASSOCIATES ■ ART DIRECTORS: PAT SAMATA, GREG SAMATA ■ DESIGNERS: PAT SAMATA, GREG SAMATA ■ PHOTOGRAPHERS: MARK JOSEPH, BOB LIEBERMAN, BOB TOLCHIN ■ WRITER: PATRICE BOYER ■ PRODUCTION MANAGER: KRISTEN ROST ■ TYPOGRAPHER: PAUL THOMPSON ■ PAPER SELECTION: MASTERART ■ PRINTER: ROHNER PRINTING ■ NUMBER OF PAGES: 20 WITH SELF-COVER ■ TRIM SIZE: 9¾ x 9¾ INCHES ■ TYPE SELECTION: FUTURA EXTRA BOLD EXTENDED, MEMPHIS EXTENDED ■ PRINT RUN: 5,000 ■

The Reece Corporation

1989 Annual Report

THE REECE CORPORATION

▲ Our annual report is primarily directed toward our stockholders, many of whom are longstanding. The report is also used for communication with our employees, customers, vendors, and some analysts. We make machines that are used in the manufacturing of clothing, and over the last few years we've been trying to stress our service to jeans manufacturers and the children's apparel industry. We also want our report to show that we are international in scope. We've had a generally good response to this book, although there's been some negative reaction to the photography. In general, I don't think this has hurt us—different things appeal to different people.

■ Unser Jahresbericht wendet sich hauptsächlich an unsere Aktionäre, die zu einem grossen Teil schon seit vielen Jahren mit dabei sind. Der Bericht dient ausserdem als Informationsdokument für unsere Angestellten, Kunden, Lieferanten und Finanzanalytiker. Wir produzieren Maschinen, die in der Textilherstellung einge-setzt werden, und während der letzten paar haben wir versucht, unsere Rolle in der Fertigung von Jeans und Kinderkleidung zu betonen. Wir wollen mit unserem Bericht auch zeigen, dass wir international tätig sind. Das Buch hat im grossen und ganzen ein gutes Echo gefunden, obwohl es einige negative Reaktionen auf die Photos gab. Ich glaube nicht, dass uns das geschadet hat – die Geschmäcke sind eben verschieden.

● Notre rapport annuel est principalement destiné à nos actionnaires, qui le sont pour la plupart depuis longtemps. Le rapport sert également de moyen de communication avec nos employés, nos clients, nos vendeurs et quelques analystes financiers. Nous fabriquons des machines utilisées dans la confection de vêtements, et durant les toutes dernières années, nous avons tâché de vendre nos produits aux fabricants de jeans, ainsi qu'à toute l'industrie de confection pour enfants. Nous voulions également que ce rapport montre le cadre international de nos activités. Dans l'ensemble, nous avons eu un bon résultat, bien qu'il y ait eu quelques réactions négatives concernant la photographie. Je ne pense pas que ceci nous ait beaucoup touché–tout le monde n'a pas les mêmes goûts.

[DONALD BLOM]

THE REECE CORPORATION: 800 SOUTH STREET, WALTHAM, MASSACHUSETTS 02254-9168 USA 617.894.9220

▲ We've been doing the Reece Corporation's annual report for approximately eleven years. In the past, they had shown photographs of their facilities and machinery in the report, but we've slowly been able to convince them to show more of the end-product—the fashion and clothing that their machines are used to make. This is the farthest we've gone with this concept so far, and I think it's the best report we've done for them. The company had not had a bad year, but they hadn't done as well as expected. They were looking for a downscaled report that would give the appearance they were saving money. And they were certainly saving money—almost $30,000 was cut from the previous year's budget, and the book went from four-color to black-and-white. Four pages of glossy stock were bound in for the photography, and the book was double-saddle bound to use a cheaper paper stock for the text pages. We also used the typewriter-like typeface to reflect the downscaled budget. The client was not happy with this report, most particularly because of the photography. We had indicated we wanted to give the book a sense of motion—a raw look. We took black-and-white photographs and copied them over and over on the photocopier to give them a sense of what we wanted to achieve. However, in the course of the shooting, I found I really like the effect of the Polapan film the photographer was using for tests, so we went with that instead of the standard black-and-white film. The result was similar to what we had shown them, but admittedly it was much more raw than they had expected.

■ Wir produzieren den Jahresbericht für die Reece Corporation seit ungefähr elf Jahren. Früher zeigte der Bericht hauptsächlich Maschinen und Werksanlagen, aber wir konnten den Kunden inzwischen davon überzeugen, das Endprodukt mehr in den Vordergrund zu stellen – die Kleider und Moden, die auf seinen Maschinen hergestellt werden. Dieses Konzept kommt in dem diesjährigen Bericht wesentlich stärker zum Ausdruck als in den vorangegangenen Jahren, und ich glaube, es ist der bislang beste Bericht, den wir für Reece gemacht haben. Das Unternehmen hatte kein schlechtes Jahr hinter sich, war aber hinter den Erwartungen zurückgeblieben. Der Kunde wollte einen etwas schlichteren Bericht, der den Eindruck vermitteln sollte, dass er mit seinem Geld sparsam umging – was in der Tat der Fall war: das Budget wurde gegenüber dem Vorjahr um $30.000 gekürzt, und das Buch wurde von Farbe auf Schwarzweiss umgestellt. Hochglanzpapier wurde nur für die vier Photoseiten eingesetzt, und die Sattelheftung sorgte dafür, dass wir billigeres Papier für die Textseiten verwenden konnten. Wir benutzten ausserdem eine schreibmaschinenähnliche Type, um das gekürzte Budget zum Ausdruck zu bringen. Der Kunde war nicht sehr glücklich mit dem Bericht, besonders wegen der Photographie. Wir hatten angedeutet, dass wir dem Buch ein Gefühl der Bewegung geben wollten – einen dynamischen, rohen Look. Wir nahmen Schwarzweissphotos und kopierten sie immer wieder auf der Kopiermaschine, um dem Kunden zu zeigen, was wir im Auge hatten. Das Ergebnis war nicht weit von dem entfernt, was wir dem Kunden gezeigt hatten, aber es war eingestandenermassen viel roher, als er erwartet hatte.

● Cela fait maintenant à peu près onze ans que nous nous occupons de la conception du rapport annuel de Reece Corporation. Auparavant, ils montraient des photographies de leurs machines et de leur équipement. Petit à petit, nous avons réussi à les convaincre de montrer davantage le produit fini, les modèles et vêtements que leurs machines pouvaient produire. C'est, je pense, le meilleur rapport que nous ayons fourni jusqu'à maintenant. L'entreprise n'avait pas eu une mauvaise année, mais pas non plus aussi bonne qu'elle s'y attendait. Ils voulaient un rapport d'apparence plus modeste afin d'avoir l'air d'économiser de l'argent. Et c'est en fait exactement ce qui s'est produit puisque le budget de l'année précédente a été réduit de 30.000 dollars et que, de la quadrichromie, le rapport est passé au noir et blanc. Quatre pages de papier brillant furent consacrées à la photographie et l'ouvrage en entier fut broché afin qu'il soit possible d'utiliser un papier bon marché pour le texte. Nous avons également employé des caractères de type machine à écrire pour refléter la modestie du rapport. Le client était mécontent du résultat, essentiellement à cause de la photographie. Nous avions précisé que nous voulions donner à la brochure une idée de mouvement, une image crue. Nous avons donc pris des photos en noir et blanc; puis, nous les avons photocopiées à outrance, pour donner une idée de ce que nous recherchions. Il n'y avait pas de différence sensible, mais je dois admettre que le résultat était tout de même un peu plus cru que prévu.

[TOM LAIDLAW]

WEYMOUTH DESIGN, INC.: 332 CONGRESS STREET, BOSTON, MASSACHUSETTS 02210 USA 617.542.2467

For 109 years Reece has been a leading manufacturer, distributor and lessor of specialized machinery, related products and services to the worldwide clothing industry. Reece is known to apparel makers around the world for its automation of the manufacture of dress and leisure clothing for men, women and children.

Reece machines produce buttonholes, feed and sew buttons and other types of sewn fasteners, cut and stitch pockets, button shirts, bag-finished garments, perform short stitching operations and blindstitch and serge many different garment parts. Reece also sells Japanese-made equipment in several key markets, which perform many operations in the garment assembly process. Various other products including shirt folding, specialized stitching, spreading and pressing equipment are distributed in local markets by certain of the Company's non-U.S. operations. In North America and selected Western European markets, the Company provides consulting services in "Just-in-Time" sewn products manufacturing under license from a Japanese company.

Reece has facilities in key locations to serve the needs of a changing international marketplace. Manufacturing facilities are located in Fall River, Massachusetts U.S.A., Gorham, Maine U.S.A., and Leiden, The Netherlands. Sales and service of products in the United States are directed by offices in Stantonsburg, North Carolina; Los Angeles, California; Dallas, Texas, and Bordentown, New Jersey and by a distribution center in Stantonsburg, North Carolina.

The Corporation also has a distribution center in Leiden, The Netherlands; sales and service operations in Canada, France, Hong Kong, India, West Germany, and the United Kingdom. An office in Miami, Florida U.S.A. directs Latin American marketing activities. Foreign manufacturing centers in other areas of the world are covered by more than 50 independent distributors and dealers who both market and service products.

Financial Highlights

Dollars in thousands except per share amounts	1989	1988	1987
Total revenues	957,192	959,570	936,978
Operating income	1,743	4,702	5,800
Settlement of plant closure dispute	1,200	—	—
Income (loss) before taxes	(923)	3,028	2,405
Net income (loss)	(1,698)	2,018	1,625
Net income (loss) per common share	(0.67)	0.79	0.64
Dividends declared per common share	0.20	0.20	—

To Our Stockholders:

Nineteen eighty-nine, most notably the final six months, was disappointing financially for The Reece Corporation. Continuing weak demand in the important North American market, combined with the effect of the stronger U.S. dollar on overseas results, depressed full-year revenues and earnings. Accordingly, our long string of consecutive year-to-year quarterly improvements in earnings was interrupted, and operating results for the year were sharply below 1988 levels.

Reece is committed to staying ahead of its competition in apparel-making technology. During 1989, we made several additions to the Series 104 eyelet-end buttonhole product line. These machines produce keyhole-style buttonholes, eyelets, and perform edge-finishing on jeans, tailored clothing and outerwear.

Revenues declined nearly four percent from the record levels of 1988. Operating results were squeezed by the stronger U.S. dollar, greater indirect- versus direct-market sales, more aggressive pricing in the face of competition, reduced rental and finance income and overall lower volumes.

Another major factor impacting our results was the settlement of a long-standing plant closure dispute. The settlement, related legal fees and other expenses, resulted in a one-time charge to earnings of $1.2 million. Our final net result was further reduced by the necessity for a consolidated tax provision, despite a pretax loss. This provision resulted from the recording of taxes on the Company's profitable foreign operations, which could not be offset by a tax credit from our domestic unit's operating losses.

For an in-depth review and discussion of our financial performance and the effect of these various factors, we direct you to the section of this report entitled "Management's Discussion and Analysis of Financial Condition and Results of Operations," beginning on page 13.

Contributing to the 1989 revenue decline was a fall-off in unit orders. Overall, unit orders for new and reconditioned Reece-brand machines were six percent below the year-earlier levels. North and Latin American markets showed unit order declines year-to-year, our European demand remained level, and the Far East showed a sharp improvement from 1988.

Not only are we developing new machines, but through the TSS system, we are arraying the more efficiently to achieve broad gains for manufacturers. With TSS, Reece's customers have been able to boost their productivity, reduce costs and inventories, and improve customer service. These improvements are necessary to meet the increasingly stringent demands of today's retailers.

A number of factors led to the slowdown that severely constrained apparel production and investment in the U.S. during 1989. The stronger dollar made imports, which had been slowing, again more attractive to retail buyers. Moreover, the consolidations and financial malaise in much of the retail industry itself brought caution to inventory investment, hurting apparel manufacturing. Finally, the overall slowing growth of the American economy and more cautious consumer spending

affected a broad segment of the clothing industry, particularly in tailored apparel production where many of our machines are marketed.

These developments combined to reduce the number of U.S. apparel makers and to restrain investment by other firms with available capacity. At the same time, our competitors from outside the U.S. which has faced pricing difficulties in the period of the weak U.S. dollar, now gained advantage at a time when customer incentives were most necessary.

Management and Cost Controls

While we consolidated our U.S. marketing and distribution operations earlier in the 1980s, the new marketplace realities have made additional cutbacks necessary. During the year, we shifted selected distribution activities from our North Carolina facility to our Maine manufacturing plant, thereby reducing costs. We also trimmed our sales, technical, and marketing support staffs in areas not critical to customer service.

We also responded to changes in market conditions. We have realigned sales territories to match the industry's restructuring, re-evaluated our direct presence in areas where the market has retrenched, developed new incentive programs and expanded training across product lines to achieve a more efficient service corps. These adjustments eventually should contribute to improving earnings in our traditional base business.

Implementing steps like these does not immediately produce financial improvements and can even increase expense levels for a period of time—an event that occurred in the latter quarters of 1989 and is continuing to a lesser extent in the early months of 1990. However, these steps should produce measurable savings over the balance of 1990.

While we were taking actions to increase efficiency and reduce costs, we also took positive steps to take advantage of opportunities in the North American and other mature markets, including France and the United Kingdom. We expanded our product base through added distribution activities and the introduction of new products.

Exclusive marketing of Toyota industrial lockstitch

machines in the Western Hemisphere began to yield results, particularly in Latin America. The Toyota reputation for quality and value is reflected in many initial placements of the premium line and is now leading to repeat orders, building a base of business for future growth. We also are marketing the line in the U.K. and France, where monthly sales are growing.

We are particularly pleased with the inroads made in marketing the Toyota Sewn Products Management System (TSS) in North America, and more recently in the U.K. and France. Installations on a broad variety of apparel applications have been completed or are underway—shortening lead times, reducing inventories, cutting defects and raising productivity. These improvements are creating major financial advantages for our apparel clients—all necessary to the competitiveness of the U.S., British and French producers.

One typical TSS user has seen a 22 percent increase in productivity, a 75 percent reduction in defects, virtual elimination of inventories and sharply improved morale. TSS has led to what one client manager calls "instant production". This is a key advantage to our customers in an age when they must quickly respond to retailers seeking to limit their inventory investment.

In addition to apparel-making machinery, Reece manufactures bagging systems which speed handling, sealing, storing, and situation of garments. We market work-handling devices that feed garments to buttonhole and button-sewing machines to speed the production of shirts and other clothing.

We have recently increased our North American and European TSS equipment and management service staffs to support this growing operation. Several major apparel producers have signed on and broad interest is developing with others. Our partner in TSS, Aisin Seiki of Japan, part of the Toyota group and the developer of the Just-in-Time total production system, is similarly dedicating more resources to work

with us on the growing business. Collectively, we look to TSS as a major means of shoring up otherwise declining market potential in the direct markets of North America and Western Europe.

In addition, we have added to our own lines with the introduction of new or enhanced Reece equipment.
- In the pocket welting area, we began shipping units to produce vest and breast pockets, a coat model of the same product, and will soon offer a machine which sews single pockets;
- A number of new eyelet-end buttonhole models were added in our Series 104 line to broaden applications with more advanced versions exhibited in prototype form;
- The Mitchell line of buttonfeeders was upgraded to ease installation and adjustment, expanding sales opportunities; and
- Maintain and strengthen inroads to our distribution centers and market welting models to improve their performance and competitiveness.

In 1989, we made important improvements in the Mitchell line to ease installation and use of these devices which automatically feed buttons, snaps and curtain rings to sewing machines. The Mitchell line accelerates the button-sewing process.

International Growth

Our new products, first marketed in the United States, are now being introduced internationally. While direct markets in France, Germany and the United Kingdom have faced, as our domestic markets have, growing imports of clothing, the international sector remained a bright spot for Reece in 1989.

Our Western European operations saw continued strong export business, offsetting domestic declines. Areas of Southern Europe, select Eastern European markets, and other regions turned in strong performances. In all our subsidiaries we shifted resources increasingly from domestic to export areas to take advantage of the opportunities.

CLIENT: THE REECE CORPORATION ■ DESIGN FIRM: WEYMOUTH DESIGN, INC. ■ ART DIRECTOR: TOM LAIDLAW ■ DESIGNER: SHERI LOPILATO ■ PHOTOGRAPHER: JOHN HUET ■ WRITER: LEONARD J. EGAN ■ TYPOGRAPHER: DANIELS PRINTING COMPANY ■ PAPER SELECTION: CIRCA SELECT, NEENAH CLASSIC LAID, INSPIRATION ■ PAPER MANUFACTURER: CONSOLIDATED, NEENAH, FOX WITHER ■ PRINTER: ACME PRINTING COMPANY ■ NUMBER OF PAGES: 36 PLUS COVER ■ TRIM SIZE: 8¼ x 11¾ INCHES ■ TYPE SELECTION: ORATOR ■ PRINT RUN: 6,000 ■ BUDGET: $65,000 ■

COHERENT

. . . .

▲ Our annual report is geared primarily toward our shareholders and the potential investor, secondarily toward our customers and our employees, many of whom are shareholders. Coherent manufactures lasers for science, medicine, and industry. We wanted to share, and hopefully infect our shareholders with, the excitement we take from our involvement with such an innovative technology, and we feel that the report text and design clearly encourages pride of ownership in Coherent. We have had a professional relationship with Steve Tolleson for three years now. He understands our markets and can relate to our needs. This relationship is helped along by the fact that we only interact with Steve Tolleson; we always have direct communication with the person in charge.

. . . .

■ Unser Jahresbericht zielt hauptsächlich auf unsere Aktionäre und potentielle Anleger und wendet sich in zweiter Linie an unsere Kunden und Angestellten, von denen viele Aktien besitzen. Coherent produziert Lasergeräte für wissenschaftliche, medizinische und industrielle Anwendungen. Wir wollten unseren Aktionären auf möglichst ansteckende Art mitteilen, wie aufregend es für uns ist, an der Entwicklung einer derartig neuen Technologie mitzuarbeiten, und nach unserem Empfinden ist es dem Text und Design des Berichts gelungen, die Teilhaberschaft an Coherent als etwas darzustellen, auf das man stolz sein kann. Wir sind seit mittlerweile drei Jahren mit Steve Tolleson geschäftlich verbunden. Er kennt unsere Märkte und kann auf unsere Bedürfnisse eingehen. Es kommt kaum zu Missverständnissen zwischen uns, was wohl auch daran liegt, dass Steve Tolleson unser einziger Ansprechpartner ist; sämtliche Design-Entscheidungen werden allein mit ihm besprochen, nicht mit seinen Angestellten.

. . . .

● Notre rapport annuel est principalement destiné à nos actionnaires et aux investisseurs potentiels, ainsi qu'à nos clients et employés, dont la plupart sont également actionnaires. Coherent fabrique des lasers pour la science, la médecine et l'industrie. Nous désirions faire partager à nos actionnaires l'enthousiasme que nous avons à utiliser une technologie aussi innovatrice; et nous avons le sentiment que le texte et le design du rapport confortent le sentiment de fierté des possesseurs d'actions de Coherent. Voilà maintenant trois ans que nous travaillons en collaboration avec Steve Tolleson. Il comprend notre marché et connait bien nos besoins. Le fait que nous traitions personnellement et exclusivement avec lui consolide encore cette relation.

[EDWINA DEROUSSE]

COHERENT: 3210 PORTER DRIVE, P. O. BOX 10321, PALO ALTO, CALIFORNIA 94393 USA 415.493.2111

TOLLESON DESIGN

▲ I have an ongoing relationship with this client, and after the initial meeting with Coherent on this report, at which I got a sense of their desires, I had no problem selling my concept. Coherent sells a complex technology to diverse markets through distinct divisions. They need a design that speaks both to the financial community and to customers. They also wanted to stress in this report that they had improved operations and product development through a decentralization of authority throughout engineering, marketing and manufacturing. To simplify presentation and make the multiple levels of communication accessible, we gave the report a layered structure. Beginning with the shareholders' letter, narrow pages of the main body of copy frame the right-hand margin of a full-size page, which showcase laser applications from each division. Conceptual photos and graphical icons, together with an opening statement, begin each section. The budget has for this report has remained relatively steady over the past three years. Here we cut costs through inexpensive paper. The financials are on bond paper, and the paper in the front of the book is not #1 grade—it's a seventy pound paper that reminds me of a photo annual from the late 50s. We did rely on the computer for typography with this design, although I have reservations about working this way, and we won't do financials in-house. The client saves money, perhaps, but I find it an inefficient process in many ways, and it's hard if you are especially appreciative of fine typography.

■ Ich arbeite schon seit einigen Jahren für diesen Kunden, und nach der ersten Besprechung hatte ich eine Vorstellung davon, was Coherent von dem Bericht erwartete. Danach hatte ich kein Problem, mein Konzept zu verkaufen. Coherent bietet über verschiedene Fachgruppen komplexe Technologien auf unterschiedlichen Märkten an. Die Firma braucht ein Design, das sowohl die Finanzwelt als auch die Kunden anspricht. Ausserdem wollte sie in diesem Bericht betonen, dass sie ihre Betriebseffizienz und Produktentwicklung durch eine Dezentralisierung der Konstruktions-, Marketing- und Produktionsleitung verbessern konnte. Um die Präsentation zu vereinfachen und um die verschiedenen Informationsebenen anschaulich zu machen, haben wir den Bericht graphisch gestaffelt. Beginnend mit dem Brief an die Aktionäre sind schmale Seiten mit dem Haupttext zwischen die vollformatigen Seiten gesetzt, auf denen Laser-Geräte aus den einzelnen Fachgruppen präsentiert werden. Konzeptionelle Photos, graphische Symbole und ein einleitender Text eröffnen jeden Abschnitt. Das Budget für diesen Bericht ist während der letzten drei Jahre mehr oder weniger gleich geblieben. Dieses Jahr haben wir zur Kosteneinsparung billigeres Papier verwendet. Die Bilanzen sind auf Schreibmaschinenpapier gedruckt, und das Papier im vorderen Teil ist eher billiges 80gm2-Papier, das mich an Photojahrbücher aus den späten 50er Jahren erinnert.

● J'ai une relation très positive avec ce client; et après une réunion préliminaire avec Coherent au sujet de ce rapport, durant laquelle j'ai pu me faire une idée bien précise de ce qu'ils désiraient, je n'ai eu aucun problème à vendre mon concept. Coherent vend une technologie assez complexe à des marchés différents, au travers de secteurs bien distincts. Ils ont besoin d'un design qui s'adresse à la fois à la communauté financière et aux clients. Dans ce rapport, ils désiraient également mettre l'accent sur le fait qu'ils ont amélioré la gestion et le développement du produit grâce à une décentralisation des départements ingénierie, marketing et fabrication. Afin de simplifier la présentation et de rendre les multiples niveaux de communication accessibles, nous avons donné à ce rapport une structure «en strates». Le rapport débute avec la lettre aux actionnaires, ensuite vient le texte principal aligné en une colonne, sur la droite de chaque page, et qui montre les applications laser de chacun des secteurs. Chaque section est illustrée par des photos conceptuelles et des images graphiques. Le budget de ce rapport est resté relativement le même ces dernières années, car nous réduisons les coûts en utilisant un papier bon marché. Nous employons du papier ordinaire pour les pages financières, et un 80 g pour les premières pages, qui me rappelle un peu les revues annuelles des années cinquante. Nous nous sommes servis d'un ordinateur pour la typographie, bien que j'aie eu quelques réserves quant à ce mode de travail, mais nous avons fait appel à l'extérieur pour la partie financière.

[STEVEN TOLLESON]

TOLLESON DESIGN: 444 SPEAR STREET #204, SAN FRANCISCO, CALIFORNIA 94105 USA 415.626.7796

CLIENT: COHERENT ▪ DESIGN FIRM: TOLLESON DESIGN ▪ ART DIRECTOR: STEVEN TOLLESON ▪ DESIGNERS: STEVEN TOLLESON, DONNA ANDERSON ▪ PHOTOGRAPHER: HENRIK KAM ▪ WRITER: LINDSAY BEAMAN ▪ TYPOGRAPHER: SPARTAN TYPOGRAPHERS ▪ PAPER SELECTION: L.O.E. NAKOSSA BOND ▪ PRINTER: ANDERSON LITHOGRAPH ▪ NUMBER OF PAGES: 54 ▪ TRIM SIZE: 7 ½ x 11 ¾ INCHES ▪ TYPE SELECTION: FUTURA, GARAMOND ▪

1989 ANNUAL REPORT

ASSOCIATED PRESS

ASSOCIATED PRESS

▲ The Associated Press is a not-for-profit news cooperative and the primary audience for the annual report is our membership: the publishers and editors of newspapers, the general managers and news directors of radio and television stations. The report goes out to a large audience (the agency has an 87 percent share of all newspapers and television stations and a 50 percent share of all radio stations), but it is an audience very familiar with the AP. Education is not a priority of this report; however, it is important that the report is used as a communications vehicle for the Associated Press staff and affiliated personnel around the world. In this report, we were trying to project an image. The Associated Press is the oldest and largest of the news organizations of its kind, but because of this we have a stodgy reputation and are not seen as innovative or high-tech. We're also unique in being a cooperative. In the midst of all the technology, we're a people-driven organization. The design of this report got across these important aspects: the AP is a twenty-four-hour organization—we're open all the time—and a very contemporary one. Last year's report was our first with Frankfurt Gips Balkind and it was a real education process for the designers. This report shows the result of that education. Despite its being radical, the concept flew with the president on the first try. And the response has been good; it's been very popular with the financial press and our employees. It's also gotten a response from old line newspaper publishers—even if they didn't like it, they noticed it.

■ Associated Press ist eine gemeinnützige Nachrichtenkooperative, und die wichtigste Zielgruppe für unseren Jahresbericht sind unsere Mitglieder: die Herausgeber und Redakteure von Zeitungen und die Direktoren und Nachrichtenchefs von Fernseh- und Radiostationen. Der Bericht wendet sich an ein ausgesprochen breites, aber mit AP gut vertrautes Publikum (zu AP gehören 87 Prozent aller Zeitungen und Fernsehstationen und 50 Prozent aller Radiosender). In diesem Bericht haben wir versucht, ein bestimmtes Image zu vermitteln. Associated Press ist die älteste und grösste Agentur ihrer Art, was leider auch bedeutet, dass wir als etwas antiquiert gelten, und unser Name nicht unbedingt für Innovation und technischen Fortschritt steht. Wir stellen auch insofern einen Sonderfall dar, als wir eine Kooperative sind. Inmitten der allgemeinen technologischen Aufrüstung sind wir eine Organisation, in der es immer noch auf den einzelnen Menschen ankommt. Das Design des Jahresberichts hat unsere Besonderheiten wirkungsvoll umgesetzt: Wir sind rund um die Uhr und rund ums Jahr geöffnet, und das Design reflektiert die Aussage, die wir vermitteln wollen – dass wir zeitgemäss und modern sind. Dies war unser zweiter Jahresbericht mit Frankfurt Gips Balkind. Das erste Jahr war eine Lernerfahrung für die Designer, und sie hat sich bei diesem Bericht wirklich bezahlt gemacht. Obwohl das Konzept des diesjährigen Berichts etwas völlig Neuartiges ist, konnte unser Präsident sich sofort dafür begeistern. Und der Bericht war ein Erfolg bei der Wirtschaftspresse und unseren Angestellten. Sogar bei den Zeitungsherausgebern alter Schule hat er Aufsehen erregt - sie mochten ihn vielleicht nicht, aber ignorieren konnten sie ihn auch nicht.

● L'Associated Press est une société cooperative d'information à but non lucratif, et le public particulièrement visé par notre rapport annuel est constitué des membres de l'association, parmi lesquels comptent les éditeurs et rédacteurs de journaux, ainsi que les directeurs de radios et de télévision. Ce rapport concerne un assez large auditoire (l'agence possède quatre-vingt-sept pour cent des parts de toutes les chaînes de télévision et de tous les journaux, et cinquante pour cent des parts des stations de radio), très proche de A.P. Avec ce rapport, nous avons tenté de projeter une certaine image de l'entreprise. L'Associated Press est la plus ancienne et la plus importante agence d'information de son espèce, mais précisément à cause de cela notre réputation n'est pas celle d'une entreprise innovatrice ou de haute technologie. Nous sommes également la seule coopérative du genre dans le monde. Au milieu de toute la technologie ambiante, nous sommes une organisation motivante pour les gens. Le design de ce rapport a bien fait comprendre certains aspects essentiels de l'A.P: nous fonctionnons 24 heures sur 24, sept jours sur sept, et notre image de marque correspond exactement à ce que nous voulons transmettre – nous sommes modernes. C'était notre second rapport annuel avec Frankfurt Gips Balkind. La première année, les designers durent surtout s'informer, et ce rapport est la preuve que tout a parfaitement fonctionné. Bien que très particulier, le concept a plu au président du premier coup. Le résultat a également été excellent, le rapport étant très populaire parmi la presse financière et nos employés.

[WENDELL WOOD COLLINS]

ASSOCIATED PRESS: 50 ROCKEFELLER PLAZA, NEW YORK, NEW YORK 10020 USA 212.621.1720

FRANKFURT GIPS BALKIND

▲ Last year was our first year with Associated Press, and that report represented an enormous change over their previous ones, which had been very average. In the first report, we tried to make their pictures look glossy. It just didn't work. This year, the report was more organic—it looks like a newspaper. We used the OCR typeface to capture a feeling of immediacy, and the report is broken into two sections—it even folds like a newspaper. Their business runs twenty-four hours a day, so we worked with the idea of a continuous image—the band that wraps around the report and then runs throughout. We broke the colors down to process. The budget was extremely limited and we couldn't afford an illustrator, so all the art was created in-house on the color photo-copier. The report was about the AP people, and five different stories are told in the front section. The financials are given in the second section. Associated Press is very happy with this report; it was a very successful effort.

■ Das letzte Jahr war unser erstes Jahr mit Associated Press, und der Bericht stellte eine gewaltige Veränderung gegenüber ihren früheren Jahresberichten dar, die ausgesprochen durchschnittlich waren. In diesem ersten Bericht versuchten wir, die Photos auf Hochglanzpapier zu drucken, und das war ein Fehler. Der diesjährige Bericht ist organischer – er sieht wie eine Zeitung aus. Wir verwendeten OCR-Lettern, um das Gefühl der Aktualität zu vermitteln, und der Bericht ist in zwei getrennte Abschnitte unterteilt – er ist sogar wie eine Zeitung gefaltet. Der Betrieb geht bei AP rund um die Uhr, und daher arbeiteten wir mit der Idee eines fortlaufenden Bildes – das Band, das den Bericht umschliesst und sich durch sämtliche Innenseiten zieht. Wir haben Farbauszüge für den Mehrfarbendruck gemacht. Das Budget war ausgesprochen begrenzt, und wir konnten uns keinen Illustrator leisten; also haben wir sämtliche Bilder hausintern auf dem Farbkopierer produziert. Der Bericht dreht sich um die Leute von AP, und im ersten Teil werden fünf verschiedene Geschichten erzählt. Der zweite Teil präsentiert die finanziellen Aktivitäten. Associated Press ist sehr glücklich mit diesem Bericht; er erwies sich als ausserordentlich erfolgreich.

● Pour la première fois l'année passée, nous avons travaillé avec l'Associated Press - ce rapport représentait un changement énorme comparé aux précédents, qui étaient extrêmement moyens. Dans le premier rapport, nous avions essayé de donner aux photos un aspect brillant. Ça n'a pas marché. Cette année, le rapport était mieux structuré. Il avait l'air d'un journal. Nous avons utilisé les caractères OCR pour capturer l'idée d'urgence; le rapport était divisé en deux sections et il pouvait même être plié comme un journal. Cette entreprise fonctionnant 24 heures sur 24, nous avons travaillé sur l'idée de la continuité de l'image, avec notamment la bande qui commence sur la couverture, court tout le long des pages et se prolonge au verso pour rejoindre son point de départ. Nous avons ensuite décomposé les couleurs pour l'impression. Le budget extrêmement limité ne nous permettant pas de nous offrir un illustrateur, tout l'artistique a été réalisé dans l'agence même, à l'aide d'un photocopieur couleurs. Les employés de l'A.P furent choisis pour être le sujet du rapport, illustré par cinq histoires différentes dans la première section. Les pages financières sont présentées dans la deuxième section. Ce rapport annuel été extrêmement satisfaisant pour l'Associated Press.

[AUBREY BALKIND]

FRANKFURT GIPS BALKIND: 244 EAST 58TH STREET, NEW YORK, NEW YORK 10022 USA 212.421.5888

WHAT A YEAR! CAN YOU IMAGINE HOW UNLIKELY, IF NOT SILLY, SOME OF 1989'S INCREDIBLE EVENTS WOULD HAVE LOOKED had they surfaced as predictions in AP's 1988 year-end wrapups?

time, AP pressed forward the top-to-bottom renewal and modernization of all news, picture, graphics and tabular services.

We tried to make you and your audiences truly eyewitnesses to history. We focus in this annual report on five AP people who played a role in that effort. We ask you to look at them for what they do, but also to look at them as representatives of the 3,000 AP people who serve you around the world.

They are AP Special

Or Mexico City newswoman Candice Hughes, who was held hostage by Panamanian military forces during the overthrow of General Noriega.

Or photographer Jeff Widener, who told the whole China story in one unforgettable frame: one man, alone, stopping that line of tanks in Beijing.

Or Warsaw Correspondent John Daniszewski, who was shot in the arm and the head in the streets of Timisoara, where he went to tell the story of the Romanian revolution.

AP's managers met the budget challenge of 1989's momentous news events. We closed the year on budget, despite an array of unforeseeable news events, with record revenue of $287.6 million. Capital spending for such projects as SelectStocks, PhotoStream, new terminals and editing systems totaled $24.5 million for the year.

Careful cost control and aggressive emphasis on developing new sources of non-traditional revenue continued to be basic to

new customized financial tables service, made its debut in 10 newspapers across the country. And it goes into more each week. We began the task of re-equipping all of our bureaus with state-of-the-art terminals and editing systems to serve you better.

In 1990, these developments and more accelerate their march into your newsrooms and ours as we work to meet the needs of a membership that has never been larger or more supportive of its news

(BEIJING) June 5—BRAVE MEN—A Chinese man stands in front of tanks down Cangan Blvd. Monday morning in front of the Beijing Hotel stopping their advance prod and pleaded for a halt to the killing. (AP ColorPhoto/mas215446tf/Jeff Widener)1989
AP LENFAX

Cyan printer. Magenta printer.

AL CHECKPOI...

> "I can't express the impact (Jeff Widener's Tiananmen Square) picture made on me and I'm sure to a lot of other people. To me it surpassed the famous sailor kissing the young lady in Times Square at V-E Day in 1945. Oh so many questions this picture asks." —Mrs. Thelma G. Rudolph, Detroit, Mich.

The Berlin Wall would come down. Non-communist governments would replace dictatorships in Eastern Europe. Chinese democratic reform would stop dead in Tiananmen Square. An oil tanker would slip its course and spill almost 11 million gallons of crude oil into Alaska's waters. The third game of the World Series would be postponed because of an earthquake.

On behalf of its members and subscribers, AP covered all that and more in 1989. At the same

Correspondent Mort Rosenblum, who provided dramatic reporting from Romania, White House Correspondent Rita Beamish, AP Network Sports Correspondent Mike Gracia, photo enterprise editor Claudia Counts and San Juan technician Pedro Collazo.

We could have chosen many others.

For example, Vienna Bureau Chief Alison Smale, who walked with the first East German woman to come west through Checkpoint Charlie.

Or the members of our business news staff who won their second consecutive John Hancock award, for their coverage of the impact of the wave of mergers and acquisitions that raced through American industry in 1989.

It was the sort of year that produced many heroes in the world, and some within AP, too, not the least of them being Terry Anderson, who as we write marks the fifth anniversary of his captivity as a hostage in Lebanon.

the finances of the cooperative.

The conversion to 9600-word-a-minute delivery of news began with a target of mid-1990 completion. PhotoStream, our new digital picture-a-minute photo service, went live in test mode and met our high expectations. We selected the AP Leaf and AP VAX Picture Desks as the photo reception equipment that can deliver the kind of photo quality members demand for the newspapers of the '90s. SelectStocks, our

cooperative. Member cooperation and news contribution remain at the heart of the enterprise.

The industry's faith in us represents a bond we are dedicated to renewing each day. It is what makes your AP different from everyone else.

Bill Keating
William J. Keating
Chairman

Lou Boccardi
Louis D. Boccardi
President and General Manager

CLAUDIA COUNTS

MIKE GRACIA

CLIENT: ASSOCIATED PRESS ■ DESIGN FIRM: FRANKFURT GIPS BALKIND ■ CREATIVE DIRECTOR: KENT HUNTER ■ DESIGNER: SAERI YOO PARK ■ PHOTOGRAPHER: CHERYL ROSSUM ■ ILLUSTRATOR: SAERI YOO PARK ■ WRITER: WENDELL WOOD COLLINS ■ PRODUCTION MANAGER: BONNIE GOLD-BERG ■ PAPER SELECTION: CORONADO MODIFIED ANTIQUE ■ PRINTER: LEBANON VALLEY OFFSET ■ NUMBER OF PAGES: 16 ■ TYPE SELECTION: OCRA ■

D E C U S

1 9 8 9

A N N U A L

R E P O R T

DIGITAL EQUIPMENT COMPUTER USERS SOCIETY

. . . .

▲ We are a volunteer society. With the annual report we try to reach the decision makers who approve volunteers' participation—the managers and directors of computing organizations and managers within Digital. The secondary audience is the membership itself. This was the very first report produced by the society. We wanted to stress that this is an organization of peers helping each other solve the specific problems of our professional lives. We also wanted to focus on the society as a whole, not on any specific activities. We're not sure how sucessful the report was. Direct evidence says it did not suceed, because in distribution it did not get into the hands of the primary audience—the managers and directors inside and outside Digital. However, since the report was distributed, we have had record-breaking meetings. We'll need to see three or four reports before we can make a judgment. I've never done this before; I write protocol stacks for a living. We put out speculative bids and had six designs submitted. The final choice was actually the first eliminated. I came back to it because the other choices looked too much like marketing literature from Digital, and I thought it important that our report have a clear, separate identity. Once the choice was made, the designer did the work. I got to make all content decisions and approve the final. All in all, it seemed a fairly painless process to me.

. . . .

■ Unsere Gesellschaft setzt sich aus freiwilligen Mitarbeitern zusammen. Mit dem Jahresbericht versuchen wir, Entscheidungsträger zu erreichen, die an der Mitarbeit von Freiwilligen interessiert sind - namentlich die Manager und Direktoren von Computer-Organisationen und die Manager von Digital. Unsere zweite Zielgruppe sind unsere Mitglieder. Dies war unser erster Jahresbericht. Wir wollten herausstreichen, dass wir eine Organisation von Menschen sind, die einander bei der Lösung spezifischer beruflicher Probleme helfen. Wir wollten uns dabei nicht auf spezielle Aktivitäten konzentrieren, sondern die Gesellschaft als Ganzes darstellen. Wir sind uns nicht ganz sicher, ob der Bericht letztlich erfolgreich war. Allem Anschein nach war er ein Fehlschlag, weil er nicht in die Hände der Hauptzielgruppe gelangte - der Manager und Direktoren innerhalb und ausserhalb von Digital. Andererseits sind unsere Zusammenkünfte seit der Publikation des Berichts besser besucht als je zuvor. Wir müssen wohl die nächsten drei oder vier Berichte abwarten, bevor wir ein endgültiges Urteil fällen können. Es war meine erste Erfahrung auf diesem Gebiet; in meinem Hauptberuf schreibe ich Protokolle. Wir veröffentlichten eine spekulative Ausschreibung, und sechs Designs wurden eingesandt. Das Design, für das wir uns zum Schluss entschieden, war ursprünglich als erstes abgelehnt worden. Ich kam darauf zurück, weil die anderen Vorschläge zu sehr an Marketing-Broschüren von Digital erinnerten. Was mir dagegen vorschwebte, war ein Bericht mit einer eigenständigen, unverwechselbaren Identität.

. . . .

● Nous sommes une société composée de volontaires. Le rapport annuel nous permet de toucher les personnes qui approuvent le volontariat: les présidents et directeurs d'entreprises d'informatique, y compris les directeurs de Digital. Les membres de la société eux-mêmes constituent notre deuxième cible. Ce rapport était le tout premier produit par la société. Nous désirions mettre l'accent sur le fait que nous sommes une organisation dans laquelle tout le monde a la même importance, où chacun aide l'autre à résoudre les problèmes spécifiques de sa vie professionnelle. Il apparaît que ce rapport a échoué dans la mesure où il n'a pas atteint notre principale audience, les directeurs extérieurs ou intérieurs à Digital. Cependant, depuis que ce rapport a été distribué, nous avons eu des réunions qui battent tous les records. Je pense que nous aurons besoin de deux ou trois rapports avant de pouvoir réellement juger de l'impact. Je n'en avais jamais fait auparavant; personnellement, ma tâche consiste à rédiger des protocoles. Après avoir demandé divers devis, nous avons reçu différentes offres, et six projets nous ont été soumis. En fait, le choix final a été le premier éliminé. J'y suis revenu ensuite, car les autres projets sélectionnés ressemblaient beaucoup trop à de la littérature marketing de Digital; or, je pensais qu'il était important que notre rapport ait une identité bien définie et parfaitement claire. Une fois le choix fait, les designers se sont occupés du reste. J'ai simplement décidé du contenu et approuvé le résultat final. La démarche m'a semblé plutôt aisée.

[RALPH STAMMERJOHN]

DIGITAL EQUIPMENT COMPUTER USERS SOCIETY: 333 SOUTH STREET, SHR #1-4/D32

SHREWSBURY, MASSACHUSETTS 01543 USA 508.841.3584

BHA DESIGN GROUP

. . . .

▲ The client put the annual report out for "spec" bids. We normally don't do work on spec, but it was a hot summer day and we were feeling particularly free-spirited, so we took off and had fun with it, creating exactly what we thought the client needed. In essence, we were working in a vacuum—the concept of "investments" was all we had to go by. The copy had already been written, the theme established. We just couldn't bear to design a typical high-tech type manual with those "hands on keyboard" shots. From what we understood, Decus was a maverick group of "techie" types, so we designed for the readership in the hope that they wouldn't ditch the annual when it came through the mail. Everyone is cost conscious these days, but this job set new standards for the word "budget." We were told we had only $70,000 for 70,000 copies, which had to include postage and mailing. They would not negotiate on the budget, so we did what we had to do—we dug deep into our collective production souls, called printers and illustrators, negotiated, and negotiated some more. I understand it was nip and tuck with approval of the design, but Ralph Stammerjohn pushed his vision through. Ultimately, he was delighted with the design, although I understand that other Decus members were caught by surprise. There's definitely a consevative contingent, but no one was indifferent, and in the end, I believe, shaking people up was Ralph's intent.

. . . .

■ Der Kunde veröffentlichte eine spekulative Ausschreibung für den Jahresbericht. Wir machen uns normalerweise nicht die Mühe, an rein spekulativen Ausschreibungen teilzunehmen, aber es war ein heisser Sommertag, und wir waren in Schöpferlaune und fingen mehr oder weniger spasseshalber an, ein Design auf die Bedürfnisse des Kunden zuzuschneiden. Das war nicht so einfach - wir arbeiteten im Grunde in einem Vakuum, denn die einzige konzeptuelle Vorgabe war der Begriff «Investitionen». Der Text und das Thema lagen bereits vor. Wir hatten keine Lust, eine typische Techno-Broschüre mit langweiligen Photos von Fingern auf einer Tastatur zu entwerfen. Das Design wurde dann mit Blick auf die Leser entworfen, die den Bericht möglichst nicht aus ihrem Briefkasten direkt in den Müll befördern sollten. Alle Welt ist heutzutage kostenbewusst, aber dieses Projekt hat neue Massstäbe für ein wahrhaft schmales Budget gesetzt. Man erklärte uns, dass wir nur $70.000 für 70.000 Hefte zur Verfügung hätten, und zwar inklusive Porto. Der Kunde gab beim Budget keinen Millimeter nach, so dass uns nichts anderes übrig blieb, als Drucker und Illustratoren anzurufen und zu feilschen. Offenbar stand die Annahme unseres Designs zunächst auf der Kippe, aber Ralph Stammerjohn konnte sich letztlich durchsetzen. Ihm gefiel das Design zum Schluss ausgesprochen gut, während andere Decus-Mitglieder aus allen Wolken fielen.

. . . .

● Le client avait demandé des devis pour son rapport annuel. D'habitude, nous ne procédons pas de cette façon, mais c'était l'été, il faisait très chaud et nous nous sentions particulièrement ouverts à toute innovation. Nous nous sommes donc lancés dans le projet, créant exactement ce que nous pensions que le client désirait. Nous avons travaillé à l'aveuglette, puisque tout ce que nous vions comme ligne directrice était un concept d'«investissement». Le texte avait déjà été écrit, et le thème établi. Il était hors de question pour nous de créer un rapport typiquement high-tech, avec le genre de photos montrant des gens en train de taper sur un clavier d'ordinateur. De plus, d'après ce que nous avions compris, Decus rassemblait un groupe de techniciens non-conformistes, qui lisaient probablement beaucoup de bandes dessinées ésotériques. Nous avons donc créé un concept spécial pour ces lecteurs, afin qu'ils ne jettent pas tout simplement le rapport annuel à sa réception. Tout le monde est très soucieux des coûts actuellement, mais ce projet a carrément donné au mot «budget» un nouveau sens. On nous a dit que nous aurions exactement 70.000 dollars pour 70.000 exemplaires, frais d'envoi et d'affranchissement inclus. Comme ils voulaient absolument s'en tenir à ce budget, il ne nous restait plus qu'à nous creuser les méninges et à négocier encore et encore avec les imprimeurs et les illustrateurs. Il m'a semblé comprendre que l'approbation finale du design avait été assez controversée, mais Ralph Stammerjohn a réussi à faire prévaloir sa vision des choses. Il était ravi du résultat, bien qu'il m'ait semblé que le reste des membres de Decus aient été passablement surpris.

[DEBORAH VAN ROOYEN]

BHA DESIGN GROUP: 215 FIRST STREET, CAMBRIDGE, MASSACHUSETTS, 02142 USA 617.576.2131

Client: DIGITAL EQUIPMENT USERS SOCIETY ■ Design Firm: BHA DESIGN GROUP ■ Art Director: DEBORAH VAN ROOYEN ■ Designers: DEBORAH VAN ROOYEN, DAVID HORTON ■ Illustrator: STEPHEN TURK ■ Writer: THE WRITESOURCE INC. ■ Production Manager: DEBORAH VAN ROOYEN ■ Typographer: TIM BARTOL ■ Paper Selection: SPECKLETONE ■ Paper Manufacturer: FRENCH PAPER CO. ■ Printer: MERIDIAN PRINTERS ■ Number of Pages: 16 PLUS COVER ■ Trim Size: 7 x 11 INCHES ■ Type Selection: GILL ULTRA BOLD SABON ■ Print Run: 70,000 ■

REINVENTING
SPECIALTY STORES

THE LIMITED

....

▲ We direct our annual report primarily to our employees, 60 percent of whom purchase shares in the company every week through a payroll deduction plan. Forty-five percent of the company is employee-owned (inclusive of the board, the chairman, Leslie H. Wexner, and the Wexner family). The financial community makes up our secondary audience. This year's report was an attempt to communicate to our employees and other stockholders the chairman's vision of where the company is and where we can go in the future. We are now at a size where we needed to adjust our report to meet the needs of the associates of each division. As we grow larger and larger as a corporation, we still want to "think small," in terms of taking the entreprenurial point of view. We want our empoyees to win one customer at a time and we want to keep close to our customers. Our motto remains that nothing happens until the customer says, "I'll take it." We received excellent feedback from our associates on this report—they approached it almost as one would a high-school yearbook; looking at their section first and then going back to read the whole thing. This was our first experience with Frankfurt Gips Balkind, and we found they were great at listening—each section really reflected the personality of the individual division. They are very creative and have their own ideas, but were open to other points of view. Equally important was the level of their interpersonal skills; they had to deal with ten marketing vice presidents, each with a different personality. They managed to not only get along with each of them, but please them all as well.

....

■ Wir wenden uns mit unserem Jahresbericht in erster Linie an unsere Angestellten, von denen 60 Prozent mittels eines Lohnabzugsverfahrens wöchentlich Aktienanteile an unserem Unternehmen kaufen. Die Finanzwelt ist die zweite Zielgruppe unseres Jahresberichts. Der diesjährige Bericht versuchte, unseren Angestellten und anderen Aktionären darzulegen, wie der Vorsitzende den gegenwärtigen Stand und die zukünftigen Möglichkeiten des Unternehmens sieht. Wir haben inzwischen eine Grösse erreicht, die es notwendig macht, dass wir unseren Bericht den Bedürfnissen der Gesellschafter jeder einzelnen Division anpassen. Da wir als Konzern immer grösser werden, liegt uns um so mehr daran, den unternehmerischen Kontakt zur Basis nicht zu verlieren. Dieser Bericht hat bei unseren Gesellschaftern ein vorzügliches Echo gefunden - er wurde mit einem ähnlichen Eifer aufgenommen wie ein Schuljahrbuch: sie haben zuerst ihren Abschnitt durchgelesen und sich dann den Rest angeschaut. Dies war unsere erste Zusammenarbeit mit Frankfurt Gips Balkind, und die Designer gingen wirklich auf unsere Vorstellungen und Erklärungen ein - jeder Abschnitt spiegelt den individuellen Charakter der verschiedenen Tochterfirmen wider. Sie sind sehr kreativ und haben ihre eigenen Ideen, aber sie waren immer offen für unsere Vorschläge. Als ebenso wichtig erwies sich ihr diplomatisches Gespür; sie mussten sich mit zehn Marketing-Vizepräsidenten und somit mit zehn völlig verschiedenen Persönlichkeiten auseinandersetzen. Es ist ihnen nicht nur gelungen, mit jedem einzelnen gut auszukommen - sie haben es geschafft, alle zehn vollauf zufriedenzustellen.

....

● Notre rapport annuel s'adresse principalement à nos employés, qui achètent chaque semaine des actions de la société selon un système de déduction sur les salaires. Notre deuxième cible est composée de toute la communauté financière. Le rapport de cette année était une tentative pour donner à nos employés et aux autres actionnaires le point de vue du président concernant la position de la société, et la direction générale à prendre dans le futur. Nous atteignons maintenant un point où le rapport doit être adapté aux besoins des membres de nos différents départements. Alors que nous prenons de plus en plus d'importance, nous voulons continuer à penser «petit» du point de vue de l'entreprise. En retour, nous avons reçu d'excellentes réactions de nos collègues au sujet de ce rapport; ils l'ont quasiment considéré comme un journal d'étudiants. Ils ont d'abord lu ce qui concernait leur propre département et se sont ensuite intéressés au reste. C'était notre première expérience avec Frankfurt Gips Balkind. L'agence nous a témoigné beaucoup d'attention et d'intérêt et elle a réussi à ce que chaque partie du rapport reflète exactement la personnalité de chaque division. Ces gens sont très créatifs et en même temps ouverts à de nouveaux points de vue. La qualité de leurs relations avec les autres était également essentielle. Ils ont dû composer avec dix directeurs de marketing, chacun ayant bien sûr une personnalité différente. Non seulement ils se sont bien entendus avec chacun d'eux, mais ils ont aussi réussi à plaire à tous.

[AL DEITZEL]

THE LIMITED, INC.: TWO LIMITED PARKWAY, P.O. BOX 16000, COLUMBUS, OHIO 43216 USA 614.479.7000

. . . .

▲ This was one tough book. Leslie Wexner, the company's chairman, has a utilitarian view of the company as a company, not as the ten different divisions that, in some cases, compete against each other. This was our first report for the client, and last year's book had reflected Wexner's utilitarian view—it had no pictures. We suggested they do something different. They needed a report that would serve them beyond just showing financials. This report could be used by the different divisions for everything from lease negotiations to recruitment. We dealt with each division president separately, therefore each division became a client—that's where the difficulty in this report lay: we had to reflect the personality of each different store in a spread, and then tie the spreads together as a book. Only one representative of the company saw the entire book. We worked with each of the division presidents to come up with a series of short words that go with the imagery, which in every case except Bendel's came from their own files. The words and pictures come together to capture the essence of the store's personality and how each suits its customer base. The body copy of a report is not just gray matter to us, we deal with expressive type. Highlighting information with the copper makes it easier to read, and the key information is easy to pick out. Despite the difficulty in dealing with so many parties on one report, everyone is happy with their division's section, and the company has received excellent response on the report as a whole.

. . . .

■ Das war ein wirklich schwieriges Buch. Leslie Wexner, der Vorsitzende, sieht das Unternehmen als nützliche Einheit, nicht als zehn verschiedene Tochterfirmen, die in einigen Fällen miteinander konkurrieren. Es war unser erster Bericht für diesen Kunden, und das Buch des Vorjahres spiegelte Wexners utilitaristische Anschauung wider - es hatte keine Bilder. Wir schlugen dem Kunden vor, etwas Neues zu versuchen, einen Bericht, der über den Zweck einer blossen finanziellen Darstellung hinausging und von den zehn verschiedenen Tochterfirmen für alles mögliche verwendet werden konnte, von Mietverhandlungen bis hin zur Rekrutierung von Personal. Wir setzten uns mit jedem einzelnen Präsidenten gesondert auseinander, so dass jede Tochterfirma einen unabhängigen Kunden darstellte - und hier lag auch die Schwierigkeit: Wir mussten die Persönlichkeit jeder einzelnen Ladenkette in einer Doppelseite darstellen und das Ganze dann zu einem Buch verbinden. Nur ein Vertreter des Unternehmens sah das Buch in seiner Gesamtheit. Die Worte und Bilder fangen gemeinsam das Wesen der einzelnen Geschäfte ein und legen dar, wie sie den Wünschen ihrer jeweiligen Kundschaft gerecht werden. Der Textsatz eines Berichts ist für uns nicht einfach eine Bleiwüste, es kommt uns auf ein ausdrucksvolles Schriftbild an. Um den Text leichter lesbar zu machen, haben wir die Schlüsselaussagen mit Kupfer herausgehoben. Es ist zwar schwierig, sich bei einem einzigen Bericht mit so vielen Parteien auseinandersetzen zu müssen, aber die einzelnen Töchter sind glücklich mit ihrem jeweiligen Abschnitt, und der Bericht als Ganzes hat in der Öffentlichkeit eine Menge Anklang gefunden.

. . . .

● Ce rapport a vraiment été dur à réaliser. Leslie Wexner, le président de la société a une vision assez utilitaire de l'entreprise et il ne la voit pas comme dix départements différents luttant parfois les uns contre les autres. Ce rapport était le premier que nous faisions pour ce client et celui de l'année dernière, il reflétait bien cette vision utilitaire de Wexner: il n'y avait aucune photo. Nous avons donc suggéré quelque chose de différent. Il était nécessaire que ce rapport soit plus qu'un simple compte rendu financier et qu'il puisse être utilisé par les différents départements, de la négociation des baux au recrutement de personnel. Nous avons négocié séparément avec chaque président de division, et par conséquent chaque division est devenue un client à part entière. C'est là que résidait tout la difficulté. Nous avons dû refléter la personnalité de chaque magasin sur une double page et ensuite, faire un livre de tout cela. Il n'y eut qu'une personne de la société à voir le travail en entier. La combinaison des mots et des photos a très bien réussi à capturer l'essence de la personnalité des magasins et la façon dont chacun est adapté à sa clientèle de base. Le contenu d'un rapport financier n'est pas simplement de la matière grise pour nous, nous utilisons également des caractères très accrocheurs. Souligner l'information avec une couleur cuivre la rend plus facile à lire et l'information-clé est ainsi aisément repérable. En dépit des difficultés rencontrées avec un tel nombre de gens intéressés par un tel rapport, chacun est content de sa section et on a enregistré d'excellents résultats.

[AUBREY BALKIND]

FRANKFURT GIPS BALKIND: 244 EAST 58TH STREET, NEW YORK, NEW YORK 10022 USA 212.421.5888

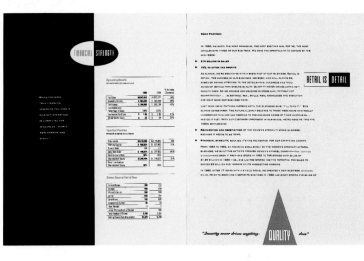

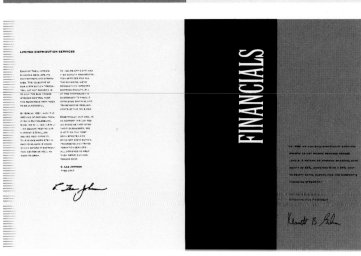

90

ANNUAL REPORT DESIGN

GESTALTUNG VON JAHRESBERICHTEN

DESIGN DES RAPPORTS ANNUELS

CHICAGO BOARD OF TRADE
1990 ANNUAL REPORT

CHICAGO BOARD OF TRADE

. . . .

▲ The primary audience for the Chicago Board of Trade's annual report is our customer base. This includes financial CFOs, CEOs, pension fund managers, mortgage brokers, and large agricultural concerns who use our commodity markets to hedge their risks. Secondarily, we send our report to the entire congressional membership in Washington D.C. as an extension of our lobbying effort. □ The purpose of the report, other than the usual imparting of financial data for the year, is to better acquaint other corporate leaders with our industry, market developments, and plan for continued growth in the future. It also serves as a prime public relations piece for our organization and our entire industry. □ The Chicago Board of Trade 1990 annual report has more than ful-filled its function. To date we have received many calls and letters from futures companies, our congressional contacts, and corporate leaders complimenting us on our efforts. We have also won several design awards on the report. □ I believe the relationship with the graphic designer is the most crucial factor in producing a successful report. Although the establishment of a theme and copy preparation are crucial elements, a good designer can make all the difference in the world between an award winning-annual and a mediocre one. Our designer directed the project to ensure that we met deadlines, contained costs, and achieved quality production results.

. . . .

■ Das Zielpublikum des Jahresberichtes des Chicago Board of Trade sind Finanzexperten, Manager, Pensionskas-senmanager, Vermittler von Hypotheken und grosse Landwirtschaftskonzerne, die unsere Rohstoffmärkte zur Ri-sikoabsicherung benützen. Zudem senden wir unseren Jahresbericht an alle Kongressabgeordneten in Washington als Zusatz zu unseren Lobby-Aktivitäten. □ Abgesehen von der Information über gewöhnliche Finanzdaten für das Geschäftsjahr zielt der Bericht darauf ab, anderen Firmenchefs unsere Industrie, die Marktentwicklungen und Pläne für weiteres Wachstum näherzubringen. Der Bericht dient auch als wichtigstes PR-Material für unsere Organisation und für die gesamte Industrie. □ Der Jahresbericht 1990 hat seine Aufgabe bestens erfüllt. Bisher haben wir zahlreiche Anrufe und Briefe von im Termingeschäft tätigen Firmen erhalten; unsere Kontaktleute im Kongress und Firmenchefs haben uns Komplimente in bezug auf den Bericht gemacht. Wir haben damit auch meh-rere Designpreise gewonnen. □ Ich bin der Meinung, dass eine gute Beziehung mit dem Designer der wichtigste Faktor für einen erfolgreichen Bericht ist. Obwohl die Festlegung eines Themas und die Vorbereitung für die Aus-gabe des Berichts sehr wichtige Elemente sind, kann ein guter Designer den Riesenunterschied zwischen einem mit Preisen ausgezeichneten und einem mittelmässigen Jahresbericht ausmachen. Unser Designer übernahm die Projektleitung und stellte sicher, dass Termine und Kosten eingehalten wurden und ein Qualitätsprodukt entstand.

. . . .

● Le principal public du rapport annuel de la Chambre de commerce de Chicago, ce sont les grands instituts fi-nanciers, les gestionnaires de fonds vieillesse, les créanciers hypothécaires et les grandes exploitations agricoles qui utilisent nos marchés de matières premières afin de couvrir leurs risques. De plus, nous envoyons notre rap-port à tous les membres du Congrès de Washington, pour étendre nos efforts en tant que groupe de pression. □ Le but de ce rapport, outre la communication des bilans financiers de l'année, est de mieux faire connaître notre fonction, l'évolution du marché et nos perspectives de croissance. C'est aussi un document de relations publiques fondamental pour notre organisation et l'industrie tout entière. □ Le rapport annuel 1990 a surpassé nos espéran-ces. A ce jour, nous avons reçu de nombreux appels et des lettres de futures sociétés, de nos relations au Congrès et de directeurs d'entreprises, nous félicitant de nos efforts. Nous avons aussi gagné plusieurs prix avec ce rap-port. □ Je crois que les bonnes relations que l'on entretient avec le designer graphique sont un facteur essentiel de réussite. Bien que le choix du thème et la préparation du texte soient des éléments cruciaux, le talent du designer fait toute la différence entre un rapport primé et un rapport médiocre. Notre designer a assumé la direction du projet, ce qui a permis de respecter les délais et de limiter les frais; il a exécuté un travail de première qualité.

[MICHAEL OAKES]

CHICAGO BOARD OF TRADE: LASALLE AT JACKSON, CHICAGO, ILLINOIS 60604 312.435.3721

VSA PARTNERS, INC.

▲ The direction for this report was collaborative. Michael Oakes of the Chicago Board of Trade stated two ideas during a session of open brainstorming which prompted the overall visual styling of the report. The first idea was to create a "look inside" feel for the operations story of the company. The second idea was a question. "Can we create a layering of imagery similar to a diagrammatic cross section of the human body?" These two ideas planted the seed to pursue the vellum-style collage direction that drives the overall styling of the book. We integrated typewritten text to tone down the complexity of the photo collage. □ With the direction being collaborative, we had little difficulty past the presentation stage to sell the idea. The hardest part came when we actually had to assemble the imagery. □ The client was extremely pleased. As a team, the client and designer were able to execute a concept which initially appeared complex and vague. But as we proceeded, the client was able to participate in the actual assemblage of the collage-style photos. This partnership led to an exciting role of participation for him. □ In general, we are noticing stricter budgets. As an office, we are experiencing a trend among clients to explore more efficient ways of producing projects. Issues relating to desktop publishing, recycled paper, and a reduction of location photography have been consistent points of economic interest among our clients. We are also producing much of our art on the Macintosh to save illustration and typesetting costs. We currently generate about 80 percent of our work on our own computer system, though we still strongly stress traditional conventions of design visualization.

■ Michael Oakes vom Chicago Board of Trade legte während einer Brainstorming-Sitzung zwei Ideen dar, die das gesamte visuelle Styling des Berichts bestimmten. Die erste Idee: ein Gefühl des «Einblicks» in die Operationen der Börse hervorzurufen. Die zweite Idee war eine Frage: «Können wir eine bildliche Darstellung ähnlich einem Querschnitt des menschlichen Körpers kreieren?» Aufgrund dieser beiden Ideen entschied man sich für pergamentartige Collagen, die das Gesamtstyling des Berichts prägen. Wir integrierten schreibmaschinengeschriebene Textpassagen, um die Komplexität der Photocollagen etwas «leichter» zu machen. □ Da die Ausrichtung des Berichtes in Zusammenarbeit mit dem Kunden erfolgte, hatten wir praktisch keine Schwierigkeiten, nach der Präsentationsphase die Idee zu verkaufen. Die schwierige Phase war, die Bilder zusammenzustellen. □ Der Kunde war äusserst zufrieden, zumal er bei der Designarbeit direkt involviert war. Als Team konnten Kunde und Designer ein Konzept umsetzen, das am Anfang sehr komplex und vage erschien. □ Allgemein stellen wir striktere Budgets fest. Als Büro sehen wir den Trend, dass Kunden effizientere Wege bei der Produktion von Projekten erkunden. Themen wie Desktop publishing, Recyclingpapier, weniger Photographien vor Ort sind immer wiederkehrende Wünsche der Kunden, um die Kosten zu reduzieren. Wir produzieren auch vieles auf dem Macintosh, um Illustrations- und Satzkosten einzusparen. Zur Zeit machen wir etwa 80 Prozent unserer Arbeit auf unseren eigenen Computersystemen, doch sind für uns die traditionellen Methoden der Designumsetzung nach wie vor sehr wichtig.

● Michael Oakes, de la Bourse du commerce de Chicago, formula deux idées au cours d'une séance de brain-storming visant à trouver le style visuel global de ce rapport. La première idée était de créer un «regard de l'intérieur» sur les opérations financières de la Bourse. La seconde idée était une question: «Pouvons-nous créer une série d'images semblables à la coupe transversale d'un corps humain?» Ces deux idées furent à l'origine du style de collage sur vélin qui domine l'ensemble du livre. Nous y avons intégré des textes tapés à la machine pour atténuer la complexité du photomontage. □ La direction ayant été très coopérative, nous avons n'avons pas eu de difficultés à vendre l'idée après la présentation. Nous eûmes par contre quelques problèmes au moment d'assembler les images. □ Le client était extrêmement content, d'autant plus qu'il était impliqué dans le processus de réalisation. Le client et le designer ont collaboré pour concrétiser un concept qui, au premier abord, semblait plutôt vague. □ Dans l'ensemble, nous constatons des budgets plus stricts. Notre bureau a noté chez les clients une tendance à rechercher des méthodes plus efficaces pour la production de leurs rapports. Les questions relatives à la C.A.O., au papier recyclé, à la réduction du nombre de photos de repérage sont d'un grand intérêt économique pour eux. Nous exécutons aussi beaucoup de nos projets sur Macintosh afin de limiter les dépenses en matière d'illustration et de typographie. Nous réalisons environ 80% de notre travail sur nos propres systèmes informatiques. Nous continuons cependant à porter nos efforts sur les méthodes traditionnelles de visualisation du design.

[DANA ARNETT]

VSA PARTNERS, INC.: 542 SOUTH DEARBORN, SUITE 202, CHICAGO, ILLINOIS 60605 312.427.6413

FUTURES AND FUTURES-OPTIONS TRADING VOLUME

	1990	1989
Agricultural Futures		
Wheat	2,676,270	3,237,769
Corn	11,423,027	9,270,784
Oats	433,567	349,836
Soybeans	10,301,905	9,634,802
Soybean Meal	4,964,471	4,486,845
Soybean Oil	4,658,302	4,800,797
Agricultural Options		
Wheat	652,941	484,952
Corn	2,114,302	1,519,164
Soybeans	2,389,382	1,975,440
Soybean Meal	181,429	112,474
Soybean Oil	136,089	101,158
Oats	7,334	—
Financial Futures		
U.S. Treasury Bonds	75,499,257	70,303,195
Ten-Year Treasury Notes	6,054,222	6,169,516
Five-Year Treasury Notes	2,533,628	1,781,680
Two-Year Treasury Notes	110,769	—
Municipal Bond Index	836,861	1,068,028
30-Day Interest Rate	61,300	68,223
Japanese Government Bonds	3,062	—
Mortgage Backed	16,848	24,815
Financial Options		
U.S. Treasury Bonds	27,315,411	20,784,019
Ten-Year Treasury Notes	536,754	1,148,194
Five-Year Treasury Notes	47,440	—
Municipal Bond Index	85,613	88,291
Japanese Government Bonds	475	—
Mortgage Backed total		13,564
Stock Index Futures		
Major Market Index	951,325	1,086,550
TOPIX	230	—
CBOE 250 Index		13,945
Metal Futures		
1000 oz. Silver	176,861	254,713
5000 oz. Silver	2,256	2,397
Kilo Gold	36,649	27,994
100 oz. Gold	7,814	75,362
Metal Options		
1000 oz. Silver	1,398	8,346
Total	154,231,543	138,351,317

Membership of the Chicago Board of Trade
(as of Dec. 31, 1990)

Full members	1402
Associate members	748
Commodity Options membership interests	643
Index, Debt and Energy membership interests	645
Government Instruments membership interests	215
Total	3643

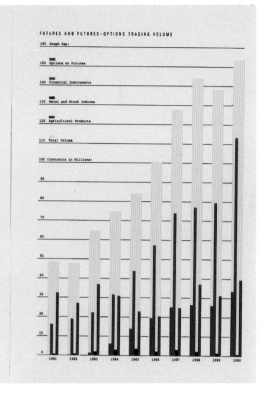

FUTURES AND FUTURES-OPTIONS TRADING VOLUME

Graph Key:

- Options on Futures
- Financial Instruments
- Metal and Stock Indices
- Agricultural Products
- Total Volume
- (Contracts in Millions)

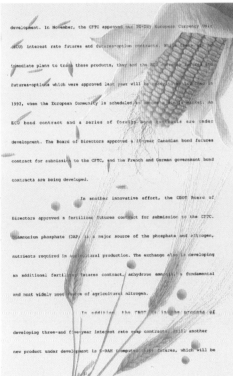

development. In November, the CFTC approved our 90-Day European Currency Unit (ECU) interest rate futures and futures-option contracts. While there are no immediate plans to trade these products, they and the ECU currency futures and futures-options which were approved last year will be reevaluated and refined in 1992, when the European Community is scheduled to become a single market. An ECU bond contract and a series of foreign bond contracts are under development. The Board of Directors approved a 10-year Canadian bond futures contract for submission to the CFTC, and the French and German government bond contracts are being developed.

In another innovative effort, the CBOT Board of Directors approved a fertilizer futures contract for submission to the CFTC. Diammonium phosphate (DAP) is a major source of the phosphate and nitrogen nutrients required in agricultural production. The exchange also is developing an additional fertilizer futures contract, anhydrous ammonia, a fundamental and most widely used source of agricultural nitrogen.

In addition, the CBOT is in the process of developing three-and five-year interest rate swap contracts. Still another new product under development is D-RAM (computer chip) futures, which will be

CLIENT: CHICAGO BOARD OF TRADE ■ DESIGN FIRM: VSA PARTNERS, INC. ■ ART DIRECTOR/DESIGNER: DANA ARNETT ■ STUDIO PHOTOGRAPHER: FRANÇOIS ROBERT ■ ARCHITECTURAL PHOTOGRAPHER: WAYNE CABLE ■ WRITERS: MICHAEL OAKES, CAROLYN HURD ■ TYPOGRAPHER: VSA PARTNERS, INC., DESIGN SYSTEMS GROUP ■ PAPER SELECTION: NORTHWEST GLOSS, VEGAS VELLUM, ESSE ■ PAPER MANUFACTURERS: POTLATCH, WITAKER CARPENTER MARQUETTE, GILBERT ■ PRINTER: THE HENNEGAN COMPANY ■ NUMBER OF PAGES: 52 ■ TYPE SELECTION: COURIER TYPEWRITER ■

LOS ANGELES DEPARTMENT OF WATER AND POWER

1989-1990 ANNUAL REPORT

RESOURCE MANAGEMENT IN THE 1990s

LOS ANGELES DEPARTMENT OF WATER AND POWER

. . . .

▲ Since it has no shareholders, the municipally owned Los Angeles Department of Water and Power has no legal requirement to prepare an annual report. But we are nonetheless answerable to a number of constituencies, including the citizens of Los Angeles (our "owners" and customers), our bondholders, and the city's elected officials. ☐ With the city in the throes of a five-year drought, we prepared last year's annual report around the theme, "Resources Management in the 1990s," which addressed an issue that is key to the Department's present and future successes: prudent stewardship of the human, natural, and financial resources that allow us to operate. We are very pleased with the execution of the theme, both in the words and the design. ☐ Our designer, Emmett Morava of Morava Oliver Berté and writer, Don Anderson, were invaluable in developing the concept and delivering last year's report. Receiving early and continuous input from management, they worked exceptionally well with the rest of the inside team. Everyone pulled together with mutual respect and produced an exceptional, professional report.

. . . .

■ Da das Los Angeles Department of Water and Power keine Aktionäre hat, ist es nicht verpflichtet, einen Jahresbericht zu erstellen. Wir sind jedoch gegenüber verschiedenen Kreisen verantwortlich, u.a. gegenüber den Bürgern von Los Angeles (unseren «Besitzern» und Abnehmern), gegenüber den Bondinhabern und der gewählten Stadtregierung. ☐ Da die Stadt mit einer fünf Jahre andauernden Trockenheit zu kämpfen hatte, wählten wir «den Umgang mit Ressourcen in den 90ern» als Thema des letztjährigen Berichtes. Es ist der Schlüssel zum gegenwärtigen und zukünftigen Erfolg unserer Behörde; das heisst kluge Verwaltung der menschlichen, natürlichen und finanziellen Ressourcen, die unsere Funktion gewährleisten. Wir sind mit der Umsetzung des Themas in Wort und Design sehr zufrieden. ☐ Unser Designer, Emmett Morava, und unser Texter, Don Anderson, waren bei der Entwicklung des Konzeptes und der Produktion des letztjährigen Berichtes hervorragende Partner. Von Anfang an erhielten sie Unterstützung vom Management, und sie arbeiteten mit dem innerbetrieblichen Team aussergewöhnlich gut zusammen, so dass die gemeinsamen Bemühungen zu einem hervorragenden Jahresbericht führten.

. . . .

● Le Department of Water and Power de la ville de Los Angeles n'ayant pas d'actionnaires, il n'est pas obligé de publier un rapport annuel d'activités. Nous avons néanmoins une responsabilité envers certains groupes, notamment les habitants de Los Angeles (nos «propriétaires» et nos clients), les porteurs d'obligations et les élus de la ville. ☐ Los Angeles souffrant de la sécheresse depuis cinq ans, nous avons préparé le rapport de l'année passée sur le sujet: «La gestion des ressources dans les années 90». C'est une question fondamentale pour le succès présent et futur de ce département: il s'agit en effet de gérer avec prudence les ressources humaines, naturelles et financières qui nous permettent d'opérer. Nous sommes très contents de l'exécution de ce projet, aussi bien au niveau du texte que du design. ☐ Bénéficiant dès le début du soutien de la direction, notre designer, Emmett Morava, et notre rédacteur, Don Anderson, qui ont tous deux participé à l'élaboration du concept et à la réalisation du rapport annuel de l'année passée, ont travaillé de manière exceptionnelle avec le reste de l'équipe de l'entreprise.

[DANIEL WATERS]

LOS ANGELES DEPARTMENT OF WATER AND POWER: 111 NORTH HOPE STREET

LOS ANGELES, CALIFORNIA 90012 213.481.4211

▲ The subject of the annual report was determined by the copywriter and the client. It's direction evolved through the collaboration between the client, copywriter, and designer. ☐ An example of the best possible way to produce a meaningful report was done in stages with all parties contributing to the process and having the maturity to accept the most appropriate solution to any given problem—even if the solution was someone else's idea. The other parties then stepped back and let the designer "design" it. The design presented to management was quickly approved because the management team had been involved in the entire development of the report. Thus, management accepted the design without any changes. ☐ Assessing a report is always difficult, however, in this case what would have normally been a difficult assignment became a success because the presentation of the information was logical and was accomplished in a manner that didn't require tremendous effort by the reader. ☐ In terms of the finances, the budget for the report was fixed, since it is a city-owned utility. Fiscal restraint was necessary, as it is with most clients. Most though, do not demand cost reductions, knowing that could hurt the quality. ☐ Part of keeping costs down and quality up is the use of computer-generated typesetting. I have no problems with this as long as the software doesn't compromise the integrity of the original foundry cut of the typefaces and it can't be "set" with the same color and dignity that the type designer intended. Overall, half our typesetting is computer-generated in-house.

■ Das Thema des Jahresberichts wurde vom Texter und vom Kunden bestimmt. Die einzuschlagende Richtung entwickelte sich durch die Zusammenarbeit zwischen dem Kunden, dem Texter und dem Designer. ☐ Der Bericht ist ein Beispiel dafür, wie ein sinnvoller Bericht produziert werden kann: Er wurde in Phasen entworfen, unter Mitarbeit aller Beteiligten, die erfahren genug waren, die jeweils beste Lösung eines Problems zu akzeptieren, auch wenn die Lösung die Idee eines anderen war. Anschliessend verhielten sich die Beteiligten zurückhaltend und liessen den Designer arbeiten. Das dem Management vorgelegte Design wurde schnell bewilligt, denn das Managementteam war in die gesamte Entwicklung des Berichts involviert gewesen. Das Management akzeptierte das Design ohne eine einzige Änderung. ☐ Einen Jahresbericht einzuschätzen ist immer schwierig. Was aber normalerweise eine schwierige Aufgabe ist, wurde bei diesem Auftrag zu einem Erfolg, weil die Information logisch und leserfreundlich präsentiert wurde. ☐ Das Budget war ein Fixum, da es sich um einen Betrieb der Stadt handelt. Es war nötig, sich finanziell einzuschränken – so wie bei vielen Kunden. Die meisten verlangen allerdings nicht eine Kostenverringerung, da sie wissen, dass dies der Qualität schaden könnte. ☐ Die Kunst, die Kosten tief und die Qualität hoch zu halten, basiert auf computergeneriertem Schriftsatz. Ich sehe da keine Probleme, solange die Software die Originalschrift nicht verfälscht und so gesetzt werden kann, wie es der Schriftentwerfer beabsichtigt hat. Im grossen und ganzen wird ungefähr die Hälfte des Satzes in unserer Firma mit dem Computer hergestellt.

● Le sujet de ce rapport annuel a été établi par le rédacteur-concepteur et le client lui-même. Sa réalisation est le fruit de la collaboration entre le client, le rédacteur et le designer. ☐ Voici là un exemple de la meilleure manière de produire un rapport: il a été réalisé par étapes avec la participation de tous les intéressés, ceux qui ont la sagesse d'accepter la solution la plus appropriée aux problèmes donnés, même si l'idée est émise par quelqu'un d'autre. En définitive, ils ont été discrets et ils ont laissé le designer «faire du design». Le projet présenté a été rapidement approuvé parce que l'équipe de la direction avait été impliquée dans le développement du rapport. Ils ont accepté le design sans un seul changement. ☐ Il est toujours difficile de juger d'un rapport, pourtant, dans le cas précis, ce qui en temps normal aurait été une commande difficile s'est avéré être un succès car la présentation de l'information était logique et ne demandait pas des efforts inouïs de la part du lecteur. ☐ En ce qui concerne l'aspect financier, le budget du rapport était fixe car cet organisme est propriété de la ville. Des restrictions furent nécessaires comme avec bon nombre de clients. La plupart ne demandent cependant pas une réduction des coûts, sachant que cela aurait des répercussions sur la qualité. ☐ La typo a été déterminée en fonction de ces limitations, mais maintenue à un bon niveau de qualité grâce à nos compétences dans l'emploi de l'ordinateur. Cela ne pose pas de problèmes aussi longtemps que le logiciel ne compromet pas l'intégrité du caractère original et qu'il peut être composé selon le désir du typographe. La moitié de notre typo est réalisée sur l'ordinateur de l'agence.

[EMMETT MORAVA]

MORAVA OLIVER BERTÉ: 2054 BROADWAY, SANTA MONICA, CALIFORNIA 90404 213.453.3523

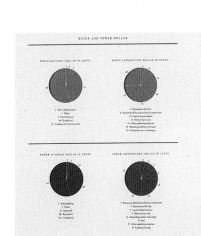

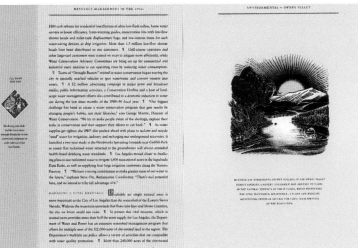

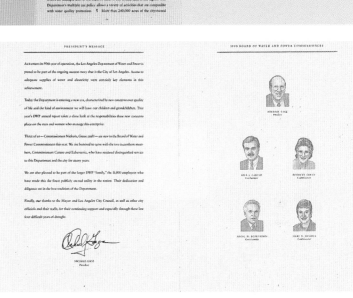

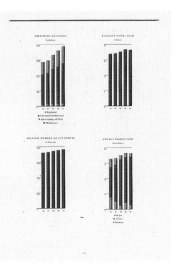

Client: THE CITY OF LOS ANGELES DEPARTMENT OF WATER AND POWER COMMISSIONERS ■ Design Firm: MORAVA OLIVER BERTÉ ■ Art Directors: EMMETT MORAVA, ROBERT SCHAEFER ■ Designer: EMMETT MORAVA ■ Illustrator: RODGER XAVIER ■ Writer: DON ANDERSON ■ Production Manager: ANDREW NAWROCKY ■ Typographer: CENTRAL TYPESETTING ■ Paper Selection: STARWHITE, EVERGREEN ■ Paper Manufacturers: CONSOLIDATED, SIMPSON ■ Printer: FRANKLIN PRESS ■ Number of Pages: 54 ■ Type Selection: SABON ■

W.M. Keck Foundation

First Light, *Ancient Light*

W.M. KECK FOUNDATION

▲ The primary audience for W.M. Keck Foundation's Annual Report is grant seekers, especially those in the fields of higher education, medical research, and science. Our secondary audience is comprised of other philanthropic institutions, fund raisers, and government agencies. ☐ Our report is expected to convey the profile of the Foundation while clearly outlining the type of programs we fund, including both our primary and secondary focuses. It is expected to tell the story of our year, including the organizations we funded, and may also feature grants that have wide appeal. ☐ We believe this book has more than fulfilled its function. With the advent of "first light" for the W.M. Keck Telescope, along with the announcement of funding for a second, it was fitting to feature the Telescope and Observatory. ☐ The relationship with our designer, Doug Oliver of Morava Oliver Berté, along with the excellent print quality and photography—supplied by Bill Varnie Photography, Inc.—were key to a successful production. With such well-chosen professionals, the result speaks for itself. These creative talents have proven themselves, as evidenced by the fact that they have produced three award-winning books.

■ Das Zielpublikum des Jahresberichtes der W.M. Keck Foundation sind Leute, die ein Stipendium beantragen, vor allem im Bereich einer höheren Ausbildung, der medizinischen Forschung und der Wissenschaft. Unser sekundäres Zielpublikum sind philantropische Institutionen, Finanzierungsvermittler und staatliche Agenturen. ☐ Unser Jahresbericht soll das Profil der Stiftung vermitteln und gleichzeitig die Art von Programmen umreissen, die wir unterstützen, einschliesslich unserer primären und sekundären Prioritäten. Er soll über die Ereignisse des Jahres berichten unter Miteinbezug der von uns unterstützten Organisationen; er kann auch über Subventionen berichten, die von allgemeinem Interesse sind. ☐ Wir glauben, dass dieser Bericht seine Funktion bestens erfüllt hat. Die Entwicklung des ersten W.M.-Keck-Teleskops und die Ankündigung der Finanzierung eines zweiten waren ein guter Grund, ein Teleskop und eine Sternwarte im Bericht aufzunehmen, zumal die Astronomie viel Presse in diesem Jahr erhielt. ☐ Die gute Beziehung mit Doug Oliver, unserem Designer von Morava Oliver Berté, die ausgezeichnete Druckqualität und die Photographien von Bill Varnie Photography, Inc. waren die Schlüsselelemente für eine erfolgreiche Produktion. Mit solchen Profis spricht das Resultat für sich. Sie haben erneut bewiesen, dass sie ein hervorragendes Team sind – bisher haben schon drei ihrer Jahresberichte Preise bekommen.

● Le rapport annuel de la Fondation W.M. Keck s'adresse en premier lieu aux chercheurs intéressés par une bourse, spécialement dans le domaine de l'enseignement supérieur, de la recherche médicale et scientifique. Ensuite viennent les autres institutions philanthropiques, les bailleurs de fonds et les pouvoirs publics. ☐ Il est supposé donner le profil de la Fondation en exposant dans les grandes lignes le genre de programmes que nous avons lancé, les projets prioritaires comme les secondaires. Il devait retracer l'histoire de la Fondation dans l'année, parler notamment des organismes que nous soutenons, et présenter les bourses qui suscitent un vaste intérêt. ☐ Nous croyons que ce livre a fait plus que de remplir cette fonction. Avec la mise au point du premier télescope W.M. Keck, en même temps que l'annonce du financement d'un second, il était normal de représenter un télescope et un observatoire dans ce rapport. ☐ Les bonnes relations que nous avons entretenues avec notre designer, Doug Oliver, de Morava Oliver & Berté, conjuguées à une qualité d'impression exceptionnelle, et les photographies de Bill Varnie Photography Inc., expliquent la réussite de ce projet. Le résultat est éloquent. Ces créatifs talentueux ont formé une remarquable équipe – la preuve, c'est que le livre qu'ils ont conçu a remporté trois prix.

[MARGARET P. BURCHETTE]

W.M. KECK FOUNDATION: 555 SOUTH FLOWER STREET, SUITE 3230, LOS ANGELES, CALIFORNIA 90071 213.680.3833

▲ In preliminary meetings held to discuss the direction of the annual report, I outlined three different conceptual themes the book could pursue. We agreed together that the first choice was the most timely, the most interesting, and the most photogenic. Once agreed upon, the problem shifted to execution. □ One of the primary objectives of the report is to present the foundation properly. The client, W.M. Keck Foundation, prides itself on a quality presentation of the foundation to its target audiences, and felt the report spoke well of the foundation and its aims. □ Generally, we are not noticing strict budgetary constraints, but by no means are they increasing. The budget, while not unlimited, is driven by the parameters. □ In a brief dozen years, I have run the gamut from setting annual reports entirely in hot metal (linotype) to setting them on a Macintosh. While computer-generated type now represents the majority of our work, I consider my familiarity with the roots of typography to be a major office strength.

■ In Vorbesprechungen über den Jahresbericht zeigte ich drei verschiedene Konzeptentwürfe, die dem Bericht zugrunde liegen könnten. Wir stimmten überein, dass das erste Konzept das zeitgemässeste, interessanteste und photogenste war. Nun blieb nur noch die Frage der Ausführung. □ Die W.M. Keck Foundation, unser Klient, ist stolz auf eine qualitativ hochstehende Präsentation der Stiftung gegenüber dem Zielpublikum und war der Meinung, dass der Jahresbericht die Stiftung und ihre Ziele positiv darstellte. □ Eines der Hauptziele des Jahresberichts war, die Stiftung angemessen zu präsentieren. Im allgemeinen spüren wir keine strikten Budgeteinschränkungen, aber die Budgets vergrössern sich auch nicht. Das Budget ist zwar nicht unlimitiert, wird aber von gewissen Bedingungen bestimmt. □ In knapp einem Dutzend Jahren habe ich die ganze Satzentwicklung von Bleisatz (Linosatz) bis zum Setzen auf dem Macintosh durchgemacht. Zwar macht computergenerierter Schriftsatz den Grossteil unserer Arbeit aus, doch ich betrachte meine Kenntnis der Grundlagen des Schriftsatzes als Stärke unserer Firma.

● Lors de réunions préliminaires concernant le rapport annuel, j'avais exposé dans les grandes lignes trois thèmes différents que le livre pourrait développer. Nous avons d'un commun accord admis que le premier choix était à la fois le plus opportun, le plus intéressant et le plus photogénique des trois. Le problème, ce fut de le réaliser. □ Le client, la Fondation W.M.Keck, est fière de la qualité de la présentation de la Fondation et ils ont eu l'impression que le rapport annuel parle bien de cette institution et de ses objectifs. □ L'un des premiers buts de ce rapport est de présenter la Fondation proprement dit. Dans l'ensemble, nous n'avons pas constaté de restrictions financières notables, mais les budgets n'augmentent certes pas. N'étant pas illimité, le budget est déterminé par certains paramètres. □ En quelques dix ans, j'ai connu toutes les phases de l'évolution, de la photocomposition (linotype) jusqu'au Macintosh. Bien que la typo conçue sur ordinateur représente maintenant la majeure partie de notre travail, je considère que ma connaissance de la typographie traditionnelle constitue un atout pour notre bureau.

[DOUG OLIVER]

MORAVA OLIVER BERTÉ: 2054 BROADWAY, SANTA MONICA, CALIFORNIA 90404 213.453.6290

CLIENT: W.M. KECK FOUNDATION ■ DESIGN FIRM: MORAVA OLIVER BERTÉ ■ ART DIRECTOR: DOUGLAS OLIVER ■ DESIGNER: DOUGLAS OLIVER ■
PHOTOGRAPHER: BILL VARIE ■ ILLUSTRATOR: ROBIN WEAVER ■ WRITER: MARGARET BURCHETT ■ PRODUCTION MANAGER: ROBIN WEAVER ■
TYPOGRAPHER: ANDRESEN TYPOGRAPHICS ■ PAPER SELECTION: REFLECTIONS, EVERGREEN ■ PAPER MANUFACTURERS: CONSOLIDATED, SIMPSON ■
PRINTER: LITHOGRAPHIX, INC. ■ NUMBER OF PAGES: 46 ■ TRIM SIZE: 11 x 14 INCHES ■ TYPE SELECTION: CENTAUR, ARRIGHI ■

BOY SCOUTS OF AMERICA, MIDDLE TENNESSEE COUNCIL

▲ Our primary audiences are our officers, executive board members, corporate and private contributors, and United Ways. Secondary audiences are program volunteers and the general public. □ We wanted the annual report to convey that we are an indispensible community resource for communicating time-tested values to young people, their families and their communities. Also, that our organization is growing and our programs, activities, and facilities are better than ever. In these ways, the design of the report fulfilled its function extremely well. □ Without question, a good relationship with the designer helped in the production of the report. The Middle Tennessee Council relies on friends for many facets of support. Chuck Creasy is a true friend to the Boy Scouts of America.

■ Das primäre Publikum unserer Jahresberichte sind unsere Mitarbeiter, der Vorstand, Firmen und private Spender sowie United Ways. Ausserdem richten sie sich an freiwillige Mitarbeiter und die Öffentlichkeit im allgemeinen. □ Der Jahresbericht sollte unsere Rolle als gemeinnütziges Unternehmen dargestellen, das sich für erprobte Werte einsetzt, die jungen Menschen, ihren Familien und den Gemeinden zugute kommen. Ausserdem wollten wir berichten, dass wir wachsen und dass unsere Programme, Aktivitäten und Einrichtungen besser denn je sind. Der Jahresbericht wurde diesen Anliegen auf hervorragende Weise gerecht. □ Zweifellos erleichterte die gute Beziehung zum Designer die Produktion des Berichtes. Chuck Creasy ist ein wahrer Freund der Boy Scouts of America.

● Notre premier public se compose de nos fonctionnaires, des membres du conseil d'administration, des cadres et des donateurs, ainsi que de United Ways. Le deuxième public est constitué des volontaires et du grand public. □ Nous voulions que le rapport annuel fasse savoir que nous sommes une association publique qui transmet aux jeunes, à leurs familles et à la communauté des valeurs qui ont fait leurs preuves. Il fallait aussi communiquer que notre organisation est en pleine croissance et que nos programmes, nos activités et nos services sont meilleurs que jamais. A cet égard, le design de ce rapport a rempli son objectif de manière tout à fait satisfaisante. □ Les bonnes relations que nous avons entretenues avec le designer ont sans nul doute facilité la production de ce rapport.

[TIM COOPER & CHUCK SIMMONS]

BOY SCOUTS OF AMERICA, MIDDLE TENNESSEE COUNCIL: 3414 HILLSBORO ROAD

NASHVILLE 37215 615.3893.9724

CHUCK CREASY CREATIVE

. . . .

▲ This is truly one of those projects that most of us would "kill" for. My client and I have worked together for over 10 years, and have built a mutual trust. ☐ I am very involved in Scouting, and I think because of that the client trusts my judgment. They have always given me complete freedom to design and execute their book each year. This freedom gives me the opportunity to allow the concept to evolve and subtlely change throughout the process. ☐ My main problem each year as I sit down to design the annual report is editing my own thinking. The subject matter on Scouting is so plentiful that I find myself coming up with two or three concepts that I like. I tuck these away and pull them out the next year for consideration. ☐ I am also very fortunate in that I have developed a relationship with a group that basically donates their services each year, from copywriting to printing. That sure takes some of the normal budget restraints away. ☐ All in all, I feel very fortunate to be able to work for this client each year and design annual reports that not only receive recognition but portray Scouting with the consideration it deserves.

. . . .

■ Dies gehört zu jenen Projekten, für die die meisten von uns «über Leichen gehen» würden. Die Zusammenarbeit mit meinem Auftraggeber dauert schon zehn Jahre und ist von gegenseitigem Vertrauen geprägt. ☐ Ich bin in der Pfadfinderbewegung sehr involviert und glaube, aus diesem Grunde vertraut der Kunde auf mein Urteil und lässt mir völlig freie Hand in der Gestaltung und Produktion. Dadurch konnte das Konzept während des ganzen Herstellungsprozesses entwickelt und leicht abgeändert werden. ☐ Die grösste Schwierigkeit für mich ist, mein eigenes Denken während der Gestaltung des Berichtes zu überwachen und zu korrigieren. Das Thema bietet so viele Möglichkeiten, dass ich schliesslich zwei oder drei Konzepte habe, die mir gefallen. Was ich nicht verwende, verschwindet in der Schublade und wird im folgenden Jahr wieder angeschaut. ☐ Es ist mir gelungen, eine Gruppe von Leuten zu finden, die ihren Beitrag, von den Texten bis zum Druck, jedes Jahr quasi als Spende geben. Das hilft natürlich im Hinblick auf die Herstellungskosten. ☐ Ich freue mich, für diesen Kunden Jahresberichte zu gestalten, die nicht nur Beachtung finden, sondern auch die Pfadfinderbewegung so darstellen, wie sie es verdient.

. . . .

● C'est véritablement un de ces projets pour lesquels on se «damnerait». Je travaille avec ce client depuis plus de 10 ans et nous avons établi des rapports de confiance mutuelle. ☐ Je suis très engagé dans le mouvement scout et je pense que c'est pour cela que le client se fie à mon jugement. Ils m'ont toujours donné la plus complète liberté pour le design et la réalisation de leur publication. Cela me donne la possiblilité de faire évoluer le concept et de procéder à de subtils changements au cours du processus d'élaboration. ☐ Mon grand problème jusqu'à ce que j'élabore ce rapport est de formuler mes propres idées. Le sujet du scoutisme est si riche qu'il m'arrive de développer deux ou trois concepts que j'aime. ☐ Je suis également très heureux d'être en relation avec un groupe qui offre gratuitement ses services chaque année, de la rédaction à l'impression. Cela permet d'éviter les restrictions d'un budget normal. ☐ En définitive, je suis très heureux de pouvoir travailler pour ce client et de concevoir des rapports annuels qui, non seulement sont bien accueillis, mais présentent le scoutisme avec le respect qu'il mérite.

[CHUCK CREASY]

CHUCK CREASY CREATIVE: 631 2ND AVENUE SOUTH, NASHVILLE, TN 37210 615.254.7991

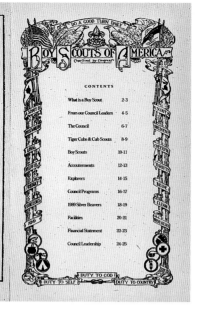
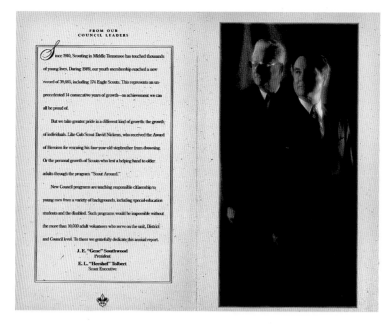
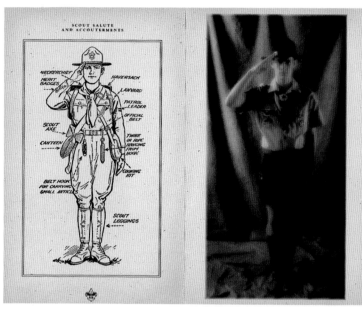
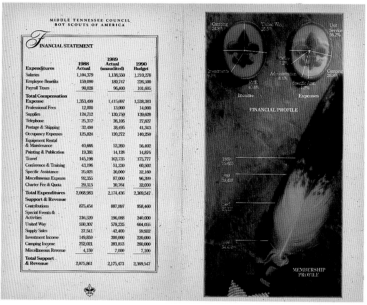
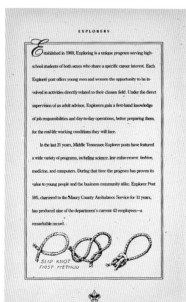
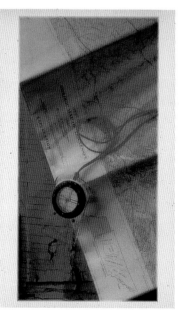

IMCERA GROUP, INC.

▲ Directed toward the investment community and our 9,600 employees worldwide, our report had three primary goals. First, build recognition for a new corporate name and identity. The company had undergone a transformation from commodity chemicals to technology-based health care business and the old name no longer described us. Second, the report was designed to highlight IMCERA's three decentralized businesses, Mallinckrodt Medical, Mallinckrodt Specialty Chemicals, and Pitman–Moore. Third, we wanted to target health care analysts in the investment community. In the past, analysts classified the company as a commodity chemical business. □ The results were measured by the recognition of IMCERA and interest in the company by Wall Street analysts and portfolio managers, the reclassification of IMCERA as a health care supplier, and ultimately by the company's stock price. □ The annual report was successful in communicating the company's new identity. It highlighted each of the three operating companies, and it reached health care analysts and portfolio managers through target mailings, initiating hundreds of inquiries about our company and what we do. IMCERA stock hit an historic high of $75 at the close of 1990, and $110 in 1991. The annual report indirectly helped these stock increases and was a great success.

■ Das Zielpublikum unseres Jahresberichtes waren internationale Anleger und unsere weltweit 9600 Angestellten. Drei Hauptziele standen im Vordergrund: 1. Aufbau der Akzeptanz und Wiedererkennung des neuen Namens des Unternehmens und der neuen Unternehmenskultur. Das Unternehmen hatte sich von einem Betrieb im chemischen Rohstoffgeschäft in eine Firma gewandelt, die auf technologische Weiterentwicklungen ausgerichtet und vornehmlich im Gesundheitswesen tätig ist. Der alte Name konnte unsere Tätigkeiten nicht mehr widerspiegeln. 2. Der Bericht sollte IMCERAs drei dezentralisierte Unternehmensbereiche herausstreichen: Mallinckrodt Medical, Mallinckrodt Specialty Chemicals und Pitman-Moore. 3. Mit dem Bericht sollten spezifisch auf das Gesundheitswesen spezialisierte Anlageberater und Analysten angesprochen werden. In der Vergangenheit hatten Analysten das Unternehmen als eine im Bereich der chemischen Rohstoffe tätige Firma eingeordnet. □ Der Erfolg zeigte sich an der Beachtung und am Interesse, das IMCERA bei Wall-Street-Analysten und Portfolio-Managern erweckte, an der Neuzuordnung IMCERAs als Zulieferer im Gesundheitswesen und schliesslich am Aktienpreis. □ Mit dem Jahresbericht gelang es uns, die neue Identität des Unternehmens bekannt zu machen. Der Bericht hob jede der drei Betriebsgesellschaften hervor, und durch ein zielgerichtetes Mailing, das Hunderte von Anfragen zur Folge hatte, erreichten wir Gesundheitswesen-Analysten und Portfolio-Manager. IMCERA-Aktien stiegen Ende 1990 auf einen Rekordpreis von $ 75, und 1991 sogar auf $ 110. Der Jahresbericht übertraf gewiss all unsere Erwartungen.

● Destiné au monde de l'investissement et à nos 9600 employés dans le monde, notre rapport avait trois objectifs. Premièrement, faire reconnaître le nouveau nom et l'identité de notre groupe. L'entreprise ayant fait l'objet d'une reconversion, passant des produits chimiques au commerce des soins de santé basés sur une technologie de pointe, l'ancien nom ne correspondait plus à rien. Deuxièmement, le rapport devait mettre en vedette les trois affaires décentralisées de l'IMCERA: Mallinckrodt Medical, Mallinckrodt Specialty Chemicals et Pitman-Moore. Troisièmement, nous voulions toucher dans la communauté des investisseurs les analystes des soins de santé. Par le passé, les analystes avaient classé notre société comme un commerce de produits chimiques. □ Ce rapport a eu pour résultat la reconnaissance d'IMCERA et l'intérêt suscité par la société auprès des analystes de Wall Street et des gestionnaires de portefeuilles, la reclassification d'IMCERA comme fournisseur de soins de santé et finalement, l'augmentation du prix des actions. □ Il a réussi a communiquer la nouvelle identité du groupe. Il présentait chacune des trois sociétés opérationnelles et il atteignit les analystes de soins de santé et les gestionnaires de portefeuilles grâce à des mailings ciblés, suscitant des centaines d'enquêtes. Le titre IMCERA a atteint un niveau historique de 75 $ à la fin 1990 et 110 $ en 1991. En définitive, ce rapport annuel aura dépassé toutes nos espérances.

[TURA COTTINGHAM]

IMCERA GROUP, INC.: 2315 SANDERS ROAD, NORTHBROOK, ILLINOIS 60062 708.564.8600

SAMATA ASSOCIATES DESIGN CONSULTANTS

▲ The direction for the IMCERA Group, Inc., 1990 Annual Report was a collaboration between us and our client. In an initial meeting with the president of IMCERA, a "three in one" concept for the book was outlined to help clarify the changing corporate structure of the company in which three independent subsidiary companies operate as a unified whole. We implemented a design for the book based on the "three in one" theme and had full client support. □ The report was so successful in clarifying and streamlining the corporate structure as well as dynamically illustrating the various products and markets of IMCERA that a large purchase of company stock resulted. Needless to say, they were extremely happy with this book. □ IMCERA had a general idea for the design of the report and formulated the budget for the project in accordance with this idea. While designing and producing the book we kept a careful eye on the budget while maintaining the high quality that IMCERA expected. □ In general, we are noticing throughout the industry that our clients have become somewhat more conservative money-wise, due to the economic recession. However, our long-term clients have continued to place great importance on high-quality corporate communications, perhaps even more so with this economic crunch. □ The typography for the IMCERA 1990 Annual Report was provided by an outside typography company. Increasingly, however, we are doing our own typography in-house on our Macintosh computers. This helps expedite the report while still adhering to quality.

■ Bei der Ausarbeitung des Konzeptes für den Jahresbericht 1990 der IMCERA-Gruppe haben wir eng mit dem Kunden zusammengearbeitet. In einem ersten Treffen mit dem Präsidenten der Firmengruppe stellten wir ein «drei-in-einem»-Konzept für den Bericht vor, das die Umstrukturierung der Firma darstellen sollte, in der drei unabhängige Tochtergesellschaften als eine Einheit funktionieren. Danach führten wir das Design für den Jahresbericht aus. Wir genossen dabei die volle Unterstützung unseres Kunden. □ Der Bericht war ausgesprochen erfolgreich, sowohl bei der Darstellung der Unternehmensstruktur als auch bei der dynamischen Illustration der verschiedenen Produkte und Märkte von IMCERA. Das schlug sich auch in einer steigenden Nachfrage nach IMCERA-Aktien nieder. Die Firma war natürlich sehr glücklich mit dem Jahresbericht. □ IMCERA hatte eine ungefähre Vorstellung, wie das Design des Jahresberichts aussehen sollte, und aufgrund dieser Vorstellung wurde das Budget festgelegt. Während unserer Arbeit am Jahresbericht haben wir immer auf das Budget geachtet und gleichzeitig versucht, die hohe Qualität beizubehalten, die IMCERA erwartete. □ Im allgemeinen fällt uns auf, dass unsere Kunden in allen Industriezweigen durch die Rezession kostenmässig konservativer werden. Doch unsere Stammkunden legen noch immer grossen Wert auf qualitativ hochstehende Unternehmenskommunikation, vielleicht aufgrund der Rezession noch stärker. □ Der Schriftsatz für den IMCERA-Jahresbericht 1990 wurde von einer Setzerei übernommen. Aber wir arbeiten für die Satzherstellung vermehrt mit unseren Macintosh-Computern.

● Les grandes orientations du rapport annuel 1990 du groupe IMCERA ont été décidées en collaboration avec le client. Lors d'une première entrevue avec le président de la firme, un concept fut défini: il prévoyait «trois livres en un seul», afin d'expliquer la restructuration de cette société, dans laquelle trois filiales indépendantes opéraient comme un tout. Nous avons réalisé un design basé sur ce thème et nous avons reçu un soutien total de la part de notre client. □ Le rapport a été tellement réussi, décrivant avec clarté les structures de l'entreprise, illustrant de manière dynamique les divers produits et marchés de l'IMCERA, qu'il en résulta une poussée des actions en Bourse. Nul besoin de souligner que nous étions extrêmement satisfaits de ce livre. □ IMCERA avait une idée générale du design de ce rapport et le budget a été établi en fonction de cette idée. Tout au long de la conception et de la réalisation, nous avons gardé un œil attentif sur le budget tout en maintenant le haut niveau de qualité que l'IMCERA attendait. □ En général, nous avons constaté dans l'industrie que les clients sont devenus un peu plus conservateurs en raison de la récession économique. Cependant, nos clients de longue date continuent à attacher une grande importance à la qualité de la communication de l'entreprise, peut-être même plus depuis le choc économique. □ La typographie du rapport annuel 1990 de l'IMCERA a été fournie par une imprimerie extérieure. De plus en plus néanmoins, nous réalisons notre propre typographie au sein de l'agence, sur ordinateur Macintosh.

[PAT SAMATA]

SAMATA ASSOCIATES DESIGN CONSULTANTS: 101 SOUTH FIRST STREET, DUNDEE, ILLINOIS 60118 708.428.8600

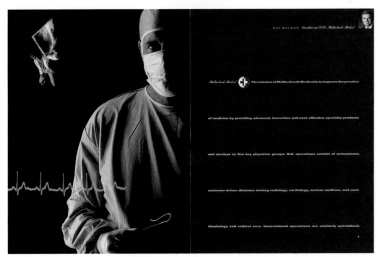

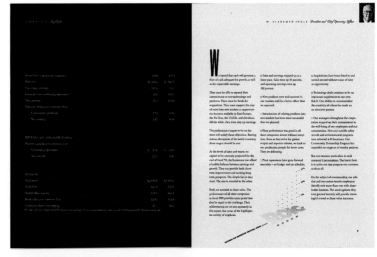

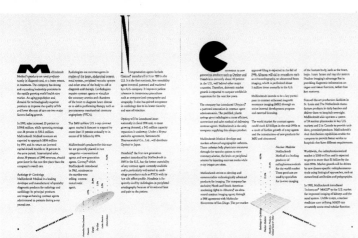

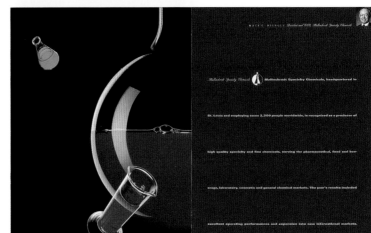

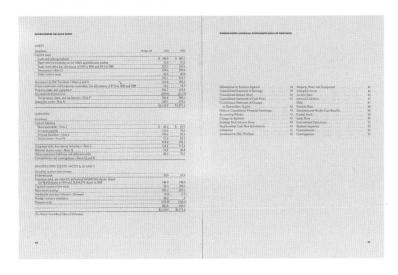

CLIENT: IMCERA GROUP, INC. ■ DESIGN FIRM: SAMATA ASSOCIATES ■ ART DIRECTOR: PAT SAMATA ■ DESIGNERS: GREG AND PAT SAMATA ■ PHOTOGRAPHER: MARK JOSEPH ■ ILLUSTRATOR: PAUL THOMPSON ■ PRODUCTION MANAGER: ANN TESON ■ TYPOGRAPHER: TYPOGRAPHIC RESOURCE ■ PAPER SELECTION: REFLECTIONS, CARNIVAL GROOVE ■ PAPER MANUFACTURERS: CONSOLIDATED, CHAMPION ■ PRINTER: GEORGE RICE & SONS ■ NUMBER OF PAGES: 60 ■ TYPE SELECTION: GARAMOND, BETHOLD SCRIPT, UNIVERS 85 ■

EG&G

ANNUAL REPORT

1990

We continue to explore the ever-emerging opportunities

offered a company with the diverse capability and capacity

that EG&G possesses. We continue to explore the ever-emerg-

ing opportunities offered a company with the diverse capabili-

ty and capacity that EG&G possesses. We continue to explore

the ever-emerging opportunities offered a company with the

diverse capability and capacity that EG&G possesses. We con-

EG&G

▲ The EG&G Annual Report sought to entice new investors by simply presenting what we do, enabling them to embrace the various pieces of our business and assisting them in understanding our corporate strategy as well as our future potential. As a communications tool for our employees, it sought to inventory our various business involvements and serve as a reminder of the "gee whiz" activities in which we engage. □ Under the direction of our designer, Harold Burch at Pentagram Design Services, Inc., we targeted our story and successfully communicated tangible, everyday applications for our very sophisticated technology and services in a very attractive manner. This was accomplished through the use of large photos—both color and black-and-white—informational copy blocks, and color diagrams of processes in which we are involved. With this combination we were able to grab the attention of all audiences. □ Professional investor interest has increased both in the dollar size of investments and the number of inquiries for further information on our ever-growing, changing business. Were we successful? Very.

■ Der Jahresbericht von EG&G sollte durch eine klare, vereinfachte Darstellung unserer Aktivitäten das Interesse neuer Investoren wecken. Dadurch konnten sie unsere diversen Geschäftsbereiche erfassen, unsere Firmenstrategie verstehen und unser Potential erkennen. Als Kommunikationsmittel für unsere Angestellten gab der Jahresbericht Auskunft über unsere verschiedenen Geschäftsverbindungen und erinnerte an die technologisch ausgeklügelten Produkte, die wir herstellen. □ Unter der Leitung von Harold Burch, unserem Designer von Pentagram, schnitten wir unsere Geschichte auf ein Zielpublikum zu und vermittelten vorstellbare, alltägliche Anwendungen für unsere hochentwickelte Technik und unsere Dienstleistungen auf attraktive Art und Weise. Wir erreichten dies durch die Verwendung grosser Photographien, von Informationsblöcken und Farbdiagrammen von Prozessen, in welchen wir engagiert sind. Mit dieser Kombination konnten wir ein sehr breitgefächertes Publikum erreichen. □ Das gestiegene Interesse professioneller Investoren zeigte sich im Investitionsumfang wie auch in der Nachfrage nach zusätzlichen Informationen über unser Unternehmen. Ob wir erfolgreich waren? Sehr sogar.

● Le rapport annuel EG&G cherchait à attirer de nouveaux investisseurs en leur expliquant ce que nous faisions, leur permettant ainsi de saisir la variété de nos activités et de comprendre notre stratégie d'entreprise et notre potentiel de développement. Comme outil de communication auprès de notre personnel, il cherchait à dresser l'inventaire de nos multiples participations commerciales et devait répertorier les activités «de pointe» dans lesquelles nous nous sommes engagés. □ Sous la direction de Harold Burch, le designer de Pentagram, nous avons conçu une histoire pouvant toucher notre public et nous avons su donner une information attrayante sur les applications quotidiennes de notre technologie et de nos services ultra-sophistiqués. Nous avons pu le faire en utilisant de grandes photos, des blocs typographiques fort instructifs et des diagrammes en couleurs des processus dans lesquels nous étions impliqués. Nous avons ainsi été en mesure d'attirer l'attention d'un vaste public. □ L'intérêt des investisseurs professionnels s'est accru si l'on considère le montant des sommes investies et le nombre de nouvelles enquêtes menées pour obtenir de plus amples renseignements sur notre entreprise. Un succès? Un grand succès.

[DEBORAH S. LORENZ]

EG&G INC.: 45 WILLIAM STREET, WELLESLEY, MASSACHUSETTS 02181-40878 617.237.5100

PENTAGRAM DESIGN SERVICES, INC.

▲ EG&G is primarily known as a hi-tech scientific company, encompassing ninety-four divisions. The company is responsible for a variety of services and products that directly or indirectly touch our lives. They produce the x-ray system used in airports, train soldiers in the use of chemical weapons protective clothing, and are responsible for the security and specialized fueling of the space shuttle. □ Our objective was to simplify the perception of EG&G and show its relevance to the average person. Pentagram developed a copy strategy that included several layers of information in addition to the operational text. We added an A to Z copy block theme that added a simplified overview of the company. We also generated diagrammatic illustrations of the more complex issues EG&G faces, and added caption blocks that became an integral part of the photo spreads. This new structure enhanced readability on many levels. □ To illustrate the diversity in the company, we employed two photographers with distinctly different styles. We contrasted two-dimensional, segmented color photographs with black-and-white shots using a great deal of depth; our anxiety level was high but the effect was visually stunning and most effective. □ The most satisfying comment came from EG&G Chairman John Kucharski, who said, that he had received compliments from many employees who stated that they had read the annual report and now fully understood their company.

■ EG&G ist hauptsächlich als High-Tech-Firma bekannt. Sie hat 94 Bereiche und zeichnet verantwortlich für ein breites Spektrum von Dienstleistungen und Produkten, die unser Leben direkt oder indirekt beeinflussen. EG&G stellt zum Beispiel Röntgensysteme für Flughäfen her, bildet Soldaten im Gebrauch von Schutzkleidung gegen Chemiekontamination aus und ist verantwortlich für die Sicherheit und die spezielle Betankung des Space Shuttle. □ Unser Ziel war es, das Bild von EG&G in der Öffentlichkeit zu vereinfachen und die Relevanz der Firma dem Durchschnittsbürger zu zeigen. Pentagram entwickelte eine Skriptstrategie, die mehrere zusätzliche Informationsebenen zum Text umfasst. □ Wir fügten ein in Blöcke aufgeteiltes Skriptthema von A bis Z hinzu, das eine vereinfachte Übersicht über die Firma erlaubt. Wir machten auch diagrammartige Illustrationen zu komplexeren Themen, in denen EG&G engagiert ist, und fügten Bildlegenden hinzu, die zu einem integralen Teil des Photobereichs wurden. Diese neue Struktur verbesserte auf vielen Ebenen die Lesbarkeit. □ Um die Vielseitigkeit innerhalb der Firma darzustellen, beschäftigten wir zwei Photographen, deren Stile sich grundsätzlich unterscheiden. Wir kontrastierten zweidimensional wirkende, fragmentartige Farbaufnahmen mit Schwarzweissphotos mit viel Tiefe. Zuerst hatten wir grosse Zweifel, doch der visuelle Effekt war schliesslich umwerfend. □ Der befriedigendste Kommentar stammt von John Kucharski, dem EG&G-Vorsitzenden: Er habe von vielen Mitarbeitern Komplimente erhalten, die den Bericht gelesen und ihm erklärt hatten, sie verstünden nun die Firma viel besser.

● EG&G, qui comprend 94 branches d'activité, est surtout réputée comme entreprise de pointe dans le secteur scientifique. Une quantité de services et de produits qui, directement ou indirectement, sont liés à notre vie quotidienne, sont du ressort de cette société. EG&G produit par exemple les systèmes de rayons X utilisés dans les aéroports; c'est elle qui entraîne les militaires qui expérimentent les vêtements de protection contre les armes chimiques; elle est par ailleurs responsable de la sécurité et du ravitaillement en carburant de la navette spatiale. □ Notre objectif était de nous adresser au lecteur moyen, en simplifiant la perception du profil de l'EG&G. Pentagram a élaboré un message comportant plusieurs niveaux d'informations. Nous avons également ajouté un bloc typo suivant une énumération «de A à Z», qui donne une vision simple de cette société. □ Nous avons aussi créé des diagrammes pour illustrer les questions les plus complexes et inséré des légendes qui sont devenues une part intégrante des doubles pages photographiques. □ Pour illustrer la polyvalence de cette société, nous avons employé deux photographes ayant des styles tout à fait différents. Les photos en couleurs fragmentées, bidimensionnelles, contrastent avec les photos en noir et blanc d'une grande profondeur. Nous étions assez inquiets au départ, mais l'effet est étonnant du point de vue visuel. □ Le commentaire le plus satisfaisant est venu du président de l'EG&G, John Kucharski, qui a déclaré qu'il avait reçu des compliments de nombreux collaborateurs: ces derniers lui ont assuré avoir lu le rapport annuel et avoir enfin complètement compris le fonctionnement de la firme.

[HAROLD BURCH]

PENTAGRAM DESIGN SERVICES, INC.: 212 FIFTH AVENUE, NEW YORK, NEW YORK 10010 212.683.7000

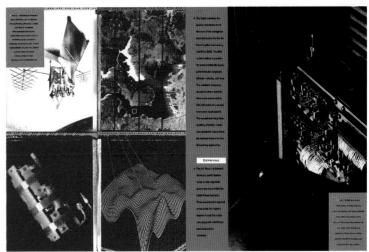

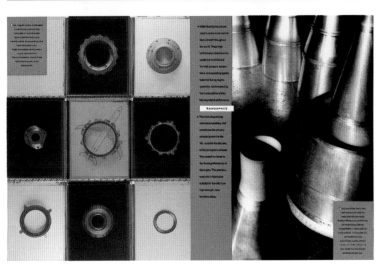

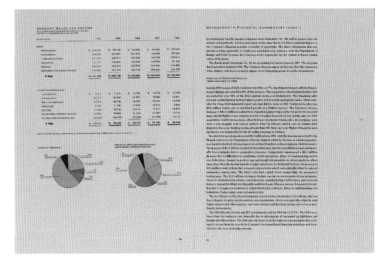

CLIENT: EG & G, INC. ■ DESIGN FIRM: PENTAGRAM ■ ART DIRECTORS: HAROLD BURCH, PETER HARRISON ■ DESIGNER: HAROLD BURCH ■
PHOTOGRAPHERS: BURTON PRITZKER, SCOTT MORGAN ■ ILLUSTRATOR: DAVID BALL ■ TYPOGRAPHER: CROMWELL ■ PAPER SELECTION:
QUINTESSENCE ■ PRINTER: COLORGRAPHICS L.A. ■ NUMBER OF PAGES: 60 PLUS COVER ■ TYPE SELECTION: TRUMP, UNIVERS, COPPERPLATE ■

Coherent 1990 annual report: twenty-five years of innovation

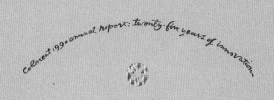

COHERENT

. . . .

▲ The primary audiences for our annual report are shareholders and potential investors; its secondary audiences are our employees and customers. □ The report stresses our long-term presence (25 years) in the laser industry in a leadership position with global strengths in delivering laser performance to all markets worldwide. □ Tolleson Design submitted one comprehensive composition. No modifications were deemed necessary, thereby demonstrating the ongoing relationship that has developed between client and designer. The report received accolades from all of our audiences.

. . . .

■ Das primäre Zielpublikum unseres Jahresberichtes sind Aktionäre und potentielle Investoren; das sekundäre Zielpublikum sind unsere Angestellten und Kunden. □ Im Jahresbericht wird unsere 25jährige Firmengeschichte als eines der führenden Unternehmen in der Lasertechnik mit Kunden in aller Welt hervorgehoben. □ Tolleson Design legte ein umfassendes Konzept vor, das ohne Änderungen akzeptiert werden konnte – ein Beweis für die ausgezeichnete Beziehung, die sich zwischen uns und dem Designer entwickelt hat. Der Bericht wurde von allen Seiten gelobt.

. . . .

● Notre rapport annuel s'adresse tout d'abord à nos actionnaires et investisseurs potentiels; le second public est constitué de nos employés et de nos clients. □ Le rapport met l'accent sur notre position de leader depuis 25 ans dans le secteur de l'industrie du laser et nos efforts pour distribuer cette technique sur les marchés du monde entier. □ Tolleson Design nous a soumis un projet global. Aucune modification ultérieure ne fut nécessaire, ce qui prouve l'entente qui s'est établie entre le client et le designer. Le rapport a reçu un écho favorable de la part de nos différents publics.

[EDWINA DERAUSSE]

COHERENT: 3210 PORTER DRIVE, P.O. BOX 10042 PALO ALTO, CALIFORNIA 94303 415.493.2111

TOLLESON DESIGN

▲ The direction and concept for the Coherent Annual Report was generated at Tolleson Design. Our understanding of Coherent's technology evolved from a longstanding relationship with the client, contributing to the ease with which the direction was accepted. It is with the help of this relationship that the report was an unequivocal success, as it met all goals set by Coherent. ☐ In terms of money, the budget parameters were given up front so there was no need for negotiation. However, because of the current weak economic conditions, there have been slimmer budgets in recent months. This is resulting in a number of cost-effective approaches that we implement in producing an annual report. Also in these times, computer-generated typesetting helps a great deal in offsetting these rising costs.

■ Tolleson Design entwickelte Stil und Konzept des Coherent-Jahresberichtes. Unsere Kenntnisse über die Technologie dieser Firma konnten wir während der langjährigen Beziehung zu diesem Kunden vertiefen, was dazu beitrug, dass unser Vorschlag mühelos akzeptiert wurde. Dank dieser langjährigen Zusammenarbeit wurde der Bericht zu einem eindeutigen Erfolg. ☐ Was die finanzielle Seite angeht, so wurde der Budgetrahmen zu Beginn festgesetzt und musste nicht ausgehandelt werden. Wegen der gegenwärtigen wirtschaftlichen Lage hatten wir in den vergangenen Monaten allgemein niedrigere Budgets als zuvor. Wir griffen deshalb zu kostensparenden Massnahmen in der Produktion. Die Satzerstellung mit Hilfe des Computers hilft z.B. eine Menge Kosten sparen.

● C'est Tolleson Design qui a dirigé et élaboré le concept du rapport annuel de Coherent. Nos relations de longue date avec le client nous ont permis d'accroître nos connaissances quant à la technologie de cette entreprise. Cela a également rendu l'acception du projet plus facile. C'est en partie à cause de ces bons contacts que le rapport a été un succès sans conteste, car il atteignait tous les objectifs de Coherent. ☐ Le budget fut établi dès le départ, si bien qu'il ne fut pas nécessaire de négocier. Vu les conditions économiques, les budgets sont plus maigres ces derniers mois. Il nous faut adopter un certain nombre de mesures qui permettent de produire un rapport annuel de manière plus économique. Heureusement, en réalisant la typo sur ordinateur, on réussit à compenser ces restrictions.

[STEVE TOLLESON]

TOLLESON DESIGN: 444 SPEAR STREET, SUITE 204, SAN FRANSISCO, CALIFORNIA 94105 415.626.7796

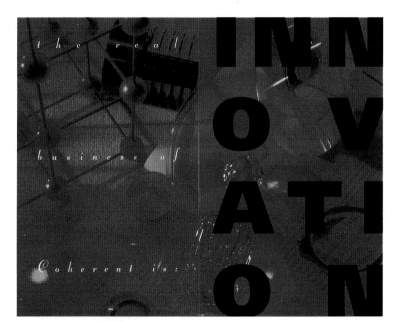

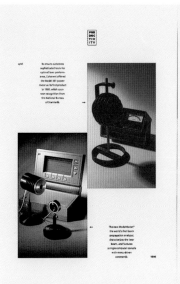

The laser industry's rapid technological changes are a constant challenge, and Coherent responds by regularly raising performance standards through design innovation. Since its founding in 1966, Coherent has scored an impressive list of "firsts" beginning with the earliest commercial high-power CO_2 laser through the first Holmium laser approved for medical procedures. New products, frequently patentable, are the Company's life blood, which it supports with product development teams in the U.S. and Europe who work directly with customers to improve existing products and develop new ones. As a result, new products released in the last three years comprise 55 percent of Coherent's 1990 revenues.

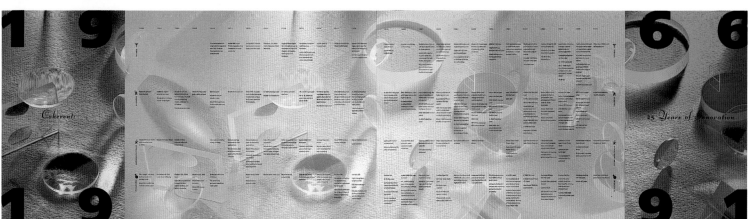

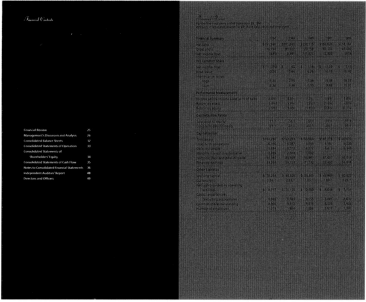

CLIENT: COHERENT ■ DESIGN FIRM: TOLLESON DESIGN ■ ART DIRECTOR: STEVE TOLLESON ■ DESIGNERS: STEVE TOLLESON, BOB AUFULDISH ■ PHOTOGRAPHER: HENRIK KAM ■ WRITER: LINDSAY BEAMAN ■ TYPOGRAPHER: SPARTAN TYPOGRAPHERS ■ PAPER SELECTION: SIMPSON STAR-WHITE VICKSBURG, S.D. WARREN WARD LUSTRO DULL ■ NUMBER OF PAGES: 49 ■ TYPE SELECTION: FRUTIGER, BERNHARD SCHÖNSCHRIFT ■

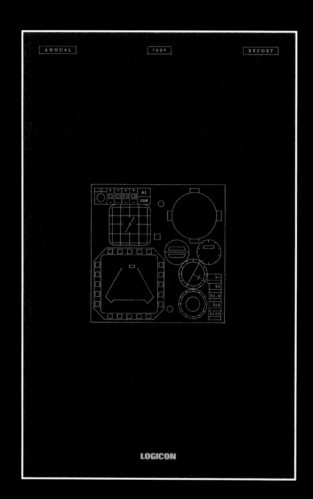

LOGICON

LOGICON

. . . .

▲ A primary objective of Logicon's annual report is to project an image of a high technology company—one totally committed to quality—involved in some of our nation's most advanced civil and defense programs. The primary audience for our report is, of course, stockholders—both institutional and individual. We also use it as a tool to interest prospective stockholders, recruit professional employees, and, in general, to gather marketing applications. A good team effort and excellent communication involving the design firm and senior company management assured the success of this project and its acceptance by the company's board of directors and its intended audiences.

. . . .

■ Hauptziel des Logicon Jahresberichtes ist, das Bild einer High-Tech-Firma zu vermitteln – einer Firma, die sich gänzlich der Qualität verschrieben hat und die in einige der modernsten Programme im Zivil- und Verteidigungsbereich der USA involviert ist. Primäres Zielpublikum sind unsere privaten und institutionellen Aktionäre. Wir brauchen den Jahresbericht aber auch als Mittel, um das Interesse potentieller Aktionäre zu wecken, qualifizierte Angestellte zu rekrutieren und als allgemeines Marketinginstrument. Gute Teamleistungen und ausgezeichnete Kommunikation zwischen der Designfirma und dem Management der Auftragsfirma sicherten den Erfolg des Projekts sowie dessen Unterstützung durch die Geschäftsleitung und ein positives Echo des Zielpublikums.

. . . .

● L'objectif principal du rapport annuel de Logicon est avant tout de donner l'image d'une entreprise de haute technologie – s'engageant à fond pour une qualité irréprochable et impliquée dans quelques-uns des programmes civils et de défense les plus avancés des Etats-Unis. Nous nous adressons d'abord bien entendu à notre public d'actionnaires, institutionnels ou privés. Nous utilisons également ce rapport comme un moyen d'attirer l'attention des actionnaires éventuels, de recruter du personnel qualifié et, en général, comme instrument de marketing. Un bon effort d'équipe et une communication excellente entre la firme de design et la direction de l'entreprise ont assuré le succès de ce projet et sa réception favorable de la part du conseil d'administration ainsi que du public visé.

[J.R. WOODHULL]

LOGICON, INC.: 3701 SKYPARK DRIVE, TORRANCE, CA. 90505-4797 213.373.0220

RUNYAN HINSCHE ASSOCIATES

▲ Logicon had no specific conceptual approach in mind when the annual report project was initiated. We discussed a number of ideas and I developed approximately three possible visual approaches. Through a series of informal meetings we developed the illustrative approach that was finally used. □ The project was very easy to sell, in fact, it more or less evolved into existence. I think everyone felt from the onset that it was the strongest visual approach. □ No specific budget requirements were discussed but it was understood that the whole project would be within the normal constraints and produced for the same amount of money as last year's annual report. In the end, the client was very pleased with the result, as all aspects of the project went smoothly including the printing and production.

■ Logicon hatte keine speziellen konzeptuellen Vorstellungen für den Jahresbericht. Wir diskutierten mehrere Ideen und entwickelten drei mögliche visuelle Lösungen. In einer Reihe informeller Besprechungen kamen wir auf die endgültige Version der Illustrationen. □ Da der Vorschlag sich mehr oder weniger von selbst entwickelte, konnte er mühelos durchgesetzt werden. Ich glaube, jeder spürte, dass dies die stärkste visuelle Lösung war. □ Das Budget war kein Diskussionsthema, aber es war klar, dass das gesamte Projekt in einem vernünftigen Rahmen bleiben und die Produktionskosten denen des letztjährigen Berichtes entsprechen müssten. Der Kunde war mit dem Resultat sehr zufrieden, da das Projekt in allen Phasen, einschliesslich der Druckphase, reibungslos ablief.

● Logicon n'avait pas de concept spécifique en tête au moment d'aborder ce rapport annuel. Nous avons discuté d'un grand nombre d'idées et j'ai développé trois concepts visuels. Au cours d'une série de réunions, nous avons mis au point une approche basée sur l'illustration, qui a été finalement adoptée. □ Le projet a été facile à vendre puisqu'il avait été élaboré peu à peu. Je crois que dès le début, tout le monde a réalisé que c'était l'approche visuelle la plus forte. □ Aucune exigence particulière n'avait été posée en matière de budget, mais il était clair que le projet devrait se faire dans le cadre des limites habituelles et être produit pour le même prix que celui de l'année passée. Le client était très content du résultat, vu que tous les aspects du projet tenaient compte de l'impression.

[JIM BERTÉ]

RUNYAN HINSCHE ASSOCIATES: 4223 GLENCOE AVENUE, SUITE A223

MARINA DEL REY, CALIFORNIA 90902 213.823.0975

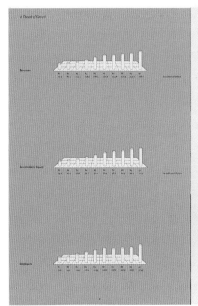

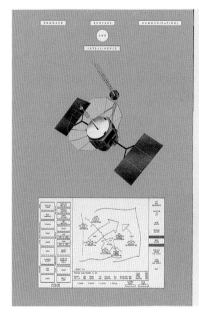

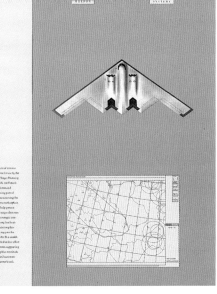

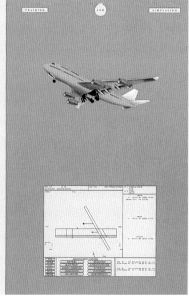

CLIENT: LOGICON, INC. ■ DESIGN FIRM: RUNYAN HINSCHE ASSOCIATES ■ ART DIRECTOR: JIM BERTÉ DESIGNER: JIM BERTÉ ■ ILLUSTRATOR: PAUL BICE, JR. ■ WRITER: LOGICON, INC. ■ PRODUCTION MANAGER: PATTY KARASAWA ■ TYPOGRAPHER: COMPOSITION TYPE ■ PAPER SELECTION: SIMPSON FILARE, POTLATCH KARMA MATTE ■ PRINTER: LITHOGRAPHIX ■ NUMBER OF PAGES: 28 ■ TRIM SIZE: 7 x 11 INCHES ■ TYPE SELECTION: GARAMOND NO. 3 ■

Report To The Community

THE CARING PROGRAM

THE CARING PROGRAM

▲ *The Caring Program—A Report to the Community*, was specifically created for financial donors, both prior and first time; both corporate and private. Secondarily, it was designed as an explicative piece to be used with the media, community agencies, program replicators, and child advocates. The report's primary message was to summarize the history and growth of The Caring Program and to state the case for its continued support. The report has been well received as a vehicle for communicating about our program. The integration of design elements and narrative content have made the report a visual masterpiece, and pleasurable for all audiences. □ The outstanding working relationship I experienced with the report designers, Rutka Weadock, contributed significantly to this excellent outcome. The design team was very receptive to my conceptual ideas and was able to express my preferences in their design approach. They were open to critical comment and sensitive to my need to change and modify. Their level of enthusiasm for the job was clear throughout the process and was conveyed in the finished product.

■ *The Caring Program – A Report to the Community* wurde speziell und zum erstenmal für private und institutionelle Spender zusammengestellt. Zudem wurde der Bericht auch als Dokumentation gestaltet, und zwar für Medien, städtische Abteilungen, Programm-Mitarbeiter und Kinder- und Jugendanwälte. Die Absicht des Berichtes war, die Geschichte und das Wachstum von The Caring Program zusammenzufassen und die Gründe für weitere Unterstützung darzulegen. Der Bericht fand ein positives Echo als Dokumentation unseres Programms. Durch die Integration von Designelementen und erzählenden Textpassagen wurde der Bericht für alle Leser zu einer interessanten Lektüre. □ Die ausgezeichnete Arbeitsbeziehung, die ich mit dem Designer Rutka Weadock hatte, trug wesentlich zum exzellenten Resultat des Berichtes bei. Das Designteam zeigte sich sehr offen gegenüber meinen konzeptuellen Ideen und konnte meine Präferenzen in ihrem Design ausdrücken. Die Designer zeigten sich offen für kritische Äusserungen und verständnisvoll für die von mir gewünschten Änderungen. Ihr Enthusiasmus für das Projekt zeigte sich während des ganzen Produktionsprozesses und schlug sich deutlich im Endprodukt nieder.

● «The Caring Program – Un rapport pour la communauté» a été spécialement créé à l'intention des anciens et des nouveaux donateurs, institutionnels ou privés, de notre institution. Deuxièmement, il a été conçu comme un document d'information pouvant être distribué aux médias, aux municipalités, à ceux qui appliquent ce programme et aux avocats d'enfants ou d'adolescents. Ce rapport avait pour principal objectif de résumer l'histoire et le développement de The Caring Program et d'exposer les arguments en faveur d'un soutien financier constant. Le rapport a été bien reçu en tant que véhicule d'information de notre programme. L'association des éléments graphiques et du texte a donné à ce rapport un aspect agréable à la lecture. □ Les relations de travail remarquables que j'ai eues avec le studio de design Rutka Weadock ont contribué de manière significative à ce résultat excellent. L'équipe des designers s'est montrée très réceptive à mes conceptions et ils ont été capables d'exprimer mes préférences dans leur design. Ils étaient très ouverts à la critique et sensibles à mes propositions de modifications. Ils ont manifesté leur enthousiasme tout au cours du processus d'élaboration et cela se ressent dans le produit fini.

[BONNIE B. KATZ]

THE CARING PROGRAM: 10455 MILL RUN CIRCLE, OWINGS MILLS, MARYLAND 21117 301.998.5823

RUTKA WEADOCK DESIGN

▲ The Caring Program Annual Report was a first-time report for this non profit subsidiary of Blue Cross & Blue Shield of Maryland. Our client gave us a directive to produce a report that would tell the story of the first three years of the program and could also be used as a fund-raising piece. With that information and a limited budget, we proceeded to develop a format and concept that could be executed economically. Our primary goal, however, was to create a piece that would convey the playful quality of children without looking frivolous. We integrated real photos with fanciful illustrations to give the piece a storybook feel. □ The client responded positively to our approach, was open to our ideas, worked closely with us to make the copy work with the design, and provided valuable insights that kept the report on target. □ We have experienced tighter budgets, financially, over the last year, especially on annual reports. This particular budget was the primary consideration in determining size, number of pages, and printing techniques of the report. We gang-separated the illustrations to save money, and it was necessary to carefully coordinate the photography and illustration so the printer could strip the two pieces of art together in a conventional fashion. □ The Caring Program Annual Report was typeset on our Macintosh computer systems.

● Der Jahresbericht für The Caring Program war der erste Bericht dieser Non-Profit-Tochter des Blue Cross & Blue Shield of Maryland. Wir erhielten den Auftrag, einen Bericht zu erstellen, der über die ersten drei Jahre des Programms informiert, und der auch als Instrument bei der Beschaffung von Spenden eingesetzt werden könnte. Auf der Basis dieser Vorgaben und eines begrenzten Budgets begannen wir mit der Entwicklung eines Gesamtkonzepts, das dem gewünschten Rahmen entsprach. Unser Hauptziel war die Darstellung des kindlich Spielerischen, ohne Frivolität. Wir kombinierten Photos mit phantasievollen Illustrationen, um dem Bericht etwas von einem Kinderbuch zu geben. □ Unser Kunde reagierte sehr positiv auf unseren Vorschlag, war offen für Ideen und arbeitete eng mit uns zusammen, um Text und Design in Einklang zu bringen. Zudem erhielten wir von ihm wertvolle Informationen, die uns erlaubten, den Bericht seiner Bestimmung entsprechend zu gestalten. □ Wir mussten im vergangenen Jahr mit noch knapperen Budgets zurechtkommen, besonders bei Jahresberichten. Das vorhandene Budget bestimmte das Format des Berichtes, die Seitenanzahl und Drucktechnik. Um Geld zu sparen, liessen wir die Lithos gruppenweise herstellen. Photos und Illustrationen mussten sorgfältig koordiniert werden, damit der Drucker beides zusammen montieren konnte. □ Der Schriftsatz wurde mit unseren Mactinosh-Computern erstellt.

● Il s'agissait du premier rapport annuel de The Caring Program, une filiale à but non lucratif des associations Blue Cross & Blue Shield of Maryland. Notre client nous avait donné pour directive de produire un rapport qui retrace l'histoire des trois premières années de ce programme, et qui puisse aussi être utilisé pour recueillir des fonds. Disposant d'un budget limité, nous avons choisi un format en fonction et élaboré un concept qui puisse être exécuté de manière économique. Mais notre premier objectif était de créer un document qui exprime l'espièglerie des enfants, sans pour autant tomber dans le frivole. Nous avons mélangé des photos avec des illustrations pleines de fantaisie afin de donner au rapport l'allure d'un livre d'histoires. □ Le client a réagi très positivement à notre proposition, il était ouvert à nos idées et il a travaillé étroitement avec nous pour que le texte aille avec le design; il nous a également donné des informations appréciables qui nous ont permis de ne pas perdre de vue l'objectif de ce rapport. □ Nous avons fait l'expérience de budgets plus modestes au cours de l'année passée, surtout pour les rapports annuels. Le format de ce rapport, le nombre de pages et les techniques d'impression ont été déterminés à partir de ce budget précis. Les typons ont été réalisés tous en même temps par mesure d'économie. Il a été nécessaire de coordonner très soigneusement la photo et l'illustration afin que l'imprimeur puisse les assembler selon des procédés tout à fait conventionnels. □ Le rapport annuel a été entièrement réalisé sur le Macintosh de notre agence.

[JOAN WEADOCK]
RUTKA WEADOCK DESIGN: 1627 EAST BALTIMORE STREET, BALTIMORE, MARYLAND 21217 301.563.2100

The Caring Program is making a vital contribution to the well-being of Maryland's children. This specially designed health care program has made it possible for children who would normally go without needed medical services to grow up strong and healthy. On the following pages you will see how the program fills a critical need, and how the generous support of local corporations, foundations and individuals has made The Caring Program a success.

The future of our society depends largely on the capacity for today's children to take their places as tomorrow's leaders. Surely the need to assure that this generation of future *A Healthy Future* leaders has access to the health care services necessary to form the foundation of good health should be of great importance to all. Unfortunately, publicly funded programs like Medical Assistance can only reach a portion of the children in need. Nationally, there are 13 million children living in poverty, but government health programs only reach half of them. Throughout Maryland, there are approximately 100,000 children ages one through 18 whose families are living in poverty but who are ineligible for Medical Assistance. These are "gray area" children — the children of the "working poor." Because of their families' limited financial resources, they frequently do not visit the doctor for routine preventive and primary health care, missing vital immunizations and basic well-child care. In many instances, their acute childhood illnesses are left unattended and the only medical care they receive is episodic services in the hospital emergency room. Prescriptions for antibiotics remain unfilled because of the expense and children are vulnerable to illnesses that will influence their lives for years to come. The Caring Program was created as a private sector initiative to reach as many Central Maryland gray area chil-

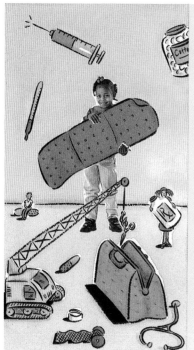

Children are referred to The Caring Program by a variety of community sources such as social workers, school nurses, and health department personnel. Children must meet certain eligibility criteria relating to age, family income, full-time student status and the lack of any other public or private health care coverage. *A Caring Response* Eligible children are then placed on a waiting list until fundraising proceeds are available to enroll them in the program. The cost to enroll a child in The Caring Program for a full year is $198, or $16.50 per month. These funds are made available through the efforts of the MBCBS Caring Foundation, the 501(c)3 fundraising arm of The Caring Program. In some instances, specific children are directly sponsored in the program by religious or community groups, relatives or friends. Children with financial sponsors who commit to a minimum 12 month sponsorship are able to access the program without experiencing the waiting list. Each month, as fundraising proceeds allow, a new group of children are enrolled in the program. Once enrolled, they receive complete instructions on how to locate a participating physician and what services are covered by the program. Since the program began in March, 1988, it has provided coverage for well-child care, immunizations, diagnostic services, sick visits and minor injury care as well as prescription drugs. Administration

MESSAGE FROM CARL J. SARDEGNA, CHAIRMAN AND CEO
BLUE CROSS AND BLUE SHIELD OF MARYLAND

Blue Cross and Blue Shield of Maryland is extremely proud of the contribution it has made to the well being of children in our community through The Caring Program. The need to have healthy youth who will lead our society into the future is of paramount importance to us all.

The Caring Program represents a perfect opportunity for BCBSM to leverage its expertise in the health services management arena while demonstrating its commitment to being a thoughtful corporate citizen.

The response of the community to this initiative has been heartening. We look forward to continued success in this effort to make every child a healthy child.

Carl J. Sardegna
Chairman and CEO
Blue Cross and Blue Shield of Maryland

Financial Report

UTILIZATION STATISTICS

	1988*	1989	1990
Covered services provided	1,012	2,689	3,913
Services per child	5.8	5.8	5.8
Average enrollment	176	488	624
Benefit expenses	$20,423	$49,615	$78,997
Covered services by category:			
Diagnostic	185	226	494
Immunizations	66	176	185
Sick/Accident visits	287	804	1,143
Well-child care	112	183	263
Prescriptions	361	1,162	1,828

*March 1 through December 31, 1988

CARING PROGRAM ENROLLMENT*

1988	1989	1990
363	676	1,219

*As of 12/31 for each year

SOURCE OF REFERRALS BY JURISDICTION

Baltimore City	50%
Baltimore County	34%
Howard County	6%
Anne Arundel County	4%
Harford County	3%
Carroll County	3%

There are an average of 1.43 children per family enrolled.

CHILDREN BY RACE

Black	48%
White	48%
Hispanic	2%
Asian	1%
Other	1%

CLIENT: THE CARING PROGRAM ■ DESIGN FIRM: RUTKA WEADOCK DESIGN ■ ART DIRECTOR: ANTHONY RUTKA ■ DESIGNER: GEORGE MIMNAUGH ■ PHOTOGRAPHER: SUZIE FITZHUGH ■ ILLUSTRATOR: MARY LYNN BLASUTTA ■ WRITER: BONNIE B. KATZ ■ PAPER SELECTION: ESSE, DARK GRAY-BLUE, WHITE ■ PAPER MANUFACTURER: GILBERT ■ PRINTER: WESTLAND PRINTERS ■ NUMBER OF PAGES: 16 PLUS COVER ■ TYPE SELECTION: BERNHARD ■

NORCEN

ANNUAL

REPORT

1 9 8 9

NORCEN

. . . .

▲ Norcen's annual report is targeted primarily at its shareholders and at Canadian and American financial analysts. It also has a lesser following among competitors and North American buy-side institutional investors. To improve our reach into this varied and sophisticated audience, we are faced with the challenge of providing a report different from those of other petroleum companies. □ For the past two years, we have used a photo essay in the middle of the report, which highlights some of the more interesting facets of the oil and gas industry. In 1990 the essay centered around the skills, experience, and talent needed to be successful in the search for oil and gas. Subsequent evaluation verifies that this section, along with the overall design of the book, did accomplish the objectives of having our annual report stand out from the crowd. □ Of course a successful design results from the collaboration between client, designer, and printer, which in this case was very effective. Good design can only be accomplished through an open and stimulating rapport among all participants in the production process. This was, indeed, the case for Norcen, Pentagram, and MacDonald Printing for the 1990 Norcen Annual Report.

. . . .

■ Norcens Jahresbericht richtet sich in erster Linie an Aktionäre und an kanadische und amerikanische Finanzanalysten. Unsere Konkurrenz und interessierte institutionelle Anleger in Nordamerika gehören zur sekundären Zielgruppe. Um dieses sehr unterschiedliche und sehr anspruchsvolle Publikum besser erreichen zu können, sahen wir uns mit der Aufgabe konfrontiert, einen Jahresbericht vorzulegen, der sich eindeutig von jenen anderer Erdölgesellschaften abhebt. □ In den vergangenen zwei Jahren haben wir dies mit einem Photo-Essay erreicht, der in der Mitte des Berichts eingefügt wurde und eine Auswahl von interessanten Aspekten der Öl- und Gasindustrie hervorhob. 1990 handelte der Photo-Essay vom Können, von der Erfahrung und vom Talent, Voraussetzungen, um bei der Suche nach Öl und Gas erfolgreich zu sein. Nachträgliche Evaluationen bewiesen, dass dieses Segment, zusammen mit dem Gesamtdesign des Berichts, tatsächlich dazu beitrug, unseren Jahresbericht von der Masse abzuheben. □ Natürlich beruht ein erfolgreiches Design auf der engen Zusammenarbeit zwischen dem Kunden, Designer und Drucker. In diesem Fall erwies sie sich als äusserst effizient. Gutes Design kann nur erreicht werden durch ein offenes und stimulierendes Verhältnis zwischen allen, die am Entstehungsprozess beteiligt sind. Dies war tatsächlich der Fall bei der Zusammenarbeit zwischen Norcen, Pentagram Design und MacDonald Printing.

. . . .

● Le rapport annuel de Norcen est avant tout destiné aux actionnaires et aux analystes financiers canadiens et américains. Il a aussi des adeptes parmi les concurrents et les investisseurs institutionnels d'Amérique du Nord. Pour améliorer notre audience auprès de ces publics variés et exigeants, nous avons dû fournir un document différent de ceux des autres compagnies pétrolières. □ Les deux dernières années, nous avions inséré au milieu du rapport un reportage photographique qui mettait en lumière quelques-unes des facettes les plus intéressantes de l'industrie du pétrole et du gaz. En 1990, ce reportage tournait autour des compétences, de l'expérience et du talent nécessaires si l'on veut connaître le succès dans la prospection de pétrole et de gaz. Une enquête ultérieure a démontré que cette partie du rapport, ainsi que le design global du livre, ont rempli leur objectif: notre rapport annuel se distinguait effectivement du lot. □ Bien sûr, un design réussi résulte d'une collaboration entre le client, le designer et l'imprimeur; dans le cas précis, elle fut très efficace. Un bon design ne peut être réalisé qu'au travers d'une relation de confiance, une émulation entre tous les participants au cours du processus de production. C'était vraiment le cas avec Norcen, Pentagram Design et MacDonald Printing pour le rapport annuel 1990.

[KEITH J. WILSON]

NORCEN, NORCEN TOWER: 715 FIFTH AVENUE SOTHWEST, CALGARY, ALBERTA, CANADA T2P 2X7 403.231.0111

. . . .

▲ Norcen's 1990 Annual Report was second in a series of reports on Canada's energy resource industry from the perspective of one of its major players. □ The overall structure of the report, including a photo essay, was established in the previous year's report. Our major responsibility was to take an outstanding report and make it more so. The photographic concept, developed between Norcen and our office, expressed the "cerebral" side of the oil business—the technicians, geologists, analysts, and engineers who rarely see an oil site. □ A series of computer-generated maps and diagrams helped explain the operational side of the business and served as a foil to Jeff Corwin's gutsy black-and-white photos. □ As usual a budget was set up after the parameters of the report were defined. □ Although the computer is an integral part of our design and production capabilities, we continue to produce most of our annual reports with outside typographers. We feel that projects of this scale and complexity, overall typographic quality, plus 'round-the-clock service and proofreading, make typographers an essential cog in creating reports.

. . . .

■ Der Norcen-Jahresbericht 1990 war der zweite Bericht in einer Serie über die Energierohstoff-Industrie Kanadas aus der Sicht eines der führenden Unternehmen. □ Die Gesamtstruktur des Berichts, der auch einen Photo-Essay beinhaltete, wurde bereits im Vorjahresbericht festgelegt. Unsere Aufgabe war es, einen hervorragenden Jahresbericht noch weiter zu optimieren. Das photographische Konzept, das in Zusammenarbeit zwischen Norcen und unserem Büro entwickelt wurde, bestand darin, die «intellektuelle» Seite der Ölindustrie zu betonen – die Techniker, Geologen, Analysten und Ingenieure, die kaum je eine Ölbohrstelle sehen. □ Eine Reihe von computergenerierten Karten und Diagrammen wurde eingesetzt, um die betriebliche Seite der Ölindustrie zu erklären. Sie dienten gleichzeitig als Gegensatz zu Jeff Corwins ausdrucksvollen Schwarzweissphotos. □ Wie üblich wurde das Budget festgelegt, nachdem das Grundkonzept feststand. □ Obwohl der Computer zu unserer Designarbeit und unseren Produktionseinrichtungen gehört, produzieren wir Jahresberichte nach wie vor mit Setzereien. Wir sind der Ansicht, dass bei Projekten dieser Grösse und Komplexität eine professionelle Setzerei aufgrund der Gesamtqualität des Schriftsatzes, des 24-Stunden-Service und des Korrekturlesens eine notwendige Komponente ist.

. . . .

● Le rapport annuel Norcen était le second d'une série de rapports sur l'industrie des ressources énergétiques du Canada, vues dans la perspective de l'un de ses principaux protagonistes. □ La structure générale, y compris un reportage photographique, avait été déterminée lors du précédent rapport. Nous devions donc faire de ce document remarquable une publication exceptionnelle. Le concept photographique élaboré en accord avec Norcen devait mettre l'accent sur le côté «intellectuel» de l'industrie pétrolière - les techniciens, les géologues, les analystes et les ingénieurs, que l'on voit rarement sur les sites pétrolifères. □ Une série de cartes et de diagrammes réalisés en P.A.O. ont permis d'expliquer le côté opérationnel de cette industrie. Elles mettaient également en valeur les superbes photos en noir et blanc de Jeff Corwin. □ Comme d'habitude, un budget avait été fixé une fois le concept défini. □ Bien que l'ordinateur fasse partie intégrante de notre design et de nos moyens de production, nous continuons à produire la plupart de nos rapports annuels avec l'aide de typographes extérieurs à l'agence. Nous pensons que pour des projets de cette ampleur et de cette complexité, les typographes sont irremplaçables, car ils garantissent une qualité irréprochable de la typographie, un service 24 h sur 24 et la correction des épreuves.

[KIT HINRICHS]

PENTAGRAM DESIGN, INC.: 620 DAVIS STREET, SAN FRANSISCO, CALIFORNIA 94111 415.981.6612

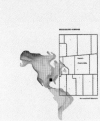

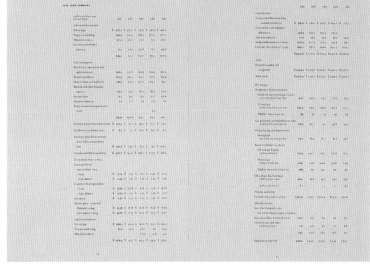

CLIENT: NORCEN ■ DESIGN FIRM: PENTAGRAM ■ ART DIRECTOR: KIT HINRICHS ■ DESIGNERS: KIT HINRICHS, PIPER MURAKAMI ■ PHOTOGRAPHER: JEFF CORWIN ■ ILLUSTRATORS: MAX SEABAUGH, HELENE MOORE ■ WRITER: DELPHINE HIRASUNA ■ PRODUCTION MANAGER: AMY CHAN ■ TYPOGRAPHER: SPARTAN TYPOGRAPHERS ■ PAPER SELECTION: QUINTESSENCE GLOSS, SIMPSON ARCHIVA, ESSENCE GLOSS ■ PAPER MANUFACTURERS: CONSOLIDATED, SIMPSON, POTLATCH ■ PRINTER: MACDONALD PRINTING ■ NUMBER OF PAGES: 78 ■ TYPE SELECTION: GARAMOND ■

CENTRE REINSURANCE

. . . .

▲ The target audience for Centre Reinsurance's Annual Report is first and foremost reinsurance brokers and their clients, who are the primary insurance companies. Of these, both the chief financial and executive officers are our main targets. ☐ In the field of reinsurance, we are creative, professional and the leader. This is exactly what we wanted conveyed in the report. With this as our primary function, we were successful in ways we never imagined. ☐ In terms of design, our relationship with the firm—WYD Design—is excellent. This is the second annual report they have worked on with us, and we feel that a good rapport is important, and manifests itself in the final product.

. . . .

■ Unser Jahresbericht richtet sich in erster Linie an Rückversicherungsagenten und ihre Kunden, die Versicherungsgesellschaften, wo wir vor allem die leitenden Angestellten im Finanzsektor und Management ansprechen wollen. ☐ Im Bereich der Rückversicherung sind wir kreativ, professionell und führend. Genau das sollte in unserem Bericht zum Ausdruck kommen. Der Bericht hat seine Funktion eindeutig erfolgreich erfüllt. ☐ Wir haben ein ausgezeichnetes Verhältnis zu dem Gestalter. Dies ist der zweite Jahresbericht, den wir gemeinsam produziert haben. Wir sind der Meinung, dass eine gute Zusammenarbeit wichtig ist und sich im Endprodukt niederschlägt.

. . . .

● Le public-cible de notre rapport annuel se compose avant tout des agents de change et de leurs clients, les compagnies d'assurances. Les responsables financiers et membres de la direction constituent notre public privilégié. ☐ Dans le domaine de la contre-assurance, nous sommes créatifs, de vrais professionnels, le leader de la branche. C'est exactement le message que le rapport devait transmettre. Ce rôle fondamental qui est le nôtre nous a apporté le succès. ☐ Nous avons eu d'excellentes relations avec l'agence. C'est le second rapport qu'ils ont élaboré pour nous. Nous pensons qu'un bon rapport est quelque chose d'important, et cela se manifeste dans le produit final.

[ANDREA HODSON]

CENTRE REINSURANCE: CUMBERLAND HOUSE, 1 VICTORIA STREET, HAMILTON HM HX BERMUDA 809.295.8501

WEISZ YANG DUNKELBERGER, INC.

· ·

▲ The concept of *The Changing Face of Reinsurance* is ours; we presented the idea to Centre Reinsurance with three other concepts that amplified the company's marketing strategy. □ The company treats us like a partner and involves us in its business. As a result, we receive a lot of information to direct and evaluate our work. We never had to *sell* one concept over another—in fact, *Changing Face* was probably the most challenging of the four concepts we presented. □ Upon completion, our client was very happy with the report. Although Centre Reinsurance is only three years old, it has become the talk of the reinsurance industry because of its innovative products and promotions. The annual report is the company's primary marketing medium and it effectively reinforces their creative position within this conservative industry. □ We began with a general budget range. Our estimate for *Changing Face* exceeded that range, but our client believed enough in the concept to shift money from his advertising budget to fund the difference. The book was then delivered within budget. □ Production-oriented clients are always looking to save a buck. Results-oriented clients are always looking for new ways to make one. Centre Reinsurance is a savvy, results-oriented client that puts more time and effort on how the report works as opposed to how much it costs.

· ·

■ Das Konzept *The Changing Face* (Das wechselnde Gesicht) stammt von uns. Wir legten diese Idee sowie drei weitere Konzepte, die die Marketingstrategie der Firma verstärken, der Centre Reinsurance vor. □ Die Firma behandelt uns wie Partner und involviert uns in ihre Aktivitäten. Resultat: Wir erhalten viele Informationen, die uns helfen, unserer Arbeit die richtige Richtung zu geben. Wir mussten unserem Kunden nie ein Konzept verkaufen – tatsächlich war wohl *The Changing Face* das anspruchsvollste der vier vorgelegten Konzepte. □ Unser Kunde war sehr zufrieden mit dem Bericht. Obwohl Centre Reinsurance erst seit drei Jahren existiert, ist es zum Gesprächsthema der Rückversicherungsindustrie geworden, und zwar wegen der innovativen Werbemittel. Der Jahresbericht ist das wichtigste Marketinginstrument der Firma, und er verstärkt effektvoll die kreative Position der Firma innerhalb dieser konservativen Industrie. □ Wir begannen mit einem allgemeinen Budgetrahmen. Unsere Kalkulationen für *The Changing Face* überschritten diesen Rahmen, doch war unser Kunde so von dem Konzept überzeugt, dass Geld für die Finanzierung der Differenz vom Werbebudget abgezweigt wurde. Dann wurde der Bericht budgetgerecht produziert. □ Produktionsorientierte Kunden versuchen immer, ein paar Dollars einzusparen; erfolgsorientierte Kunden suchen immer neue Wege, um ein paar Dollars zu verdienen. Centre Reinsurance ist ein erfolgsorientierter Kunde mit Köpfchen, für den der Erfolg des Berichts wichtiger ist als dessen Kosten.

· ·

● Le concept du rapport annuel, *The Changing Face of Reinsurance*, était notre idée; nous l'avons présentée à Centre Reinsurance avec trois autres concepts qui développaient la stratégie de marketing de cette compagnie d'assurances. □ Celle-ci nous a traité comme un partenaire et nous a fait participer à ses activités. Cela nous a permis de disposer d'une quantité d'informations pour notre travail. Nous n'avons jamais dû vendre le concept à notre client – en fait, *The Changing Face* était probablement le plus stimulant des quatres projets proposés. □ Une fois terminé, notre client était très satisfait de ce rapport. Bien que Centre Reinsurance n'a que trois ans d'existence, elle fait parler d'elle dans le secteur des assurances à cause de ses innovations et de sa publicité. Le rapport annuel est le premier outil de marketing de cette compagnie et il renforce effectivement sa position créatrice dans un secteur plutôt conservateur. Nous avons commencé avec un budget d'ensemble. Nos estimations dépassaient ces prévisions, mais le client était convaincu et il a puisé dans son budget publicitaire afin de payer la différence. Le budget fut ensuite respecté. □ Les clients axés vers la production cherchent toujours à sauver la mise. Ceux qui se concentrent sur le succès cherchent de nouvelles méthodes pour gagner plus. Centre Reinsurance est un client plein de bon sens, soucieux des résultats: ils attachent plus d'importance à l'efficacité du rapport qu'à son coût.

[RANDELL SMITH]

WEISZ YANG DUNKELBERGER, INC.: 61 WILTON ROAD, WESTPORT, CONNECTICUT

06880 203.227.2627

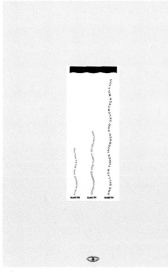
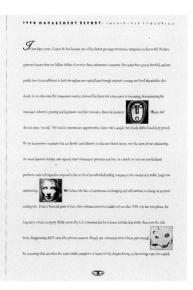

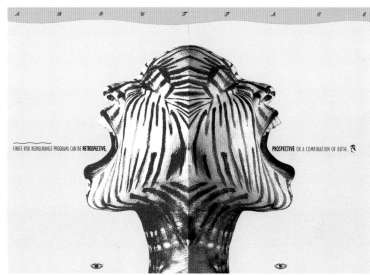
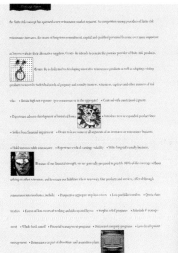
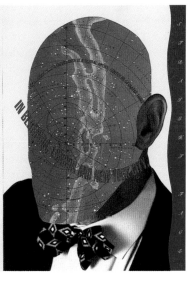

CLIENT: CENTRE REINSURANCE ■ DESIGN FIRM: WYD DESIGN ■ ART DIRECTORS: FRANK OSWALD, RANDALL SMITH ■ DESIGNERS: RANDALL SMITH, FRANK OSWALD ■ PHOTOGRAPHERS: WILLIAM DUKE, IAN MACDONALD SMITH, DICK SCOTT STEWART, JOHN PINDERHUGHES, GUNTER RAMBOW, GEOF KERN ■ ILLUSTRATORS: JOHN MARTINEZ, SETH JABEN ■ WRITER: FRANK OSWALD ■ PRODUCTION MANAGER: SUZIE YANNES ■ TYPOGRAPHER: WYD DESIGN, IMAGING TECHNOLOGIES ■ PAPER SELECTION: MOHAWK INNOVATION, KIMBERLY-CLARK BUCKSKIN ■ PRINTER: DANIELS PRINTING ■ NUMBER OF PAGES: 24 ■ TRIM SIZE: 10¼ x 14¼ INCHES ■ TYPE SELECTION: SNELL ROUNDHAND, LITHOS, COPPERPLATE BOLD, NEW CALEDONIA, CAMPANILE, ARQUITECTURA ■

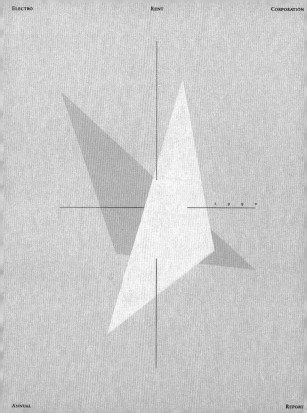

1 9 9 0

ELECTRO RENT CORPORATION

....

▲ At Electro Rent, our report must be developed to inform shareholders and potential shareholders of the state of the company at a fixed instant in time. Secondly, our report is sent to customers and reviewed very carefully by our vendors who—like all our competitors who judge their own performance—are interested in our financial condition and plans for the next year. □ In 1990 our annual report needed to move in a different direction from the previous year. More importantly, the intensity needed to drop a register. I did not want the colors to be as bold; in fact, we wanted a far more subtle report. The pace of business had slowed somewhat and I wanted our readers to have a feeling of much greater caution and concern on our part. The use of pastels, the squares, rectangles, and triangles—the building blocks of graphic design—represented the aspects of stability we wanted to present to the reader. The year 1990 was one of reflection, not of excitement. □ This year our designer was given almost a blank sheet in deciding the report's direction. Obviously the tone needed to be more understated, but we let him move in his own direction. In the end he decided upon a marvelous innovation—to have an embossed page that worked on both sides, which meant the printer had to position each page perfectly. It worked! We continued the process of sharing ideas between ourselves and the printer and improving the product until the project had been completed.

....

■ Unser Jahresbericht soll Aktionäre und potentielle Anleger über den Zustand der Firma zu einem bestimmten Zeitpunkt informieren. Zudem wird er unseren Kunden zugestellt und von unseren Verkäufern sorgfältig studiert. Sie sind, wie alle unsere Konkurrenten, die ihre eigenen Leistungen beurteilen müssen, an unserer Finanzsituation und an den Plänen für das nächste Jahr interessiert. □ 1990 musste unser Jahresbericht eine andere Richtung einschlagen als im Vorjahr. Noch wichtiger war, dass er etwas weniger «intensiv» sein musste. Ich wollte, dass die Farben etwas weniger kräftig waren – wir wollten einen viel subtileren Bericht. Der Geschäftsgang hatte sich etwas verlangsamt, und ich wollte bei unseren Lesern den Eindruck erwecken, dass auf unserer Seite viel mehr Sorgfalt und Vorsicht herrschte. Die Verwendung von Pastellfarben, von Quadraten, Rechtecken, Dreiecken – den Elementen des graphischen Designs – standen für die Stabilität, die wir den Lesern vermitteln wollten. 1990 war ein Jahr der Reflexionen und Betrachtungen und nicht der Aufregung. □ Dieses Jahr hat der Designer praktisch keine Instruktionen für die Gestaltung des Jahresberichts erhalten. Natürlich sollte der Ton zurückhaltender sein, aber ansonsten liessen wir ihm praktisch alle Freiheiten. Schliesslich entschied er sich für eine grossartige Innovation: Seiten mit Prägung, die bei Ansicht auf der Vorder- und Rückseite einen Sinn ergibt. Dies bedeutete, dass der Drucker jede Seite ganz genau positionieren musste. Und es funktionierte! Wir involvierten den Drucker bis zum Schluss in unsere Planung, so dass der beste Weg für die Ausführung gefunden werden konnte.

....

● Pour Electro Rent, ce rapport annuel devait être conçu de manière à informer les actionnaires actuels et potentiels de l'état de la société et remémorer certains événements. D'autre part, notre rapport est envoyé aux clients et examiné très attentivement par nos vendeurs; comme tous nos concurrents qui évaluent leurs propres performances, ceux-ci sont intéressés par notre situation financière et nos projets pour l'année à venir. □ En 1990, notre rapport annuel devait marquer un changement de direction par rapport à l'année passée. Il devait surtout être moins tape-à-l'œil. Je ne voulais pas de couleurs trop criardes; en fait, nous désirions un rapport beaucoup plus subtil. Les affaires tournaient au ralenti et je voulais que nos lecteurs aient un sentiment de plus grande prudence et de responsabilité de notre part. La technique du pastel, les carrés, les rectangles et les triangles, ces pierres angulaires du design graphique, symbolisaient l'impression de stabilité que nous voulions donner au lecteur. 1990 aura été une année de réflexion, d'observations. □ Nous avons pratiquement laissé carte blanche à notre designer. A l'évidence, le ton devait être plus modéré, mais nous l'avons laissé suivre sa propre direction. A la fin, nous avons décidé d'une innovation fabuleuse, à savoir des pages gaufrées utilisables des deux côtés, ce qui signifiait que l'imprimeur devait mettre en place chaque page parfaitement. Cela a marché! Nous n'avons cessé d'échanger nos points de vue avec l'imprimeur et nous avons ainsi été en mesure d'améliorer le produit jusqu'au dernier moment.

[DANIEL GREENBERG]

ELECTRO RENT CORPORATION: 6060 SEPULVEDA BOULEVARD, VAN NUYS, CALIFORNIA 91411 818.787.2100

MORAVA OLIVER BERTÉ

....

▲ In designing the report for Electro Rent, I worked directly with the Chairman of the Board, Dan Greenberg. Dan is a hands-on kind of guy, and likes to be very involved in creation, thus the direction for the annual report was definitely a collaborative effort. The project evolved slowly over a series of meetings, and we produced a variety of design ideas for consideration. In terms of selling this concept, I had no problems because of this collaborative effort. ☐ The client normally likes bolder, brighter graphic approaches. This year, however, the report was an obvious departure. Due to a down year, we agreed to have a rather subdued approach featuring charts that were integrated into the copy. I would say the client liked it, but not necessarily loved it. ☐ Our budgets are not any tighter than before, however, our clients are re-evaluating the quantities and size of their books, thereby saving money on printing and mailing costs. With Electro Rent, they wanted the budget to be in-line with previous years and wanted to save money wherever they could by not being needlessly frivolous. In the end it was a great success.

....

■ Bei der Gestaltung des Jahresberichtes für Electro Rent arbeitete ich direkt mit dem Verwaltungsratsvorsitzenden, Dan Greenberg, zusammen. Dan ist ein Pragmatiker und schätzt es, voll involviert zu werden. Somit war das Grundkonzept für den Jahresbericht eindeutig ein Gemeinschaftsprodukt. Es entwickelte sich im Laufe mehrerer Sitzungen, und wir führten mehrere visuelle Konzepte als Vorschlag aus. Natürlich hatte ich keine Schwierigkeiten, das Grundkonzept durchzusetzen, da es ja gemeinsam entwickelt worden war. ☐ Dieser Kunde schätzt eigentlich einen kräftigeren, farbenfroheren graphischen Stil. Dieses Jahr jedoch sollte sich der Bericht von den bisherigen abheben. Das Jahr war nicht gut gewesen, und wir entschieden uns deshalb für eine zurückhaltende graphische Lösung mit im Text integrierten Diagrammen und Tabellen. Ich würde sagen, der Kunde war zufrieden, wenn auch nicht übermässig begeistert. ☐ Allgemein sind unsere Budgets nicht straffer als zuvor, aber die Auftraggeber überdenken immer öfter die Auflage der Jahresberichte und das Format, was Einsparungen beim Druck und beim Postversand bedeutet. Im Falle von Electro Rent sollte das Budget den vergangenen Jahren entsprechen, und wo immer möglich sollten durch Vermeidung allen überflüssigen Beiwerks Einsparungen erzielt werden.

....

● Pour la conception du rapport annuel d'Electro Rent, j'ai travaillé directement avec le président du conseil d'administration, Dan Greenberg. Il adore s'occuper de création, aussi la réalisation de ce rapport annuel fut-elle le résultat de nos efforts conjugués. Le projet prit forme petit à petit et nous avons proposé un évantail d'idées. Je n'ai eu aucun problème à vendre le concept à cause de cette collaboration. ☐ D'habitude, ce client préfèrait un style graphique plus audacieux, plus vif. Cette année par contre, le rapport dérogeait à cette règle. En cette période de récession, nous sommes tombés d'accord pour adopter un ton plus retenu dans la présentation des graphiques intégrés au texte. Je dirais que le client a bien aimé cette solution – sans plus toutefois. ☐ Nos budgets ne sont pas plus restreints qu'auparavant, cependant, les clients réexaminent le nombre et la taille de leurs publications, économisant ainsi sur l'impression et les frais postaux. Chez Electro Rent, ils voulaient que le budget soit aligné sur celui des années précédentes, tout en économisant là où c'était possible, sans pour autant manquer de sérieux.

[JIM BERTÉ]

MORAVA OLIVER BERTÉ: 2054 BROADWAY, SANTA MONICA, CALIFORNIA 90404 213.453.6290

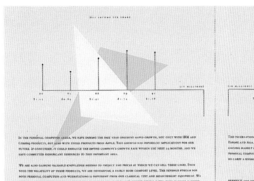
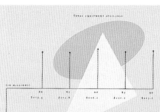

C L I E N T : ELECTRO RENT CORPORATION ■ D E S I G N F I R M : RUNYAN.HINSCHE.ASSOCIATES ■ A R T D I R E C T O R : JIM BERTÉ ■ D E S I G N E R : JIM BERTÉ ■ P H O T O G R A P H E R : MAXINE GOMBERG ■ P R O D U C T I O N M A N A G E R : PATTY KARASAWA ■ T Y P O G R A P H E R : COMPOSITION TYPE ■ P A P E R S E L E C T I O N : KROMECOAT COVER, 6 PT. KARMA ■ P R I N T E R : LITHOGRAPHIX ■ N U M B E R O F P A G E S : 26 PLUS COVER ■ T Y P E S E L E C T I O N : BEMBO ■ P R I N T R U N : 9,000 ■

Annual Report

The Progressive Corporation

1990

THE PROGRESSIVE CORPORATION

. . . .

▲ The primary audience for our company's annual report is current and prospective employees, shareholders, and our secondary audiences include any and all parties interested in the corporation and industry in general. In addition to furnishing our year end financial results we wanted our report to provide some insights into our philosophies, core values, and the way our corporation thinks. Using this as a guide, our report fulfilled its function superbly, thanks in part to the design firm of Nesnadny & Schwartz. They played an essential and indispensible role in the creation and production of the report. Without them we would not only lack a creative and artistic report, it would have been just another document with charts, facts, and figures. We were unique and the outcome showed it.

. . . .

■ Zielpublikum unseres Jahresberichtes sind in erster Linie die gegenwärtigen und zukünftigen Mitarbeiter sowie Aktionäre; in zweiter Linie richtet er sich an alle, die sich für unsere Firma oder Branche interessieren. Neben der Information über das Geschäftsjahr und die finanziellen Ergebnisse sollte unser Bericht Aufschluss über unsere Firmenpolitik, -einstellung und Werte geben. Auf der Basis dieser Richtlinien erfüllte der Bericht seine Funktion hervorragend, was teilweise das Verdienst von Nesnadny & Schwartz ist. Sie spielten bei der Kreierung des Berichtes eine unentbehrliche Rolle. Ohne sie hätten wir keinen künstlerischen Jahresbericht, sondern das übliche Dokument mit Tabellen, Fakten und Zahlen. Wir hatten Einzigartiges geleistet, und das manifestierte sich.

. . . .

● Le rapport annuel de notre société est tout d'abord conçu pour nos employés, actuels et potentiels, ainsi que nos actionnaires; il s'adresse en second lieu à tous ceux qui s'intéressent à notre entreprise et à l'industrie en général. Ce rapport comporte les résultats et les bilans financiers de l'année, mais en plus, nous voulions donner quelques apperçus de la philosophie de l'entreprise, de nos valeurs fondamentales, de nos visions. Tenant compte de ces objectifs, notre rapport a magnifiquement rempli sa fonction, en grande partie grâce au design du studio Nesnadny & Schwartz. Ils ont joué un rôle essentiel, indispensable, dans la création et la production de ce raport. Sans eux, ce document n'aurait pas la même qualité artistique, il aurait été uniquement l'un de ces documents quelqonques où s'alignent diagrammes, données et graphiques. Notre entreprise est unique et le résultat le prouve.

[PETER B. LEWIS]

THE PROGRESSIVE CORPORATION: 6000 PARKLAND BOULEVARD, MAYFIELD HEIGHTS, OHIO 44124 216.464.6000

NESNADNY & SCHWARTZ

. . . .

▲ After several meetings with Progressive, we proposed "protection" and "risk" for the thematic approach to the publication and as key words for artists to respond to. As words that sum up important aspects of the insurance process, they were seen simultaneously as both relevant to the company, while providing the artists with a broad range of interpretation and creative freedom. In addition to the key words, the only direction that the artists were given was the number of pieces required and the deadline for completion. ☐ There were no difficulties in the approval process regarding the design recommendations we made. The response to the book has been very favorable from not just the client, but their various audiences and the design community as well. ☐ Monetarily speaking, the budget was reviewed and established before the project began. The report was delivered under budget and ahead of schedule.

. . . .

■ Nach mehreren Sitzungen mit Progressive schlugen wir als Thema des Jahresberichts und als Schlüsselwörter für den Künstler «Schutz» und «Risiko» vor. Dies sind wichtige Aspekte des Versicherungsprozesses – sie werden als relevant für die Firma betrachtet und bieten dem Künstler ein breites Interpretationsfeld und kreative Freiheit. Neben den Schlüsselausdrücken bestanden die einzigen Instruktionen an den Künstler darin, die Anzahl der benötigten Berichte termingerecht fertigzustellen. ☐ Nennenswerte Schwierigkeiten bei der Bewilligung der eingereichten Designempfehlungen gab es keine. Die Reaktionen auf den Jahresbericht waren positiv, sowohl von der Firma als auch vom Zielpublikum und der Designergemeinde. ☐ Das Budget wurde vor Projektbeginn besprochen und erstellt. Der Jahresbericht wurde unter den budgetierten Kosten und vor dem Schlusstermin fertiggestellt.

. . . .

● Après plusieurs rencontres avec Progressive, nous avons proposé la «protection» et le «risque» comme thèmes dominants de cette publication, les artistes devant s'inspirer de ces deux mots-clés. Ils résument des aspects importants du processus même de l'assurance et nous avons estimé qu'ils convenaient à cette entreprise, tout en fournissant aux artistes un vaste éventail d'interprétations et de liberté créatrice. En plus de ces mots, la seule directive qui leur fut donnée concernait la quantité d'images et la date limite d'achèvement. ☐ Il n'y eut aucune difficulté notoire; nos recommandations furent approuvées. L'écho a été très favorable, de la part du client comme des divers publics et du milieu des designers. ☐ D'un point de vue financier, le budget a dû être révisé et aménagé. Le rapport a été réalisé dans les limites de cette somme et nous avons même eu de l'avance sur notre programme.

[MARK SCHWARTZ]

NESNADNY & SCHWARTZ: 10803 MAGNOLIA DRIVE, CLEVELAND, OHIO 44106 216.791.7721

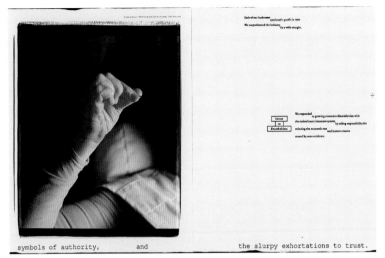

symbols of authority, and the slurpy exhortations to trust.

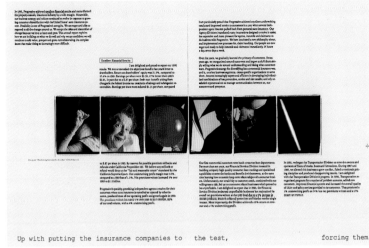

Up with putting the insurance companies to the test, forcing them

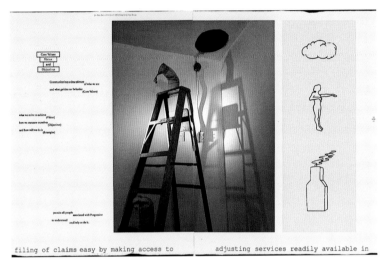

filing of claims easy by making access to adjusting services readily available in

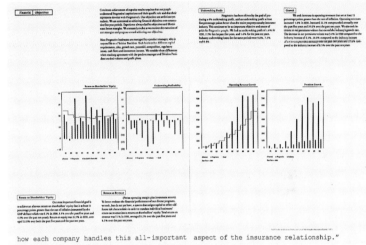

how each company handles this all-important aspect of the insurance relationship."

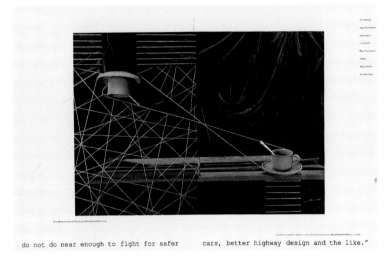

do not do near enough to fight for safer cars, better highway design and the like."

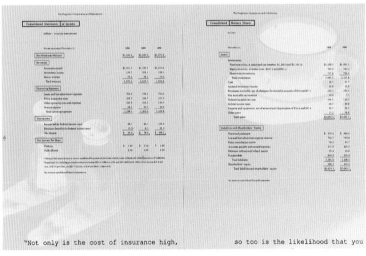

"Not only is the cost of insurance high, so too is the likelihood that you

CLIENT: THE PROGRESSIVE CORPORATION ■ DESIGN FIRM: NESNADNY & SCHWARTZ ■ CREATIVE DIRECTORS: MARK SCHWARTZ, JOYCE NESNADNY ■ DESIGNERS: JOYCE NESNADNY, JENNIFER DYE ■ PHOTOGRAPHERS: BRUCE CHARLESWORTH, EVERGON, JO ANN CALLIS, DAVID LENINTHAL, STEPHEN FRAILEY, ZEKE BERMAN, ROBERT CUMMING, WILLIAM WEGMAN ■ WRITER: PETER B. LEWIS, THE PROGRESSIVE CORPORATION ■ PRODUCTION MANAGER: MARK SCHWARTZ ■ TYPOGRAPHER: TYPESETTING SERVICES, INC. ■ PAPER SELECTION: S.D. WARREN CAMEO DULL WHITE ■ PRINTER: FORTRAN PRINTING ■ NUMBER OF PAGES: 64 ■ TRIM SIZE: 8 ½ x 11 INCHES ■ TYPE SELECTION: GARAMOND, COURIER ■

UNIVERSAL FOODS CORPORATION

1990
ANNUAL
REPORT

A Different
Kind
of
Food
Company

UNIVERSAL FOODS CORPORATION

▲ Since the annual report is the one time each year when our shareholders get a comprehensive review of the return on their investment in the company, they remain our primary audience. Secondary audiences are many—potential shareholders, employees, customers, suppliers, bankers, insurance brokers, media, community leaders, and recruits—as the annual report is the only piece of corporate, descriptive literature we produce. □ We wanted the report to explain that Universal Foods is a different kind of food company. As a supplier to the branded food companies and food service industry, we do not have "brand" name recognition in the consumer market. Yet our products are just as highly regarded by our customers as theirs are by the general public. □ With this in mind, our report fulfilled its function with the assistance of our designer. Good relationships with suppliers helps to produce a better product. It is important to spell out objectives clearly and stay in close touch during the entire production process.

■ Mit dem Jahresbericht erhalten die Aktionäre einmal im Jahr einen umfassenden Überblick über die Rendite des von ihnen investierten Kapitals. Deshalb bleiben sie unser wichtigstes Zielpublikum. Das sekundäre Zielpublikum ist breitgefächert: potentielle Aktionäre, Angestellte, Kunden, Lieferfirmen, Bankleute, Versicherungsagenten, Medien, Politiker und mögliche Arbeitskräfte. Der Jahresbericht ist nämlich die einzige Literatur, die wir herausgeben. □ Mit dem Jahresbericht 1990 wollten wir zeigen, dass Universal Foods eine ungewöhnliche Nahrungsmittelfirma ist. Als Lieferant für Firmen mit Markenartikeln und für die Zulieferungsindustrie werden wir beim Konsumenten nicht als Marke erkannt. Und doch werden unsere Produkte von unseren Kunden genauso hoch eingeschätzt wie deren Produkte vom Konsumenten. □ Mit dieser Idee als Basis hat unser Jahresbericht seine Aufgabe durch die Mithilfe des Designers erfüllt. Gute Beziehungen zum Lieferanten (in diesem Falle dem Lieferanten des Designs) helfen immer, das Produkt noch zu verbessern. Es ist wichtig, die Ziele genau zu artikulieren und während des ganzen Entwicklungs- und Produktionsprozesses in engem Kontakt mit ihm zu bleiben.

● Pour nos actionnaires, le rapport annuel représente la seule occasion chaque année d'avoir un compte-rendu détaillé du rendement de leurs investissements: ceux-ci constituent donc notre public principal. Ensuite, il intéresse les nombreux actionnaires potentiels, les employés, clients, fournisseurs, banquiers, courtiers en assurances, les médias, les politiciens et la main-d'œuvre potentielle. Le rapport annuel est en effet le seul document concernant l'entreprise que nous publiions. □ Nous voulions expliquer au travers de ce rapport 1990 que la Universal Foods est une entreprise de produits alimentaires différente des autres. En tant que fournisseurs des grandes marques et de l'industrie de sous-traitance dans le domaines des denrées alimentaires, notre marque n'est pas reconnue comme telle par le marché des consommateurs. Et pourtant, nos produits sont aussi bien appréciés par nos clients qu'ils le sont par le public. □ Avec l'aide de notre designer, notre rapport a rempli sa fonction. De bonnes relations avec les fournisseurs aident toujours à fabriquer un meilleur produit. Il est important d'expliquer bien clairement ses objectifs et de suivre attentivement le développement complet et le processus de production.

[PAULA C. NORTON]

UNIVERSAL FOODS CORPORATION: 433 EAST MICHIGAN STREET, P.O. BOX 737

MILWAUKEE, WISCONSIN 53201 414.271.6755

SAMATA ASSOCIATES DESIGN CONSULTANTS

. . . .

▲ The direction of the Universal Foods 1990 Annual Report was presented to the client by our firm after an initial meeting to determine a set of objectives for the book; primarily to clearly identify the nature of the company's products and markets. □ Universal Foods Corporation is in the food industry, but its products are so specialized that it often has trouble communicating to the public exactly what its products and markets are. Readers of the 1990 Annual Report do not even have to read the text to get this information. The theme of the book, "A Different Kind of Food Company," is clearly illustrated by the split-page photos. We had no trouble whatsoever in gaining Universal Foods' support of our project ideas, and they were very pleased with the results. The report successfully fulfilled the objectives the company set out to accomplish. □ As with virtually all of our clients, Universal Foods wanted the best possible annual report produced within the budget. Budget parameters were given up front and a design for the book was developed that fit within those parameters while accomplishing the established objectives. Generally, our clients still want well-designed, high-quality pieces but pay close attention to where the dollars are going. □ The Universal Foods Corporation's 1990 Annual Report was one of the projects which was typeset completely on our in-house Macintosh computer system. More frequently we are doing our own typography for our clients.

. . . .

■ Wir legten das Konzept für den Jahresbericht 1990 der Universal Foods Corporation dem Kunden nach einer ersten Sitzung über die Zielsetzung des Berichts vor. Hauptziel war, die Art der Produkte der Firma und die Märkte klar zu identifizieren. □ Universal Foods Corporation ist in der Nahrungsmittelindustrie tätig, aber die Produkte sind so spezifisch, dass die Firma oft Mühe hat, dem Publikum klar zu vermitteln, welches ihre Produkte und Märkte sind. Der Leser des Jahresberichts 1990 muss nicht einmal die Textpassagen anschauen, um diese Information zu erhalten. Das Thema des Berichts, «Eine ungewöhnliche Nahrungsmittelfirma», ist durch die Photoseiten deutlich illustriert. Wir hatten absolut keine Schwierigkeiten, Unterstützung für unsere Projektideen von Universal Foods Corporation zu erhalten – und die Firma war sehr zufrieden mit dem Resultat. Der Bericht erfüllt die von der Firma gesetzte Zielsetzung. □ Wie praktisch alle unsere Kunden wollte Universal Foods Corporation den bestmöglichen Jahresbericht innerhalb des budgetierten Rahmens. Budgetrichtlinien waren von Anfang an vorgegeben, und dementsprechend wurde ein Design entwickelt, das diese Bedingungen und die Zielsetzungen erfüllt. Generell wollen die Kunden noch immer gutes Design und hochstehende Qualität, doch werden die Ausgaben genauer überwacht. □ Der Jahresbericht 1990 von Universal Foods Corporation war eines jener Projekte, die komplett auf unserem Macintosh gesetzt wurden. Immer öfter kreieren wir auch neue Schriften für unsere Kunden.

. . . .

● Les grandes lignes du rapport annuel 1990 d'Universal Foods Corporation ont été présentées au client par notre firme lors d'une première rencontre visant à déterminer une série d'objectifs au sujet de cette publication. Il s'agissait avant tout d'identifier clairement les produits et les marchés de l'entreprise. □ Universal Foods Corporation travaille dans le secteur alimentaire, mais ses produits sont tellement spécialisés qu'il a souvent été difficile de communiquer exactement au public leur nature et leurs marchés. Les lecteurs du rapport annuel 1990 ne sont pas obligés de lire le texte pour obtenir des informations. Le thème, «Une entreprise alimentaire différente des autres», est clairement illustré par des photos structurant la page. Notre projet a été soutenu sans problème par Universal Foods Corporation et ils ont été ravis des résultats. Le rapport a rempli les objectifs que l'entreprise avait fixés. □ Comme pratiquement tous nos clients, Universal Foods Corporation voulait le meilleur rapport annuel possible sans dépasser le budget prévu. Les exigences budgétaires ont été déterminantes et le design de cette publication a été élaboré en fonction de ces données, tout en réalisant les objectifs établis. Généralement, nos clients veulent des documents bien conçus, d'une haute qualité, mais ils surveillent de près les dépenses. □ Le rapport annuel 1990 de la Universal Foods Corporation a été l'un des projets que nous ayons complètement réalisés sur le Macintosh de l'entreprise. De plus en plus fréquemment, nous créons nous-mêmes la typo pour nos clients.

[PAT SAMATA]

SAMATA ASSOCIATES DESIGN CONSULTANTS: 101 SOUTH FIRST STREET, DUNDEE, ILLINOIS 60118 708.428.8600

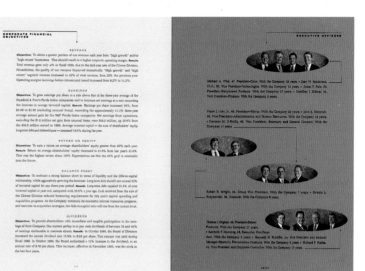

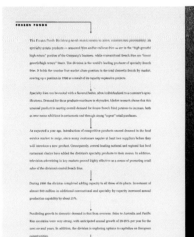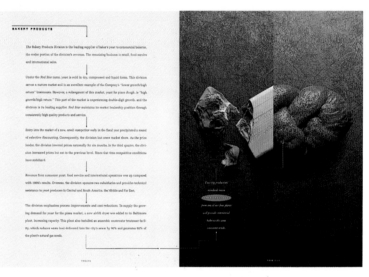

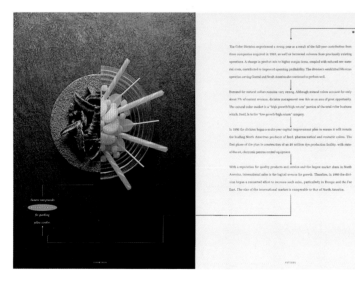

Client: UNIVERSAL FOODS CORPORATION ■ Design Firm: SAMATA ASSOCIATES ■ Art Directors/Designers: GREG AND PAT SAMATA ■ Photographers: SANDRO MILLER, MARC NORBERG ■ Writer: PAULA NORTON ■ Production Manager: JANE MCMILLIAN ■ Typographer: SAMATA ASSOCIATES ■ Paper Selection: CENTURA, EVERGREEN ASH ■ Paper Manufacturers: CONSOLIDATED, SIMPSON ■ Printer: DIVERSIFIED GRAPHICS ■ Number of Pages: 38 ■ Type Selection: MELIOR, GARAMOND, UNIVERS ■

1990 ANNUAL REPORT

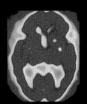

NATIONAL MEDICAL ENTERPRISES, INC.

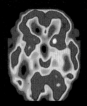

THE DECADE OF THE BRAIN

NATIONAL MEDICAL ENTERPRISES, INC.

. . . .

▲ The primary audience for the annual report is the company's shareholders. While we try to skew the report to the individual shareholder, our strategy is to communicate effectively with both individual and institutional shareholders. Our secondary audiences include employees, prospective employees, governmental agencies, physicians, legislators, and insurance companies. □ We wanted to identify NME with leading-edge research on the brain and its functions, and brain diseases and their treatments. For several years, NME's psychiatric subsidiary, Psychiatric Institutes of America had been the fastest-growing segment of the company. By focusing on the brain, we could focus more attention on the success of that segment. □ The report did fulfill its function. It communicated NME's committment to quality care by highlighting the outstanding physicians who work at NME hospitals and by placing the company in the forefront of brain research and the treatment of brain malfunctions and maladies. □ In dealing with our designer—The Jefferies Association—we had an outstanding relationship. It was their imagination, creativity, and drive that convinced us to use symbolic illustrations to powerfully portray brain maladies and positively connect these images to the work being done at NME hospitals.

. . . .

■ Das primäre Zielpublikum unseres Jahresberichts sind unsere Aktionäre. Wir versuchen zwar, den Bedürfnissen des individuellen Aktionärs gerecht zu werden, unsere Strategie aber besteht darin, eine effiziente Kommunikation sowohl mit dem individuellen als auch mit dem institutionellen Anleger herzustellen. Das sekundäre Zielpublikum umfasst Angestellte, zukünftige Mitarbeiter, öffentliche Stellen, Ärzte, Gesetzgeber und Versicherungsgesellschaften. □ Unser Anliegen war, NME mit Spitzenforschung über das Gehirn und seine Funktionen, Gehirnkrankheiten und deren Behandlung zu identifizieren. Seit einigen Jahren ist NMEs Tochterunternehmen, Psychiatric Institutes of America – im Bereich der Psychiatrie tätig – das am schnellsten wachsende Segment des Unternehmens. Indem wir uns auf das Gehirn konzentrierten, konnten wir diesen Erfolg besser herausstreichen. □ Der Jahresbericht erfüllte seine Funktion. NMEs Engagement für ein qualitativ hochstehendes Gesundheitswesen wurde veranschaulicht, indem die hervorragenden Ärzteteams der NME-Krankenhäuser vorgestellt wurden und die führende Rolle des Unternehmens in der Gehirnforschung und der Behandlung von Krankheiten und Funktionsstörungen des Gehirns erfolgreich vermittelt werden konnte. □ Mit unserem Designteam – The Jefferies Association – hatten wir ein optimales Verhältnis. Dank ihres Vorstellungsvermögens, ihrer Kreativität und Energie konnten sie uns davon überzeugen, im Bericht symbolische Illustrationen für die Darstellung von Gehirnkrankheiten einzusetzen und diese Bilder positiv mit der Arbeit in den NME-Krankenhäusern in Verbindung zu bringen.

. . . .

● Le premier public de notre rapport annuel est celui des actionnaires de la société. Bien que nous essayions d'attirer plutôt l'attention des actionnaires privés, notre stratégie consiste à communiquer aussi bien avec les actionnaires privés que les actionnaires institutionnels. En second, nous nous adressons à notre personnel, aux employés potentiels, aux administrations, aux médecins, législateurs et compagnies d'assurances. □ Nous voulions identifier NME à la recherche de pointe sur le cerveau, sa fonction, les maladies cérébrales et leur traitement. Depuis quelques années, la filiale psychiatrique de NME, Psychiatric Institutes of America est le secteur le plus dynamique de notre société. En nous concentrant sur le cerveau, nous pouvions mettre l'accent sur le succès. □ Le rapport a rempli sa fonction. Il expliquait l'engagement de NME en faveur de la qualité des soins, mettant en vedette les médecins remarquables qui travaillent dans nos hôpitaux; par ailleurs, il positionne NME à l'avant-garde de la recherche sur le cerveau et du traitement des maladies et des mauvais fonctionnements du cerveau. □ Nous avons eu d'excellentes relations avec le studio de design, The Jefferies Association. Ils ont su, grâce à leur imagination, leur créativité, nous convaincre d'utiliser des illustrations symboliques pour présenter de manière impressionnante les maladies du cerveau, et relier positivement ces images au travail qui s'accomplit dans les hôpitaux NME.

[DAVID OLSON]

NATIONAL MEDICAL ENTERPRISES, INC.: 2700 COLORADO AVENUE

SANTA MONICA, CALIFORNIA 90404 213.315.8000

THE JEFFERIES ASSSOCIATION

· ·

▲ In the NME Annual Report, the concept of the "decade of the brain" was a management concept; the execution was our concept. We suggested using an NME expert to talk about each of the four areas of the brain that NME was interested in. We proposed using a series of different illustrations to begin each article, but all unified because of the integrity of art, the size of the human head, and the power that each illustration would generate. While the idea of using these strong illustrations was slightly foreign to the company, the effectiveness of using them in communicating their concept was recognized and immediately endorsed by the senior management. All subsequent images would come from the highest tech exploration and diagnostic equipment in NME's arsenal and graphics, which we produced to emphasize internal programs. □ As we all know, various industries are experiencing major budgetary difficulties. Our mix of clients, with the exception of a few, have not pulled in their budgets. They are producing annuals that communicate their companies' strengths. In our report, the budget was built around the concept, but it was tightly controlled and adhered to thanks, in part, to the computer-generated type we produced out-of-house.

· ·

■ Beim NME-Jahresbericht stammte das Konzept «Das Jahrzehnt des Gehirns» von der Geschäftsleitung; die Ausführung beruhte auf unserem Konzept. Wir schlugen vor, einen NME-Experten heranzuziehen, der über die vier Zonen des Gehirns schreiben sollte, an denen NME interessiert ist. Wir schlugen weiter vor, jeden neuen Artikel mit anderen Illustrationen zu beginnen, die aber alle aufgrund der wahrheitsgetreuen Darstellung, der Grösse des menschlichen Kopfs und der Aussagekraft jedes einzelnen Bildes eine Einheit bilden würden. Die Idee, solche Illustrationen zu benützen, war für die Geschäftsleitung zwar ungewöhnlich, doch sie sah ein, dass die Illustrationen bei der Vermittlung des firmeneigenen Konzepts sehr effizient sein würden. Alle Bilder stammen aus NMEs Spitzentechnologie-Forschung und aus den firmeneigenen Diagnostikgeräten. Die Graphiken dienen zur Erläuterung interner Vorgänge. □ Wie wir alle wissen, befinden sich verschiedene Industriebereiche in einer schwierigen Situation. Mit wenigen Ausnahmen haben unsere Kunden die Budgets für Jahresberichte aber nicht gekürzt. Sie wollen weiterhin Jahresberichte, die dem Publikum die Stärken ihrer Firmen erfolgreich vermitteln. Für diesen Jahresbericht wurde das Budget nach Absegnung des Konzepts aufgestellt, aber es wurde streng kontrolliert, und wir haben uns daran gehalten, zum Teil dank computergenerierter Schriften, die ausser Haus produziert wurden.

· ·

● Dans le rapport annuel de NME, le concept de la «Décennie du cerveau» provenait de la direction; nous nous sommes chargés de l'exécution. Nous avons suggéré de demander à un expert de NME de parler de chacune des quatres régions du cerveau auxquelles NME s'intéresse. Puis, nous avons proposé d'insérer différentes illustrations au début de chaque article, mais qui présentaient une certaine unité grâce à leur style, la taille de la tête et leurs qualités expressives. Bien que l'idée d'utiliser ces illustrations ait été plutôt étrangère à l'entreprise, la direction a immédiatement reconnu leur efficacité à communiquer le concept. Toutes les images ultérieures proviennent des programmes de recherche génétique et des instruments de diagnostic de NME. Des graphiques nous ont permis de mettre en lumière les programmes de l'entreprise. □ Chacun le sait, de nombreuses industries connaissent des difficultés financières. Nos clients, sauf quelques exceptions, n'ont cependant pas réduit leurs budgets. Ils produisent des rapports annuels qui communiquent les efforts de leur entreprise. Dans ce rapport, le budget a été déterminé par le concept, mais il a été en partie respecté grâce à la typo produite sur ordinateur à l'extérieur.

[C. CLAUDIA JEFFERIES]

THE JEFFERIES ASSOCIATION: 430 SOUTH WESTMORELAND AVENUE

LOS ANGELES, CALIFORNIA 90020 213.388.4002

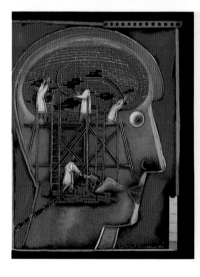

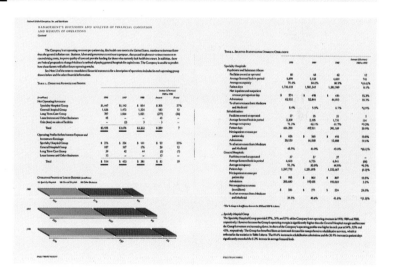

The Decade of the Brain

MONITORING THE CENTRAL NERVOUS SYSTEM DURING SURGERY

Today, it would be unthinkable to perform surgery without monitoring a patient's heartbeat, respiration and blood pressure. We are now entering a period when the monitoring of a patient's brain activity will become equally commonplace . . . Certain procedures lend themselves toward specific monitoring of certain portions of the central nervous system . . . We foresee a day when neurological monitoring will be a routine portion of any neurosurgical procedure. Monitoring the function of the tissue being surgically manipulated enhances the safety of such procedures and will, no doubt, aid in the development of more sophisticated forms of surgery . . .

Dr. Frank Culicchia, right

Dr. Theo Berenzen

Today, it would be unthinkable to perform surgery without monitoring a patient's heartbeat, respiration and blood pressure. We are now entering a period when the monitoring of a patient's brain activity will become equally commonplace. As a team, the neurologist and the neurosurgeon have been working together to develop new and better techniques for monitoring neurological activity during surgery.

Monitoring brain activity can be vitally important in surgery involving the brain's vascular network, or the removal of tumors within or surrounding the brain. Monitoring function of the spinal cord is equally important when surgery is performed within or around this vital structure. Obviously, with the patient under a general anesthetic, it is not possible to ask him to move his arm or leg, or ask him if he can hear a sound while surgery is taking place. Other means must be utilized to monitor the brain's function.

The electroencephalogram (EEG), which records the brain's electrical activity, is the primary device

for monitoring. It is similar to the electrocardiogram, which records the electrical activity of the heart. Another form of monitoring, evoked potentials, involves stimulating a nerve within the arm or leg and recording the electrical activity of the brain as this nerve is stimulated.

Surgery involving the central nervous system, which includes the brain and spinal cord, places this tissue at risk of injury. This injury may take the form of a paralysis, loss of vision, speech impairment, personality and memory changes, among others. Identifying and avoiding such problems is the goal of neurological monitoring.

EEG signals can be compressed into very simplified form that can be followed over periods of time while the patient is under a general anesthetic. Changes in the electrical signals may indicate if brain tissue is in jeopardy. Adjustments at the time these changes are identified may avoid permanent injury.

In special cases, the brain's electrical activity is decreased with medications. This artificial reduction in the electrical activity results in lower requirements for oxygen and other necessary metabolic substances, since the tissue is put "to rest." This technique is particularly

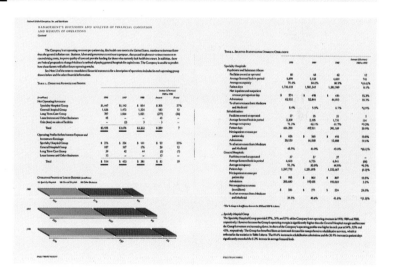

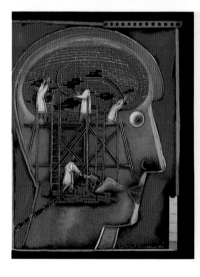

CLIENT: NATIONAL MEDICAL ENTERPRISES, INC. ■ DESIGN FIRM: THE JEFFERIES ASSOCIATION ■ ART DIRECTOR: RON JEFFERIES ■ DESIGNER: C. CLAUDIA JEFFERIES ■ ILLUSTRATORS: JOEL PETER JOHNSON, ANDRZEJ DUDZINSKI, TOM CURRY, NORM WALKER ■ WRITER: DAVID OLSON ■ PRODUCTION MANAGER: C. CLAUDIA JEFFERIES ■ TYPOGRAPHER: CAPCO ■ PAPER SELECTION: REFLECTIONS GLOSS ■ PAPER MANUFACTURER: POTLATCH ■ PRINTER: GEORGE RICE & SONS ■ NUMBER OF PAGES: 52 ■ TYPE SELECTION: BEMBO ■

Overview
of the Group's
companies

Analysis ● ● ●
of the marketing
services sector
in the 1990s

WPP Group plc

Annual Report & Accounts 19 90

Performance
for the year to
31 December 1990

*'The purpose of all WPP Group companies
is to add value and worth to clients' businesses through
the management of the imagination'*

WPP GROUP, PLC

. . . .

▲ The primary audiences for our annual report—shareholders, institutions, analysts, journalists, and media marketers—are no less important than our secondary ones—employees, equity and non-equity holders, directors, graduates and suppliers. ☐ WPP Group is in the marketing services sector and knows more about this than any other. The group, itself a "financial brand," has within it many of the most famous and successful "professional brands" in the field of marketing services—each with its own skills and its own identity. ☐ It was important that the look and style of the report should reflect the philosophy—value and worth—of clients' businesses through the management of imagination. Appropriate to the more austere economic climate of the period, the approach was crisp, elegant, and deliberately monochromatic, focusing on the financial performance and corporate issues. ☐ In all respects the report was a success due to the good relationship we had with the designer, who fully understood and contributed to the report. Changes requested by the client were considered thoughtfully and constructively; imaginative solutions were always sought for problems as they arose. The designer retained the design integrity of the report while never resorting to temperament.

. . . .

■ Unser Jahresbericht richtet sich vor allem an unsere Aktionäre, an Institutionen, Analysten, Journalisten und Marketingfachleute im Medienbereich. An zweiter Stelle stehen – aber nicht weniger wichtig – die Angestellten: sowohl jene, die gleichzeitig Aktionäre sind, als auch solche, die es nicht sind; Verwaltungsräte, Studienabgänger und Zulieferbetriebe. ☐ Die WPP Group ist im Marketingbereich tätig und verfügt auf diesem Gebiet über ein beträchtliches Know-how. Die Hauptgesellschaft, ein Finanzunternehmen, vereinigt viele der berühmtesten und erfolgreichsten Marketingfirmen – wobei jede Firma ihre eigene Identität und ihre Spezialbereiche bewahrt hat. ☐ Es war ausserordentlich wichtig, dass der Jahresbericht vom Stil und Aussehen her unsere Unternehmensphilosophie widerspiegelt – durch ein kreatives Management, das bestrebt ist, die Geschäftsinteressen der Kunden optimal wahrzunehmen. Dem raueren Wirtschaftsklima entsprechend haben wir einen knappen, sauberen, eleganten Stil gewählt, mit Absicht schwarzweiss, und uns auf den finanziellen Geschäftsgang und auf Unternehmensfragen konzentriert. ☐ In jeder Hinsicht ist unser Jahresbericht ein Erfolg, dank der guten Zusammenarbeit mit dem Designer, der unseren Auftrag begriff und in der Lage war, Ideen beizusteuern. Unsere Änderungswünsche wurden sorgfältig und konstruktiv überdacht und bei auftauchenden wurden Problemen kreative Lösungen gesucht. Wir arbeiteten in einer sachlichen Atmosphäre, und dem Designer gelang es, die Integrität des Designs zu bewahren.

. . . .

● Le public principal de notre rapport annuel – actionnaires, institutions, analystes et responsables du marketing publicitaire – est tout aussi important que celui des employés, des détenteurs de titres boursiers ou de ceux qui ne le sont pas, des membres du conseil d'administration, des étudiants et des fournisseurs. ☐ Le groupe WPP travaille dans le secteur du marketing et ses connaissances en la matière sont considérables. La maison mère, elle-même un institut financier, comprend quelques-unes des marques les plus célèbres et les plus prospères dans le domaine du marketing – chacune ayant son propre savoir-faire et son identité. ☐ Il importait que le look et le style du rapport se fassent l'écho de notre philosophie: c'est en faisant marcher leur imagination que les clients de valeur font des affaires. L'approche caustique, claire, élégante, de ce document volontairement monochrome, se concentrant sur les performances financières et les questions touchant la marche de l'entreprise, était particulièrement appropriée au climat d'austérité économique de cette période. ☐ A tous points de vue, ce rapport aura été un succès, notamment grâce aux bonnes relations que nous entretenions avec le designer, qui sut comprendre parfaitement la commande et apporter ses idées personnelles. Les modifications souhaitées par le client ont été prises en considération de manière constructive; des solutions imaginatives ont été données aux questions au fur et à mesure qu'elles surgissaient. Le designer a conservé le design du rapport dans son intégrité sans jamais tergiverser.

[MARTIN SORRELL]

WPP GROUP PLC: 27 FARM STREET, LONDON, ENGLAND W1X 6RD 44-71 493.6819

SAMPSON TYRELL LTD.

. . . .

▲ The annual report for WPP Group had to reflect a satisfactory rather than an exceptional trading performance but still convey a sense of confidence and authority. The black-and-white analytical approach that we set up on the front cover, along with bold "chapter introduction" spreads and crisp, cool layouts, was well-received by the client as it hit exactly the right balance of economy and style. □ We suggested combining two documents used in last year's report: the Group financial statement and the companies book. This was a responsible idea given the current trading conditions. It presented a very challenging, creative problem as to how we could present the individual nature of 48 Group companies with some degree of cohesion. We decided to ask every company to submit three numerical facts about themselves. In consultation with each, we then selected one of these based on its visual potential, using the criteria of business effectiveness, wit, or skill-based facts. These were deliberately the only six pages in the annual report that were in full color. We wanted to use an element of surprise—although the report primarily addressed financial and corporate issues. It was important that readers were reminded of the scale and expertise of the companies that make up the Group. As imagined, it was demanding both logistically and creatively. The report turned out to be a success, as the head of WPP wrote us to say he was looking forward to next year's report. □ We judged that the report should be less lavish than in previous years, so the budget was based accordingly. This budget is typical of all our clients in general, as they are looking for added value and cost-effective design solutions.

. . . .

■ Der Jahresbericht der WPP-Gruppe musste eine zufriedenstellende, aber nicht sehr bemerkenswerte Aktienkursentwicklung reflektieren, dennoch aber Zuversicht und Autorität ausstrahlen. Der analytische Stil in Schwarzweiss, der den Umschlag bestimmte, die ausdrucksvollen Einführungsseiten für die einzelnen Kapitel und das frische, klare Layout gefielen dem Kunden sehr, da diese Elemente eine Harmonie zwischen Wirtschaftlichkeit und Stil erzielten. □ Wir schlugen vor, das Design zweier Dokumente des letztjährigen Berichts wiederzuverwenden: das der Gruppenbilanz und das des «Companies' Book». Diese Idee war durchaus sinnvoll angesichts der Aktienkursentwicklung. Das wohl anspruchsvollste kreative Problem bestand darin, die Individualität der 48 Firmen der Gruppe mit einem gewissen Mass an Kohäsion darzustellen. Wir beschlossen, jede um drei numerische Fakten zu bitten. Eine davon wurde visuell umgesetzt, und zwar auf den einzigen sechs Farbseiten des Jahresberichts. Wir wollten einen Überraschungseffekt erzielen – obwohl sich der Bericht vornehmlich auf Unternehmens- und Finanzfragen konzentrierte. Es war wichtig, die Leser auf Umfang und Können der einzelnen Firmen aufmerksam zu machen. Wie man sich vorstellen kann, war diese Aufgabe sowohl in logistischer als auch in kreativer Hinsicht sehr anspruchsvoll. Der Jahresbericht, bewusst weniger luxuriös gestaltet als in früheren Jahren, war ein Erfolg, und der Geschäftsführer von WPP schrieb uns, er freue sich bereits auf den nächstjährigen Bericht.

. . . .

● Le rapport annuel du groupe WPP devait traduire des résultats commerciaux satisfaisants plutôt qu'exceptionnels, tout en inspirant l'idée de confiance et de compétence. Nous avons adopté un style analytique en noir et blanc, de la couverture jusqu'aux audacieuses doubles pages de l'introduction, une mise en pages décontractée qui fut bien perçue par le client car elle procédait d'un subtil dosage entre économie et style. □ Nous avons suggéré de réutiliser deux documents du précédent rapport: le bilan financier du groupe et le «Livre de la société». C'était une idée raisonnable vu les conditions commerciales actuelles. Il fallait présenter le caractère individuel des 48 entreprises du groupe avec une certaine cohésion. Nous avons décidé de demander à chacune de nous soumettre trois faits chiffrés. Avec leur accord, nous en avons ensuite sélectionné un en nous appuyant sur son potentiel visuel, sur des critères d'efficacité commerciale. Ces six pages sont à dessein les seules en quadrichromie. Nous voulions jouer sur l'effet de surprise – bien que le rapport ait surtout eu trait à des questions financières et institutionnelles. Il convenait de rappeler aux lecteurs la taille et la compétence des entreprises qui constituent ce groupe. Le rapport s'est avéré être un succès lorsque la direction de la WPP nous a écrit pour nous annoncer qu'elle espérait que nous ferions le prochain. □ Nous avons estimé que ce rapport devait être moins luxueux que ceux des années passées; c'est un budget typique pour des clients qui demandent des solutions de design économiques.

[DAVID FREEMAN]

SAMPSON TYRELL LIMITED: 6 MERCER STREET LONDON WC2H 9QA GBR 071.379.7124

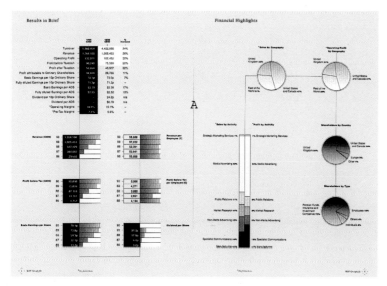

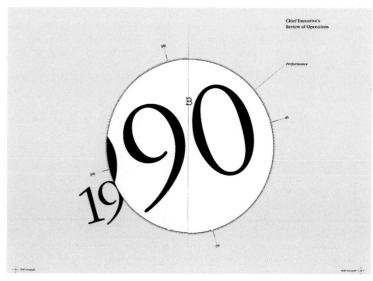

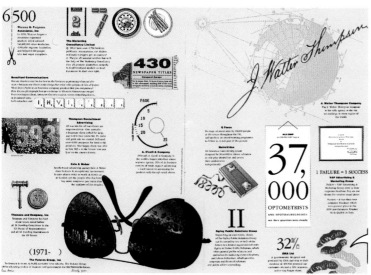

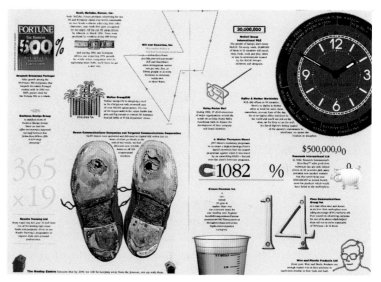

CLIENT: WPP GROUP PLC ■ DESIGN FIRM: SAMPSONTYRRELL LIMITED ■ ART DIRECTOR: DAVID FREEMAN ■ DESIGNERS: JOHN HENRY, SHAUN WESTGATE ■ PHOTOGRAPHERS/ILLUSTRATORS: VARIOUS ■ WRITER: MARTIN SORRELL ■ PAPER SELECTION: CONSORT ROYAL SILK ■ PAPER MANUFACTURER: DONSIDE PAPER ■ PRINTER: ROYAL CITY LTD ■ NUMBER OF PAGES: 64 ■ TYPE SELECTION: HELVETICA BLACK, GARAMOND STEMPLE ■

ANNUAL

REPORT

1989

THE

CHILDREN'S

HOSPITAL

OF

PHILADELPHIA

THE CHILDREN'S HOSPITAL OF PHILADELPHIA

. . . .

▲ For The Children's Hospital of Philadelphia, 1989 was a year of firsts—in building equipment, programming, and research. The purpose of The Children's Hospital's 1989 Annual Report was to showcase the highlights and the employees who were responsible for making it happen. ☐ The primary audience for the report was the donor, and the secondary audiences were physician alumni, referring physicians, employees, and government officials. The objectives of the annual report were different for each group; however, for all audiences we wanted to reflect the philosophy of senior management—businesslike, yet committed to patient care, their families, and referring physicians. ☐ A good relationship with the designer was important in producing the annual report. If you and the designer share the same philosophies and ideas, it is easier for the philosophies of the organization to be carried through.

. . . .

■ Für das Children's Hospital of Philadelphia war 1989 ein Jahr der Erneuerungen – in bezug auf das Gebäude, die Einrichtung, das Programm und die Forschung. Das Ziel des Jahresberichtes 1989 bestand darin, diese Höhepunkte vorzustellen und auch die Angestellten, ohne die diese Erneuerungen nicht stattgefunden hätten. ☐ In erster Linie richtet sich der Jahresbericht an die Geldgeber, in zweiter Linie an Mediziner, die gerade das Studium abgeschlossen haben, an einweisende Ärzte, Angestellte und öffentliche Stellen. Zwar waren unsere Zielsetzungen verschieden; doch wir wollten allen Gruppen die Philosophie der Klinikleitung darstellen – einerseits die Orientierung nach unternehmerischen Richtlinien und Wirtschaftlichkeit, andererseits die Verpflichtung zum Dienst am Patienten, sowie gegenüber seiner Familie und den einweisenden Ärzten. ☐ Eine gute Beziehung zum Designer war ausserordentlich wichtig bei der Entstehung des Jahresberichts. Wenn der Designer die Einstellung und die Ideen des Auftraggebers teilt, kommt der Geist der Organisation im Endprodukt viel besser zum Tragen.

. . . .

● Pour le Children's Hospital de Philadelphie, 1989 aura été une année d'innovations – en ce qui concerne nos bâtiments, nos programmes et notre recherche. Le but du rapport annuel 1989 était de mettre en lumière les temps forts de l'année et de présenter le personnel hospitalier sans lequel cet institut ne pourrait fonctionner. ☐ Notre public se composait tout d'abord des bailleurs de fonds, puis des anciens membres de l'équipe des médecins, des médecins actuels, des employés et des services publics. L'objectif du rapport annuel différait suivant chaque groupe; mais, aux uns comme aux autres, nous voulions donner une idée de la philosophie de la direction: travailler en respectant les règles propres aux entreprises, être au service des patients, de leurs familles et des médecins. ☐ Nos bonnes relations avec le designer ont joué un rôle important pour la production de ce rapport annuel. Il est plus facile d'exprimer la philosophie d'une organisation si vous partagez les mêmes vues que le designer.

[TAMARA L. CALKINS]

THE CHILDREN'S HOSPITAL OF PHILADELPHIA: 34TH STREET AND CIVIC CENTER BOULEVARD

PHILADELPHIA, PENNSYLVANIA 19104 215.590.1000

▲ Several conceptual approaches were presented to achieve our primary goal of reinforcing the position of The Children's Hospital of Philadelphia as a major institution in the pediatric health care arena. □ Events such as the opening of the John D. Wood Pediatric Ambulatory Care Center, implementation of a pediatric liver transplant program, acquisitions of state-of-the-art communication systems, and unparalleled research and educational programs were interwoven by the use of dramatic portrait photographs of the doctors, nurses, and employees who made it all possible. Additional photography reinforced the hospital's renowned reputation for programs, patient care, education, and research. □ The colors for the book were extracted from the interior color palette of the new ambulatory care center. The overall tone and feel of the book was sensitive, understated, and was well received.

■ Verschiedene Konzepte wurden dem Auftraggeber präsentiert, um unser primäres Ziel zu erreichen: die Darstellung des Children's Hospital of Philadelphia als wichtige Institution in der Pädiatrie. □ Ereignisse wie die Eröffnung des John D. Wood Pediatric Ambulatory Care Centre (pädiatrisches, ambulantes Behandlungszentrum), die Realisation eines Lebertransplantationsprogramms für Kinder, der Erwerb eines hochmodernen Kommunikationssystems und die unübertroffenen Forschungs- und Ausbildungsprogramme wurden zu einer Einheit verschmolzen mit dramatischen Porträtphotographien der Ärzte, Krankenschwestern und Mitarbeiter, die das alles erst möglich machen. Zusätzliche Photographien betonten den soliden Ruf des Krankenhauses in den Bereichen der Gesundheitsprogramme, Patientenbetreuung, Ausbildung und Forschung. □ Die Farbpalette des Jahresberichts reflektierte die Farben der Innenräume des neuen ambulanten Behandlungszentrums. Grundstimmung und Ausstrahlung des Jahresberichts waren weich, gefühlvoll, dezent, und er wurde sehr gut aufgenommen.

● Afin de réaliser notre premier objectif, renforcer la position du Children's Hospital de Philadelphie comme une institution d'importance dans le domaine de la pédiatrie, nous avons présenté plusieurs approches du sujet. □ Des événements tels que l'ouverture du Centre de soins ambulants John D. Wood, le lancement d'un programme de transplantation du foie pour les enfants, l'achat de systèmes de communication sophistiqués et des programmes de recherche et de formation sans précédent étaient évoqués dans les photos spectaculaires des docteurs, des infirmières et des employés de l'hôpital. D'autres images soulignaient la réputation de l'hôpital, célèbre pour la qualité des soins, l'éducation et la recherche. □ Les couleurs du rapport sont en harmonie avec celles de l'intérieur du Ambulatory Care Center. La tonalité d'ensemble et le style sont plutôt discrets et il a été fort bien reçu.

[RALPH BILLINGS]

GUNSELMAN & POLITE: 1400 NORTH FRANKLIN STREET, WILMINGTON, DELAWARE 19806 302.655.7077

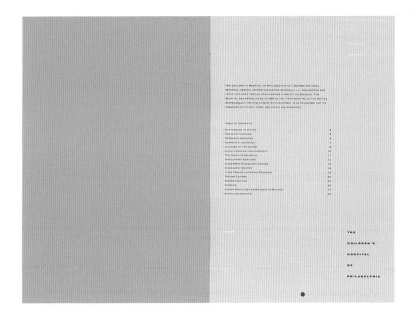

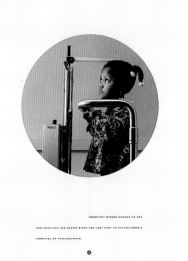

CLIENT: THE CHILDREN'S HOSPITAL OF PHILADELPHIA ■ DESIGN FIRM: GUNSELMAN + POLITE ■ ART DIRECTOR/DESIGNER/PRODUCTION MANAGER: MICHAEL GUNSELMAN ■ PHOTOGRAPHER: ED ECKSTEIN ■ WRITER: JOAN DELCOLLO ■ TYPOGRAPHER: COMPOSING ROOM ■ PAPER SELECTION: POTLATCH KARMA, MIAMI MEDALLION ■ PRINTER: LEBANON VALLEY OFFSET ■ NUMBER OF PAGES: 44 ■ TYPE SELECTION: UNIVERS 73, COPPERPLATE 32/BC ■

· ·

▲ American National Corporation is a commercial bank serving companies located in the Chicago area, southeast Wisconsin, and northwest Indiana. In the defined markets, there are approximately 30,000 companies within our targeted sales size; primarily, with annual sales of $5 to $150 million; secondarily with sales of $500,000 to $5 million. American National Corporation's annual report is focused entirely on these markets. □ The strategy in our annual report was to communicate our market leadership position, which was achieved through our strong customer focus. This was demonstrated by our full-service capabilities serving a diverse range of businesses. □ Our report was the single most important communications tool used by our commercial bankers, and both its copy and design were consistent with our business philosophy and the image we project. In the end, the report surpassed its expectations thanks in part to our designers. The solid relationship we have formed with them is based on their talent and professionalism, and had enabled us to minimize the time we spent on the day-to-day issues related to the reports production. The designer had a good understanding of American National Corporation and our markets.

· ·

■ Die American National Corporation ist eine Geschäftsbank, deren Kunden Unternehmen mit Sitz in Chicago und Umgebung, im Südosten von Wisconsin und im Nordwesten von Indiana sind. In diesen Märkten gibt es etwa 30 000 Unternehmen, die aufgrund ihrer Verkaufszahlen als Kunden für uns in Frage kommen: in erster Linie Unternehmen mit jährlichen Verkaufszahlen von $5 bis $150 Millionen, in zweiter Linie solche mit Verkaufszahlen zwischen $500 000 bis $5 Millionen. Unser Jahresbericht richtet sich spezifisch an diese Zielmärkte. □ Die Strategie, die wir diesmal verfolgt haben, bestand darin, unsere marktführende Position hervorzuheben, die wiederum auf unserer starken Kundennähe beruht. Dies wird durch unser umfassendes Dienstleistungsangebot vermittelt, das von den unterschiedlichsten Unternehmen beansprucht wird. □ Unser Jahresbericht ist das wichtigste Kommunikationsmittel, das uns zur Verfügung steht, und sowohl Inhalt als auch Design stimmen überein mit unserer Geschäftsphilosophie und dem Unternehmensbild, das wir nach aussen projizieren. Der Jahresbericht übertraf unsere Erwartungen, und dies ist zum Teil unseren Designern zu verdanken. Das solide Verhältnis, das wir mit ihnen aufgebaut haben, basiert auf ihrem Können und ihrer Professionalität, die es uns ermöglichte, den Zeitaufwand für die täglichen Fragen im Zusammenhang mit der Entstehung des Berichts zu optimieren. Der Designer besass ein gutes Einfühlungsvermögen für die American National Corporation und die Märkte, die wir bedienen.

· ·

● L'American National Corporation est un établissement de crédit au service des entreprises de la région de Chicago, du sud-est du Wisconsin et du nord-ouest de l'Indiana. Ce marché comporte environ 30 000 entreprises qui ont le volume d'affaires requis: tout d'abord, celles qui ont des chiffres de vente annuels de 5 à 150 millions de dollars; en second, celles qui tournent autour de 500 000 $ à 5 millions de dollars par an. Le rapport annuel de l'American National Corporation se concentre exclusivement sur ces marchés. □ Notre stratégie visait à faire connaître notre position de leader dans cette branche, un succès qui repose sur nos contacts étroits avec la clientèle. Cela s'explique par les capacités multiples de nos services qui répondent aux besoins de tout un éventail d'entreprises. □ Notre rapport annuel est l'outil de communication le plus important utilisé par notre établissement; le texte et le design sont adaptés à notre conception des affaires et à l'image que nous projetons. Finalement, le rapport aura surpassé toutes nos attentes, en partie grâce à nos designers. Les solides relations que nous avons établies avec eux se basaient sur leur talent et leur professionnalisme, ce qui nous a permis de réduire au minimum le temps que nous devions consacrer aux questions journalières concernant la production du rapport. Le designer a vite compris la nature de l'American National Corporation et des marchés auxquels nous proposons nos services.

[R. RENEE MCKENNA]

AMERICAN NATIONAL BANK AND TRUST COMPANY OF CHICAGO: 33 NORTH LASALLE STREET
CHICAGO, ILLINOIS 60690 312.661.5000

CROSBY ASSOCIATES, INC.

. . . .

▲ Regarding the basic concept, the American National Corporation Annual Report is a collaboration between client and designer, although theme and design direction is developed and recommended by the designer. This year, the concept featuring bank customers in their business environments—combining pastel, illustrated backdrops and portrait photography—was not difficult to sell or execute. We did produce an actual situation test shot prior to getting the final go-ahead from senior management. □ Monetarily, our budget is determined before the development and approval of design concepts. We had to be very creative and careful in keeping within the constraints of the budget. In general, clients tend to be more budget conscious than in previous years—as a result of the current economic conditions. □ The book was not designed on the computer even though we have full computer capabilities. Our client was pleased with the final result and we are looking forward to working on next year's annual report.

. . . .

■ Das Grundkonzept für den Jahresbericht der American National Corporation entstand in Zusammenarbeit mit dem Kunden, wobei Thema und Gestaltung vom Designer vorgeschlagen und entwickelt wurden. Das Konzept des diesjährigen Jahresberichts, das sich auf Kunden der Bank in ihrer geschäftlichen Umgebung konzentrierte und diese in einer Kombination von pastellfarbenen Hintergründen und Porträtphotographien zeigte, bereitete weder beim Verkauf der Idee noch bei der Durchführung Schwierigkeiten. Wir machten Testbilder von realen Situationen, bevor wir von der Geschäftsleitung endgültig grünes Licht für unsere Idee erhielten. □ Was das Finanzielle betrifft, stand das Budget bereits vor der Entwicklung und der Genehmigung des Designkonzepts fest. Wir waren gezwungen, sehr kreativ und vorsichtig damit umzugehen, um es nicht zu überschreiten. Im allgemeinen sind Kunden budgetbewusster als in den vergangenen Jahren. □ Das Design des Jahresberichts entstand nicht auf dem Computer, obwohl die notwendige Infrastruktur dafür vorhanden gewesen wäre. American National war sehr zufrieden mit dem Endprodukt, und wir freuen uns bereits auf die Zusammenarbeit für den nächsten Jahresbericht.

. . . .

● Pour ce qui est du concept de base, le rapport annuel de l'American National Corporation résulte d'une collaboration entre le client et le designer, bien que l'élaboration du sujet et la réalisation du design aient été confiées au designer. Le rapport de cette année, qui montrait des clients de la banque dans leur cadre de travail, combinant des toiles de fond colorées au pastel et des photographies de portrait, ne fut pas trop difficile à vendre ni à exécuter. Nous avons produit des épreuves du projet final avant d'obtenir le feu vert de la direction. □ Du point de vue financier, notre budget était déterminé avant l'élaboration et l'acception du concept. Il nous a fallu faire preuve de créativité et de prudence pour respecter ces contraintes de budget. En général, les clients ont tendance à faire beaucoup plus attention à ces questions que les années passées. Le design de ce rapport annuel n'a pas été conçu sur ordinateur bien que nous ayons toutes les compétences pour le faire. Notre client était enchanté du résultat final et nous nous réjouissons à l'avance de travailler sur le rapport de l'année prochaine de cette société.

[JACKLIN PINSLER]

CROSBY ASSOCIATES: INC., 676 NORTH ST. CLAIR, #1805, CHICAGO, ILLINOIS 60611 312.951.2800

CLIENT: AMERICAN NATIONAL CORPORATION ■ DESIGN FIRM: CROSBY ASSOCIATES, INC. ■ ART DIRECTOR: JACKLIN PINSLER ■ DESIGNER: JACKLIN PINSLER ■ PHOTOGRAPHER: TOM LINDFORS ■ ILLUSTRATOR: PAM ROSSI ■ WRITER: RENEE MCKENNA ■ PRODUCTION MANAGER: BARB HOLBERT ■ TYPOGRAPHER: MASTER TYPOGRAPHERS ■ PAPER SELECTION: REFLECTIONS, STARWHITE ■ PRINTER: BRADLEY PRINTING ■ NUMBER OF PAGES: 40 ■ TRIM SIZE: 8½ x 11 INCHES ■ TYPE SELECTION: GARAMOND SIMONCINI, UNIVERS 67 ■

ARCO

Alaska

Lower 48 States

United Kingdom

Indonesia

Australia

Europe

1990 ANNUAL REPORT

ARCO

. . . .

■ ARCOs Jahresbericht richtet sich in erster Linie an unsere Aktionäre. Da der grösste Teil der Unternehmensaktien von Banken, Investmentfonds und ähnlichen Unternehmen gehalten werden, besteht unser Zielpublikum aus anspruchsvollen Investoren mit fundierten Kenntnissen der Petroleumindustrie. In zweiter Linie sollte der Jahresbericht das Unternehmen ARCO zukünftigen Investoren, Geschäftspartnern oder Mitarbeitern vorstellen. □ Das Konzept des Jahresberichts 1990 sah die Darstellung eines zukunftsorientierten Unternehmens vor, in dem soziales Bewusstsein, technologische Errungenschaften und Geschäftsinstinkt hoch eingeschätzt werden. Wir wollten sowohl die finanziellen und technologischen Erfolge des Unternehmens als auch unsere führende Rolle in der Industrie porträtieren, ohne den menschlichen Aspekt der Organisation zu vernachlässigen. □ Die computergenerierten Illustrationen zeugen von einem hohen technischen Niveau, und die Zitate der Geschäftsleitung geben Einblick in die Denkprozesse des Unternehmens. Im Brief an die Aktionäre zeigen die Photos, in denen sowohl der Vorstandsvorsitzende als auch der Präsident anstatt allein im Sitzungszimmer zusammen mit Mitarbeitern gezeigt werden, dass sich ARCO um seine Mitarbeiter kümmert und somit auch um seine Zukunft. Diese Darstellung im Jahresbericht entspricht der Realität einer aktiven Geschäftsleitung, der die Mitarbeiter wichtig sind. □ Designer und Geschäftsleitung müssen eng zusammenarbeiten, von der Konzeptdiskussion bis zu den letzten Besprechungen und der endgültigen Produktion. Ohne ein gutes Verhältnis zwischen Auftraggeber und Designer wäre die Produktion eines Jahresberichts eine Katastrophe und auch nicht der Mühe wert.

. . . .

● Le rapport annuel ARCO est conçu et réalisé en premier lieu pour les actionnaires. La majorité des actions sont détenues par les banques, les fonds d'investissements et autres instituts du même genre. Ceux qui reçoivent donc ce rapport ont une ample connaissance de l'industrie pétrolière. En second lieu, le rapport annuel ARCO sert d'introduction à tous ceux qui songent à investir dans cette société, à nos partenaires commerciaux et à nos collaborateurs. □ Le rapport annuel 1990 a été conçu de manière à montrer une société qui va de l'avant, où la conscience sociale, les performances techniques et un sens aigu des affaires sont hautement appréciés. Nous voulions présenter les succès financiers et techniques, aussi bien que le rôle de leader de l'entreprise au niveau industriel, sans négliger les aspects humains de l'organisation. Nous pensons que cette mission a été remplie. □ Les illustrations réalisées sur ordinateur témoignent d'une technique sophistiquée et les citations des cadres permettent de comprendre le processus de décision. Dans la Lettre aux actionnaires, des photos qui mettent en scène le président et le président-directeur général en pleine action, au milieu du personnel, révèlent une société soucieuse des hommes et des femmes qui y travaillent et de leur avenir. Le rapport montrait avec justesse une direction active, qui se préoccupe de ses employés. □ Les relations entre les représentants de la société et le designer ont été essentielles pour le succès du rapport annuel. De l'acceptation du concept aux révisions et à la production finale, le designer a dû travailler en étroite collaboration avec les cadres. Sans une bonne relation entre le client et le designer, un rapport annuel serait un désastre et ne vaudrait pas la peine, ni pour les uns, ni pour les autres.

▲ ARCOs annual report is designed and produced with the ARCO stockholder as its primary audience. The majority of the company's shares are held by banks, investment funds and the like. Therefore, those who receive the annual are sophisticated investors with breadth of knowledge in the petroleum industry. Secondarily, the ARCO annual report serves as an introduction to ARCO for those who are considering investing in the company, doing business with, or pursuing a career with ARCO. □ The 1990 annual report was designed to show a forward-looking company where social consciousness, technical achievements, and business acumen were highly valued. We wanted to portray the company's financial and technological successes as well as its leadership role in the industry while reflecting human aspects of the organization. We believe that this mission was fulfilled. □ The computer-generated artwork displayed a level of technical sophistication and the management quotations provided insight into the corporate thought process. Through the Letter to the Stockholders and the accompanying photographs, in which both the Chairman and the President were photographed in action with ARCO employees rather than in the boardroom, ARCO revealed a company concerned about its people and, through them, its future. This accurately reflected an active management which was involved with the people. □ The relationship between company representatives and the designer was vital to the success of the annual report. From the point of concept agreement to the reviews and final production, the designer must work closely with the management. An annual report without a good client/designer relation would be a disaster and not worth the effort on either side.

[LODWRICK COOK]

ARCO: 515 SOUTH FLOWER STREET, LOS ANGELES, CALIFORNIA 90051 213.486.3738

▲ Our client had some definite ideas that they wished to have communicated in their 1990 annual report. They wanted a book that represented their leading position, financially and technologically, in the oil industry. They wanted to include maps showing world involvement and quotes from management which would highlight achievements and humanize the message. □ The client encouraged us to forget the previous restrictions and break from tradition in order to represent a vigorous, forward-thinking company. Our original idea for the graphics was to use landsat images in order to make the maps more unique and promote the idea of the leading-edge technology that ARCO uses in exploration and other facets of the company's business development. □ Because of the vast area that had to be shown and the difficulty of controlling the images aesthetically, we dropped the landsat idea and proposed the concept of using the computer as the common medium for developing the imagery. We discovered that through experimentation we could develop maps on the computer that resembled landsat images. By using techniques which emphasized digitization and pixelization, we converted black-and-white line drawings and artwork to color, thus creating a commonality to all of the imagery in the book and underlining the technological look. □ The budget of this book was based on very strict, up-front parameters, which needed to be adjusted slightly after we changed the medium for creating the graphics. In general, we are experiencing budgets that are tighter in some industries, but for most moderation and caution is the key. Success was the outcome of the ARCO annual report.

■ Unser Kunde hatte ganz bestimmte Ideen, die im Jahresbericht 1990 berücksichtigt werden mussten. Der Jahresbericht sollte die führende Marktposition der Firma im finanziellen und im technologischen Bereich der Ölindustrie darstellen. Er wollte ferner Karten zur Illustration der weltweiten Betätigung der Firma, und er wollte durch Zitate der Geschäftsleitung Leistungen des Unternehmens hervorheben und der Gesamtbotschaft des Berichts einen menschlichen Aspekt verleihen. □ Der Kunde ermunterte uns, Restriktionen vergangener Jahre zu ignorieren und mit der Tradition zu brechen, um auf diese Weise eine visionäre, vorausdenkende Firma zu porträtieren. Wir dachten ursprünglich an den Einsatz von Satellitenbildern für die Landkarten, womit gleichzeitig die Spitzentechnologie dargestellt worden wäre, die ARCO bei der Ölsuche und in anderen Bereichen einsetzt. □ Die Grösse des darzustellenden Gebiets und die schwierige Bildkontrolle sprachen jedoch gegen diese Idee. Wir entdeckten, dass wir mit dem Computer Bilder herstellen konnten, die Satellitenbildern sehr ähnlich sind. Dank der Anwendung von Digitalisierungs- und Pixelauflösungstechniken gelang es uns, schwarzweisse Strichzeichnungen und Illustrationen farbig wiederzugeben. Damit erzielten wir nicht nur eine Kontinuität bei den Illustrationen, sondern konnten auch dem Bericht ein «technologisches» Aussehen verleihen. □ Das Budget beruhte auf einem sehr strikten, im voraus festgelegten Rahmen. Viele Industriebereiche haben niedrigere Budgets, doch den meisten geht es um einen zurückhaltenden Eindruck. Der ARCO-Jahresbericht war ein durchschlagender Erfolg.

● Notre client avait une idée bien précise de ce qu'il désirait communiquer dans ce rapport annuel 1990. Ils voulaient un livre qui expose leur position de leader dans le secteur de l'industrie pétrolière, aussi bien sur le plan financier que technologique. Des cartes devaient évoquer l'internationalité d'ARCO et des citations de la direction mettre l'accent sur les réalisations et humaniser le message. Le client nous invita à oublier les restrictions antérieures et à rompre avec la tradition en représentant une société en bonne santé et tournée vers l'avenir. Nous eûmes l'idée d'utiliser des images-satellites afin de rendre les cartes plus originales et de promouvoir l'idée d'une technologie de pointe, celle qu'ARCO utilise dans la prospection pétrolière et le développement commercial de l'entreprise. □ A cause du vaste domaine qui devait être abordé et de la difficulté de contrôler l'esthétique des images, nous avons renoncé à cette idée et nous avons proposé d'utiliser l'ordinateur. Nous avons découvert qu'en expérimentant, nous pouvions élaborer des cartes qui ressemblent à des images-satellites. En employant des techniques qui mettent l'accent sur les signes digitalisés et les pixels, nous avons transposé en couleurs des dessins au trait et des illustrations en noir et blanc, créant une unité de l'image et soulignant le côté technologique d'ARCO. □ Le budget de ce livre avait été fixé dès le début; il dut être légèrement ajusté après que nous ayons changé de support pour la conception graphique. En général, nous faisons l'expérience de budgets plus modestes dans certaines industries; pour la plupart, la modération est de mise. Le rapport annuel a été extrêmement bien accueilli.

[C. CLAUDIA JEFFRIES]

THE JEFFRIES ASSOCIATION: 430 SOUTH WESTMORELAND AVENUE, LOS ANGELES, CALIFORNIA 90020 213.388.4002

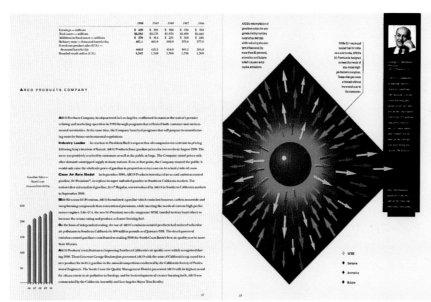

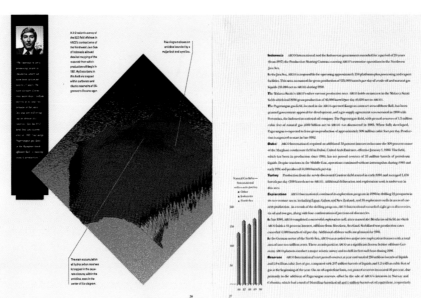

CLIENT: ARCO ■ DESIGN FIRM: THE JEFFERIES ASSOCIATION ■ ART DIRECTOR: RON JEFFERIES ■ DESIGNER: SCOTT LAMBERT ■
PHOTOGRAPHER: KEITH WOOD ■ ILLUSTRATOR: HANK FISCHER ■ WRITER: LINDA DOZIER ■ PRODUCTION MANAGER: SCOTT LAMBERT
■ TYPOGRAPHER: ARCO TYPESETTING ■ PAPER SELECTION: POTLATCH VINTAGE GLOSS, SIMPSON EVERGREEN COATED,
EVERGREEN ■ PRINTER: GEORGE RICE & SONS ■ NUMBER OF PAGES: 72 ■ TYPE SELECTION: ITC BASKERVILLE, UNIVERS ■

PERFORMING

THE ART OF

BUSINESS

BANKING

COMMERCEBANCORP

· ·

▲ CommerceBancorp sought to communicate a corporate message that would appeal not only to our primary audience of shareholders and customers, but to prospective customers and market analysts as well. ☐ While we operate in a highly regulated, traditional industry with conservative images, CommerceBancorp wanted an annual report delivered to audiences which demonstrated, in a very creative way, that we not only play by the rules, we continually move ahead by sticking to them. We felt that the use of illustration for graphs accurately communicated that we are a progressive institution. ☐ The annual report certainly met its objectives and we received many positive comments about it. We felt this was due to our design firm taking the time to understand our company's "personality." Without this insight, a representative report would not have been possible. Having a good working relationship with the design firm was essential in producing a successful annual report.

· ·

■ CommerceBancorp wollte eine Botschaft, die nicht allein das primäre Zielpublikum von Aktionären und Kunden anspricht, sondern auch potentielle Kunden und Marktanalysten. ☐ Zwar operieren wir in einer strikt regulierten und traditionellen Industrie mit konservativen Werten, doch CommerceBancorp wollte einen Jahresbericht, der den Lesern auf kreative Art zeigt, dass wir uns nicht nur an die Regeln halten, sondern uns dabei auch fortwährend weiterentwickeln. Wir waren überzeugt, dass Graphiken die Tatsache, dass wir eine progressive Institution sind, angemessen vermitteln. ☐ Der Jahresbericht hat seinen Zweck erfüllt, und wir erhielten viele positive Kommentare. Wir glauben, dass dies unserer Designfirma zu verdanken ist, die sich die Zeit nahm, die «Persönlichkeit» unseres Unternehmens zu erfassen. Ohne diesen tiefen Einblick wäre ein repräsentativer Jahresbericht nicht möglich gewesen. Eine gute Beziehung mit der Designfirma war ausschlaggebend für den Erfolg des Jahresberichts.

· ·

● L'intention de CommmerceBancorp était de transmettre des informations qui s'adressent non seulement à notre public principal d'actionnaires et de clients, mais aussi aux clients potentiels et aux analystes de marché. ☐ Bien que nous opérions dans un secteur strictement réglementé, traditionnel, qui a une image conservatrice, CommerceBancorp voulait offrir à ces différents publics un rapport annuel qui démontre de manière créative que non seulement, nous respectons les règles, mais que cela ne nous empêche pas d'aller de l'avant. Nous étions convaincus qu'en utilisant l'illustration pour les graphiques, nous communiquions exactement ce que nous étions, une institution progressive. ☐ Le rapport annuel a satisfait ces objectifs et nous avons reçu de nombreux commentaires positifs à son sujet. Nous estimons que c'est dû au fait que la firme de design a pris le temps de comprendre la «personnalité» de notre entreprise. Sans cela, il n'aurait pas été possible de réaliser un rapport représentatif. Avoir de bonnes relations avec la firme de design est la chose essentielle pour produire un rapport annuel réussi.

[CLYDE H. GOSSERT]

COMMERCEBANCORP: 1201 DOVE STREET, NEWPORT BEACH, CALIFORNIA 92660 714.557.1012

LARRY PAO DESIGN

▲ The direction for the 1990 annual report was provided by CommerceBancorp. The theme of the "Art of Business Banking" was one the bank had used for other promotions and provided us with a direction largely open to illustration. The annual report was intended for use as a marketing tool as well as a financial report, and the bank had built a solid reputation in a troubled industry by adhering to business banking basics—thus, performing the art of business banking. ☐ The illustrations gave appropriate attention to the bank's financial performance. Six concepts were presented, with the executed version the most adventuresome of the six. Needless to say, we were very pleased when the president of the bank selected the executed version without hesitation. The officers were thrilled with it and the framed illustrations now hang in the bank's corporate offices. The illustrations were also applied to the covers of the quarterly reports, and to greeting cards used for bank correspondence. Budget parameters were established up-front, with a request made that our execution not exceed the budget of the 1989 annual report. Cost-effective computer-generated typography was used, with the majority of our typesetting performed in this manner.

■ Die Ausrichtung des Jahresberichts 1990 wurde von CommerceBancorp festgelegt. Zwar hatte die Bank das Thema «Die Kunst des Geschäftsbanking» bereits für andere Werbezwecke benützt, doch liess es uns einen breiten Spielraum für Illustrationen. Der Jahresbericht sollte sowohl Marketinginstrument als auch Finanzbericht sein. Die Bank hatte sich einen guten Ruf in einer von Schwierigkeiten gezeichneten Industrie erworben, indem sie sich an die Grundlagen des Geschäftsbanking hielt und so auch die Kunst des Geschäftsbanking praktizierte. ☐ Die Illustrationen stellten die finanziellen Leistungen der Bank angemessen dar. Sechs Konzepte wurden vorgelegt, und das ausgeführte ist das «abenteuerlichste» von allen. Selbstverständlich waren wir sehr erfreut, als der Präsident der Bank ohne zu zögern dieses Konzept auswählte. Die Mitarbeiter waren begeistert, und die gerahmten Illustrationen hängen nun in den Büros des Hauptsitzes. Die Illustrationen wurden auch für die Umschläg der Vierteljahresberichte und für Gruss- und Glückwunschkarten der Firma verwendet. Das Budget wurde von Anfang an festgelegt. Forderung: Das Budget des Jahresberichts 1989 darf nicht überschritten werden. Es wurde kostengünstiger, computergenerierter Schriftsatz verwendet. Wir machten den Grossteil der Setzarbeit mit dem Computer.

● Les grandes lignes du rapport annuel 1990 ont été définies par la CommerceBancorp. Le thème de «L'art des affaires bancaires» avait été utilisé pour d'autres opérations de promotion, mais il offrait de vastes possibilités pour les illustrations. Ce document devait pouvoir être employé aussi pour le marketing et comme rapport financier. D'autre part, cette banque jouit d'une solide réputation dans un domaine qui connaît des difficultés: elle est en effet restée fidèle aux grands principes de gestion des banques – pratiquant par conséquent «l'art des affaires bancaires». ☐ Les illustrations ont permis d'attirer l'attention sur les performances financières de cet institut. Six concepts ont été présentés, dont un rendu du plus aventureux des six. Nul besoin de dire combien nous avons été ravis lorsque le directeur de la banque a sélectionné ce projet sans hésiter. Les membres du comité directeur étaient vraiment aux anges et les illustrations encadrées ornent maintenant les bureaux de la banque. Ces dernières ont été aussi utilisées sur les couvertures des rapports trimestriels et des cartes de vœux. Les conditions budgétaires avaient été fixées dès le départ; on nous avait demandé expressément de ne pas dépasser le montant du rapport 1989. Une typo économique, réalisée sur ordinateur, comme la plupart de nos textes, a été adoptée.

[SUZANNE PAO]

LARRY PAO DESIGN INC.: 151 KALMUS, SUITE J2, COSTA MESA, CALIFORNIA 92626 714.557.1012

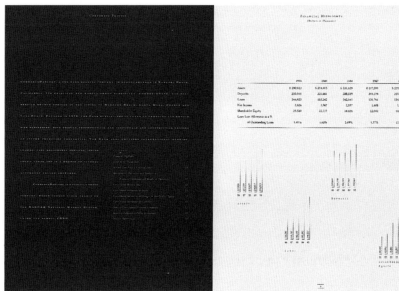

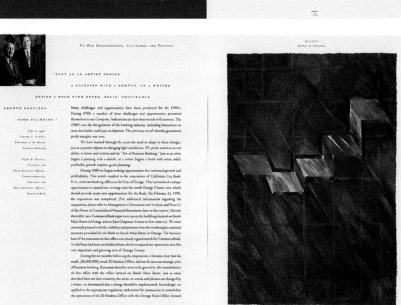

CLIENT: COMMERCEBANCORP ■ DESIGN FIRM: LARRY PAO DESIGN, INC. ■ ART DIRECTOR: LARRY PAO, MICHAEL DULA ■ DESIGNER: LARRY PAO, MICHAEL DULA ■ PHOTOGRAPHER: LONNIE DUKA ■ ILLUSTRATOR: FANGFANG LI GUO ■ WRITER: COMMERCEBANCORP ■ PRODUCTION MANAGER: LARRY PAO DESIGN, INC. ■ TYPOGRAPHER: MACINTOSH, ADOBE FONTS ■ PAPER SELECTION: POTLATCH QUINTESSENCE ■ PRINTER: LITHOGRAPHIX, INC. ■ NUMBER OF PAGES: 32 PLUS COVER ■ TRIM SIZE: 8 ½ x 11 INCHES ■ TYPE SELECTION: CENTAUR, ENGRAVURE ■

GENDEX CORPORATION

ANNUAL REPORT

1991

GENDEX

▲ We are an innovative and progressive company, and fiscal 1991 was a milestone year for us. We acquired a company one-and-a-half times our size, identified synergies rarely found in acquisitions, and gained depth of management. We consolidated our manufacturing facilities from four plants to two and managed through a weak economy. Our opportunity for the future is to adapt our operations to this challenging environment without disrupting the strategic momentum of our business. Our annual report needed to reflect these elements. ☐ Existing and potential institutional and retail shareholders are our primary audiences. Our customers, followed by our suppliers and employees are the secondary audiences. ☐ Our design team is very progressive and also brings a great wealth of annual report experience to the table. A good relationship with them is key. We feel we worked extremely well together to produce a book that is a financial report, a sales and marketing tool, and a work of art all rolled into one.

■ Für unsere innovative und fortschrittliche Firma war das Geschäftsjahr 1990/91 ein Meilenstein in der Firmengeschichte. Wir erwarben ein Unternehmen, das eineinhalbmal grösser als unsere Firma ist. Es gelang uns, Synergien wahrzunehmen, die selten bei Übernahmen realisiert werden können, und wir waren in der Lage, in bezug auf das Management an Tiefe zu gewinnen. Unsere Produktionskapazitäten konnten von vier auf zwei Produktionsanlagen konsolidiert werden, was sich für uns als Vorteil in der geschwächten Wirtschaftslage erwies. Wir müssen nun die Gelegenheit wahrnehmen, unseren Betrieb an das rauhere Wirtschaftsklima anzupassen, ohne unsere Ziele aus den Augen zu lassen. Im Jahresbericht 1991 wollten wir all diese Elemente wiedergeben. ☐ Bestehende und potentielle institutionelle Investoren sowie Einzelanleger sind unser Hauptpublikum. Unsere Kunden (sowohl Verteiler als auch Ärzte), gefolgt von unseren Zulieferern und Mitarbeitern, bilden das sekundäre Publikum. ☐ Unser Designerteam ist sehr progressiv und bringt breite Erfahrungen im Bereich der Jahresberichtsproduktion mit. Der Schlüssel zum Erfolg liegt in einem guten Arbeitsverhältnis. Wir sind der Überzeugung, dass die Zusammenarbeit mit dem Designerteam hervorragend geklappt hat bei der Produktion dieses Jahresberichtes, der ein Finanzbericht, ein Verkaufs- und Marketinginstrument sowie auch ein Kunstwerk ist – alles in einem.

● Nous sommes une entreprise innovatrice et progressiste, et l'année commerciale 1991 aura été décisive pour nous. Nous avons racheté une société qui fait une fois et demie notre taille, nous avons identifié des synergies que l'on trouve rarement dans des acquisitions et gagné en profondeur au niveau de la direction. Nous avons renforcé nos moyens de production en passant de quatre usines à deux, ce qui constitue un atout dans une situation économique difficile. Nous avons ainsi l'occasion d'adapter nos activités à ces conditions sans interrompre le rythme de nos affaires. Notre rapport annuel devait refléter tous ces éléments. ☐ Les actionnaires institutionnels et privés, actuels et potentiels, constituent notre premier public. Nos clients (les distributeurs et les docteurs), suivis par nos fournisseurs et notre personnel, constituent notre audience secondaire. ☐ Notre équipe de designers est très dynamique et elle apportait avec elle une expérience appréciable en matière de rapports annuels. Nos bonnes relations avec eux expliquent tout. Nous estimons avoir extrêmement bien travaillé ensemble pour produire un livre qui est à la fois un rapport financier, un outil de ventes et de marketing et, qui plus est, une œuvre d'art.

[JOHN J. MCDONOUGH]
GENDEX: 901 WEST OAKTON STREET, DES PLAINES, ILLINOIS 60018-1884 708.640.4800

SAMATA ASSOCIATES DESIGN CONSULTANTS

▲ After initial meetings with our client to discuss their strategies for positioning the company within their markets, we presented the concept for this annual report, which was met with wholehearted approval. ☐ We did not have any difficulty in selling the design or execution of the annual report to Gendex. Throughout the project, our client was very supportive and enthusiastic about our ideas. We have repeatedly received commendations and positive feedback from Gendex and from others outside the company that have seen the annual report. ☐ From the very beginning, the Gendex Annual Report project was formulated and executed within strict budgetary parameters. Materials, suppliers, and production methods were carefully considered with financial limitations in mind. Generally with all of our clients we are noticing some type of budgetary "belt tightening," but in the case of Gendex, we were made aware, up-front, of the budget and we proceeded to design and produce the book accordingly. ☐ In terms of production, we are increasingly utilizing our in-house Macintosh system to provide typography services for our clients. As more of our staff members have increased their expertise in this area, we are able to take on more projects involving complex typography. The Gendex Annual Report was typeset completely in-house.

■ Nachdem wir uns mehrmals mit dem Kunden getroffen hatten, um seine Marktstrategien zu diskutieren, stellten wir das Konzept für den Jahresbericht vor. Die Firmenleitung stimmte dem Konzept voll und ganz zu. ☐ Wir hatten keinerlei Schwierigkeiten, das Konzept zu verkaufen und den Jahresbericht für Gendex zu produzieren. Während des ganzen Projektes unterstützte uns der Kunde und war begeistert von unseren Ideen. Wir erhalten auch immer wieder Lob und positive Kritik von Gendex und anderen ausserhalb der Firma, die den Jahresbericht gesehen haben. ☐ Von Anfang an wurde der Gendex-Jahresbericht einem strikten Budgetrahmen unterworfen. Materialien, Zulieferer und Produktionsmethoden wurden unter Berücksichtigung der finanziellen Richtlinien strengstens evaluiert. Im allgemeinen gilt es wohl für alle unsere Kunden, dass sie in irgendeiner Weise den Gürtel enger schnallen, doch bei Gendex wurde uns das Budget von Anfang an mitgeteilt. Wir haben Design und Produktion des Jahresberichts dem Budget angepasst. ☐ Im Produktionsbereich gehen wir immer mehr dazu über, unseren Kunden Schriftsatz anzubieten, den wir auf unseren Macintosh-Computern herstellen. Da unsere Mitarbeiter in diesem Bereich immer besser mit dem Computer umgehen können, können wir vermehrt Projekte annehmen, die komplexen Schriftsatz beinhalten. Der Gendex-Jahresbericht wurde vollumfänglich firmenintern gesetzt.

● Après les premières rencontres avec notre client pour discuter des stratégies de positionnement de l'entreprise sur le marché, nous avons présenté le concept de ce rapport annuel et il a suscité une approbation sans réserve. ☐ Nous n'avons rencontré aucune difficulté à vendre le design et à produire ce rapport annuel pour Gendex. Tout au long du projet, notre client nous a soutenu et s'est enthousiasmé pour nos idées. Nous avons à maintes reprises reçu des éloges et des réactions positives de la part de Gendex et d'autres personnes extérieures à l'entreprise qui avaient vu le rapport annuel. ☐ Dès le début, un budget rigoureux avait été établi. Les matériaux, les fournisseurs et les méthodes de production furent choisis en fonction de ces contraintes budgétaires. Dans l'ensemble, nous constatons que certains clients «se serrent la ceinture», mais dans le cas de Gendex, nous avons respecté le budget et conçu le design de ce livre en fonction de cela. ☐ En termes de production, nous utilisons de plus en plus le Macintosh afin de réaliser la typographie pour les clients. Comme de nombreux membres de notre équipe ont des compétences toujours plus vastes dans ce domaine, nous sommes capables de nous charger de projets qui demandent une typographie complexe. Le rapport annuel Gendex a été imprimé dans son intégralité au sein de l'agence.

[PAT SAMATA]

SAMATA ASSOCIATES: 101 SOUTH FIRST STREET, DUNDEE, ILLINOIS USA 60118 708.428.8600

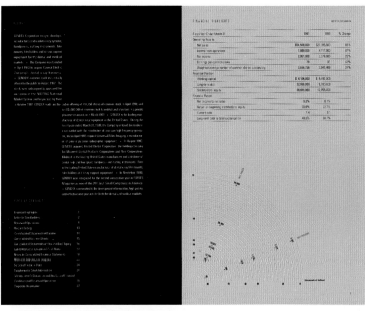

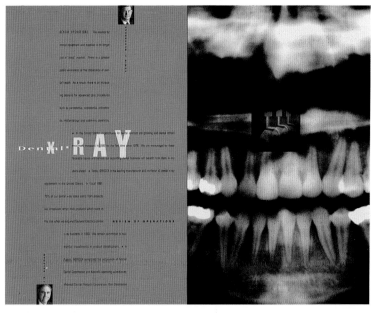

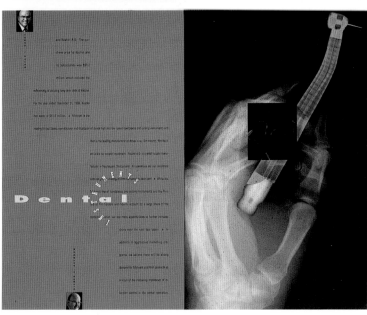

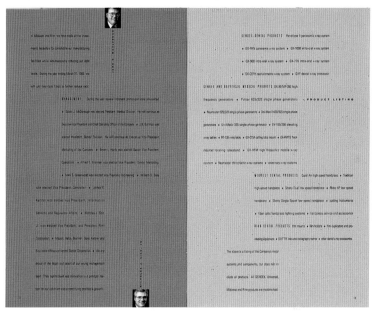

CLIENT: GENDEX CORPORATION ■ DESIGN FIRM: SAMATA ASSOCIATES ■ ART DIRECTORS/DESIGNERS: GREG AND PAT SAMATA ■ PHOTOGRAPHER: MARK JOSEPH ■ WRITER: ALLISON MCDONOUGH ■ PRODUCTION MANAGER: JANE MCMILLAN, K.C. YOON ■ PAPER SELECTION: KARMA, GENESIS ■ PAPER MANUFACTURERS: POTLATCH, CROSSPOINTE ■ PRINTER: GREAT NORTHERN DESIGN PRINTING ■ NUMBER OF PAGES: 28 ■ TYPE SELECTION: UNIVERS 39, 47, 57, 75 ■ TRIM SIZE: 7 ³/₄ x 12 ■

THE DALLAS ZOO

▲ The primary audience for this report is the 15,000-plus membership of the Dallas Zoological Society. The secondary audiences are the corporations, foundations, and philanthropic institutions that the Society petitions for monetary support. ☐ One of the difficulties in producing an annual report for the Dallas Zoo is this: most designers and graphics companies see the Zoo as a wonderful opportunity to express long-suppressed feelings about animals and the environment. In the past, the result has been reports that portray animals as cute, scary, circus-like, or anthropomorphic. The Dallas Zoo is an institution committed to the preservation of wild places and wild animals; the Zoo espouses the idea that animals should be respected as animals, not as objects put into an environment to amuse humans. I generally have a hard time reigning in designers who want to show the Zoo in a different light as it is easy to succumb to trendy interpretations. ☐ The annual report for 1989 functioned well on one level. It informed audiences through written word about the work going on at the Zoo. I personally do not feel that the design, including the way the type was set, imparted a suitable dignity to the Zoo's image. In general, I like the piece, and Peterson and Company—particularly Scott Ray—who worked very hard to please the client.

■ Das primäre Zielpublikum dieses Jahresberichts sind die über 15 000 Mitglieder der Dallas Zoological Society. Das sekundäre Publikum besteht aus den Unternehmen, Stiftungen und gemeinnützigen Institutionen, die von der Zoologischen Gesellschaft um finanzielle Unterstützung angegangen werden. ☐ Eine der grössten Schwierigkeiten bei der Produktion eines Jahresberichts für einen Zoo ist folgende: Die meisten Design- und Graphikunternehmen betrachten den Zoo als eine wunderbare Gelegenheit, um lang unterdrückten Gefühlen über Tiere und Umwelt freien Lauf zu lassen. In der Vergangenheit entstanden so Jahresberichte, in denen die Tiere entweder süss, furchterregend, zirkusähnlich oder menschenähnlich porträtiert wurden. Der Zoo von Dallas ist eine Institution, die es sich zur Aufgabe gemacht hat, wilde Tiere und ihre natürliche Umgebung zu schützen; Tiere sollten als Tiere respektiert und nicht als Objekte betrachtet werden, die in einer künstlichen Umgebung zum Vergnügen der Menschen zur Schau gestellt werden. Im allgemeinen muss ich darum kämpfen, die Designer unter Kontrolle zu halten, die den Zoo lieber in einem anderen Licht zeigen möchten. Es ist leicht, den gängigen Interpretationen zu verfallen. ☐ Der Jahresbericht 1989 informierte das Publikum im Textteil über die laufenden Arbeiten im Zoo. Ich persönlich bin der Ansicht, dass es im Design und im Schriftsatz nicht gelang, dem Image des Zoos die gebührende Würde zu verleihen. Doch im grossen und ganzen gefällt mir der Jahresbericht, und ich bin zufrieden mit Peterson and Company, insbesondere mit Scott Ray, der sich sehr bemüht hat, den Kunden zufriedenzustellen.

● Ce rapport s'adresse en tout premier lieu aux 15 000 et quelques membres de la Dallas Zoological Society. En second viennent les entreprises, les fondations et institutions philanthropiques auxquelles notre organisation sollicite un soutien financier. ☐ La production d'un rapport annuel pour le zoo de Dallas présentait notamment la difficulté suivante: la plupart des studios de design pensaient que cela serait pour eux une merveilleuse occasion d'exprimer des sentiments longtemps refoulés sur les animaux et l'environnement. Le résultat, dans le passé, ce furent des rapports annuels qui présentaient les animaux soit comme une attraction, donnant le frisson, des animaux de cirque, ou alors selon une conception anthropomorphique. Le zoo de Dallas est une institution chargée de la protection des espaces et des animaux sauvages. Il soutient cette idée que les animaux devraient être respectés en tant que tels, et non comme des objets mis dans la nature pour amuser les humains. D'une manière générale, j'ai eu du mal à réfréner des designers qui voulaient montrer le zoo sous un éclairage différent. Il est si facile de succomber aux interprétations à la mode. ☐ Le texte du rapport annuel 1989 informait le public du travail qui se fait dans le zoo. Personnellement, je ne trouve pas que le design et la manière dont la typo a été utilisée, donnaient une image du zoo assez respectable. Dans l'ensemble pourtant, le résultat me plaît et j'ai apprécié Peterson and Company, et plus particulièrement Scott Ray qui a travaillé d'arrache-pied pour nous donner toute satisfaction.

[KATHLEEN CRIST]

THE DALLAS ZOOLOGICAL SOCIETY: 621 EAST CLARENDON, DALLAS, TEXAS 75203-2996 214.943.2771

▲ For the Dallas Zoo's annual report, the only direction given to me was to show the animals in a realistic way—if illustrated. They did not want circus-like drawings or cartoon animals but an earthy feel with the use of recycled paper. Other than that it was left up to me. It was my direction to have a more graphic cover rather than a realistic drawing. I wanted to visually thread several animals and man together with one graphic image. The eyes were the perfect common element which worked with the word, "zoo." I didn't have difficulty in selling the idea to the client, because I did stick to the general feel they wanted. Actually, the two hardest selling points were the vertical headlines and the fact that I didn't want to feature some of the poor quality photographs they wanted me to use in the front of the book. Fortunately, the photos had little to do with the copy. In the end the client loved the illustrations, the flow of the book, and the fact that it was easy to read—which it is important because a large part of their contributors are elderly. □ I was given the total budget up-front which actually set the direction of the book more than any other factor. The problem facing us today is that clients still expect the same high-quality work after tightening their budgets. □ The report was done on our Macintosh computer system, along with most of our other work. All of the financials of the annual reports, however, are still done on the conventional typesetting equipment.

■ Die einzige Anweisung, die ich für das Design des Jahresberichts für den Dallas Zoo erhielt, lautete, die Tiere möglichst real darzustellen – in den Illustrationen. Zirkusähnliche Zeichnungen oder Comicsfiguren lehnte der Kunde ab. Mit dem Gebrauch von Recycling-Papier sollte ein «erdiges» Gefühl erzielt werden. Ich wollte einen Umschlag, der eher in Richtung Graphik als in Richtung realistische Zeichnung geht. Auf visuelle Art sollten Tiere und Menschen in einem graphischen Bild zusammengezogen werden. Die Augen waren das gemeinsame Element, das auch mit dem Wort «Zoo» kombinierbar war. Ich hatte keine Schwierigkeiten, dem Kunden die Idee zu verkaufen, weil ich mich an die Grundstimmung hielt, die dem Kunden vorschwebte. Die zwei grössten Probleme waren die vertikalen Headlines und die Tatsache, dass ich einige der schlechten Photographien nicht benutzen wollte, die der Kunde vorgesehen hatte. Glücklicherweise hatten die Photographien wenig mit dem Text zu tun. Am Ende war der Kunde ganz glücklich mit den Illustrationen, dem Aufbau und Tenor und mit der Leserfreundlichkeit. Letzteres war wichtig, weil ältere Leute einen Grossteil der Geldgeber ausmachen. □ Das Gesamtbudget stand vor der Auftragserteilung fest und war ausschlaggebend für das Gestaltungskonzept. Das Problem ist, dass Kunden trotz Budgetkürzungen die gewohnte Qualität erwarten. □ Wie die meisten unserer Arbeiten erstellten wir auch diesen Bericht mit einem Macintosh. Für das Kapitel über Finanzen wurden konventionelle Satzmethoden eingesetzt.

● Pour le rapport annuel du zoo de Dallas, la seule directive qui m'ait été donnée était, si nous utilisions des illustrations, de représenter les animaux de manière réaliste. Ils ne voulaient pas de dessins dans le style de ceux du cirque ou des animaux de bandes dessinées; ils désiraient transmettre l'idée de la nature en utilisant un papier recyclé. Sinon, j'avais carte blanche. Ce fut ma décision d'adopter un dessin plus graphique qu'illustratif sur la couverture. Je voulais réunir visuellement l'homme et l'animal en une seule image. Les yeux constituaient le dénominateur commun idéal qui aille avec le mot «zoo». Je n'ai pas eu de difficultés à vendre l'idée au client parce qu'elle collait avec le ton général qu'ils comptaient donner. Les points les plus délicats concernaient les titres à la verticale et le fait que je ne voulais pas faire figurer certaines photos médiocres de leur choix en première page. Heureusement, les photos n'avaient pas grand-chose à voir avec le texte. A la fin, le client fut satisfait des illustrations, du plan du livre et de sa lisibilité, car une grande partie des donateurs sont assez âgés. □ Le budget fut fixé dès le départ, ce qui détermina le contenu. Le problème aujourd'hui, c'est que les clients attendent la même qualité malgré des budgets réduits. □ Ce rapport a été exécuté sur Macintosh, comme presque tout notre travail du reste. Les chapitres financiers cependant ont été réalisés au moyen de techniques typographiques traditionnelles.

[SCOTT RAY]

PETERSON & COMPANY: 2200 NORTH LAMAR STREET, SUITE 310, DALLAS, TEXAS 75202 214.954.0522

RESEARCH

Research has been an integral part of the Zoo's agenda for many years. In 1989, the Zoo curators and staff continued to pursue aggressively their research goals, guided by the Research Master Plan. The Plan was established to co-ordinate both new and on-going research at the Zoo. ➤ Zoo curators and staff regularly publish papers in scientific journals of record, such as the *International Zoo Yearbook* and the *Bulletin of Psychonomics*; they also routinely present papers and monographs at scientific conferences and seminars, such as the American Society of Ichthyology meeting, the AAZPA conference, and meetings of the Texas Parks and Wildlife Department. ➤ In 1989, the Zoo hosted a seminar, "Applying Behavioral Research to Animal Management," for the second consecutive year. Thirty-two scientists and zoologists representing 24 zoos from across the United States and as far away as Australia spent eight days at the Zoo attending lectures and conducting research. The purpose of the workshop was to offer participants an opportunity to study methods of research on animal behavior in zoos and to encourage the study of captive animal behavior. ➤ The opening of the Wilds of Africa has allowed the Zoo unprecedented opportunities to study animals in two different environments. Many of the Zoo's mammals were moved to unfenced, open habitats in the Wilds from more confining enclosures in ZooNorth. The Zoo staff used this once-in-a-lifetime opportunity to do pre- and post-occupancy studies of the gorillas, the mandrill baboons, and the okapi. A mother/infant study is being carried out on the okapi, as well as on the Speke's gazelle, the slender-horned oryx, and the dik-dik. ➤ Mammal research in 1989 included the Gorilla Ethology Study, an examination of the Zoo's four lowland gorillas which will provide a descriptive catalogue of many of their behaviors. ➤ In 1989, telemetry studies with the red (lesser) panda continued, as did the Zoo's participation in Chimpanzoo. The Chimpanzoo project collects data on captive chimps in various zoos and compares this data with information on wild chimps; it was created by Jane Goodall and her research teams in Africa and the United States. ➤ In 1989, the Bird Department conducted a study on the space utilization of a breeding pair of Goliath herons, to use as a pre-model for designing exhibit space in the Wilds of Africa. Bird Department staff continued field research on the black-capped vireo habitats in Texas. ➤ The Reptile Department continued studies on feeding and behavior of the bushmaster, as well as studying predatory behavior in this snake. The department also collected data on perch selection of the green tree python and conducted a study of Texas rat snakes.

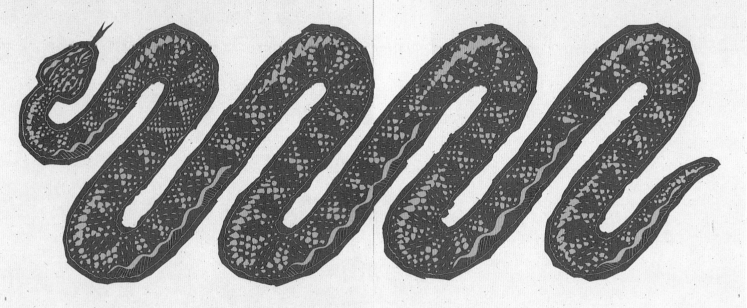

Client: THE DALLAS ZOOLOGICAL SOCIETY ■ Design Firm: PETERSON & COMPANY ■ Art Director/Designer: SCOTT RAY ■ Illustrators: JACK UNRUH, JAMES NOEL SMITH, CATHIE BLECK, BRYAN PETERSON, GREG KING ■ Writer: KATHLEEN CRIST ■ Typographer: CREATIVE TYPE ■ Paper Selection: SIMPSON EVERGREEN ■ Printer: HICKS PRINTING ■ Number of Pages: 16 ■ Type Selection: ITC FENICE ■

NIKE, INC. 1990 ANNUAL REPORT

NIKE, INC.

....

▲ The primary audience consists of current and prospective NIKE shareholders. Currently 80 percent of NIKE's publically traded shares are owned by institutional investors, and our investor relations efforts are focused on retaining as many of them as possible while also attracting additional long-term investors. Secondary audiences include retailers, consumers, banks, suppliers, and our own employees who were the main focus of the 1990 annual report. □ The goal of NIKE's 1990 Annual Report was to portray the spirit of NIKE's people as creative and innovative. NIKE had experienced a record year in sales and earnings, and had established itself as the biggest sports and fitness company in the world. We wanted to communicate to our readers that our employees, utilizing team work, are the driving force behind the footware and apparel products. Similarly, we wanted to recognize the various employee groups who made it happen. We received positive feedback from many different sources that indicated a completely successful report. □ NIKE enjoys a unique situation in that we have our own in-house graphic design department. The woman who designed the 1990 annual report [Ann Schwiebinger] has been the lead designer for each of the last four years and has worked as an assistant on the project in prior years. Obviously, this results in a very good relationship and a natural understanding of the company and how to communicate the desired message visually and in print. I feel this relationship is extremely critical to the report's success.

....

■ Primäres Zielpublikum sind unsere Aktionäre und zukünftige Anleger. Zur Zeit werden 80% der öffentlich gehandelten NIKE-Aktien von institutionellen Investoren gehalten. Unsere Bemühungen in bezug auf Investorenbeziehungen konzentrieren sich darauf, soviele institutionelle Investoren wie möglich zu behalten und gleichzeitig weitere langfristige Investoren zu gewinnen. Das sekundäre Publikum umfasst Detailhändler, Verbraucher, Banken, Zulieferer und unsere eigenen Angestellten, die im Brennpunkt des Jahresberichts 1990 standen. □ Ziel des NIKE-Jahresberichts 1990 war, die NIKE-Leute als kreativ und innovativ zu porträtieren. NIKE verzeichnete für 1990 Rekorde beim Verkauf und Gewinn und hat sich als die weltweit grösste Sport- und Fitnessfirma etabliert. Wir wollten klarmachen, dass unsere Angestellten durch Teamarbeit die treibende Kraft hinter den Schuh- und Bekleidungsartikeln sind. Gleichzeitig wollten wir aber auch allen Angestelltengruppen, die den Erfolg ermöglicht hatten, Anerkennung zollen. □ Wir erhielten ein positives Echo aus verschiedenen Kreisen – Beweise für einen erfolgreichen Jahresbericht. □ NIKE hat eine firmeninterne Abteilung für graphisches Design. Ann Schwiebinger, die den Jahresbericht 1990 gestaltet hat, zeichnete schon für die Berichte der vergangenen vier Jahre verantwortlich und hatte vorher als Assistentin beim Projekt mitgearbeitet – eine gute Voraussetzung für die Zusammenarbeit und tiefgreifende Kenntnisse der Firma sowie das Gespür für die richtige visuelle Umsetzung der Botschaft.

....

● Notre premier public se compose des actionnaires présents et futurs de NIKE. Actuellement, 80% des actions NIKE sont possédées par des investisseurs institutionnels: nous nous efforçons de les fidéliser tout en cherchant également à attirer d'autres investisseurs à long terme. Ensuite viennent les détaillants, les consommateurs, les banques, les fournisseurs et nos propres employés; le rapport annuel 1990 était consacré à ces derniers. □ Notre objectif était de donner une idée de la créativité des collaborateurs de cette marque. NIKE a connu des ventes et des bénéfices record en 1990; elle s'est en outre positionnée sur le marché comme la plus grande marque de sport et de fitness dans le monde. Nous voulions faire savoir que, derrière notre ligne de chaussures et de vêtements de sport, ce sont nos employés, qui travaillent en équipe, qui sont la force motrice de l'entreprise. Nous voulions rendre hommage aux diverses catégories de collaborateurs qui ont contribué à son essor. □ Nous avons reçu des échos positifs de sources différentes. □ NIKE jouit d'une situation exceptionnelle: nous avons en effet notre propre département de design. Ann Schwiebinger qui a conçu ce rapport annuel était notre designer préférée depuis quatre ans et elle avait travaillé comme assistante sur les projets des années passées. Notre réussite provient manifestement de nos excellentes relations, de sa compréhension de l'entreprise et de sa façon de communiquer le message souhaité au moyen de l'image et du texte. Je pense que ceci est fondamental pour le succès du rapport.

[RON PARHAM]

NIKE, INC.: 1 BOWERMAN DRIVE, BEAVERTON, OREGON 97005-6453 503.671.6453

▲ The overall direction for the report comes from Nike, but there is a great deal of collaboration along the way. In this case, the focus was on the employees behind Nike, and my job was to represent all of them (not just the senior management) in an unpredictable and irreverent way. ☐ When I first presented the idea of using pictures from photo booths in an annual report, it took some people a little while to get used to. We all agreed, though, that we wouldn't be Nike if we didn't keep pushing things a little bit more to the extreme than the average company. ☐ In terms of budgetary constraints, with this report it was adjusted slightly higher because of the dynamic concept. I know that in working on Nike's annual report, they want to push the limit of creativity *and* adhere to their budgets.

■ Die allgemeine Ausrichtung des Jahresberichts kommt von der Nike-Geschäftsleitung, aber während des Entstehungsprozesses geschieht vieles in enger Zusammenarbeit. In diesem Fall standen die Angestellten von Nike im Brennpunkt. Meine Aufgabe war es, sie alle auf überraschende, unkonventionelle Art darzustellen (und nicht nur das obere Management). ☐ Als ich zum ersten Mal vorschlug, in Passbildautomaten aufgenommene Photographien im Jahresbericht zu verwenden, brauchten einige Leute eine Weile, um sich an diese Idee zu gewöhnen. Wir stimmten aber alle überein, dass wir nicht Nike wären, wenn wir nicht mutiger wären als ein Durchschnittsunternehmen. Die Budgetvorgaben wurden aufgrund des Konzepts leicht nach oben korrigiert. Ich weiss, dass Nike im kreativen Bereich das Optimum erreichen möchte und gleichzeitig im Rahmen des Budgets bleiben will.

● L'orientation d'ensemble vient de Nike, mais nous avons coopéré tout au long du projet. Dans le cas précis, l'accent était mis sur le personnel de cette firme et mon travail consistait à les représenter tous (et pas seulement les membres de la direction), d'une manière inattendue et irrévérencieuse. ☐ Lorsque j'ai suggéré d'utiliser des photos d'identité dans un rapport annuel, certains ont mis du temps à se faire à cette idée. Mais nous étions tous d'accord sur le fait que nous ne serions pas Nike si nous ne poussions pas les choses un peu plus loin que n'importe quelle entreprise moyenne. En ce qui concerne les contraintes budgétaires, il a fallu augmenter légèrement la somme prévue. Je sais que chez Nike, ils veulent repousser les limites de la créativité tout en respectant le budget.

[ANN SCHWEIBINGER]
NIKE DESIGN: 3700 S.W. MURRAY BOULEVARD, BEAVERTON, OREGON 97005 503.671.6800

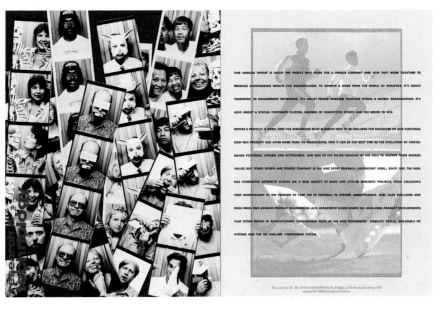

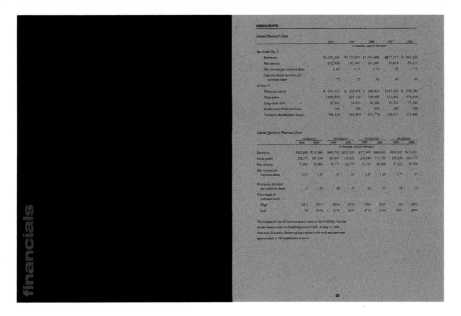

CLIENT: NIKE, INC. ■ DESIGN FIRM: NIKE DESIGN ■ ART DIRECTOR/DESIGNER: ANN SCHWIEBINGER ■ PHOTOGRAPHERS: DENNIS MENARCHY, PHILIP NEWTON, MICHAEL O'NEILL, GEORGE HOLZ, PEGGY SIROTA, CHRIS NOBLE, DAN LANGLEY, DEBORAH TURBEVILLE, THE EMPLOYEES OF NIKE & COLE HAWN ■ WRITER: LORI SEVERSON ■ PRODUCTION MANAGER: TERRY KELLY ■ TYPOGRAPHER: V.I.P. TYPOGRAPHERS ■ PAPER SELECTION: ZANDERS ICONOLUX, FRENCH SPECKLETONE ■ PRINTER: IRWIN HODSON ■ NUMBER OF PAGES: 40 ■ TYPE SELECTION: FUTURA, GARAMOND ■

Komag Annual Report 1990. Survival through continuous improvement. Success through innovation.

KOMAG, INC.

▲ Komag's 1990 Annual Report was designed with our shareholders—present and potential—in mind. The document was also written to help other stockholders, specifically customers, employees, and suppliers better understand Komag's past success and future challenges. The 1990 annual report was designed to help explain in non-technical terms what we do, how big we are, and why 1990 was a successful year. □ Building upon a four year, strong partnership with Tolleson Design, we found that the continuity of working with one firm sped the writing and design process. A solid understanding of our management style and company enabled Tolleson De-sign to recommend a format and approach that was effective and acceptable to the company. Through the use of an extended eight-page President's Letter, a four-page gatefold spread, and effective graphic illustrations and text, our graphic design firm helped to achieve our goals. A good relationship with them was crucial to its success.

■ Komags Jahresbericht für 1990 richtet sich in erster Linie an unsere Aktionäre, auch an potentielle. Ausserdem soll er anderen Anteilhabern, vor allem Kunden, Angestellten und Lieferanten, ein klareres Bild von Komags bis-herigem Erfolg und den zukünftigen Herausforderungen vermitteln. In allgemeinverständlicher Sprache sollte der Jahresbericht 1990 erklären, was wir machen, wie gross wir sind und warum 1990 ein erfolgreiches Jahr war. □ Wir konnten auf einer vierjährigen guten geschäftlichen Beziehung zu Tolleson Design aufbauen und stellten fest, dass diese Kontinuität der Zusammenarbeit der Text- und Design-Erstellung zugute kam. Eine solide Kenntnis un-serer Geschäftspolitik und -tätigkeit ermöglichte Tolleson Design ein inhaltliches und visuelles Konzept vorzu-schlagen, das für unsere Zwecke geeignet war und von der Geschäftsleitung akzeptiert wurde. Durch den Einsatz des auf acht Seiten präsentierten Briefes der Geschäftsleitung, einer Doppelseite mit Auslegern sowie graphischer Illustrationen und eines geeigneten Textes trug die Designfirma dazu bei, unsere Zielsetzungen zu verwirklichen.

● Nous avons conçu le rapport annuel 1990 de la Komag en gardant à l'esprit nos actionnaires – actuels et poten-tiels. Ce document a également été écrit pour aider d'autres actionnaires, plus exactement des clients, des em-ployés et des fournisseurs, à mieux comprendre les raisons du succès de l'entreprise et ses plans pour l'avenir. Il devait faire comprendre en termes simples ce que nous faisions, quelle était notre taille, et pourquoi l'année 1990 avait été une réussite. □ Travaillant en collaboration étroite avec Tolleson Design depuis quatre ans, nous avons observé que cette continuité accélérait le processus de rédaction et de design. Comprenant parfaitement notre style de management et le fonctionnement de la Komag, Tolleson Design a pu nous conseiller un format et un style qui fassent de l'effet et soient acceptés par l'entreprise. En décidant de réserver huit pages à la Lettre du pré-sident, en utilisant des illustrations et un texte efficaces, le studio de design nous a aidé à réaliser nos objectifs.

[DAVID ALLEN]

KOMAG INC.: 275 SOUTH HILLVIEW DRIVE, MILPITAS, CALIFORNIA 95035 408.946.2300

TOLLESON DESIGN

▲ While the direction and conceptual theme was developed in-house, it was born out of a longstanding relationship with the client. Tolleson Design has developed a clear sense of the client's business and target markets; therefore, our direction stemmed directly from our knowledge of their technology. Moreover, a four-year collaboration between Tolleson Design and business writer Lindsay Beaman makes for a strong marriage of graphic and text solutions. □ Due to the current economic situation, we have received budgets that are much smaller than in previous years. This has necessitated "creative" solutions to supplement the expenses. For this particular report, the overall budget was built up-front and was slightly modified due to changes in the report positioning. □ Overall, the client has been most pleased with this annual report, as it succeeded in representing their voice and marketing direction.

■ Zwar wurden die Richtlinien und das Konzept für den Jahresbericht hausintern entwickelt, doch entstanden sie aus einer langjährigen Beziehung zum Kunden. Tolleson Design hat klare Vorstellungen des Geschäftes und der Zielmärkte von Komag. Deshalb basierte unser Konzept unmittelbar auf diesen Kenntnissen. Ausserdem garantierte die vierjährige Zusammenarbeit mit dem Texter Lindsay Beaman ausgezeichnete Lösungen im graphischen und Textbereich. □ Aufgrund der Wirtschaftslage war das Budget kleiner als in anderen Jahren. Das forderte «kreative» Lösungen als Ausgleich. Beim vorliegenden Jahresbericht wurde von Anfang an ein Gesamtbudget festgelegt, das wegen Änderungen im Bericht leicht modifiziert werden musste. □ Der Kunde war im allgemeinen sehr zufrieden mit dem Jahresbericht, der mit Erfolg die Firma und ihre Marketingziele repräsentiert.

● Bien que les directives et le concept de ce rapport aient été élaborés par notre studio, ils sont le résultat d'une longue collaboration avec le client. Tolleson Design a ainsi pu se faire une idée très nette des affaires de son client et des marchés visés. En l'occurrence, notre projet se basait directement sur la connaissance que nous avions de leurs capacités technologiques. En outre, l'équilibre entre le graphisme et le texte est le fruit de quatre années de coopération entre Tolleson Design et le directeur commercial, Lindsay Beaman. □ En raison de la situation économique, nous avons eu des budgets plus restreints que les années précédentes. En compensation, il a fallu trouver des solutions «créatives». Le budget d'ensemble du rapport avait été établi d'avance et il dut être légèrement modifié à cause des changements apportés au cours de la réalisation. □ Dans l'ensemble, le client a été très satisfait de ce rapport annuel, en ce sens qu'il réussissait à représenter les idées de la firme et les objectifs du marketing.

[STEVE TOLLESON]

TOLLESON DESIGN: 444 SPEAR STREET #204, SAN FRANCISCO, CALIFORNIA 94105 USA 415.626.7796

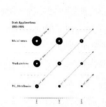

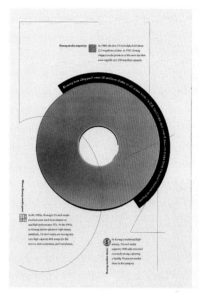

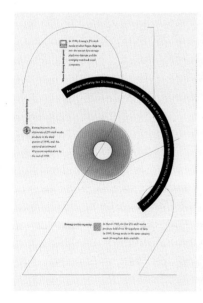

CLIENT: KOMAG ■ DESIGN FIRM: TOLLESON DESIGN ■ ART DIRECTOR: STEVE TOLLESON ■ DESIGNERS: STEVE TOLLESON, BOB AUFULDISH ■ PHOTOGRAPHER: HENRIK KAM ■ WRITER: LINDSAY BEAMAN ■ TYPOGRAPHERS: STEVE'S HOUSE OF TYPE, SPARTAN TYPOGRAPHERS ■ PAPER SELECTION: WARREN LOE DULL, STRATHMORE AMERICANA ■ PRINTER: LITHOGRAPHIX ■ NUMBER OF PAGES: 44 ■ TYPE SELECTION: SABON, MEMPHIS ■

"A **WOMAN** *is a being who has discovered her own* **NATURE.**"

Jean Giraudoux, France

Tambrands Inc.

1990 Annual Report

TAMBRANDS, INC.

▲ In creating the 1990 annual report, the Tambrands design team had two constituencies in mind. The first was the shareholder group, consisting primarily of institutional investors and investment analysts, and secondarily of individual investors. The second constituency was made up of Tambrands' ultimate customers; namely, the women who use the Company's feminine protection products. □ The annual report needed to reflect Tambrands' dedication to the female consumers who support the company's brand franchise, while communicating the facts and figures required by shareholders for an understanding of corporate results. □ The theme of the 1990 annual report was the relationship of women to the natural environment. This theme emphasized the Company's concern for the customers who purchase its products and for the environment. Photography, illustration, and text all supported the theme. The main photo spreads showed women in natural settings in four different seasons and in the four different parts of the world that make up Tambrands' major markets. Quotations from poets of the different regions supported the theme. □ As the designers of the annual report, Frankfurt Gips Balkind (FGB) was largely responsible for its success as a communications device. Understanding Tambrands' commitment to its female consumers, FGB created a design that communicated that concern on several levels, while presenting a consistent image that broke the standard annual reports mold. At the same time, FGB achieved a clear and interesting presentation of a great deal of relevant information for Tambrands' shareholders. Overall, the report achieved the Company's goals.

■ Bei der Konzeption des Jahresberichtes 1990 dachte das Designteam von Tambrands an zwei Zielgruppen: zum einen an die Aktionäre – in erster Linie institutionelle Investoren und Investment-Analytiker; zum anderen an die Endverbraucher – die Frauen, die die Monatshygieneartikel der Firma verwenden. □ Der Jahresbericht sollte sowohl das fürsorgliche Bemühen Tambrands um die Frauen zeigen, die dieser Marke vertrauen, als auch Fakten und Zahlen, die die Aktionäre über das Geschäftsergebnis informieren. □ Thema des Jahresberichtes 1990 war das Verhältnis der Frauen zu ihrer natürlichen Umwelt. Dadurch liess sich auch die fürsorgliche Einstellung des Unternehmens gegenüber den Konsumentinnen und der Umwelt zum Ausdruck bringen. Photographische und gezeichnete Illustrationen sowie der Text bezogen sich auf dieses Thema. Die Photoseiten zeigen Frauen in der Natur, aufgenommen in den vier Jahreszeiten und in vier verschiedenen Regionen der Welt, Tambrands' wichtigsten Märkten. Zitate von Dichtern aus verschiedenen Regionen unterstützten das Thema. □ Frankfurt Gips Balkind (FGB) gestalteten den Bericht und waren somit für seinen Erfolg als Kommunikationsinstrument verantwortlich. Der Bericht trägt Tambrands' Bemühen um seine weiblichen Kunden auf verschiedenen Ebenen Rechnung, und er hebt sich von den üblichen Jahresberichten ab. Gleichzeitig gelang FGB eine klare und interessante Darstellung einer grossen Menge wichtiger Informationen. Insgesamt erfüllte der Jahresbericht die Zielsetzung der Firma.

● En créant le rapport annuel 1990, l'équipe de design de Tambrands visait deux publics. Le premier était celui du groupe des actionnaires, composé tout d'abord d'investiteurs institutionnels et d'analystes financiers, et deuxièmement d'investisseurs privés. Notre second public était celui des derniers clients de Tambrands, à savoir les femmes qui utilisent nos produits de protection féminine. □ Le rapport annuel devait refléter l'engagement de Tambrands auprès des consommatrices, tout en communiquant les données et les chiffres nécessaires aux actionnaires pour comprendre les résultats de l'entreprise. □ Le rapport annuel 1990 avait pour thème la relation des femmes à la nature. Il mettait l'accent sur le fait que l'entreprise se préoccupe des femmes et de l'environnement. Les photographies, les illustrations et le texte avaient tous trait à ce sujet. Les doubles pages de photos montraient des femmes dans des décors naturels à quatre saisons différentes et dans les quatre parties du globe qui constituent les marchés principaux de Tambrands. Des citations de poètes de ces pays illustraient le sujet. □ Le succès de ce rapport annuel en tant qu'outil de communication est directement imputable à Frankfurt Gips Balkind (FGB), l'agence qui l'a conçu. Comprenant l'engagement de Tambrands envers les consommatrices, FGB a créé un design qui exprime cet effort sur plusieurs plans, tout en présentant une image solide qui sorte de l'ordinaire. FGB a réussi en même temps à faire une présentation concise et intéressante d'une grande quantité d'informations, à l'intention des actionnaires de Tambrands. Dans l'ensemble, le rapport annuel a rempli les objectifs de l'entreprise.

[PAUL E. KONNEY]

TAMBRANDS INC.: 777 WESTCHESTER AVENUE, WHITE PLAINS, NEW YORK 10604 914.696.6000

FRANKFURT GIPS BALKIND

. . . .

▲ The 1990 Tambrands, Inc. Annual Report was a continuation of the company's renewed focus on the needs and issues concerning women. (Tambrands is the global manufacturer of Tampax sanitary products.) This theme serves as a broad communication platform from which secondary themes will be developed each year. ☐ The previous year's book had introduced the company's new mission statement, illustrated by fine art images of women throughout history. ☐ This year the company wanted to highlight its concern for the environment, specifically the relationship between women and nature. We expressed this both in poetry and photo illustration. Elisabet Zeilon was commissioned to create images relating to the four seasons as viewed by women from four regions of the world. Lush, layered images were reproduced on a recycled, uncoated paper stock, in keeping with the report's theme.

. . . .

■ Der Jahresbericht 1990 für Tambrands, Inc. war eine Fortsetzung der Konzentration auf die Bedürfnisse von Frauen. (Tambrands ist der Hersteller von Tampax.) Dies ist das Grundthema, von dem aus sekundäre Themen Jahr für Jahr entwickelt werden. ☐ Im Bericht des vergangenen Jahres ging es um die Formulierung dieses Grundanliegens; als Illustrationen dienten Porträts von grossen Frauen der Geschichte. ☐ Dieses Jahr wollte die Firma ihre Sorge um die Umwelt zum Ausdruck bringen, insbesondere die Beziehung der Frauen zur Umwelt. Wir drückten dies durch Poesie und photographische Illustrationen aus. Elisabet Zeilon erhielt den Auftrag, die vier Jahreszeiten, so wie sie von Frauen aus vier Regionen der Welt erlebt werden, im Bild auszudrücken. Üppige, vielschichtige Bilder wurden auf ungestrichenem Umweltpapier gedruckt, im Einklang mit dem Thema des Berichtes.

. . . .

● Le rapport annuel 1990 de Tambrands, Inc. continuait de se concentrer sur les besoins des femmes (Tambrands est le fabricant de Tampax). Ce thème général, à partir duquel sont développés de nouveaux sujets secondaires chaque année, sert de base à la communication de l'entreprise. ☐ Le rapport de l'année passé, illustré d'images de femmes au travers de l'histoire, avait permis de présenter les nouveaux objectifs de Tambrands. ☐ Cette année, l'entreprise voulait mettre en lumière son souci de l'environnement, et plus spécialement, la relation des femmes à la nature. Nous avons exprimé cela au moyen de poèmes et de photos. Elisabet Zeilon a été chargée de créer des images ayant trait aux quatre saisons, telles qu'elles sont vécues par des femmes des quatre continents. Ces images luxueuses ont été reproduites sur un papier recyclé non couché, qui convenait particulièrement bien au sujet.

[KENT HUNTER]

FRANKFURT GIPS BALKIND: 244 EAST 58TH STREET, NEW YORK, NEW YORK 10022 USA 212.421.5888

Our Mission Summarized

1
TO BE THE LEADING SUPPLIER OF ALL TYPES OF TAMPONS WORLDWIDE.

2
TO ACHIEVE SHARE AND MARKET GROWTH OBJECTIVES THROUGH PRODUCT IMPROVEMENTS AND LINE EXTENSIONS.

3
TO BE THE LOW-COST PRODUCER WHILE MAINTAINING HIGH PRODUCT QUALITY.

4
TO DIVERSIFY ONLY IF OPPORTUNITIES OFFER NEAR-TERM PROFITABILITY.

Selected Financial Data

Years Ended December 31 (in thousands, except per share amounts)	1990	1989	1988	1987	1986
Net sales	$631,511	$583,408	$563,347	$515,611	$475,520
Operating income	149,926	27,899	131,585	124,148	116,679
Net earnings	97,760	1,719	85,276	76,601	69,130
Per share	2.30	.04	1.91	1.73	1.56
Cash distributions to shareholders	46,977	46,115	43,471	40,693	38,279
Per share	1.11	1.04	.98	.92	.86
Shareholders' equity	249,173	284,456	352,930	313,934	260,303
Total assets	381,029	411,002	465,306	408,236	363,655
Net cash provided by operating activities	118,692	97,890	99,926	65,111	79,958
Capital expenditures	39,158	14,896	16,833	22,170	28,063

Per share amounts have been restated to reflect a two-for-one stock split effected in the form of a 100% stock dividend in December 1990.

SUMMER

"In the sea
nothing lives to itself...
each living thing is
LINKED
with all
that surrounds it."
Rachel Carson, USA

Review of Operations

TAMBRANDS HAS OPERATIONS IN FIVE MAJOR AREAS: NORTH AMERICA, SOUTH AMERICA, WESTERN EUROPE, EASTERN EUROPE, AND ASIA/PACIFIC. WE WILL REVIEW SIGNIFICANT DEVELOPMENTS IN EACH OF THESE AREAS.

North America

WE UNDERTOOK MAJOR INITIATIVES IN 1990 TO STRENGTHEN THE TAMPAX FRANCHISE IN THE UNITED STATES, CANADA, AND MEXICO. THESE INITIATIVES SUCCEEDED, AND THE TAMPAX TAMPON BUSINESS IN NORTH AMERICA IS WELL-POSITIONED FOR CONTINUED GROWTH.

IN THE UNITED STATES, WE LAUNCHED THREE SIGNIFICANT PROJECTS IN 1990: 1. TO REDUCE PROMOTIONAL SELLING AND TRADE INVENTORIES; 2. TO INTRODUCE TAMPAX COMPAK TAMPONS; AND 3. TO REDIRECT OUR MARKETING EFFORTS TO FOCUS ON TEENS.

OUR PROGRAM TO REDUCE PROMOTIONAL SELLING AND TRADE INVENTORIES HAS ACCOMPLISHED ITS GOALS. IN 1990, PROMOTIONAL SALES WERE 22% LOWER THAN 1989, EVEN THOUGH ATTRACTIVE DISCOUNTS WERE OFFERED TO THE TRADE TO SUPPORT OUR INTRODUCTION OF COMPAK TAMPONS. BY YEAR-END, TRADE INVENTORIES HAD BEEN REDUCED. SHIPMENTS TO THE TRADE WERE AT THE LEVEL OF CONSUMER PURCHASES. BENEFITS OF THIS SUCCESSFUL PROGRAM INCLUDE HIGHER MARGINS, BETTER PRODUCTION PLANNING, AND MORE EFFECTIVE MANAGEMENT OF OUR CONSUMER MARKETING ACTIVITIES.

THE TAMPAX TAMPON SHARE OF THE U.S. TAMPON MARKET AT YEAR-END WAS 54% IN DOLLARS, AND 59.3% IN UNITS. THE TAMPON SHARE OF THE SANITARY PROTECTION MARKET INCREASED FROM 37% TO 37.9% YEAR-TO-YEAR, AND THE SIZE OF THE OVERALL SANITARY PROTECTION MARKET INCREASED FROM $1.6 BILLION TO $1.7 BILLION.

THE NEW TAMPAX COMPAK TAMPON WAS INTRODUCED NATIONALLY LAST SUMMER. THE PRODUCT HAS A PATENTED, TELESCOPING PLASTIC APPLICATOR THAT IS ONE-THIRD SHORTER THAN OUR STANDARD APPLICATOR, YET IT CONTAINS A FULL-SIZE TAMPAX TAMPON. FOR COMFORT AND DISCRETION, THE COMPAK TAMPON IS A SUPERIOR PRODUCT.

COMPAK TAMPONS HAVE BEEN ENTHUSIASTICALLY ACCEPTED BY 98% OF OUR KEY TRADE CUSTOMERS. BASED ON EARLY MARKET SHARE DATA, WE BELIEVE THIS PRODUCT WILL BUILD OUR TAMPAX TAMPON BUSINESS IN THE UNITED STATES. FOR PERSPECTIVE, COMPAK TAMPONS ENJOY AN 8.4% UNIT SHARE OF THE MARKET IN CANADA, WHERE THEY WERE INTRODUCED NATIONALLY IN LATE 1988.

THE REDIRECTION OF OUR U.S. MARKETING EFFORTS TO

IRIS
MUNZII
United States
Common name:
Iris

U.S. sanitary
protection market:
$1.7 billion.
• Tampax share: 37.9%.
• Tampax share of
tampon market: 59.3%.

The number of female teens in the United States is growing at three times the rate of total menstruating females.

FOCUS ON TEENS INVOLVED MANY ACTIVITIES, BUT THE KEY ELEMENT WAS EDUCATION. WE HAVE INCREASED OUR SUPPORT TO EDUCATION SUBSTANTIALLY, FOCUSING ON THE FORMATIVE 12- TO 13-YEAR-OLD AGE GROUP. WE WILL REACH 1.3 MILLION TEENS THROUGH THIS PROGRAM BY YEAR-END 1991. OUR EDUCATION STRATEGY IS THREE-FOLD: 1. PRIMARILY TO EDUCATE YOUNG TEENS ABOUT PUBERTY AND MENSTRUATION; 2. TO EXPLAIN TAMPON USE TO FEMALE TEENS AND PROMOTE TRIAL USAGE OF TAMPAX TAMPONS; AND 3. TO DIRECT FIRST-TIME USERS TO THE BEST TAMPAX PRODUCT FOR THEIR NEEDS.

IN ADDITION TO OUR DIRECT EDUCATION EFFORTS, WE HAVE INTRODUCED A 24-HOUR, TOLL-FREE TELEPHONE NUMBER FOR TEENS IN THE UNITED STATES AND CANADA, STAFFED BY WOMEN TRAINED TO RESPOND TO QUESTIONS ABOUT MENSTRUATION AND OUR PRODUCTS.

OUR ADVERTISING AND PUBLIC RELATIONS ACTIVITIES ALSO HAVE BEEN REDIRECTED TO BETTER REACH TEENS. AN EXAMPLE IS OUR SPONSORSHIP OF THE U.S. WOMEN'S SWIMMING TEAM. WE HAVE PRODUCED A VIDEO SPECIFICALLY AIMED AT TEEN SWIMMERS THROUGHOUT THE COUNTRY WHO ARE INVOLVED IN LOCAL, STATE, AND REGIONAL CHAMPIONSHIPS.

THE POPULATION OF TEENAGE WOMEN, NOW NEARLY 12 MILLION STRONG IN THE UNITED STATES, IS GROWING AT THREE TIMES THE RATE OF THE TOTAL POPULATION OF MENSTRUATING FEMALES. THE POPULATION OF MENSTRUATING FEMALES WILL GROW TO 78 MILLION OVER THE NEXT 10 YEARS.

THE IMPORTANCE OF TEENS TO THE CONTINUED GROWTH OF OUR TAMPAX FRANCHISE IS CLEAR. THIS IS THE AGE WHEN WOMEN MAKE THEIR LONG-TERM CHOICE OF FEMININE PROTECTION PRODUCT, FORMING THE BASIS FOR THE STRONG BRAND LOYALTY IN THE TAMPON CATEGORY.

OUR PLANS FOR 1991 INCLUDE CONTINUED EXPANSION OF OUR EDUCATION PROGRAM AND OTHER TEEN MARKETING ACTIVITIES. WE ALSO EXPECT TO INCREASE THE USE OF ENVIRONMENTAL THEMES IN OUR ADVERTISING, BUILDING ON THE SUCCESS OF OUR ENVIRONMENTAL TV COMMERCIAL THAT AIRED ON THE 20TH ANNIVERSARY OF EARTH DAY IN 1990. THE COMMERCIAL EMPHASIZED THAT TAMPAX FLUSHABLE TAMPONS ARE THE ONLY APPLICATOR TAMPONS THAT ARE BOTH FLUSHABLE AND BIODEGRADABLE. WE ARE PROUD THAT TAMBRANDS' FLAGSHIP BRAND HAS BEEN ENVIRONMENTALLY FRIENDLY FOR 55 YEARS.

TAMBRANDS WILL CONTINUE TO DEVELOP TAMPON PRODUCT IMPROVEMENTS AND LINE EXTENSIONS, LIKE THE COMPAK TAMPON. THE MOST RECENT EXAMPLE IS THE TAMPAX COMFORT SHAPED FLUSHABLE TAMPON, WHICH PROVIDES IMPORTANT ADVANTAGES OVER ALL EXISTING TAMPON PRODUCTS. THIS NEW PRODUCT COMBINES THE ENVIRONMENTAL BENEFITS OF AN ALL-PAPER APPLICATOR WITH A ROUNDED TIP, WHICH PROVIDES THE EASE OF INSERTION OF A PLASTIC APPLICATOR TAMPON.

IN CANADA, PROGRAMS WERE SUCCESSFULLY IMPLEMENTED IN 1990 TO REDUCE TRADE INVENTORIES AND PROMOTIONS, AND TO FOCUS MARKETING ACTIVITIES ON TEENS. OUR CANADIAN COMPANY ALSO INTRODUCED DOWNSIZED PACKAGING. SHIPMENTS IN CANADA WERE FLAT ON A YEAR-TO-YEAR BASIS, DUE TO THE REDUCTION OF TRADE INVENTORIES AND DOWNSIZING. THE TAMPAX SHARE OF THE CANADIAN TAMPON MARKET AT YEAR-END STOOD AT 61.2%.

IN MEXICO, OPERATING INCOME WAS MODESTLY POSITIVE IN 1990, A SIGNIFICANT IMPROVEMENT OVER 1989 RESULTS. TAMPAX TAMPON SHIPMENTS AND THE TAMPAX TAMPON SHARE OF THE MARKET INCREASED SUBSTANTIALLY. OUR SHARE REACHED 82% IN 1990, COMPARED WITH 73.6% IN 1989.

South America

OUR BRAZILIAN SUBSIDIARY OPERATED PROFITABLY IN 1990, FOR THE SECOND YEAR IN A ROW. TAMPAX TAMPONS REACHED NATIONAL DISTRIBUTION IN SEPTEMBER, ACHIEVING A 20% SHARE OF THE MARKET BY YEAR-END, AND 28% IN OUR ORIGINAL MARKET IN RIO DE

Worldwide operating margins increased from 22% in 1988 to 23% in 1990.

U.S. Female Teen Population Trends (IN MILLIONS): 11.9 (1990), 12.8 (1995), 13.7 (2000)

Operating Income (IN MILLIONS): $131.6 (1988), $27.9 (1989), $149.9 (1990)

CLIENT: TAMBRANDS, INC. ■ DESIGN FIRM: FRANKFURT GIPS BALKIND ■ ART DIRECTOR: KENT HUNTER ■ DESIGNER: STEVEN FABRIZIO ■ PHOTOGRAPHERS: ELISABET ZEILON, MARK JENKINSON ■ ILLUSTRATOR: MONICA RANGNE ■ WRITER: DEBORAH CAPUA ■ PRODUCTION MANAGER: FRED BARD ■ TYPOGRAPHER: FRANKFURT GIPS BALKIND ■ PAPER SELECTION: EVERGREEN ■ PAPER MANUFACTURER: SIMPSON ■ PRINTER: BRADLEY ■ NUMBER OF PAGES: 36 PLUS COVER ■ TRIM SIZE: 11 x 9 INCHES ■ TYPE SELECTION: BAUER BODONI ■

ANNUAL REPORT ILLUSTRATION

ILLUSTRATION FÜR JAHRESBERICHTE

ILLUSTRATION DES RAPPORTS ANNUELS

(THIS SPREAD) ILLUSTRATOR: STEVE JOHNSON ■ MEDIUM: OIL ■ CLIENT: LINCOLN BANCORP ■ DESIGN FIRM: BESSER JOSEPH PARTNERS ■ ART DIRECTORS: DOUGLAS JOSEPH, RIK BESSER ■ DESIGNER: DOUGLAS JOSEPH ■

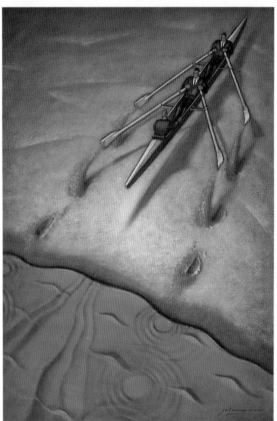

(OPPOSITE TOP) Illustrator: JOHN KLEBER ■ Medium: AIRBRUSH ■ Client: PINNACLE WEST CORPORATION ■ Design Firm: CAMPBELL & FISHER DESIGN INC. ■ Art Directors: GREG FISHER, MIKE CAMPBELL ■ (OPPOSITE CENTER) Illustrator: SAM MORROW ■ Medium: PENCIL ON PAPER ■ Client: PRINCE'S TRUST ■ Design Firm: MICHAEL PETERS LITERATURE LTD. ■ Art Director/Designer: PETER CHODEL ■ (OPPOSITE BOTTOM) Illustrator: RAUL COLON ■ Medium: COLORED PENCIL ON PAPER ■ Client: JOHNSON & HIGGINS ■ Design Firm: FRANKFURT GIPS BALKIND ■ Art Directors: AUBREY BALKIND, KENT HUNTER ■ Designer: THOMAS BRICKER ■ (ABOVE) Illustrator: BRAD HOLLAND ■ Medium: ACRYLIC ON CANVAS ■ Client: APPLIED MATERIALS ■ Design Firm: JACOBS FULTON DESIGN GROUP ■ Art Director: CAROL FULTON ■ Designers: GEOFF AHMANN, TOM HAYES ■

CAPTAIN COLLAZMENT
VIDEO FILM
MERCHANDISING
THE WONDER YEARS & JERRY

(OPPOSITE) ILLUSTRATOR: ANTHONY RUSSO ■ MEDIUM: SCRATCHBOARD ■ CLIENT: PYRAMID TECHNOLOGY ■
DESIGN FIRM: ALTMAN & MANLEY ■ ART DIRECTOR: PAUL HUBER ■ DESIGNERS: PAUL HUBER, ALBERT DOWNS,
BRENT CROXTON ■ (ABOVE) ILLUSTRATOR: SANDRA DIONISI ■ CLIENT: TURNER BROADCASTING SYSTEM,
INC. ■ DESIGN FIRM: CORPORATE REPORTS, INC. ■ ART DIRECTOR: JEFF GOLD ■ DESIGNER: JEFF GOLD ■

(ABOVE) ILLUSTRATOR: DANIELLE SURPRENANT ■ MEDIUM: PEN & INK ■ CLIENT: LAVALIN INDUSTRIES INC. ■ DESIGN FIRM: GRAPHISME LAVALIN ■ ART DIRECTOR: NÉLU WOLFENSOHN ■ (OPPOSITE) ILLUSTRATOR: BRIAN CRONIN ■ MEDIUM: PEN & INK, WATERCOLOR ■ CLIENT: WEITEK CORPORATION ■ DESIGN FIRM: ALTMAN & MANLEY ■ ART DIRECTORS: BRENT CROXTON, PAUL HUBER ■ DESIGNERS: BRENT CROXTON, ALBERT DOWNS, PAUL HUBER ■

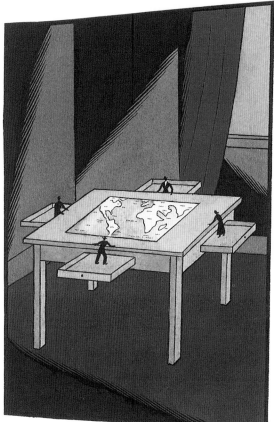

(ABOVE) ILLUSTRATOR: GUY BILLOUT ■ MEDIUM: WATERCOLOR & AIRBRUSH ■ CLIENT: ASSURANCEFORENINGEN GARD ■ DESIGN FIRM: TATHAM PEARCE ■ ART DIRECTOR: DAVID PEARCE ■ DESIGNERS: JULIE FELLOWES, DAVID PEARCE ■

(ABOVE) ILLUSTRATOR: SIMON NG ■ MEDIUM: ACRYLIC & OIL ON MASONITE ■ CLIENT: PETRO-CANADA INC. ■ DESIGN
FIRM: GOTTSCHALK & ASH INTERNATIONAL ■ ART DIRECTOR: PETER STEINER ■ DESIGNER: HÉLÈNE L'HEUREUX ■

(OPPOSITE) ILLUSTRATOR: TOM CURRY ■ CLIENT: WEITEK CORPORATION ■ DESIGN FIRM: HUBER & HUBER ■ DESIGNERS: PAUL HUBER, ALBERT DOWNS ■ (ABOVE) ILLUSTRATOR: CATHIE BLECK ■ MEDIUM: SCRATCHBOARD ■ CLIENT: REPUBLIC NEW YORK CORPORATION ■ DESIGN FIRM: BLOCH GRAULICH WHELAN INC. ■ ART DIRECTOR/DESIGNER: DAVID BLOCH ■

ILLUSTRATOR: JOE FLEMING ■ CLIENT: EDS ■ ART DIRECTOR: GARY DANIELS ■ CREATIVE DIRECTOR: DICK MITCHELL ■

ANNUAL REPORT PHOTOGRAPHY

PHOTOGRAPHIE FÜR JAHRESBERICHTE

PHOTOGRAPHIE DES RAPPORTS ANNUELS

(TOP LEFT) Photographer: JAY MAISEL ■ Camera Format: 35 MILLIMETER ■ Film: KODACHROME ■ Client: NATIONALE-NEDERLANDEN ■ Design Firm: MCDOUGALL ASSOCIATES INC. ■ Art Director: JOHN MILANO ■ Designer: JOHN MILANO ■ (TOP RIGHT) Photographer: RON BAXTER SMITH ■ Camera Format: 4 x 5 INCHES ■ Film: KODAK EKTACHROME 64 ■ Client: NORTHERN TELECOM LIMITED ■ Design Firm: PENTAGRAM DESIGN ■ Art Director: WOODY PIRTLE ■ Designer: JENNIFER LONG ■ (BOTTOM LEFT) Photographer: ARTHUR MEYERSON ■ Camera Format: 35 MILLIMETER ■ Film: FUJICHROME 50 ■ Client: BATTLE MOUNTAIN GOLD COMPANY ■ Design Firm: SAVAGE DESIGN GROUP ■ Art Directors: PAULA SAVAGE, KENNY RAGLAND ■ (BOTTOM RIGHT) Photographer: JIM BARBER ■ Camera Format: 8 x 10 INCHES ■ Film: KODAK ECKTACHROME 64 ■ Client: REEBOK INTERNATIONAL INC. ■ Design Firm: CORPORATE ANNUAL REPORTS INC. ■ Art Director: LESLIE A. SEGAL ■ Designer: VICTOR RIVERA ■

PHOTOGRAPHER: R. J. MUNA ■ CAMERA FORMAT: 2 ¼-INCH SQUARE ■ FILM: KODAK T-MAX 100 ■ CLIENT: FURON CO. ■ DESIGN FIRM: THE JEFFERIES ASSOCIATION ■ ART DIRECTOR: RON JEFFERIES ■ DESIGNER: JULIE MARKFIELD ■

(ABOVE) Photographer: TIM SIMMONS ■ Camera Format: 2 ¼ INCH SQUARE ■ Film: ILFORD FP4 ■ Client: FREEDOM HOUSE ■ Design Firm: EMERSON, WAJDOWICZ STUDIOS, INC. ■ Art Director: JUREK WAJDOWICZ ■ Designers: LISA LAROCHELLE, JUREK WAJDOWICZ ■ (OPPOSITE, ALL IMAGES) Photographer: JOHN CLARIDGE ■ Camera Format: 6 X 7 CM ■ Film: KODAK TRI-X 400 ■ Client: MACINTYRE ■ Design Firm: KB DESIGN ■ Art Director: KAREN BLINCOE ■ Designers: SIMON DRYLAND, KAREN BLINCOE ■

(TOP LEFT & RIGHT) PHOTOGRAPHER: JEFF CORWIN ■ CAMERA FORMAT: 2 ¼ INCH SQUARE ■ FILM: AGFA-PAN 100 ■ CLIENT: ST. VINCENT MEDICAL CENTER ■ DESIGN FIRM: THE WARREN GROUP ■ ART DIRECTOR: LINDA WARREN ■ DESIGNERS: THOMAS DEVINE, LINDA WARREN ■ (BOTTOM LEFT) PHOTOGRAPHER: BRIAN K. SNIDER ■ CLIENT: ENERGEN CORPORATION ■ DESIGN FIRM: EGN ADVERTISING ■ ART DIRECTOR: D. BARRETT DELOZIER ■ (BOTTOM RIGHT) PHOTOGRAPHER: HARRY DEZITTER ■ CAMERA FORMAT: 6 x 12 CM; 135 MILLIMETER LENS ■ FILM: KODAK EKTACHROME EPR 120 ■ CLIENT: THE TIMBERLAND COMPANY ■ DESIGN FIRM: TOMLINSON ADVERTISING DESIGN INC. ■ ART DIRECTOR/DESIGNER: BILL TOMLINSON ■ (OPPOSITE) PHOTOGRAPHER: THOMAS SENNETT ■ CLIENT: MAUI LAND & PINEAPPLE COMPANY ■ DESIGN FIRM: DEUTSCH DESIGN, INC. ■ ART DIRECTOR: PETER DEUTSCH ■

ANNUAL REPORTS 4

ENTRY DEADLINE: APRIL 30, 1993 | EINSENDESCHLUSS: 30. APRIL 1993 | DATE LIMITE D'ENVOI: 30 AVRIL 1993

All annual reports, capability brochures, public interest reports, and other corporate public relations material produced in a brochure format for 1990. ELIGIBILITY: All work published between April 30, 1991 and April 30, 1992.

Alle Jahresberichte einer Firma oder Organisation (Tabellen und Diagramme, Illustrationen und Photos). IN FRAGE KOMMEN: Alle Jahresberichte und ähnliche Firmenpublikationen für Öffentlichkeitsarbeit in Form von Broschüren von 1991 bis 1992.

Tous travaux publiés en relation avec le rapport annuel d'une entreprise ou d'une organisation. ADMISSION: Tous les rapports annuels et autre rapports destinés au grand public publiés sous forme de brochure en 1991 ou en 1992.

RULES

By submitting work to GRAPHIS, the sender grants permission for his or her publication in any GRAPHIS book, as well as any article in GRAPHIS magazine, or any advertisement, brochure, or other printed matter produced specifically for the purpose of promoting the sale of these publications.

ELIGIBILITY: All work produced in the 12-month period previous to the submission deadlines.

WHAT TO SEND: Please send the printed piece (unmounted but well protected). Do not send original art. For large, bulky or valuable pieces, please submit color photos or (duplicate) slides. Entries cannot be returned. Only in exceptional cases and by contacting us in advance will material be sent back.

HOW AND WHERE TO SEND: Please tape (do not glue) the entry form provided (or copy)-with full information-on the back of each piece. Entries can be sent by air mail, air parcel post or surface mail. Please do not send anything by air freight. Declare, "No Commercial Value" on packages, and label "Art for Contest." The number of transparencies and photos should be indicated on the parcel. (If send by air courier, please mark "documents, Commercial Value 00.00").

TEILNAHMEBEDINGUNGEN

GRAPHIS erhält die Erlaubnis zur Veröffentlichung der eingesandten Arbeiten sowohl im entsprechenden Jahrbuch als auch in der Zeitschrift GRAPHIS oder für die Wiedergabe im Zusammenhang mit Besprechungen und Werbematerial für GRAPHIS-Publikationen.

IN FRAGE KOMMEN: Alle Arbeiten von Fachleuten und Studenten.

WAS EINSENDEN: Bitte senden Sie uns das gedruckte Beispiel (gut geschützt). Senden Sie keine Originale. Bei unhandlichen, umfangreichen und wertvollen Sendungen bitten wir um Farbphotos oder Duplikat-Dias. Bitte beachten Sie, dass Einsendungen nicht zurückgeschickt werden können (Ausnahmen möglich).

WIE SCHICKEN: Bitte befestigen Sie das vorgesehene Etikett (oder Kopie) - vollständig ausgefüllt - mit Klebstreifen (nicht mit Klebstoff) auf der Rückseite jeder Arbeit. Bitte per Luftpost oder auf normalem Postweg einsenden. Keine Luftfrachtsendungen. Deklarieren Sie «ohne jeden Handelswert» und «Arbeitsproben für Wettbewerb». Die Anzahl der Dias und Photos sollte auf dem Paket angegeben werden (bei Luftkurier-Sendungen vermerken Sie «Dokumente, ohne jeden Handelswert»).

MODALITÉS D'ENVOI

Par votre envoi, vous donnez expressément à GRAPHIS l'autorisation de reproduire les travaux reçus aussi bien dans le livre en question que dans le magazine GRAPHIS, ou dans tout imprimé concernant des comptes rendus ou du matériel publicitaire sur les publications GRAPHIS.

ADMISSION: Sont acceptés tous les travaux de professionnels et d'étudiants.

QUE NOUS ENVOYER: Veuillez nous envoyer un exemplaire imprimé. N'envoyez pas d'originaux. Pour les travaux de grand format, volumineux ou de valeur, veuillez nous envoyer des photos ou des duplicata. Veuillez noter que les travaux ne peuvent pas être retournés, sauf dans des cas exceptionnels et si vous nous en avisez à l'avance.

COMMENT ET OU ENVOYER: Veuillez scotcher (ne pas coller) au dos de chaque spécimen les étiquettes ci-jointes (ou photocopies) dûment remplies. Envoyez les travaux de préférence par avion, ou par voie de surface. Ne nous envoyez rien en fret aérien. Indiquez «Sans aucune valeur commerciale» et «Echantillons de spécimens pour concours». Le nombre de diapositives et de photos doit être indiqué sur le paquet. (Pour les envois par courrier, inscrire «Documents, sans aucune valeur commerciale».)

ENTRIES

SINGLE ENTRY: North America: US $15.00
All other countries: SFr. 15.00
CAMPAIGN ENTRY: (3 or more pieces) North America: US $35.00 All other countries: SFr. 35.00

Please make checks payable to GRAPHIS PRESS CORP. ZURICH and include in parcel. These fees do not apply to students, if copy of student identification is included. (For entries from countries with exchange controls, please contact us.) A confirmation of receipt will be sent to each entrant, and all entrants will be notified whether or not their work had been accepted for publication. By submitting work you qualify for a 25% discount on the purchase of the respective book. Please send your entries to:

GEBÜREN

SFR. 15.--/DM 15.-- Für Einzelne Arbeiten
SFR. 40.--/DM 40.-- Für Kampagnen Oder Serien (Mehr als 3 stück)

Bitte senden Sie uns einen Scheck (SFr.-Schecks bitte auf eine Schweizer Bank ziehen) oder überweisen Sie den Betrag auf PC Zürich 80-23071-9 oder PSchK Frankfurt 3000 57-602. Diese Gebühren gelten nicht für Studenten. Senden Sie bitte eine Kopie des Studentenausweises. (Für Einsendungen aus Ländern mit Devisenbeschränkungen bitten wir Sie, uns zu kontaktieren.) Jeder Einsender erhält eine Empfangsbestätigung und wird über Erscheinen oder Nichterscheinen seiner Arbeit informiert. Durch Ihre Einsendung erhalten Sie 25% Rabatt auf das betreffende Buch. Herzlichen Dank für Ihre Mitarbeit. Bitte senden Sie Ihre Arbeiten an folgende Adresse:

DROITS D'ADMISSION

SFR. 15.00 Pour les envois concernant un seul travail
SFR. 40.00 Pour chaque série de 3 travaux ou davantage

Veuillez joindre à votre envoi un chèque tiré sur une banque suisse ou verser ce montant au compte chèque postal Zurich 80.23071.9. Les étudiants sont exemptés de cette taxe. Prière de joindre une photocopie de la carte d'étudiant. (Si vous résidez dans un pays qui connaît le contrôle des changes, veuillez nous contacter préalable-ment.) Nous vous ferons parvenir un accusé de réception. Vous serez informés par la suite de la parution ou non-parution de vos travaux. Votre envoi vous vaudra une réduction de 25% sur l'annuel en question. Veuillez faire parvenir vos travaux à l'adresse suivante: